MILTON STUDIES
XXII

MILTON
STUDIES
XXII ❧ *Edited by*
James D. Simmonds

UNIVERSITY OF PITTSBURGH PRESS

MILTON STUDIES

is published annually by the University of Pittsburgh Press as a forum for Milton scholarship and criticism. Articles submitted for publication may be biographical; they may interpret some aspect of Milton's writings; or they may define literary, intellectual, or historical contexts — by studying the work of his contemporaries, the traditions which affected his thought and art, contemporary political and religious movements, his influence on other writers, or the history of critical response to his work.

Manuscripts should be upwards of 3,000 words in length and should conform to the *MLA Style Sheet*. Manuscripts and editorial correspondence should be addressed to James D. Simmonds, Department of English, University of Pittsburgh, Pittsburgh, Pa. 15260.

Milton Studies does not review books.

Within the United States, *Milton Studies* may be ordered from the University of Pittsburgh Press, Pittsburgh, Pa. 15260.

Overseas orders should be addressed to Feffer and Simons, Inc., 100 Park Avenue, New York, N.Y. 10017, U.S.A.

Library of Congress Catalog Card Number 69-12335

ISBN 0-8229-3541-4

US ISSN 0076-8820

Published by the University of Pittsburgh Press, Pittsburgh, Pa. 15260

Feffer & Simons, Inc., London

Manufactured in the United States of America

CONTENTS

MILTON STUDIES

XXII

WHAT IS THE PERSONA DOING IN
L'ALLEGRO AND *IL PENSEROSO?*

Herbert J. Phelan

CRITICS HAVE noted before that the onlooker in Milton's *L'Allegro* and *Il Penseroso* is solitary. Samuel Johnson was the first to suggest that the persona in these two poems is an outsider: "Both Mirth and Melancholy are solitary, silent inhabitants of the breast that neither receive nor transmit communication; no mention is therefore made of a philosophical friend or a pleasant companion. The seriousness does not arise from any participation of calamity, nor the gaiety from the pleasures of the bottle."[1] And in our own time Don Cameron Allen seconds Johnson's view: "Johnson is right; the poet is as lonely as God and to some extent he shares God's stasis."[2] But neither of these critics investigates thoroughly the implication of his statement: neither takes care to locate just where the persona is when he is speaking, to whom he is speaking, or what he is doing inside the world of the poems. This oversight causes both critics to make unwarranted assumptions. Johnson assumes that

The man of *chearfulness* having exhausted the country tries what "towered cities" will afford, and mingles with scenes of splendor, gay assemblies, and nuptial festivities; but he mingles a mere spectator as, when the learned comedies of Jonson or the wild dramas of Shakespeare are exhibited, he attends the theatre.

The *pensive* man never loses himself in crowds, but walks the cloister or frequents the cathedral. (*LEP*, pp. 166–167)

Allen assumes much the same thing, though he is more hesitant than Johnson to commit himself unequivocally to this proposition. Concerning *L'Allegro*, he says, "In the city he [the persona] is also a spectator if the things that he witnesses there are real at all" (*HV*, p. 8). But no sooner does he hesitate to admit the actuality of the events being described in the poem than he contradicts himself by assuming that the persona "attends the theater; he listens to concerts" (*HV*, p. 8). And in a comment on the "solitary" qualities of both poems he says, "I have said that these poems have little social quality, that the poet lives to himself. It is for this reason that 'Il Penseroso' gains in power; it is much more solitary and, hence, a more personal poem" (*HV*, p. 10).

In the above excerpts both Johnson and Allen make the false as-

3

sumption that the persona is to be seen in all of the scenes that are described in the two poems. It is my contention, however, that Milton does not let us see the persona in all of the scenes, but rather lets us see him as physically present in only some of them, while other scenes are viewed as only figments of his imagination.

My specific objective in this essay is to follow the persona through the poems and to take note, by means of a careful analysis of the verbal clues, of his relationship to the events that he is describing. This procedure will do much more than simply disprove Johnson's and Allen's claim that the persona actually visits the "Towred Cities" or "walks the cloister"; it will, I hope, reveal the persona's relationship to all the events that he is describing and serve as a corrective influence that will prevent future critics from making unwarranted assumptions about the persona's involvement in the world of the poem.

A useful hypothesis for analyzing the persona's whereabouts in the poems is one which states that both *L'Allegro* and *Il Penseroso* are in some ways analogous to a film which uses the five following techniques: (1) the off-screen narrator; (2) a character on-screen who is participating in "real" events; (3) dream visions; (4) quick cuts (including flashbacks) from one scene to another; and, in *Il Penseroso*, (5) slow dissolves. However, this analogy must be explained in some detail, because obviously neither poem is a film — only filmlike in certain respects. The persona as off-screen narrator occurs in those passages where he is addressing the personification of an abstract ideal. In *L'Allegro* this technique is used when the persona addresses "loathed Melancholy" in lines 1–10, "Mirth" and her crew in lines 11–40, and "Mirth" alone in lines 135–52.[3] Similarly, the persona in *Il Penseroso* addresses "vain deluding joyes" in lines 1–10, and Melancholy (often by means of an epithet) in lines 11–55 ("divinest Melancholy"),[4] lines 103–20 ("sad Virgin"), lines 131–66 ("Goodness"), and lines 175–76 ("Melancholy").

The persona's physical presence on-screen occurs in *L'Allegro* whenever he is describing a natural scene and is using either a present participle (with the subject "I" and the auxiliary verb understood) or a first-person-possessive pronoun to place himself within that scene. A subtle distinction must be made, however, between the two ways this technique is used in the poem. Some activities, such as those occurring in lines 41–56, seem to be taking place in the present as we read; others, such as those occurring in lines 57–69, are introduced by adverbial modifiers (in this case "Som time") which suggest that the persona is not actually engaged in the activity at the present time, but is recalling — and describing — a realistic scene in which he has been actually present in the past. In both types of realistic scenes the vividness (or concreteness) of the natural details and the persona's use of either the present participle or the first-person-possessive pronoun seem actually to place him within a realistic setting. In *Il Penseroso* the persona employs the first-person-personal pronoun (which the persona in *L'Allegro* never does) much more often than the first-person-possessive pronoun to place himself within a realistic scene (e.g., in lines 65–72), although he also employs the first-person-possessive pronoun for this purpose (e.g., in lines 85–86). However, it must be pointed out (and this is an important point) that the persona also uses the first-person-personal pronoun to place himself within nonrealistic scenes (scenes that I shall describe in the next category — dream visions).

In *L'Allegro* the dream visions occur in those passages in which the persona describes events but does not use a first-person-possessive pronoun as a verbal indicator that he himself is actually present in the scenes. The dream visions occur in lines 79–150. In *Il Penseroso* these scenes can be distinguished from the on-screen scenes in three ways. First, the persona makes it quite clear that he is asking Melancholy to make it possible for him to be in certain places in which he has hitherto never been and to do certain things he has hitherto never done. Second, he describes these scenes in language that creates either a more abstract or a more mythological/pastoral setting, or both. The following brief passages illustrate the differences between the two types of scenes. First, an on-screen scene:

> I walk unseen
> On the dry smooth-shaven Green,
> To behold the wandring Moon,
> Riding neer her highest noon,
> Like one that had bin led astray
> Through the Heav'ns wide pathles way. (65–70)

Next, a dream-vision scene, in which the persona invokes Melancholy's aid and the allusions create a pastoral setting:

> me Goddess bring
> To arched walks of twilight groves,
> And shadows brown that *Sylvan* loves
> Of Pine, or monumental Oake,
> Where the rude Ax with heaved stroke,
> Was never heard the Nymphs to daunt,
> Or fright them from their hallow'd haunt. (132–38)

Or third (a special case — see lines 167–74), he uses the word "may" — while musing to himself — in describing a scene in which he hopes that he will eventually find himself. But more about this later.

The quick cut (which sometimes includes the flashback) occurs whenever the persona suddenly changes scenes without using a transitional passage. In *L'Allegro* this technique is used in lines 53, 57, 69, 81, 89, 100, 117, 125, and 131; in *Il Penseroso*, in lines 65, 73, 77, 85, 131, 155, and 167.

One technique used in *Il Penseroso* but not in *L'Allegro* is the dissolve. This technique is used to blend or meld scenes together. The first instance occurs in lines 56–64. In the lines where the persona says, "'Less *Philomel* will deign a Song, / In her sweetest, saddest plight, / Smoothing the rugged brow of night, / While *Cynthia* checks her Dragon yoke, / Gently o're th' accustom'd Oke," we are not sure at first whether the persona is continuing to address Melancholy, or is beginning to describe a realistic visual scene. My contention is that he is doing both, and, thus, the persona continues to address Melancholy after line 55, "And the mute Silence hist along, / 'Less *Philomel* will deign a Song" (55–56), while at the same time dissolving into a scene that will culminate in the realistic visual image of "th' accustom'd Oke" in line 60. After line 60, the persona addresses the "Sweet Bird" directly in lines 61–64 — the nightingale being, presumably, in or near the "Oke." What makes this passage an instance of the dissolve technique is that the word for nightingale is first given not in its common form (as is the case in the analogous passage in *L'Allegro*, line 41, where the bird mentioned is designated straightaway in its common form: "Lark"), but in its mythological form. Therefore, we are not at first sure whether "Philomel" belongs in the company of Melancholy and her companions (Peace, Quiet, Spare Fast, and the Cherub Contemplation) in their imaginary and abstract world of the persona's imagination, or whether we are to treat Philomel as a real nightingale in a real garden. Nor does the mention of "*Cynthia*" in line 59 help us fix the moon in a realistic setting. It is only in line 60 that the first truly realistic image — "th' accustom'd Oke" — appears, thus suggesting to the reader that Philomel and Cynthia may indeed be a real nightingale and the real moon in a real natural setting. (The word "accustom'd" should be especially noted in this phrase because it suggests that the persona is referring to an "Oke" with which he is actually familiar rather than merely conjuring one up in his imagination.) The "realness" of the scene is further established in lines 61–70, when the persona drops the use of mythological terminology and calls the nightingale simply "Sweet Bird" in line 61 and "Chauntress" in line 63, and the moon simply "Moon" in line 67. The other occurrence of the dissolve technique is found in lines 85–103, and will be dealt with below. I turn now to a detailed discussion of the two poems.

In the first forty lines of *L'Allegro*, the persona is heard but not seen. He is a disembodied voice who, in lines 1–10, exorcises "loathed Melancholy" from the world of the poem and condemns this vile personification to dwell in a "dark *Cimmerian* desert." The persona's disembodied voice then hails the "Goddess fair and free, / In Heav'n ycleap'd *Euphrosyne*, / And by men, heart-easing Mirth" (11–13), and asks her to come to him and bring along her companions. Next, he beseeches Mirth to let him live with her and her "crue . . . In unreproved pleasures free . . . if I give thee honour due" (38, 40, 37).

After invoking Mirth and her "crue," the persona is now ready to make his appearance in the real world.

In lines 41–42, he begins describing a realistic scene: "To hear the Lark begin his flight, / And singing startle the dull night." Immediately thereafter, he places the lark in a particular location: "From his watchtowre in the skies, / Till the dappled dawn doth rise" (43–44). (It should be noted that in both passages the time of day is also established.) Through the use of auditory and visual imagery, the persona creates a scene in the real world into which he soon places himself by the use of a first-person-possessive pronoun: "Then to com in spight of sorrow / And at *my* window bid good morrow" (45–46; my italics). This scene is further delineated when he mentions the sound of a cock crowing, and then gives a brief visual description of it:

> While the Cock with lively din,
> Scatters the rear of darknes thin,
> And to the stack, or the Barn dore,
> Stoutly struts his Dames before.   (49–52)

At line 53, the persona makes a quick cut, by means of auditory imagery, to earlier times within the same location, when he recalls:

> Oft list'ning how the Hounds and Horn
> Chearly rouse the slumbring morn,
> From the side of som Hoar Hill,
> Through the high wood echoing shrill.   (53–56)

The times alluded to in this passage occur in the indefinite, generalized past, since the word "Oft" suggests that they are not occurring at the same time the persona is listening to the lark and the cock. But the concreteness of the imagery forces the reader to hear the sounds of the hounds and the horn as though they were occurring during one single time span in the present. Thus a legitimate quick cut occurs, and, as in a film, the reader relives a past event along with the persona as though it were occurring, as it were, right before his eyes. There is no reason to assume, however, that the persona is not hearing—or recalling having heard—these sounds through his window, because there is no indication within these lines that the location has shifted—only the time.

A quick cut which does change the location occurs in lines 57–58, when the persona creates a visual scene in which he is "Som time walking not unseen / By Hedge-row Elms, on Hillocks green." (Again note that the time alluded to occurs in the indefinite, generalized past.) In lines 59–68, the persona provides more concrete details which bring this scene to life. He describes the sun "Roab'd in flames, and Amber light," against whose "Eastern gate" he himself is walking, and then provides the reader with a brief but realistic description of what is occurring nearby:

> While the Plowman neer at hand,
> Whistles ore the Furrow'd Land,
> And the Milkmaid singeth blithe,
> And the Mower whets his sithe,
> And every Shepherd tells his tale
> Under the Hawthorn in the dale. (63–68)

Of particular interest in this passage is the persona's relationship with the people he is describing. The fact that he uses only the generic names of the rustics and quotes nothing they say verbatim is a strong indication that he is aloof from what he sees.

Next, the persona describes other pastoral scenes that he sees. Again, the reader gets the feeling that the persona is present in the scene because of his use of the first-person-possessive pronoun in line 69: "Streit mine eye hath caught new pleasures." Also, the reader senses that the persona is moving farther away from other human beings: his description of the clouds on the barren mountains suggests that he has climbed far above the common haunts of men—even rustics—and his description of a panoramic scene confirms this suggestion. The entire passage reads as follows:

> Streit mine eye hath caught new pleasures
> Whilst the Lantskip round it measures,
> Russet Lawns, and Fallows Gray,
> Where the nibling flocks do stray,
> Mountains on whose barren brest
> The labouring clouds do often rest:
> Meadows trim with Daisies pide,
> Shallow Brooks, and Rivers wide.
> Towers, and Battlements it sees
> Boosom'd high in tufted Trees. (69–78)

If my reading is correct, this is the last time the reader feels the persona's actual presence in a scene. From lines 79 to 134 the reader senses his presence only as a daydreamer—with one brief exception in lines 81–82; or, to use a film metaphor, the reader is allowed, by a series of dream visions, to see the persona's thoughts acted out in scenes. There are three main reasons for reading the lines this way. First, the persona does not use the first-person-possessive pronoun in this section to place himself within a scene. Second, the scenes he describes are clearly inspired by chivalric or pastoral modes, or by his literary interests. And third, whereas he refers in lines 77–78 to his eye which sees "Towers, and Battlements . . . Boosom'd high in tufted Trees," in line 79 he indicates that he is daydreaming when he uses the phrase "perhaps som beauty lies" in one of the towers that he sees in line 77. The "perhaps" denotes that he does not actually see the "beauty," but is only imagining her presence within the tower. Also, it might be noted that after using "perhaps," the persona imagines the "beauty" being seen not by his own eyes, but by some indefinite "neighbouring eyes" (80). Since the persona does not actually say that he sees the people who see the "beauty," he further enhances the dreamlike quality of the scene he is describing.

Lines 81–82, "Hard by, a Cottage chimney smokes, / From betwixt two aged Okes," is the last real scene the persona describes from his vantage point on the mountain. In a sense, the reader leaves the persona on the mountain top, and then begins to take a dream-journey with him, in which the persona first imagines an idyllic scene taking place in the cottage, and then, by means of associative leaps, imagines other scenes.

The persona begins his scene at the cottage by imagining that the cottage is the one "Where *Corydon* and *Thyrsis* met" (83). He then peoples the scene with two other stock characters from the pastoral convention: Phillis and Thestylis. Corydon and Thyrsis are eating, while Phillis leaves her bower to help Thestylis "bind the Sheaves" (88). This brief scene ends at line 89 when the persona quick cuts to an earlier season within the same locale. Into this scene he places "many a youth, and many a maid," who are "Dancing in the Chequer'd shade" (95–96). Young and old then join in the rustic merrymaking until nightfall, at which time they retire indoors to drink "Nut-brown Ale" (100) and recount various fairytales (101–14). This scene ends at lines 115–16, when the revelers go to bed. We might notice before continuing that the feeling we have that we are watching a dream vision is further enhanced by the persona's use of parallel and balanced antitheses of universals—youth / maid, young / old—which give to the scene a contrived and unparticularized quality: a strategy that he will employ again in the next section when he sets the scene in the "Towred Cities."⁵

A minor interpretive problem arises at the beginning of the next scene. The persona begins by saying, "Towred Cities please us then" (117). The first-person-plural pronoun "us" might lead the reader to believe that the persona is actually placing himself within this scene, and inviting the reader to join him. However, the plural noun "Cities" argues against this interpretation. The persona could not possibly be in more than one city at a time, and so his statement that "Towred Cities please us then" ought to be read in the sense that he is making an imaginative leap from a contemplation of country life to a contemplation of city life. Also it should be noted that the persona's view of the countryside in lines 57–79 is one that could be realistically taken in by a single observer in a single viewing. The scenes of city life, on the contrary, do not give the reader the impression that a single observer is seeing them himself. Rather, they give the impression that they are being conjured up in the persona's mind; or, to use the words of the persona himself, that they are "Such sights as youthful Poets dream" (129). In other words, the persona is strongly hinting (even if he does not come right out and say so) that the sights he is describing in lines 117–28 ("the busie humm of men," the "throngs of Knights and Barons bold," the contests "Of Wit, or Arms," and the marriage mask where "*Hymen* oft appear[s]") are being conjured up in his own mind. Furthermore, the persona's use of the subjunctive mood in line 125, "There let *Hymen* oft appear," reinforces the interpretation that what is being described is contrary to fact.

After this brief vision of festive city life is an even briefer vision of a theatrical event: "Then to the well-trod stage anon, / If *Jonsons* learned Sock be on, / Or sweetest *Shakespear* fancies childe, / Warble his native Wood-notes wilde" (131–34). There are two points here that mitigate against the possibility that the persona is actually present at the theater. First, the persona does not put himself into the scene by using the first-person-singular pronoun. And second, the subjunctive phrase, "If *Jonsons* learned Sock be on" suggests that an actual play is not taking place. The persona is saying, in other words, that he can imagine himself going to the theater if Jonson or Shakespeare is being performed, but that he is not actually doing so at the present time. In short, if my theory about the persona's dream vision is correct, he is not in the city at all.

Beginning with line 135, the persona once again addresses Mirth with his disembodied voice. Gone are the evocations of place and human activity as he makes his request of Mirth:

> And ever against eating Cares,
> Lap me in soft *Lydian* Aires,
> Married to immortal verse

> Such as the meeting soul may pierce
> In notes, with many a winding bout
> Of lincked sweetness long drawn out,
> With wanton heed, and giddy cunning,
> The melting voice through mazes running;
> Untwisting all the chains that ty
> The hidden soul of harmony.   (135–44)

Even though "the Greeks condemned the *Lydian* mode as sentimental and conducing to effeminacy,"[6] there is no hint in this passage that the Lydian mode is anything other than what the persona desires from Mirth. Indeed, it is just such a mode that will allow him to untwist "all the chains that ty, / The hidden soul of harmony." So efficacious are "*Lydian* Aires" to the persona's way of thinking, that if he were to master them, then

> *Orpheus* self may heave his head
> From golden slumber on a bed
> Of heapt *Elysian* flowres, and hear
> Such streins as would have won the ear
> Of *Pluto*, to have quite set free
> His half regain'd *Eurydice*.   (145–50)

But the persona has still not attained the capabilities of a master comic poet, for Orpheus still sleeps and Eurydice remains in Hades.

In short, what I hear in lines 135–50 is the return of the persona's disembodied voice, in which he addresses Mirth directly and asks her to grant him the power to write great comic poetry — poetry so enthralling that it will have life-giving powers. In lines 151–52, the persona continues his direct address to Mirth by offering to enter into a bargain with her. He says that if Mirth can grant him "these delights" — presumably meaning the delights attendant on his being able to write great comic verse and not the physical and imaginative delights he has already experienced in lines 41–135 — then he means to live with her. It is possible to argue, I suppose, that the persona is asking Mirth to grant him all the delights that he has experienced in the poem; however, the clause "if thou canst give" means that Mirth still has not granted them to him. *L'Allegro* thus ends with the persona playing the role of supplicant to Mirth, and asking her to grant him the gift of comic poetry (and perhaps the other delights as well).

Concerning the two poems, Allen says that they "have little social quality . . . the poet lives to himself. It is for this reason that 'Il Penseroso' gains in power; it is much more solitary and, hence, a more personal poem . . . his experiences of night as he relates them in the second poem were certainly more keenly felt than the experiences recounted in 'L'Allegro'" (*HV*, p. 10). He then cites, among other passages, lines 127–30 — "usher'd with a shower still, / When the gust hath blown his fill, / Ending on the rustling Leaves, / With minute drops from off the Eaves" — and says in defense of his above statement, "These lines have in them a conviction of observation that is quite beyond that of the traditional descriptions of the first poem" (*HV*, p. 11). He then goes on to say, "'Il Penseroso' is a more mature poem than 'L'Allegro' . . . [it] is the poem of a poet who has found his way. It magnifies some of the insights of 'L'Allegro,' but it is the work of a man who is almost free from the sterile melancholy that once invested him. In the second poem, Milton is not only purged of his black bile but of his academic obligations; he is cultivating his 'trim Gardens' in the 'retired leasure' that is proper to his temperament" (*HV*, pp. 11–12).

I have quoted this passage from *Harmonious Visions* because I feel that Allen is correct in his assessment that *Il Penseroso* is the more powerful and more mature of the two poems. However, I feel that Allen could have been more precise in his analysis of those factors which contribute to *Il Penseroso*'s success. As it is, he relies on his own rather impressionistic response to the poem to support his claim. I feel, on the contrary, that it is possible to support the contention that *Il Penseroso* is the more mature, more personal, more sophisticated of the two poems without recourse to the conjecture that it was written at Horton after Milton had "purged . . . his black bile . . . [and] his academic obligations." My own contention is that it is the better of the two poems because it exhibits a higher degree of verbal sophistication. Two main factors are involved in this contention. First, the persona's use of the dissolve technique merges some of the sections together in a smoother manner than does his use of the quick cut in *L'Allegro*; and second, the persona's use of the first-person-personal pronoun in the dream visions gives the poem a more "personal" tone. The effect of these two techniques — especially the latter — is to render *Il Penseroso* a poem in which the persona sounds as though he is more intimately concerned with attaining his goal than is the persona in *L'Allegro*, who disassociates himself from the activities he is describing in his dream visions.

For the first fifty-five lines of *Il Penseroso*, however, the poem establishes a close parallel to the first forty lines of *L'Allegro*. In lines 1–10 the off-screen disembodied voice of the persona again exorcises a vile personification — this time "vain deluding joyes" — from his life, and bids them to "Dwell in some idle brain." After banishing "deluding joyes" from his life, the disembodied voice continues: "But hail thou Goddess, sage and holy, / Hail divinest Melancholy" (11–12). Later, the persona asks her to bring with her "Peace, and Quiet" (45), "Spare Fast" (46), "The Cherub Contemplation" (54), and "mute Silence" (55). Unlike the persona in *L'Allegro*, however, the persona in *Il Penseroso* does not expressly bid Melancholy to admit him to her "crue," but rather seems content to have her and her attendants merely assemble. One reason, perhaps, that the persona does not overtly ask Melancholy to let him join her and her companions is that, through the use of the dissolve technique in lines 56–64, the persona is able to have her and her companions join him, as it were, by the use of a more subtle means than direct request. I have already mentioned above how the dissolve technique operates in this passage, but perhaps it would be a good idea here to quote the passage in full, along with the preceding five lines, and analyze more precisely what is taking place. Lines 51–64 read:

> But first, and chiefest, with thee bring,
> Him that yon soars on golden wing,
> Guiding the fiery-wheeled throne,
> The Cherub Contemplation,
> And the mute Silence hist along,
> 'Less *Philomel* will deign a Song,
> In her sweetest, saddest plight,
> Smoothing the rugged brow of night,
> While *Cynthia* checks her Dragon yoke,
> Gently o're th' accustom'd Oke;
> Sweet Bird that shunn'st the noise of folly,
> Most musical, most Melancholy!
> Thee Chauntress oft the Woods among,
> I woo to hear thy Even-Song.

As noted above, the line which begins to create a scene with visual imagery, "'Less *Philomel* will deign a Song," is much more subtly woven into the fabric of the poem than its parallel line, "To hear the Lark begin his flight," is in *L'Allegro*. The most important thing to notice here is that line 56 makes perfectly good sense if read as a continuation of the lines preceding it. The persona, in other words, after asking Melancholy to bring her companions along in "Silence,"[7] immediately qualifies that statement by saying, in so many words, that he would not mind if the silence were broken by Philomel's singing. Another thing to notice is that *Philomel* is the mythological name for nightingale, whereas *lark* is the generic name for the bird that startles "the dull night." Also, as I noted earlier, the persona's use of the mythological term *Cynthia* for "moon" further reinforces the reader's feeling that he is still suspended between an unreal, invisible world, the inhabitants of which the persona is still addressing off-screen, and the real world, which the persona is beginning to create through the use of visual imagery in line 56 and in which he will appear in line 64. The question therefore begins to arise in line 56: Where exactly is the persona? He is, I believe, both continuing his invocation to Melancholy while at the same time beginning to create a visual scene in the real world — culminating with his use of the generic word "Oke" in line 60 and "Bird" (a nonmythological reference to the nightingale) in line 61. In others words, the persona is still speaking off-screen while a visual scene in which he will appear in line 64 is being developed. The overall effect of lines 56–64 is to merge subtly the world of Melancholy with the real world in which the persona is wooing "to hear" the song of a real nightingale. It is this subtle merging — or dissolving — of the "Melancholy section" of the poem with the "real world section" that permits the persona to dispense with a request to Melancholy to let him join her. In other words, Melancholy and her companions join the persona in the real world rather than being separated from it by the persona's use of a quick cut, as are Mirth and her "crue" in lines 40–41 of *L'Allegro*.

After the dissolve is completed, we find ourselves in the real world of the "accustom'd Oke," where the persona himself soon appears by use of the first-person-personal pronoun "I" in line 64. Then, using the device we are familiar with from *L'Allegro*, the persona quick cuts to another scene in lines 65–66: "And missing thee [the nightingale], I walk unseen / On the dry smooth-shaven Green." One should note that in describing what he sees from the "Green," the persona uses the word "Moon," not "Cynthia," in line 67: "To behold the wandring Moon." The persona is now firmly established in the real world. However, there is still in the real world a subtle echo from the world of Melancholy. The persona, in his description of the moon shining through a cloud — "And oft, as if her head she bow'd, / Stooping through a fleecy cloud" 71–72) — uses the same metaphor of the bowed head looking down at earth that he uses to describe Melancholy in lines 43–44: "With a sad Leaden downward cast, / Thou fix them [her eyes, see line 40] on the earth as fast." I believe it is safe to say that by the end of line 72 Melancholy can be felt pervading the real world of *Il Penseroso* to a much greater degree than Mirth does the real world of *L'Allegro*.

In line 73 the persona quick cuts to another scene. As in *L'Allegro*, he uses the word "Oft" to flashback to a scene in which he is not at present situated, but in which he has often been situated in the past: "Oft on a Plat of rising ground, / I hear the far-off *Curfeu* sound, / Over some wide-water'd shoar, / Swinging slow with sullen roar" (73–76). Also note that, as in lines 53–56 of *L'Allegro*, so here, too, the persona relies heavily on auditory imagery to create the scene for the reader.

The persona uses a quick cut again at lines 77–78 to change both the place and the weather conditions: "Or if the Ayr will not permit, / Som still removed place will fit." On these colder nights we see the persona in his lodging

> Where glowing Embers through the room
> Teach light to counterfeit a gloom,
> Far from all resort of mirth,
> Save the Cricket on the hearth,
> Or the Belmans drowsie charm,
> To bless the dores from nightly harm.   (79–84)

With the sound of the bellman's bell blessing "the dores from nightly harm," we leave the persona in the realistic world of the poem and enter with him into his dream visions. The dream visions are all conjured up as part of the persona's second invocation to Melancholy which begins on line 85 and continues, with one brief interruption, to the end. Unlike *L'Allegro*, in which the persona conjures up a series of dream visions between lines 79 and 134 before beginning his second invocation to Mirth at line 135, all the dream visions in *Il Penseroso* are subsumed under the persona's invocation to Melancholy, which begins with the request "Or let my Lamp at midnight hour, / Be seen in some high lonely Towr" (85–86). The key word in this passage is "let." This word denotes that a request is being made of Melancholy, and it is linked grammatically with the word "let" in line 97 in the passage "Som time let Gorgeous Tragedy / In Scepter'd Pall com sweeping by" (97–98), which in turn is linked grammatically to the word "raise" in line 104 in the passage "But, O sad Virgin, that thy power / Might raise *Musaeus* from his bower" (103–04). The second invocation begins subtly because we do not know for certain whether the two "lets" are addressed to Melancholy, or whether the persona is using "let" merely as a verbal means of introducing his own dream vision, as he does in *L'Allegro*, line 125: "There let *Hymen* oft appear." It is not until we read the words, "But, O sad Virgin" and notice that another request — the third in the series so far — is being made of her that we realize that the first two passages containing "let" are also to be taken as a request of Melancholy to transport the persona to places he has actually never been to before. The "Towr," all that happens there, and all that happens afterward, are all figments of the persona's imagination.

It is in the imaginary tower that the persona begins to imagine the course that his future intellectual/poetic life might take. And it is there, too, that he does something that the persona in *L'Allegro* does not do — he places himself within the dream vision by means of the first-person-personal pronoun "I," which he does for the first time in line 87. If *Il Penseroso* is, as Allen claims, a "more personal poem" — and I think it is — then a major reason is that the persona more closely envisions himself as being active within the dream vision he creates than is the persona in *L'Allegro*. And what he envisions himself doing is devoting himself to "high studies" (see *Var.*, p. 323). He sees himself spending long nights[8] in the tower studying the mystical writings of Hermes Trismegistus in lines 86–88 and Plato's writings concerning "immortal souls" (see *Var.*, p. 324) in lines 89–92. In lines 93–97, the persona desires to gain knowledge of the "*Daemons* that are found / In fire, air, flood, or under ground."

In lines 97–98, we note another interesting departure from *L'Allegro*. Whereas in *L'Allegro* the persona imagines himself *going* "to the well-trod stage" if the comedies of Jonson or Shakespeare are being performed, here the persona is bidding Melancholy to "let Gorgeous Tragedy / In Scepter'd Pall com sweeping by" within the confines of his tower. That is, in lieu of any verbal clues to the contrary, he is asking that Melancholy send Tragedy to him, not stating that he intends to go to the theater to watch a tragedy performed. The reader can only imagine that the persona intends to enjoy a tragedy by reading one or by seeing a performance in his mind's eye, since he does not say specifically how he intends to apprehend it.

Not to burden the reader with a detailed analysis of what all the various allusions mean (a job performed in the *Variorum*), let me just outline briefly what the persona is doing in the remainder of this section. In lines 103–04, the persona asks Melancholy to "raise *Musaeus* from his bower," or, in lines 105–08, "bid the soul of *Orpheus* sing." The persona makes a third alternative request in lines 109–15 when (in an allusion to Chaucer's *Squire's Tale*) he asks her to summon up Chaucer with the words "Or call up him that left half told / The story of *Cambuscan* bold." The persona ends his series of requests by asking Melancholy to "call up" (the verb phrase "call up" in line 109 takes both "him" in line 109 and "great *Bards*" in line 116 as direct objects) "great *Bards*" who might enlighten him with songs "Where more is meant then meets the ear" (120). He then sums up his hope that he will be able to study long nights in his tower with a brief apostrophe to night: "Thus night oft see me in thy pale career" (121).

In lines 122–30 the persona, still in his tower, describes the dawn of a new day. Then in lines 131–33 he both makes another request of Melancholy (whom he refers to here as "Goddess") and uses a quick cut to change location: "And when the Sun begins to fling / His flaring beams, me Goddess bring / To arched walks of twilight groves." The scene in the groves is that of a pastoral landscape — "Where the rude Ax with heaved stroke, / Was never heard the Nymphs to daunt, / Or fright them from their hallow'd haunt" (136–38) — where the persona, who had sought a resting place in a "covert by some Brook" (139), falls asleep with the request that Melancholy "let som strange mysterious dream, / Wave at his Wings in Airy stream, / Of lively portrature display'd, / Softly on my eye-lids laid" (147–50). Through the use of a quick cut in line 151 the persona jumps ahead in time to his awakening — "And as I wake . . ." — and then, still under the spell of this enchanted "haunt," imagines that some unseen power is playing music for his benefit: "sweet musick breath / Above, about, or underneath, / Sent by som spirit to mortals good, / Or th' unseen Genius of the Wood" (151–54).

The persona again makes both a request of Melancholy and uses a quick cut to change the scene in lines 155–56: "But let my due feet never fail, / To walk the studious Cloysters pale." After briefly describing the "Cloyster" in lines 157–60, the persona makes the request of Melancholy that she bring him to ecstasy through religious music:

> There let the pealing Organ blow,
> To the full voic'd Quire below,
> In Service high, and Anthems cleer,
> As may with sweetness, through mine ear,
> Dissolve me into extasies,
> And bring all Heav'n before mine eyes. (161–66)

Something odd occurs at line 167, for the persona suddenly seems to change the tactic that he has been using since line 85 of introducing his dream-vision sequences with a request of Melancholy. Lines 167–168 — "And may at last my weary age / Find out the peacefull hermitage" — seem to be a reverie in the mind of the persona rather than an actual request of Melancholy — the word "may" denoting a wish rather than a request. It is interesting to note that both the line that introduces the passage describing the "hermitage" (167) and the line introducing the passage in which the persona states what he hopes to accomplish there (170) contain the word "may." I can only guess at the reason for this, but it just may be that the persona, in visualizing his final attainment "To something like Prophetic strain" (174), feels that this final triumph is almost too great for him to request even of the goddess Melancholy.

Perhaps he feels that if Melancholy can grant him everything that he asks of her, then this final, triumphal attainment just might come to pass, too. In any case, he ends the poem by offering to enter into a bargain with Melancholy (in much the same manner that the persona offers to enter into a bargain with Mirth in the last two lines of *L'Allegro*) by stating the conditions under which he will become her votary: "These pleasures *Melancholy* give, / And I with thee will choose to live" (175–76).

One of the things I hope I have achieved in this essay is to offer a corrective to critical views, like those of Johnson and Allen, which are based in part on a faulty assumption of where the persona is, what he does, and to whom he speaks. I think that my analysis has shown, for instance, that these two poems cannot be thought of as one long poem, that their structure is not "based on a daily but continued ascent" (*HV*, p. 17). To the contrary, they ought to be read as separate poems because it seems apparent from my analysis that the persona in both poems does not achieve his ultimate desire. Therefore, even if we were to grant that the personae in both poems are indeed one and the same (an assumption that is reasonable to make in light of the fact that Milton wrote the poems as companion pieces expressing two possible paths that a young poet might tread), we cannot thereby assume that it is necessary for him to educate himself by becoming a comic poet before he can become a serious poet. Thus, I cannot agree with Allen when he says, "By a continued mounting of the slopes of the intellect from common experience, to intellectual experience, to religious inspiration, the poet trusts to arrive at the supreme poetic gratification" (*HV*, p. 17). In order for the poems to be read in this manner, the persona would have to achieve his ultimate goal in each. This he does not do.

This point can be further elucidated if we note the mistake that Allen makes when he says, concerning the persona in *L'Allegro*, that he "attends the theater; he listens to concerts. His interest in men and their daily affairs is passive, almost disinterested" (*HV*, p. 8). The persona does not attend the theater, he does not listen to concerts, and his interest in the affairs of men is purely imaginative. In short, since the persona has not yet experienced the common pleasures about which he speaks, he can hardly be said to mount "the slopes of the intellect from common experience" in *L'Allegro* to the more sublime experiences — culminating in "the supreme poetic gratification" — of *Il Penseroso*.

Another thing I hope I have achieved is an analysis of the verbal clues in the two poems which make it possible to account more explicitly for some of the effects that certain critics have intuited but which they have not satisfactorily explained. Johnson, for example, is basically right when he says that "Both Mirth and Melancholy are solitary, silent inhabitants of the breast that neither receive nor transmit communication" (*LEP*, p. 166), but he does not explain that one of the major reasons for the persona's solitude is that some of the things he sees and does — for example, going to the theater — are nothing more than dream visions. So, too, Allen is correct in noting that "the transition in 'Il Penseroso' between the invitation to Contemplation and Silence and the phrase 'Less Philomel will deign a song' is more fluid and skillful. The poetic components of 'Il Penseroso' seem to glide out of each other by brilliant acts of association" (*HV*, p. 10). However, he does not analyze the persona's verbal ingenuity in the entire passage (56–72) in which these lines occur. Allen is also correct in stating that *Il Penseroso* is "a more personal poem" than *L'Allegro*, but he does not analyze the reasons why this is so — relying instead on his own rather impressionistic response (noted above) to substantiate his claim.

I cannot help but agree with Johnson when he says that these two poems "are two noble efforts of imagination" (*LEP*, p. 167). What I have tried to show is that they are also two poems which exhibit an extraordinary degree of verbal ingenuity and that this verbal ingenuity can be appreciated more fully if we pay close attention to just where the persona is, what he does, and to whom he speaks.

University of Florida

NOTES

1. Samuel Johnson, *Lives of the English Poets*, ed. George Birkbeck Hall (Oxford, 1905), vol. I, p. 166. Hereafter cited in the text as *LEP*.

2. Don Cameron Allen, *The Harmonious Vision* (Baltimore, 1954), p. 4. Hereafter cited in the text as *HV*.

3. All quotations of *L'Allegro* and *Il Penseroso* are from *The Works of John Milton*, ed. Frank Allen Patterson et al. (New York, 1931–38), vol. I, part 1, pp. 34–46.

4. Lines 56–60 in *Il Penseroso*, it may be argued, ought to be included here. However, they present special problems for analysis in light of my hypothesis because, as Don Cameron Allen rightly states "The poetic components of 'Il Penseroso' seem to glide out of each other by brilliant acts of association" (*HV*, p. 10). These problems will be dealt with later.

5. I am indebted to Professor Ira Clark of the University of Florida for bringing this fact to my attention.

6. *A Variorum Commentary on the Poems of John Milton*, ed. Merritt Y. Hughes (New York, 1972), vol. II, part 1, p. 304. Hereafter cited in the text as *Var*.

7. I am, of course, defining the word *hist* (in line 55) as "the so-called optative subjunctive (expressing Il Penseroso's wish) with *Silence* as its subject, the sense being 'And may Silence move along (with the whole group) admonishing noiselessness the while.'" For a brief discussion of the problems involved in defining *hist* see *Var.*, p. 319, from which the above passage is quoted.

8. "Since *the Bear* (Ursa major) never sets but becomes invisible with daylight, the phrase ['out-watch the Bear'] implies 'keep watch till daybreak' (Keightley)." *Var.*, p. 323.

MILTON'S USE OF AQUINAS IN *COMUS*

James Obertino

I N   A N essay on *Comus*, Georgia Christopher has argued that the
masque can be profitably considered in terms of Reformation theology: "If . . . we approach *Comus* with the Reformation assumption that
nature is inimical to grace and that virtue is extrinsic to man, the masque
will appear remarkably coherent."[1] Reading chastity as a "pervasive metaphor for faith" is an important part of Christopher's argument because
this reading supports the split between nature and grace she sees throughout the masque.[2] My essay will argue that *Comus* can be more adequately
read if one recognizes in it the continuity of nature and grace, with chastity important as a virtue in its own right, as well as a pervasive meton-
ymy for charity, which binds Creator and creature, grace and nature
together.[3] While Christopher aligns Milton with the Reformation, I will
attempt to show that Milton's primary theological source throughout the
masque is St. Thomas Aquinas rather than Luther or Calvin. The theology of *Comus* shows so many parallels with St. Thomas that one is
pressured either to conclude that Milton knew Aquinas well from his Cambridge days (jocular references to the schoolmen in Prolusion Three suggest how much a part of the curriculum they were) or that Milton at
least happens to agree with him on several key points. A few critics have
recently recognized that Milton's praise of Spenser as a better teacher
than Aquinas is not a left-handed compliment to Spenser, preferring
him to a nugatory Aquinas, but rather a valuation of Spenser above even
St. Thomas.[4]

The ambivalence of nature in *Comus* is well known. At one extreme
there is nature as Comus sees it, where the natural pleasures of the senses
cause his followers their "native home [to] forget, / And roll with pleasure in a sensual sty" (76–77), the nature whose fecundity offers Comus
matter for his seductive argument that "her waste fertility" (729) is only
"to please and sate the curious taste" (714).[5] The Attendant Spirit's early
disdain for the world, to him a "dim spot" (5), a low place that a heavenly aristocrat from "Regions mild of calm and serene Air" (4) would
rightly spurn, were it not for his errand to help the virtuous who aspire
to reach heaven, appears appropriately to respond to the misuse of nature
that Comus represents. But as the masque progresses, the Attendant Spirit

21

proves to be most knowledgeable about the extraordinary salvific powers remaining in nature, powers that even his celestial intelligence must resort to in order to free the Lady so the little company he guides can reach their destination. Not the least of these powers is haemony, "a small unsightly root, / But of divine effect" (629–30). Later, the Attendant Spirit will appeal to Sabrina, who is various things, among them a personality, associated with nature's flowers and waters, who works to protect human beings and the animals that serve them: she

> oft at Eve
> Visits the herds along the twilight meadows,
> Helping all urchin blasts, and ill-luck signs
> That the shrewd meddling Elf delights to make,
> Which she with precious vial'd liquors heals.
> For which the Shepherds at their festivals
> Carol her goodness loud in rustic lays.   (844–50)

Thus nature in *Comus* is far from being in Christopher's words "inimical to grace"; in fact, nature in *Comus* has within it forces through which grace operates to help people's lives, supervening the destructive use of nature that Comus represents. The beneficent powers of nature to nurture and protect are an aspect of that "most innocent nature" (762) the Lady has in mind when she rebuts Comus's argument for sensual indulgence that he bases on natural fertility. The Lady appeals to a nature whose "provision" (a term suggesting that Providence and nature can be near allied) for her "children" requires only that they govern themselves according to the natural virtue of temperance. This nature

> Means her provision only to the good
> That live according to her sober laws,
> And holy dictate of spare Temperance.   (765–67)

As this essay will try to show, the natural virtue of temperance is closely connected throughout the masque with the supernatural virtue of charity. As the Lady remarks, the intemperate refuse charity, of which the highest form, for St. Thomas, is man's love of God.[6] The greedy

> Ne'er looks to Heav'n amidst his gorgeous feast,
> But with besotted base ingratitude
> Crams, and blasphemes his feeder.   (777–79)

The misuse of nature's abundance also violates the other kind of charity, love of other people, because the excessive appetites of "some few" deprive "every just man that now pines with want" (768). The masque strongly suggests that nature should be properly and temperately used, rather than regarded as an enemy allied with evil, as in the formulation, "the world, the flesh, and the devil."

It is hard to know precisely where the world of the masque is located in terms of Christian theory. The Attendant Spirit is a daimon rather than an angel, and Milton's mature theology in *Paradise Lost* and *De Doctrina* gives no positive place to daimons or goddesses such as Sabrina. Nevertheless, the masque also locates itself in the historical Christian present of its original viewers, the Bridgewater family. The children in the masque journey to their father's, the earl's house, and while their father's house may symbolize their heavenly father's house, the audience is not to lose track of the historical identity of the characters and their immediate destination in Wales. The Lady appeals to faith and hope, and her substitution of "chastity" for "charity" inevitably puts the reader in mind of the three principal Christian virtues. The easy movement the masque makes from classical to Christian and back again — Sabrina, for example, is a saint as well as a goddess — coincides with the graceful identifications of the natural and supernatural orders one also finds. This continuity between natural and supernatural is characteristic of St. Thomas, according to Thomas Gilby (*ST* XXXIV, p. xvi).

The Lady's making temperance a virtue arising from nature's "sober laws" follows St. Thomas's ideas that "since every judgment of human reason is derived in some way from natural reason, it must necessarily follow that all moral precepts belong to the law of nature" (*ST* 1a2ae 100.1, XXIX, p. 58), and "each man's reason naturally dictates that he should act virtuously" (*ST* 1a2ae 94.3, XXVIII, p. 84). Thus the Lady's resistance to Comus is natural, that is, in accord with the best potentials of human nature, despite the fallenness of man; and reason, which the Lady uses abundantly in her retorts to Comus, dictates that nature's laws be followed. As St. Thomas remarks, "There is in man an inclination to good that accords with the nature of his reason" and "the order of the precepts of the law of nature accords with the order of natural inclinations" (*ST* 1a2ae 94.2, XXVIII, p. 82). Aquinas's confidence in the capacity of postlapsarian man to continue to be drawn to God through his fallen nature differs markedly from the pessimism of Calvin, who insists that "through Adam's sin we are so alienated from God that all our faculties are corrupt and vicious: I call the faculties of the soul, intelligence and reason, will and judgment: all these were perverted when Adam turned from God."[7] Milton is closer to Aquinas than to Calvin in his prose as well as in *Comus*; in *Tetrachordon*, he writes of the "most innocent lesson of nature"; in the *Doctrine and Discipline of Divorce* of "blameles nature" (*CM* III, p. 511) and the "faultles innocence of nature" (*CM* III, p. 397).[8] Milton's confidence in the potential for good even in the hearts of fallen men is most clearly seen in *De Doctrina:* "the law of God is either written or unwritten. The unwritten law is no other than that law of nature given originally to Adam, and of which a certain remnant, or imperfect illumination, still dwells in the hearts of all mankind" (*CM* XVI, p. 101).[9]

The debate between Comus and the Lady centers on opposing points of view about the purposes of nature and of human life, yet these viewpoints, seemingly so unlike, will be partially reconciled in the epilogue. Much of Comus's argument is based on deriving rules for human conduct from natural fecundity: "Wherefore did Nature pour her bounties forth, / . . . But all to please, and sate the curious taste?" (710–14). Comus's Epicureanism ignores the differences between people and animals, reason and appetite. He features consumption rather than stewardship or temperance as the chief dictate of nature. As he sees it, if people refuse to consume what nature produces, then nature "would be quite surcharg'd with her own weight, / And strangl'd with her waste fertility" (728–29). The sexual enjoyment that Comus claims to offer is the conclusion of an argument that calls for the eating of birds to avoid overburdening the earth and continues by paralleling food and sex, but this argument contains a logical problem: sexuality freely indulged in will produce only more life, and thus "burden" the earth even more. Sabrina will, later in the masque, show the fusion of the order of nature and the order of grace, a possibility that Comus does not recognize in his rather mechanical model of nature as production and consumption. The character of Sabrina will suggest that chastity, even virginity, can be in accord with the laws of nature. Even the nature that Comus invokes is not completely outside the divine order — it follows the command to be fruitful and multiply — but it knows nothing of the Pauline assertion that continence has its legitimate place in God's plan.

Food and sex are equated throughout the debate between Comus and the Lady; for her to accept his drink is tantamount to yielding her body, as she well knows. The use of food as a metaphor for sexuality also occurs in St. Thomas: "What food is for man's well being, such is sexual intercourse for the welfare of the human race" (*ST* 2a2ae 153.2, XLIII, p. 192). Comus pursues the food-sex parallel throughout his temptation, and in responding to him, the Lady rejects gluttony as much as lechery. Temperance is the virtue Comus tests, and sobriety and chastity are two of its salient faces in the masque. Milton in *De Doctrina* remarks that "the virtue which prescribes bounds to the desire for bodily gratification, is called temperance. . . . Under temperance are comprehended sobriety and chastity, modesty and decency. Sobriety consists in abstinence from immoderate eating and drinking" (*CM* XVII, p. 213). The Lady's awareness that to choose to drink the cup of Comus's "brewed enchantments" (706) is to choose degeneration recalls the Attendant Spirit's earlier remark on Comus's "baneful cup"

> whose pleasing poison
> The visage quite transforms of him that drinks,
> And the inglorious likeness of a beast
> Fixes instead, unmolding reason's mintage
> Character'd in the face. (526–30)

The emphasis the Attendant Spirit places on the correspondence between the loss of reason and the loss of beauty one also sees in Aquinas: "Intemperance is most disgraceful for two reasons. First, because it is most repugnant to human excellence, since it is about pleasures common to us and the lower animals. . . . Secondly, because it is most repugnant to man's clarity and beauty; inasmuch as the pleasures of intemperance dim the light of reason from which all clarity and beauty of virtue arises" (*ST* 2a2ae 142.4, XLIII, p. 46). The Lady's insistence that "that which is not good, is not delicious / To a well-govern'd and wise appetite" (704–05) recalls St. Thomas's idea that temperance restrains man from things which seduce the appetites from obeying reason (*ST* 2a2ae 141.2, XLIII, p. 10). In the Lady's circumstances, tired and hungry though she is, total abstention from all that Comus offers her is appropriate. St. Thomas approvingly quotes Augustine: "The temperate man looks to the need not only of this life but also of his duty" (*ST* 2a2ae 141.6.3, XLIII, p. 26); the Lady's duty includes her remaining a virgin until she is married. Aquinas also suggests that what is right depends on the probable consequences of action: "To consider a situation with an eye to its consequences in practice is proper to human reason" (*ST* 2a2ae 57.3, XXXVIII, p. 12). The Lady's temporary fasting in Comus's bower accords with St. John Chrysostom, whom Aquinas approvingly cites, "For those who wish to contemplate wisdom, fasting is a delight."[10] Fasting is the right response to the Lady's trial, but the epilogue will show that delight is not forever renounced by the faithful and that joy can legitimately include the pleasures of the senses.

The Lady's insistence that Comus "canst not touch the freedom of my mind" (664) fits both St. Augustine's idea that chastity is a virtue of the mind[11] and Aquinas's concept that chastity both refers to abstaining from sexual acts inappropriate to one's condition and is a comprehensive virtue as well: "Taking chastity in this sense, it is a general virtue, because every virtue withdraws the human mind from . . . union with unlawful things. Nevertheless, *the essence of this chastity consists principally in charity* and the other theological virtues whereby the mind is united to God" (*ST* 2a2ae 151.2, XLIII, p. 160; my emphasis). Thus the Lady agrees with Aquinas that chastity is first of all a condition of consciousness; her substitution of "chastity" for "charity" earlier in the masque (215), a substitution the *Variorum* authors term "outrageous,"[12] makes good sense because chastity metonymically stands in the masque for other virtues, including charity, as the epilogue suggests. Chastity is the necessary basis for Christian liberty, "the freedom of my mind," because it allows the soul to join with God in charity, which in its highest form is "the friendship of man and God" (*ST* 2a2ae 23.1, XXXIV, p. 6). What Comus invites the Lady to do is dangerous for several reasons: he would compromise her social status as Bridgewater's virgin daughter, he would deprive her of her maidenhead (a loss St. Thomas considers irreparable, even by God, though the bodily organ be restored [*ST* 2a2ae 152.3.3, XLIII, pp. 178–80]), and most seriously, he would compromise her Christian liberty by exciting her lust (though he claims this forfeiture would make her his "Queen," 265, Comus's kingdom is a part of the City of Man rather than the City of God), which would deprive her of her reason. Milton agrees with Aquinas about the primacy of reason in maintaining one's position within the City of God: "Reason is also choice," Raphael tells Adam (*PL* III, 108), and Aquinas observes, "Among the vices of intemperance, venereal sins are most deserving of reproach because of the disobedience of the genital organs, and because in this way especially reason is absorbed" (*ST* 2a2ae 151.4.3, XLIII, p. 166).

As Rosemond Tuve has noticed, then, Comus's temptation is aimed as much at the Lady's soul as at her body.[13] The Lady's vehement rejection of Comus, calling him "Fool" (663) and "false traitor (690), and telling him "Thou are not fit to hear thyself convinc't" (792) might seem to suggest that Comus has won at least a partial victory over the Lady's charity, which is the essence of chastity; the Lady's anger against Comus could be taken as at odds with her insistence that temperance includes self-restraint. The Lady's outrage, however, can be justified in terms of St. Thomas's understanding of magicians and the appropriate response to them. A sorcerer, notes Aquinas, uses apparitions and deceptions contrary to reason to achieve his ends; these means are "often used to further lustful intercourse" (*Opera* V, p. 248). St. Thomas also remarks that while charity dictates a sinner should be loved, when a sinner "falls into great wickedness and becomes incurable," then friendliness has no place;

in fact sinners so depraved should be put to death (*ST* 2a2ae 25.6, XXXIV, p. 98). Milton in *De Doctrina* agrees with St. Thomas on the limitations of charity: "hatred . . . is in some cases a religious duty; as when we hate enemies of God, or the church" (*CM* XVII, p. 259). Comus's character suggests little possibility of redemption. He alone, of all the characters of the masque, embodies concupiscence as Calvin understands it, natural viciousness, a fertile, active principle of sin.[14]

The Lady's anger against Comus is thus justifiable and adult. Her maturity is further shown by her prudence. She does not respond as if personally offended when Comus argues that her refusal to mate with him because she values virginity — "List Lady, be not coy, and be not cozen'd / With that same vaunted name Virginity" (737–38) — is at bottom selfish:

> Beauty is nature's coin, must not be hoarded,
> But must be current, and the good thereof
> Consists in mutual and partak'n bliss,
> Unsavory in th'enjoyment of itself. (739–42)

Instead of countering that her love of chastity is not selfish, she refuses to defend her amour-propre, countering that Comus "hast nor Ear nor Soul to apprehend / The sublime notion and high mystery / . . . [of] the sage / And serious doctrine of Virginity" (784–87). Milton's understanding of prudence is based on Aquinas, but goes beyond him. St. Thomas remarks that "prudence provides both the faculty for good works and the right use of appetite"; moreover, prudence "is right reason in regard to actions that may be done," concerning itself with the purpose of actions (*ST* 1a2ae 57.4, XXIII, p. 50). In *De Doctrina*, Milton observes, "Prudence is that virtue by which we discern what is proper to be done under the various circumstances of time and place. . . . This quality is an indispensable seasoning to every virtue" (*CM* XVII, p. 37). Proper self-love is not selfish because it is ultimately directed toward the love of God: "the love of man towards himself consists in loving himself next to God, and in seeking his own temporal and eternal good" (*CM* XVII, p. 201). What appears to Comus as selfish in the Lady is nothing more than the quality Raphael advises Adam to cultivate: "Oft-times nothing profits more / Than self-esteem, grounded on just and right / Well manag'd" (*PL* VIII, 571–73).

While both the Lady and Comus would probably agree with Milton that "the law of nature . . . is sufficient of itself to teach . . . whatever is intrinsically good" (*CM* XV, p. 117), Comus's appeal to nature's laws shows a wholly carnal understanding of them. His appeal to nature

(710–753) ranges over much of the scale of being: men, minerals, plants, animals, and fish are all mentioned. But the use he makes of the chain of being is rather different from Raphael's, who observes, "In contemplation of created things / By steps we may ascend to God" (*PL* V, 511–12). Comus's use of nature only to furnish matter for seduction recalls Calvin's idea that man's natural viciousness of heart leads him to make wrong and corrupted use of all beautiful created things with which God has filled the world, drawing his material for pride from the gifts that should lead him to piety.[15] The Lady's rebuttal of Comus bases itself on another interpretation of nature; she remarks, "do not charge most innocent nature, / As if she would her children should be riotous / With her abundance" (762–64). The Lady, like St. Thomas, knows that correct behavior for human beings and for animals is very different: "there is one kind of order for rational creatures under divine providence and another for irrational creatures" (*Opera* V, p. 252). Against the riotously fertile nature Comus finds, the Lady proposes another model that accepts natural copiousness and adds to it another principle:

> she, good cateress,
> Means her provision only to the good,
> That live according to her sober laws
> And holy dictate of spare Temperance.   (765–68)

The Lady, like St. Thomas, makes temperance a natural and reasonable virtue, in accord with human desires and suggested by intelligent observation: in human beings "the order of our natural tendencies is the order of the law of nature," which is in accord with reason (*ST* 1a2ae 94.2, XXVIII, p. 80). Comus's insistence on the copiousness of nature alone, ignoring her reasonable aspects, suggests an immature understanding. Played by Alice Egerton at age fifteen, almost grown up by seventeenth-century standards, the Lady's response to Comus sounds like the voice of adult reason addressing a clever but rather childish suitor. St. Thomas, like Milton, considers intemperance a childish sin because children easily give in to their appetites, refusing to listen to reason that advises control of desires (*ST* 2a2ae 142.2, XLIII, p. 38). By manifesting adult self-control instead of childish self-indulgence, the Lady confirms herself in her adult social role.

The Lady's ability to resist Comus is clearly seen in her refusal to fall, shown emblematically by her remaining seated in the chair. That she is attracted to him despite her reason is shown by her inability to stand, which can be best understood in terms of Milton's use of St. Thomas's ideas about the power of virtue and the nature of appetite.

The Elder Brother's remark, "Virtue could see to do what virtue would / By her own radiant light" (373–74), echoes Aquinas: "the law of nature is nothing other than the light of the intellect put in us by God, so that we may know what to do and what to avoid" (*Opera* XVI, p. 97). Thus the Elder Brother's confidence in virtue is not misplaced, and the Lady does not boast when she says to Comus, "Thou canst not touch the freedom of my mind" (664). What the Elder Brother and the Lady both neglect to consider is that she is a woman living after the Fall. While Milton shows that nature in *Comus* has preserved much of its aboriginal goodness, there are still frequent references aligning it with the postlapsarian dispensation. On the one hand, nature recalls prelapsarian order: the woods are "kind" and "hospitable" (187), the sky filled with "Stars, / That nature hung in Heav'n" (197–98); on the other hand, the consequences of the Fall are also evident: night is "thievish" (195) and the woods "tangl'd" and full of "blind mazes" (181). Nature is the realm of haemony and Sabrina, but it is also the abode of Comus and his rout. For all of Aquinas's confidence in the continuing goodness and power of nature and natural impulses despite the Fall, he does note that "On top of this law [of reason], the devil has sown another, the law of concupiscence. Frequently the law of concupiscence corrupts the law of nature and the plan of reason" (*Opera* XVI, p. 97). St. Thomas's use of "frequently" separates him from those who would, like Calvin, stress the complete corruption of nature and human reason. In fact, Aquinas emphasizes the power of good to continue in the natural order despite the workings of evil: "Evil belongs neither to the perfection of the universe, nor is it part of the order of the universe, except accidentally because of an accompanying good" (*ST* 1a 48.1, VIII, p. 110). His emphasis on the continuing power of goodness despite evil contradicts Luther's belief that Satan is the master of the world and Calvin's idea that human nature is totally depraved. And Milton follows Aquinas in both these matters. Thus the Elder Brother is partly right when he asserts, "Virtue may be assail'd but never hurt" (589); the action of the masque suggests that the Lady cannot be harmed so long as she continues to choose good. The Elder Brother's next assertion, "Surpris'd by unjust force but not enthrall'd" (590), is not correct. The Lady is enthralled by Comus, despite her mental resistance. A breakdown of mind-body coordination occurs, and she is unable to rise from her seat, despite her firmness of purpose.[16] St. Thomas accounts for lapses in mind-body coordination by noting that the will naturally wants what is good according to reason, just as the concupiscible appetite wants what is pleasing to the senses (*Opera* V, p. 335), but the reason's ability to control the appetites is limited: "that a man wants not to lust and nevertheless lusts derives from a disposition of the body by which the sensitive appetite is impeded from perfectly following the command of reason. The Apostle [St. Paul] says, 'I see another law in my members, fighting against the law of my mind' [Rom. 7.22]" (ST 1a2ae 17.7, XVII, p. 200). The Lady's appetite, not her reason, desires what Comus offers, and her appetite lies so far beneath her reason that she is perhaps not much aware of how strongly her body is tempted. More than one critic has noted that the Lady has been attracted to Comus on a level below reason. Her seat, Sabrina observes, is "smear'd with gums of glutinous heat" (917); that this statement can be read as evidence of arousal has been noted by G. Wilson Knight, Richard Neuse, and Edward Le Comte.[17] The force of Comus's "clasping charm" (853) is also ambiguous and can support either the idea that the Lady is restrained by necromancy or by Comus's seductive presence because "charm" in Milton's time could refer either to sexual fascination or the occult (OED). The amphiboles of "gums of glutinous heat" and "charm" fit Milton's purpose of showing a Lady humanly recognizable as a daughter of Eve without overtly offending the daughter of the earl. That a woman can avoid sin while suffering internal disturbances because of temptation and require external help because of these disturbances can also be seen in Paradise Lost, Book V, 95–128, where Adam comforts Eve following her diabolic dream. As in Comus, a tempter appeals to a woman below the level of rational choice. Eve requires Adam's healing words, just as the Lady requires Sabrina's healing actions.[18]

Part of what Comus offers is reasonable: sexual activity is a legitimate aspect of God's universe; but Comus's way of offering this activity reason must reject. While a recent interpretation of the masque suggests that "the law obeyed in Comus forbids the sexual life,"[19] sexuality is not ultimately repudiated in Comus; the epilogue suggests a reconciliation between the claims of sexuality and chastity. In fact, the younger Milton's acceptance of the goodness of sex can be seen in The Doctrine and Discipline of Divorce: "the guiltles instinct of nature" (CM III, p. 500) and "the radical and innocent affections of nature" (p. 499). Milton's belief in the validity of the sex drive agrees with St. Thomas for whom concupiscence (the desire for pleasure) is not, depending on context, necessarily bad: "concupiscence is . . . a desire for something good" (ST 1a2ae 77.4, XXV, p. 172). Calvin's understanding of concupiscence is altogether different: it throws man's life into violent and lawless movements "which war against the order of God" (Inst. I, p. 518); moreover, Calvin maintains that since the whole of man is concupiscence (Inst. I, p. 218), there is no moderating principle of reason in human nature to offset the fierceness of desire. Luther too considers human nature to be totally depraved;

"the scholastic statement that 'the natural powers are unimpaired' is a horrible blasphemy" and "Memory, will, and mind we have indeed; but they are most depraved and most seriously weakened . . . they are utterly leprous and unclean."[20] Aquinas, on the other hand, more positive about human potential, distinguishes between the superfluous concupiscence of intemperance (*ST* 2a2ae 142.1, XLIII, p. 36) and the healthy pleasure which is the legitimate object of temperance. Milton agrees that both passion and pleasure have their appropriate purposes, and each must be part of the temperate life: "Wherefore did he create passions within us, pleasure round about us, but that these rightly temper'd are the very ingredients of vertu?" (*CM* IV, p. 319).

The internal conflict between reason and appetite in the Lady does not manifest itself on the level of speech; it is evident only in her immobility. Like Eve, she is inwardly perturbed, requiring assistance, but not fallen.[21] To restore the Lady to complete freedom is to heal the breach between what she rationally knows and wants and what her lower appetites want. Sabrina, a young virgin like the Lady, has had her own senses rectified after her death as part of her transfiguration by Nereus,

> Who piteous of her woes, rear'd her lank head,
> And gave her to his daughters to imbathe
> In nectar'd lavers strew'd with Asphodel,
> And through the porch and inlet of each sense
> Dropt in Ambrosial Oils till she reviv'd
> And underwent a quick immortal change,
> Made Goddess of the River.   (836–42)

According to Aquinas, one consequence of the resurrection will be a quickening and perfecting of bodily senses (*ST* 1a2ae 3.3, XVI, pp. 66–68). Because Sabrina first experiences something like death, oils, used in the rite of extreme unction, are appropriate for the regeneration of her senses. The Lady, still alive, will have her senses purified by water, which, through Sabrina's agency in a ceremony suggesting baptism, becomes the emblem for grace indwelling in nature.[22] St. Thomas considers a sacrament to be a "healing remedy" or "spiritual medicine" (*ST* 3a 61, LVI, p. 38); the function of the sacrament of Baptism is regeneration or rebirth through water (*Opera* XVI, p. 119). To restore the Lady to complete freedom, Sabrina must heal her senses and the rest of her body that has unwillingly been excited by Comus. This rectification will heal the gap that has opened between the conscious desires of her reason and the hidden desires of her body:

> Thus I sprinkle on thy breast
> Drops that from my fountain pure

> I have kept of precious cure,
> Thrice upon thy finger's tip,
> Thrice upon thy rubied lip;
> Next this marble venom'd seat
> Smear'd with gums of glutinous heat
> I touch with chaste palms moist and cold.
> Now the spell hath lost his hold.   (911–19)

The Lady's freedom is literally reborn of water. Her concern with temperance, the general virtue under which chastity — and chastity's specific application to her situation as an unmarried woman, virginity — are subsumed, is made complete by the purification of her senses, so that her body can more adequately correspond to the freedom of her mind. Milton follows Aquinas who writes that "the good of mankind is to live according to reason" and that "temperance signifies a certain temperateness or moderation, that reason appoints to human operations and passions"; moreover, "the special object of temperance," he continues, "is healthy pleasure in the sensation of touch" (*ST* 2a2ae 141.1, 2, 5, XLIII, pp. 6, 8, 22). Sabrina specifically sprinkles areas of the Lady's body where tactile sensations are especially acute: breast, fingers, lips, and genitals (which are decorously referred to as "seat"). The Lady has not been willingly incontinent; nevertheless, the necessary intervention of Sabrina, despite the soundness of the Lady's reason and will in resisting Comus, recalls St. Thomas: "knowledge alone does not suffice to cure the incontinent man, for he needs the inward assistance of grace which tempers concupiscence, besides the external remedy of admonition and correction, which induce him to . . . resist his desires, so that concupiscence is weakened" (*ST* 2a2ae 156.3.2, XLIV, p. 28). Sabrina heals the conflict that has been stirred up between the Lady's reason and her body: "the quality and disposition of the body is not subject to reason's rule, and thus the movements of the sensitive appetite are prevented from being entirely subject of reason" (*ST* 1a2ae 17.7, XVIII, p. 200). The freeing of the Lady from her captivity naturally follows from the reintegration of body and mind that Sabrina brings about. Having passed through death herself, Sabrina stands fully in both the natural and supernatural realms, beyond death and yet fully identified with a local river. She is at once human, "a Virgin pure," participating as the Lady does in what remains of prelapsarian rectitude, "guiltless" (829) of the fault for which she is pursued, yet also "a gentle Nymph" (824) and "Goddess of the River" (842).

Sabrina, as Douglas Bush has noted, shows "the necessity of grace as well as rational virtue."[23] But the grace she provides is allied with nature through the operation of something like a sacrament, rather than her being above nature in the rather Platonic way the Lady expects assistance from disembodied forms of faith, hope, and chastity (213–15). Some assistance does come from the supersensible realm; the Attendant Spirit's function is essential. His knowledge leads the rescuers to haemony and Sabrina. But his agency is shown to be not enough. Grace must also work through nature. John Knott observes, "Sabrina's power to release the Lady . . . , though it may suggest the operation of Christian grace . . . seems to spring from the river itself. It is as though Sabrina by virtue of her own purity can call upon a power for goodness latent in the natural world."[24] While haemony, like Sabrina, suggests the positive powers remaining hidden in nature despite the Fall, it is not sacramental because although it causes Comus to flee, it has no power to heal the Lady. That haemony is a real plant available in Western Britain, as Charlotte Otten has shown, reinforces this idea.[25] The identification of Sabrina with grace is encouraged by the text: the Attendant Spirit says, after Sabrina has worked the release of the Lady, "Come Lady, while Heaven lends us grace, / Let us fly this cursed place" (938–39).

Milton's opinion in *De Doctrina* is that baptism is for "the bodies of believers who engage themselves to pureness of life," which the Lady's prayer (213 ff.) suggests she has done prior to the entry of Sabrina, "immersed in running water, to signify their regeneration" (*CM* XVI, p. 169), which occurs for the Lady as she regains her mobility. Milton does not in *De Doctrina* make sacraments the vehicle of grace; a sacrament is a "visible sign," a "figure" (*CM* XVI, pp. 165, 199), which "can neither impart salvation or grace" of itself, but is "given as a pledge or symbol to believers of the actual blessings" (p. 201). Nevertheless, the functioning of Sabrina in *Comus* seems closer to St. Thomas's belief that baptism is an instrumental cause of grace (*ST* 3a 62.1, LVI, pp. 52–54). Aquinas also believes that a sacrament "has a certain hidden holiness, and in this sense a sacrament is a sacred secret" (*ST* 3a 60.1, LVI, p. 6). Sabrina's power is also hidden; only the Attendant Spirit knows of her presence "under the glassy, cool, translucent wave" (861). If Sabrina's power confers freedom, liberating like grace, so also is it, in both Milton's and Aquinas's terms, a sign, though each of them interprets "sign" differently. St. Thomas writes, "a sacrament properly is that which is planned to *signify* our sanctification. In this, three things can be considered: the actual *cause* of our sanctification, which is the Passion of Christ, the *form* of our sanctification, which consists in grace and the virtues, and the ultimate *end* of our sanctification, which is eternal life" (*ST* 3a 60.3, LVI, p. 10, my emphasis). While Sabrina's watery realm in the "smooth Severn stream" (835) suggests something of the easy harmony of prelapsarian nature, "the most innocent nature" the Lady speaks of (762), there is in Sabrina that which also suggests the virgin martyr. She is allied with this world through her identification both with nature — in the Attendant Spirit's invocation of her (859–66) and in her song (890–901) — and with history as the Attendant Spirit rehearses the story of her pursuit and death (824–32). At the same time, she is identified also as supernatural, immaterial,

> Thus I set my printless feet
> O'er the Cowslip's Velvet head,
> That bends not as I tread,   (896–98)

and immortal (841). Sabrina's historical personality, her virginity, her innocent death, and her subsequent transfiguration and immortality all suggest that she is a type of Christ. Her sovereignty over the Severn corresponds to Christ's priestly function and her martyrdom recalls Christ's. Like Christ, she is a good shepherd, concerned with the nurturing of life in her realm; though "Goddess of the River"

> still she retains
> Her maid'n gentleness, and oft at Eve
> Visits the herds along the twilight meadows,
> Helping all urchin blasts, and ill-luck signs
> That the shrewd meddling Elf delights to make,
> Which she with precious vial'd liquors heals.   (842–47)

The sacramental healing of the Lady fits Aquinas's idea that the power of Christ works through the sacraments (*ST* 3a 64.3, LVI, p. 110), and the sacrament of baptism is especially appropriate for the Lady because baptism signifies "spiritual cleansing" (*ST* 3a 60.6, LVI, p. 22).

The association of Sabrina with water, and thus with mobility, flexibility, and softness, stands as a necessary counterweight to balance the Lady's embodiment of chastity as a too militantly rigid virtue. The Elder Brother mentions goddesses from classical mythology whose business it is to guard chastity, yet both Diana and Minerva have some rather frightening attributes. Diana, like Sabrina, is a virgin and like Sabrina governs nature, but while Sabrina "with moist curb sways the smooth Severn stream" (835), Diana, "queen o' th' Woods" (446), presides over savage beasts: "tam'd the brinded lioness / And spotted mountain pard" (443–44). Nothing in Sabrina corresponds to Diana's "dread bow" (441); Sabrina is far too gentle for armament. Her gentleness and softness also distinguish her from Minerva, whose "snaky-headed *Gorgon*-shield / . . .

freez'd her foes to congeal'd stone" (447–48). How unlike are Sabrina's "soft alluring locks" (882) and "the loose train of . . . amber-dropping hair" (863). Diana and Minerva, stern, dreadful goddesses, are supernatural counterparts for the Lady's initial conceptions about what her unassisted virtue can accomplish; what she needs (and gets) to free her from immobility is someone like Sabrina, who is both kindly and protective, associated with water rather than with stone.

In Sabrina, rational adherence to chastity is fully integrated with a regenerated body, incorporeal as it is. Aquinas emphasizes the importance of incarnation — the flesh of Christ's body, his bodily resurrection, and the transformation of sacramental bread and wine into this body, integrating the natural world with the world of grace (*ST* 3a 61.1, 62.5, 78.3; LVI, pp. 38, 68; LVIII, pp. 176–80). Sabrina embodies the reintegration of nature with perfected reason that for the faithful lies on the other side of death, and yet, through her merit as a saint, she can still help the living (*ST* 3a 25.6, L, p. 202). Comus has attempted to destroy the Lady's integrity, the cooperation of her body with her mind's allegiance to divine precept, and he has in part succeeded through the unwilled response of her body. This response Sabrina corrects. That Sabrina enjoys corporeity, however subtle, is important. The emphasis on her senses (839) and her hair (863, 882, 927) stresses, even in her regenerate state, a physicality as refined perhaps as that of the angels in *Paradise Lost,* and very different from the disembodied ideal of chastity that occurs to the Lady when she addresses the "unblemish't form" of chastity (215). Sabrina exists in the masque partly to correct the excessively transcendental focus the Lady has given to her experience. Expecting rescue in a gloomy wood, the Lady's thoughts of faith, hope, and chastity lead her to reflect that God "Would send a glist'ring Guardian, if need were, / To keep my life and honor unassail'd" (219–20). Comus shows up soon afterward; nevertheless, the Lady's prayer is also answered in the way she intends: a "glist'ring Guardian" in the person of the Attendant Spirit does come to help rescue her. But the Attendant Spirit's reliance on haemony and Sabrina suggests that the Lady needs to learn that powerful goodness also exists at one's feet on earth as well as over one's head in heaven. Sabrina proves, as the Lady has argued in her rebuttal against Comus's understanding of nature, that there is no necessary dichotomy between nature and grace, provided that nature is rightly used. The sacramental, physical nature of Sabrina fits what the Lady needs to learn: that virtue can be absolutely self-sufficient only when mind and body work perfectly together, an impossibility for postlapsarian man or woman, even the staunch Lady.

The nature of both Comus and Sabrina is sensuous. While Comus appeals to the Lady's natural appetites and apparently offers the Lady a drink made of all natural ingredients — "spirits of balm, and fragrant Syrups mixt" (674) — Sabrina's use of nature is to "save" (866), through her sacramental combining of nature (water) with grace to heal the Lady so that she can stand. Sabrina also serves to teach the Lady the incompleteness of her assumptions about the locus of redemptive power, which is in nature as much as in the heavens. Sabrina's function as both healer and teacher fits Aquinas's understanding of the sacraments: "by the institution of the sacraments, man in harmony with his nature learns through sensible things. He is humbled by recognizing that he is subject to physical things, inasmuch as he gets help through them, and he is even preserved from physical harm through the healthy partaking of the sacraments" (ST 3a 61.1, LVI, p. 38).

The rising of the Lady from her seat prepares the reader for the consummation of her journey. There is not in *Comus*, unlike *Paradise Lost*, an immediately obvious emphasis on education; nevertheless, the Attendant Spirit has shown the audience that learning and teaching are possible. The Attendant Spirit has learned about haemony from "a certain shepherd lad" who taught him about herbs in payment for his singing; the Attendant Spirit also learned about Sabrina from Meliboeus, another shepherd. That the Attendant Spirit, early in the masque so disdainful about the earth, has been taught by shepherds, who are at once humble and knowledgeable about the hidden potencies that exist in nature, suggests that education is a concern of the masque. As the Attendant Spirit has learned from shepherds, so he, disguised as one, teaches the brothers what needs to be done to drive off Comus and rescue the Lady. That the Lady learns is suggested both by the enormous amount of experience she has undergone and her silence following her rescue, implying that she needs time to assimilate what has happened. The most obvious indication that the Lady has learned from her trials and rescues comes from the Attendant Spirit, who reintroduces her parents, appropriately saying that she, as well as her brothers, have "goodly grown" (968). The Lady's knowledge before she meets Comus was sufficient to allow her to refute his argument and repulse seduction; this sufficiency shows that her parents have done their duty educating her. But the Lady's knowledge has not been strong enough to free her from the fascination Comus has exerted. Nevertheless, her ability to avoid falling, plus the actions of others, arising both from love of her and love of virtue, make possible her liberation. The masque clearly shows that the concern of others is no substitute for self-reliance. The Lady must resist for a time, depending on her own resources. Milton agrees with Aquinas, who observes that, while well regulated home and social relationships are indispensable for the proper welfare of each person, domestic and political prudence do not supply the lack of personal prudence (*Opera* XXI, p. 210). While Sabrina's function is to reintegrate the Lady's body with her knowledge of what is right, once her rescue is complete, she can be completely reintegrated only in the society to which she properly belongs, her father's household, which is both the local expression of the City of God and the community to which she rightly adheres as her father's daughter. G. H. Carrithers has correctly emphasized the importance of community in *Comus*;[26] Milton accords with Aquinas, who observes, "man is a social animal, having many wants he cannot supply for himself. By living with others, he is helped to the good live" (*Opera* XXI, p. 2). The Lady's full reintegration in the human community is celebrated through images of reappearing light, "Come let us haste, the Stars grow high" (956), after "the Stygian darkness" of Comus, and movement, the "rural dance" of the shepherds and the "victorious dance" (952, 974) as the Lady and her brothers celebrate the fact that virtue is free to enjoy as well as stable to avoid falling.

Even after the rescue of the Lady and with the approaching reunion with her family, there are hints that nature will continue to mix the ingredients of trial with blessedness. The Attendant Spirit leads his group to "holier ground," but he must first take them "through this gloomy covert wide" (945). As he does, light increases, "the Stars grow high," but darkness is not banished, for "night sits monarch yet in the mid sky" (956–57). The Attendant Spirit announces to Lord and Lady Egerton that all that has transpired has helped to perfect their children, by its having "tri'd their youth" (970), recalling Milton's concept, "that which purifies us is triall, and triall is by what is contrary" (*CM* IV, p. 311). If "youth" is tried in the masque, perhaps the audience is encouraged to recognize that later times in life will have their trials too. "The crown of deathless praise" (983) which the Attendant Spirit says the young people have won belongs to their present victory and reminds one that the final crown they aspire to achieve lies ahead, after the trials of their whole lives' journey have been gone through.

The interconnectedness, even the interpenetration, of nature and grace suggested by Sabrina does not disappear in the epilogue despite the pattern of ascent there that has so frequently been commented upon. Woodhouse first remarked on "the ascent through the order of nature to the order of grace"; Rajan, Reesing, and Roston have all commented upon ascent in the epilogue.[27] The paradisal garden that Attendant Spirit describes includes processes that recall earlier events in the masque. The beauties of "eternal Summer" are guaranteed by the stewardship of Iris, who, very much like Sabrina, tends nature through her benevolence:

> *Iris* there with humid bow,
> Waters the odorous banks that blow
> Flowers of more mingled hue
>
> · · · · · · · · · ·
>
> And drenches with *Elysian* dew
> (List mortals, if your ears be true)
> Beds of *Hyacinth* and Roses.   (992–98)

The dew of Iris recalls the moist white magic of Sabrina; each of them works to assure fertility within her own realm. In the garden of Iris, we find Venus and Adonis. Venus would appear to symbolize here the principle of generative love. She awaits the healing of Adonis, "waxing well of his deep wound" (1000), whose injury corresponds to the Lady's wounding by Comus. Implicitly, recovery for the Lady will, at the proper time, enable the fruition of generative love that Adonis will enjoy with Venus when he awakens. This hint is exquisitely tactful — the audience will understand if their ears be true. Milton was perhaps aware that nine of Alice Egerton's sisters married between the ages of seventeen and twenty-two and that Alice was approaching marriageable age.[28] The epilogue shows that the Lady's chastity, known to her most appropriately at the current time of her life as virginity, will endure even when virginity is transmuted into chaste marriage, "for marriage must not be call'd a defilement" (*CM* III, p. 306).

In the paradisal garden of the epilogue, time and process continue to go on. "Far above" this garden "in spangled sheen,"

> Celestial *Cupid* her fam'd son advanc't,
> Holds his dear *Psyche* sweet entranc't.   (1003–05)

Though the Attendant Spirit has now soared in his description above the earthly paradise he initially describes, he continues to address the same concerns. The marriage of Cupid and Psyche in heaven, "far above in spangled sheen," both ratifies the more earthly and physical unions of Venus and Adonis, as well as the Lady and her implied future husband, and shows the delightful circumstances of chaste marriage, "Youth and Joy" (1011), which image may also point toward the offspring the Lady may some day produce. Marriage may later, as virginity does now, ensure the continuation of chastity. The engendering of children in marriage is chaste, as well as delightful, fulfilling God's ordinance to be fruitful and multiply. Like Venus and Adonis, Cupid and Psyche are identified with the generative principle in the cosmos. Far surpassing Comus's understanding of nature in terms of lust, with indiscriminate gratification of the appetite the sole means to pleasure, the union of Cupid and Psyche is a social act; the "free consent the gods among" (1007) publicly ratifies their union and shares their joy, quite unlike the love in a closet that Comus offers the Lady.

Cupid and Psyche remind the reader of the trial and testing that Psyche underwent before her marriage to Cupid could be possible, a testing and trial that was not without her making some mistakes. Nevertheless, she finally was allowed to marry Cupid. The Lady too has been tried and tested, proving to be both virtuous and maculate. The waiting that Psyche and Venus must endure before they can enjoy union with their beloveds recalls the delay the Lady experienced while waiting to be rescued. In the matter of delay and testing, as in marriage and generation, the epilogue suggests that heaven may be like earth; the ascent from earth to heaven brings no reversal or annulment of all conditions creatures must experience. The celebratory emphasis of the epilogue does show that trials and testing bear the glorious fruits of joy and freedom.

Milton's suggestion of the fulfillment that chastity makes possible follows Aquinas, who discusses chastity not as a self-punishing restraint but rather as a necessary means to happiness: "the end and rule of temperance is itself happiness" (*ST* 2a2ae 141.6.1, XLIII, p. 26). The most complete happiness can be found only in love: Aquinas suggests that no one has joy unless he lives in love (*Opera* XVI, pp. 98–99). The epilogue suggests that the outcome of chastity is not "lean and sallow Abstinence" (709) as Comus insists, but rather joy, delight, and freedom. The Lady and her brothers are happy finally to be free of Comus's enchantments, but greater happiness still awaits them; in Aquinas's words, "delight perfects happiness as beauty does youth" (*Opera* VII, p. 556). The pattern of ascent in the epilogue is not so much from nature to grace as through increasing discoveries of delight, none of which repudiates an earlier, "lower" delight. Milton does not oppose mind to body in the epilogue; while Sidney suggests the power of "knowledge to lift up the mind from the dungeon of the body to the enjoying his own divine essence,"[29] Milton's masque suggests how one joy may follow another as life progresses without denying the body's legitimate claims. The key to the delight that Milton assures the temperate is to be found through love, which he terms "the summe of all commands, and the perfection" (*CM* IV, p. 186), agreeing with Aquinas that it is love which perfects the will and orders it to the perfection of happiness (*Opera* VII, p. 556).

The emphasis on love in the epilogue provides for the audience the necessary corrective to the Lady's earlier "faith, hope and chastity." While the masque has shown the importance of both chastity and charity, the epilogue reinforces what we have learned. The emphasis on love — Sabrina's love of virgins, the Attendant Spirit's love of the virtuous, the brothers' love of the Lady, the loves of Venus and Adonis, Cupid and Psyche — recalls the orthodox Christian position on love (1 Cor. xiii), which in Aquinas takes this expression: "charity is more excellent than faith or hope, and consequently than all the virtues" (ST 2a2ae 23.6, XXXIV, p. 24). While the epilogue suggests that marriage will be an appropriate action in the Lady's future, Milton does not follow Aquinas completely in the treatment of the relationship of marriage to supreme bliss. The Attendant Spirit rejoices in a mobility, a freedom that enables him to soar from "the green earth's end" to "the corners of the Moon" (1014–17). The felicity of liberty he enjoys may be qualified by the commitments of the married estate the Lady will some day enter, but this freedom, the highest delight of which is the contemplation of God, is not forfeited by the married. While he does not exclude all spiritual pleasures from the married, Aquinas notes, "the higher powers, namely reason and will," which lead men to the knowledge of God, "are most grievously disordered by lust" (ST 2a2ae 153.5, XLIII, p. 200); however, the married state need not know lust, which "consists essentially in exceeding the order and mode of reason in the matter of venereal acts" (ST 2a2ae 153.5, XLIII, p. 196). Nevertheless, Aquinas stresses that the highest felicity for mankind, the contemplation of God, is more readily available to celibates than householders: "holy virginity abstains from all venereal pleasures in order more freely to have leisure for divine contemplation" (ST 2a2ae 152.2, XLIII, p. 174). Milton's understanding of this issue is rather different. The same high felicity and freedom available to celibate contemplatives may be known by those who marry: "celestiall songs" will be heard by those who are "not defil'd with women, which doubtlesse means fornication: For mariage must not be call'd defilement" (CM III, p. 306). The freedom which the Attendant Spirit says virtue rejoices in — "Love virtue, she alone is free" (1019) — complements the obligations, stability, and patience that marriage implies. It recalls Milton's insistence that true freedom is Christian liberty, which can be attained only by aligning one's will with God in a relationship the Scripture depicts as marriage.

The difficulty of the epilogue may in part arise from the young Milton's preference for the Spenserian dark conceit, where the obscurity of the images fits the sublimity of the subject matter. The images of idealized earth and heaven in the epilogue transcend the limits of the rational arguments that various characters have so far advanced about the power of chastity. Without rejecting reason, the epilogue literally soars beyond it. Milton's practice here has a rationale in Aquinas, who, while highly valuing the role of reason in religious life, remarks that reason has its limits: "some supernatural knowledge is necessary" (*ST* 2a2ae 2.3.1, XXXI, p. 74); "love is the end (*terminus*) of knowledge" (*ST* 2a2ae 27.4.1, XXXIV, p. 172). Since the highest form of love leads to supreme wisdom, which is the knowledge of God (with chastity serving to guarantee the direction of attention toward the highest good), and supreme knowledge is itself love, some mystery in the epilogue fits its subject. The difficulty of the epilogue may relate to Aquinas's suggestions (*ST* 1a 37.1, VII, p. 80) that language often falls short of adequately depicting the mysteries of love.

Central Missouri State University

NOTES

1. Georgia Christopher, *Milton and the Science of the Saints* (Princeton, 1982), p. 33. William Kerrigan argues that *Comus* suggests a split between the natural and divine orders (*The Sacred Complex: On the Psychogenesis of "Paradise Lost"* [Cambridge, Mass., 1983], pp. 20, 27). Maryann McGuire, while deeming Christopher's approach "suggestive," finds that it "argues for too rigid conformity on Milton's part to Protestant orthodoxy" (*Milton's Puritan Masque* [Athens, Ga., 1983], p. 6); McGuire's observation that in *Comus* Milton "described a world in which the divine infuses the natural" (p. 77) differs remarkably from Christopher.

2. *Milton and the Science of the Saints*, p. 39.

3. A. S. P. Woodhouse's readings have been most influential in establishing this tradition. The seminal essays, "The Argument of Milton's *Comus*," *UTQ*, XI (1941), 46–71, and "*Comus* Once More," *UTQ*, XIX (1950), 219–23, are reprinted in John S. Diekhoff, ed. *"A Maske at Ludlow": Essays on Milton's "Comus"* (Cleveland, 1968). Following Woodhouse are Arthur Barker, *Milton and the Puritan Tradition* (Toronto, 1942); William Madsen, "The Idea of Nature in Milton's Poetry," in Richard B. Young et al., *Three Studies in the Renaissance: Sidney, Jonson, Milton*, Yale Studies in English, no. 138 (New Haven, 1958), pp. 181–283; and Eric LaGuardia, *Nature Redeemed: The Imitation of Order in Three Renaissance Poems* (The Hague: 1966). James Andrew Clark, "Milton Naturans, Milton Naturatus: The Debate Over Nature in *A Maske Presented at Ludlow*," *Milton Studies*, XX, ed. James D. Simmonds (Pittsburgh, 1984), pp. 3–25, appeared too late for me to consider in this essay.

4. Paul Dowling, "'The Scholastick Grosnesse of the Barbarous Ages': The Question of the Humanism of Milton's Understanding of Virtue," pp. 59–72, and Ellen Goodman, "Sway and Subjection: Natural Causation and the Portrayal of Paradise in the *Summa*

Theologica and *Paradise Lost*," pp. 73–87. Both these studies appear in John Mulryan, ed. *Milton and the Middle Ages* (East Brunswick, 1982).

5. The text of Milton's poetry cited throughout this essay is Merritt Y. Hughes ed., *John Milton: Complete Poems and Major Prose* (Indianapolis, 1957).

6. *Summa Theologiae*, ed. Thomas Gilby et al. (New York, 1964–69), 2a2ae 23.1, XXIV, p. 8. Hereafter cited in the text as *ST*. All translations of Aquinas are mine.

7. *Corpus Reformatorum*, ed. W. Baum et al. (Bransvigae, 1864), LVI, p. 488.

8. All quotations of Milton's prose are from *The Works of John Milton*, ed. Frank Patterson et al. (New York, 1931–38), cited in the text as *CM*.

9. John Reesing observes that Milton "throughout his career . . . refers to Nature as a standard of pure and faultless morality" (*Milton's Poetic Art: "A Mask," "Lycidas," "Paradise Lost"* [Cambridge, Mass., 1968], p. 3). By "Nature" Reesing means prelapsarian nature, which is *Comus*, as in the theology of Aquinas, still persists despite the distortions in it arising from original sin.

10. *Opera Omnia* (New York, 1948), XV, p. 81, hereafter cited in the text as *Opera*.

11. *City of God*, trans. Marcus Dods (New York, 1948), I, pp. 15–22, II, pp. 91–92.

12. A. S. P. Woodhouse and Douglas Bush, eds. *A Variorium Commentary on the Poems of John Milton*, gen. ed. Merritt Y. Hughes (New York, 1972), II, iv, 808.

13. *Images and Themes in Five Poems by Milton* (Cambridge, Mass., 1957), p. 140.

14. *Institutes of the Christian Religion*, trans. Henry Beveridge (Grand Rapids, 1970), I, p. 218, hereafter cited in the text as *Inst.*

15. *Commentaries on the First Twenty Chapters of the Book of the Prophet Ezekiel*, trans. Thomas Myers (Edinburgh, 1850), II, p. 111.

16. Two important interpretations of the Lady's immobility are Richard Neuse, "Metamorphosis and Symbolic Action in *Comus*," *ELH*, XXXIV (1967), 49–64, and Sears Jayne, "The Subject of Milton's Ludlow *Mask*," *PMLA*, LXXIV (1959), 533–43. A reading attempting to reconcile the two is William A. Oram, "The Invocation of Sabrina," *SEL*, XXIV (1984), 121–41.

17. G. Wilson Knight, *The Burning Oracle* (London, 1939), pp. 168–69; Neuse, "Metamorphosis," 57; Edward Le Comte, *Milton and Sex* (New York, 1978), pp. 1–2.

18. In *Milton's Eve* (Urbana, 1983), pp. 90–91, Diane McColley discusses the Puritan treatment of the idea that "the lower faculties" can desire an action without sin, so long as the will does not accede.

19. Kerrigan, *Sacred Complex*, p. 20.

20. *Works*, ed. Jaroslav Pelikan (St. Louis, 1953), XII, p. 308; I, p. 61.

21. Christopher argues that the Lady's immobility derives from the persistence of grace despite sin, *Milton and the Science of the Saints*, p. 53.

22. Woodhouse first noticed that Sabrina provides an infusion of grace, though he excluded baptism, "*Comus* Once More," in Diekhoff, *Essays*, p. 76.

23. *John Milton* (New York, 1964), p. 54.

24. *Milton's Pastoral Vision* (Chicago, 1971), pp. 121–22.

25. While haemony, like Sabrina, suggests the positive powers remaining hidden in nature despite the Fall, it is not sacramental because, though it causes Comus to flee, it has no power to heal the Lady. That haemony is a real plant available in western Britain, as Charlotte Otten has shown ("Milton's Haemony," *ELR*, V [1975], 81–92) reinforces this idea.

26. "Milton's Ludlow Mask: From Chaos to Community," *ELH*, XXXIII (1966), 23–42.

27. Woodhouse, "The Argument of Milton's *Comus*," in Diekhoff, p. 36; Balachan-

dra Rajan, "Comus: The Inglorious Likeness," *UTQ*, XXXVII (1967–68), 129–30; Reesing, *Milton's Poetic Art*, p. 7; Murray Roston, *Milton and the Baroque* (Pittsburgh, 1980), p. 46.

28. William Parker, *Milton: A Biography* (London, 1968), p. 791.

29. Philip Sidney, *An Apology for Poetry*, ed. Geoffrey Shepherd (London, 1965), p. 104.

TOWARD *PARADISE LOST:*
TEMPTATION AND ANTICHRIST
IN THE ENGLISH REVOLUTION

Jun Harada

THE PURPOSE of my essay is to search for a possible link between Milton the revolutionary and Milton the bard in his execution of the theme of temptation in *Paradise Lost*. First, I confess that my general approach to the subject is akin to Christopher Hill's historical and author-contextual methodology: "The poems will not speak for themselves unless we understand his ideas in their context. . . . I believe that Milton's ideas were more directly influenced than is usually recognized by the events of the English Revolution in which he was an active participant."[1] This is the basis upon which I try to elucidate how some of Milton's experiences during the Revolution influenced the temptation scene in *Paradise Lost*.[2]

However, Hill's interpretation and mine differ with regard to such basic matters as Milton's concepts of innocence, ignorance, and the manner of temptation. Hill says, "Intuitive understanding of God's purposes, and consequent obedience to them, was expected of Adam and Eve. One of Milton's problems which he did not solve, was to differentiate between unfallen innocence and ignorance. In his conversation with Raphael Adam's mental processes are not different from those in his postlapsarian discussion with Michael" (pp. 378–79). Milton's alleged confusion of unfallen innocence with fallen ignorance is the basis of Hill's equating the innocent Adam's fall with the ignorant revolutionary leaders' failure: "It is at such points that the analogy with the English Revolution may help. Blame for its failure, in Milton's eyes, rested with its leaders. They ought to have abstained from certain temptations—from avarice and ambition—and they and their followers ought to have known that God so wished. If they ought to have had this intuitive knowledge, so *a fortiori* ought unfallen Adam" (ibid.).

The sin of ignorance which Hill derives from the *Christian Doctrine* is not the primary cause of Adam's fall in Milton's system of ideas. The sin of falling is clearly defined in *Christian Doctrine* as "evil desire, or the will to do evil and the evil deed itself."[3] The sin of ignorance to

45

which Hill ascribes the main cause of the Fall is understood by Milton as a subordinate term to explain the loss of innocence, which was unfallen man's original condition: "Anyway their loss was a consequence of sin, rather than a sin itself; or if it was a sin, it was only a sin of ignorance, because they did not expect for a moment that they would lose anything good by eating the fruit" (YP VI, p. 390). Thus ignorance is not a principal sin that accounts for man's Fall, but rather a minor constituent of the complex mechanism of the Fall. This may be why it is placed in an additional clause preceded by "if it was a sin."

Hill's concepts of unfallen innocence and fallen ignorance are not effective tools for elucidating the problem of temptation and fall with which Milton was centrally concerned in both the arena of the Revolution and the visionary world of poetry. The central concept should be sought first not in the one tempted but in the Tempter himself, because it was Satan's fraud that aroused an evil desire in man and led him to yield to it in the original temptation. This evil desire must be the sin most responsible for the Fall of Eve and Adam. Hill's direct overlapping of literary and extraliterary material does not help to elucidate but rather confuses the point at issue. A solution to the problem of the Fall is not to be found by reducing it to an analogy of the revolutionary leaders' failure but is to be sought in Milton himself and in his involvement with the failure of the revolutionary leaders.

On Milton's own problem with the Revolution, Hill merely perpetuates the old story of a split between Milton's conscious and unconscious selves, the latter being of the devil's party: "Satan, the battle ground for Milton's quarrel with himself, saw God as arbitrary power and nothing else. Against this he revolted: the Christian, Milton knew, must accept it. Yet how could a free and rational individual accept what God had done to his servants in England? On this reading, Milton expressed through Satan (of whom he disapproved) the dissatisfaction which he felt with the Father (whom intellectually he accepted)" (pp. 366–67).

God's unjust dealing with his servants supposedly invited Milton's hidden revolt against him. Such speculation is not convincing. Milton begins The Tenure of Kings and Magistrates with a statement of his belief in man's full responsibility for his own deeds: "If men within themselves would be govern'd by reason, and not generally give up thir understanding to a double tyrannie, of Custom from without, and blind affections within, they would discern better, what it is to favor and uphold the Tyrant of a Nation" (YP III, p. 190). Here at the start of this antimonarchical tract he argues that the fallen ignorance of degenerates who are not governed by reason is the cause of their subjugation to tyranny. Those people have a propensity to fall because of their innate ignorance. Such ignorance, however, could be overcome by their faith in Christ who sacrificed himself to save those ignorant sinners. Thus their subjugation to a tyrant is their own responsibility, not to be ascribed to God. Milton had no occasion to express through Satan any dissatisfaction with what God had done to his servants.

Milton was not directly concerned with Satan in the actual arena of the Revolution, but he was concerned with Antichrist, Satan's entrusted apocalyptic Beast. The first premise of my discussion is that any element of an epic must be filtered through the poet's built-in mythopoeic apparatus and his patterned experience before it is realized as an external art form. Such raw materials as the revolutionary leaders' failure or the fiction of Milton's unconscious revolt against God are alien insertions by a critic. My second premise is that the theme of the temptation must have been experienced within Milton's inner being in such a fatal way that he was himself inevitably but innocently involved in worldly powers by having trusted in them more than once. This may be the way the English Revolution influenced the development of Satan and of the temptation theme in the epic.

I

Milton's misgivings about the Revolution found vent as early as August 1646 in a sonnetto *On the New Forcers of Conscience under the Long Parliament*. In it Presbyterians were not so much likened to as matched with the prelates, yesterday's enemy they found and threw off, says Milton, only "to seize the widow'd whore plurality / From them whose sin ye envied, not abhorr'd."[4]

The sonnetto makes another comparison between the Presbyterians and the papists who once maneuvered the minority Protestant delegates into drafting the Confession of Faith at the Council of Trent in 1563. Likewise, the Presbyterians forced the minority Congregationalists into a similar sort of confession of faith at the Westminster Assembly in 1643, two years before the composition of the sonnetto. Their guilefulness is, according to Milton, "worse than those of Trent." Both comparisons are reconfirmed in the last line of the poem: "*New Presbyter* is but *Old Priest* at large."

The sonnetto goes on to ask the Presbyterians an incriminating question: "Dare ye for this adjure the Civil Sword / To force our Consciences that Christ set free?" Their spiritual predecessors were the Jewish clergy at the time of Christ, who, to quote Milton in *Sonnet XII*, "Still revolted when truth would set them free" from the bondage of the letter of the Law. They denied and crucified him with the help of the secular sword of a Roman procurator. The Presbyterians similarly use state power to deny liberty of conscience. By comparing the Presbyterians to the preceding Antichristian forcers of conscience, the poet prophesies their destruction.

The Antichrist loomed up with an utterly different mask at each critical stage in the persecution of Christian believers. He was recognized in the English Reformation in the historical line of world-dominant powers, such as the Roman empire or emperor at the time of the apostles' hardships, the pope or papacy in the age of the Protestants' sufferings, and the Episcopal prelates in the period of the Puritans' persecutions. In the marginal notes to the Geneva Bible is found "the first empire Roman was as the pattern: the second empire is an image and shadow thereof."[5] At the outbreak of the Revolution in 1640 the Presbyterian-dominated Parliament passed the Root and Branch Petition to terminate the Episcopal Prelacy by labeling them "members of the Beast."[6]

Following this apocalyptic bestial image of Antichrist, Milton indicted the prelates in his first tract *Of Reformation in England* in May 1641: "If the splendor of Gold and Silver begin to Lord it once againe in the Church of England; wee shall see *Antichrist* shortly heere, though his chiefe Kennell be at Rome" (YP I, p. 590). The same method is used to identify Charles I with Antichrist in *The Tenure* in February 1649: "we read how the Dragon gave to the beast *his power, his seate, and great authority:* which beast so autoriz'd most expound to be the tyrannical powers and Kingdoms of the earth" (YP III, 210). Milton goes on to indict the Presbyterians for their royalized apostasy, their Antichristian, deceitful activities of siding with the king they once fought and even imprisoned: "He [Charles I] who but erewhile in the Pulpits was a cursed Tyrant, an enemie to God and Saints . . . is now, though nothing penitent or alter'd from his first principles, a lawfull Magistrate, a Sovran Lord, the Lords anointed, not to be touch'd, though by themselves imprison'd" (YP III, p. 197). Three months later Milton accused them again in *The Observation on the Article of Peace*. The Presbyterian rule was "the next immediate way to make the Church lift a Horn against the State and claim an absolute and undepending Jurisdiction." Thus finally identifying them with the Beast, Milton repeatedly discloses the Antichristian nature of the Presbyterians. He says, "as from like advantage and occasion . . . the Pope hath for many ages done; and not only our Bishops were climing after him, but our Presbyters also, as by late experiment wee find" (YP III, p. 320).

Milton is telling us by these resolute indictments that the Presbyterians were arch enemies of the Revolution within the revolutionary camp, betraying themselves as Antichristian at the very moment of their parliamentary ascendancy over the Antichrist, King Charles I. Milton's frontal attack on the Presbyterians never slackened throughout almost all the tracts he wrote after 1649, but continued until *The Considerations Touching the Likeliest Means* in August 1659: "These our new reformed English Presbyterian divines, against thir own cited authors, and to the shame of thir pretended reformation, would engross to themselves all tythes by statute . . . to impose upon us a Judidaical ceremonial law . . . more complying with a covetous clergie, then any of those Popish kings and parlaments alleged" (YP VII, p. 295). Within this brief passage is compressed Milton's final critical assessment of the royalized Presbyterians.

It should be pointed out that he stops impeaching them in *The Readie and Easie Way* in April 1660. This time he resorts to warning them of possible retaliation by the son of the executed king and by the Popish and Episcopal forces if they were to be restored: "Especially what can this last Parlament expect, who having receiv'd lately and published the covenant, have reengag'd themselves, never to readmit Episcopacie: which no son of Charls returning, but will most certainly bring back with him, if he regard the last and strictest charge of his father . . . among which he accounted Presbyterie one of the chief . . . how will he keep faith to us with disobedience to him?" (Y VII, pp. 457–58). The passage shows Milton's desperate but vain efforts to rally to the anti-Stuart campaign all the people who might suffer reprisals at the restoration of the Stuarts. He reminds the Presbyterians, yesterday's enemy, of what the late king had thought of them and of what they had done to him. It may seem strange that such a determined anti-Presbyterian as Milton should switch abruptly to an amiable voice, but this is the voice of the realist-strategist Milton who tried by all means to organize a united front against the enemy of Christ at the deathbed of the Commonwealth in April 1660.

His warning discloses his fundamental attitude toward the Presbyterians in his strategic map of the revolutionary war. In it they are situated not as the real Antichrist such as Charles I or the papists but as an Antichristian wing, which he understood very well was highly precarious in its opportunistic nature. In the map there are ranged the reactionary, feudalistic monarch, papists, and prelates on one hand and the modern democratic, petit bourgeois Levellers, utopian-socialist Diggers, and other radical sectaries on the other. In between stand the established, conservative, gentry-class Presbyterians and the newly-risen propertied class, the Independents. It is these middle groups that Milton once trusted in, despaired of, and then finally appealed to at the last stage of the abortive Revolution — but in vain. He says, "I may say the antipathie which is in all kings against Presbyterian and Independent discipline? for they hear the gospel speaking much of libertie; a word monarchie and her bishops both fear and hate" (YP VII, p. 458). He tried to move the two middle wings to the side of the Gospel. Thus his final appraisal of the Presbyterians is that they are not essentially a principal embodiment of Antichrist but a deserted apostate ally.

It is characteristic in politics that a middle party is by nature circumspect and expedient between the two extremes. Especially when it happens to get power, it will move not on a professed principle but in a self-centered way because of the sudden disorder of an existing power mechanism. We can see such modernistic, pragmatic behavior in the Presbyterians and the Independents. It was the age of the rise of modern politics, the theory of which was founded by Machiavelli and developed by Milton's contemporary, Hobbes. Milton did not, however, see this new trend of the European governing system with new understanding. He saw it in the traditional framework of the Hebraic-Christian myth of Satan-Antichrist. Milton was a last Renaissance man. Yet this older Christian-humanist view gave him a more comprehensive means of understanding the complicated revolutionary situation than the practical, segmented, modern way of viewing each field for its own sake. The Presbyterians' betrayal was comprehended by him not only on a contemporary, ecclesiastical, and political level but also in a deeper religious, moral, historical, and poetical context. The following remark by Milton may bear witness to this.

A little more than a year after the sonnetto Milton digressed in Book III of *The History of Britain* about the desperate state of the Presbyterians, then at their political peak dominating the Long Parliament. He saw conditions in the first four months of 1646 as a close parallel to those of the fifth century in England: "as they [causes stemming from ruler, priest, and people] brought those antient natives to miserie and ruin by libertie which rightly us'd might have made them happie, so brought they these of late after many labours, much blood-shed, & vast expence, to ridiculous frustration, in whom the like defects, the like miscarriages notoriouslie appear'd, with vices not less hatefull or inexcusable" (YP V, p. 443). The historical similarities between them in the interval of twelve centuries are not a mere analogy in Milton's system of ideas. They are a consanguine inheritance of ingorance by the people in England: "as wine and oyle are imported to us from abroad, so must ripe understanding and many civil vertues bee imported into our minds from forren writings & examples of best ages" (YP IV, 451). The kind of knowledge which he thought his people were wanting is "the heroic wisdom which is requir'd" to surmount "far the principles of narrow politicians" (YP IV, p. 451). It is the knowledge of "Antient and illustrious deeds, invincible against money, vain titles, impartial to friendships and relations" (YP IV, p. 451). We see that, as early as the latter half of the 1640s, Milton was serious about expressing an imminent need of an epic which could meet the degenerate minds of contemporary parliamentary leaders. Though a subject for the epic was not specified, what he had in mind must have been one that could confront the issue of the Antichristian degeneration of the Presbyterians who were then ruling the nation. He did not, however, seem to have intended to write such an epic himself at this time, referring instead to "forren writings and examples of best ages."

II

The Independents whom Milton so much trusted as to join them disappointed him as bitterly as had the Presbyterians. This experience first took the form of a sonnet addressed to Lord General Cromwell in May 1652. In it he reminds Oliver that "new foes arise / Threatening to bind our souls with secular chains." As the full title of the sonnet shows, the "new foes" are some leading Independent ministers who formed the Committee for the Propagation of the Gospel to control dissenting private preachers or personal believers and to propose the setting up of an Independent state church. It originated with Cromwell's designation of John Owen as its head. And Milton was examined by the Committee on the charge of licensing a Socinian pamphlet, *Racovian Catechism*, which the Committee called "blasphemous, erroneous and scandalous" and ordered all the copies to be burnt.[7] Milton's indictment of the Committee members as new foes is partly based upon the unhappy experience he actually suffered. The sonnet reveals Milton's encounter with another Antichristian force in the midst of his own party's central authority. It should be pointed out that he understood each of the different enemies as one aspect of the apocalyptic Beast's historically repetitive appearances.

Milton is careful to exempt Cromwell from blame and goes so far as to entreat him to "Help us to save free conscience from the paw / Of hireling wolves whose gospel is their maw." The sonnet, by itself, seems to contain nothing to arouse any suspicion of Milton's critical attitude toward Cromwell, though he must have known well that Cromwell was an initiating and most influential member of the Committee. To understand the sonnet properly, it should be read along with another sonnet addressed to Sir Henry Vane on July 3 in the same year, less than two months after the sonnet to Cromwell.

Both sonnets begin with the same manner of hailing the addressee and develop the same theme of liberty of conscience exactly at the same fourth stress in the first line of the third quatrain. Such an elaborate pattern is found only in these two among Milton's twenty-three English sonnets. The use of the same theme and the same pattern seems not accidental but intended. But the motifs running through the sonnets are strikingly different. In the Cromwell sonnet Milton appeals to the Lord General saying "yet much remains / To conquer still; peace hath her victories / No less renown'd than war." But in such a seemingly humble way he is really urging Cromwell to side against the Committee he himself formed. These lines work to intensify an emphasis on the virtue of peace in the following thrid quatrain and to tone down the praise for Cromwell's battlefield victories. In such a complicated manner the motif of admonition-criticism of the addressee emerges as the poet's really intended meaning in the Cromwell sonnet.

In contrast, there is no complicated motif in the Vane sonnet. While starting the theme of the liberty of conscience at the same point, Milton does not break the eulogy motif as in the former sonnet. He continues to praise the addressee quite properly according to the decorum of encomium: "besides, to know / Both spiritual power and civil, what each means / What severs each, thou hast learnt, which few have done." The continual praise is further heightened at the closing: "Therefore on thy firm hand Religion leans / In peace, and reckons thee her eldest son." The conclusion undoubtedly signifies that Milton had Vane, not Cromwell, in mind as the reckoned eldest son of Christian liberty.

A comparative analysis of the two sonnets discloses that Milton was already not wholly confident in Cromwell as early as two years before he was to serve him as secretary. Masson tells us that "at that time there was some doubt among many which way Cromwell would go" and "those who thought he would be against the ministers' side misconstrued Cromwell even then, and ought to have known his opinion better."[8] Recently, Honigmann has placed Milton among those who misconstrued Cromwell, saying that he "no doubt sincerely admired Cromwell" in the sonnet.[9] It is, however, highly doubtful that Milton, who was so gravely concerned with liberty of conscience as to have dedicated his life wholly to this cause, should have been blind at this time to the role Cromwell played for and within the Committee.

It should be remembered that Cromwell, who reportedly declared at that time that "he had rather that Mohametanism were permitted amongst us than that one of God's children should be persecuted,"[10] was one who had said in a letter to the governor of Edinborough on September 12, 1650, two years before the composition of this sonnet, that "If [anyone speaks] blasphemously or to the disturbance of the public peace, let the civil magistrate punish him."[11] It is understandable that such an ambiguous person as Cromwell should have led many people to misconstrue him.

One reason Milton's relationship with Cromwell has been examined in some detail here is that it seems to be one of the distressingly annoying problems with which Milton had to grapple throughout the course of the Revolution. A related reason is that, in the light of his poetics, which places great importance on a poet's experience (discussed later), the relationship seems to have prepared for him a motif of temptation different from that of the Presbyterians' case for an epic. *Paradise Lost* was very likely under serious consideration during the time of the two sonnets' composition and was to be started probably in 1658.[12]

When he impeached the Presbyterians, Milton went so far as to openly mention some of their names. But as far as Cromwell was concerned, he strictly kept himself from uttering any critical word against him throughout his lifetime except through the complicated admonition in the sonnet and in *The Second Defence of the English People*, a discussion of which follows. This tacit reservation was kept after Cromwell's death as well, with the one exception of an implicit but most vigorous attack upon his regime, but still not directly on the man, in *Considerations Touching the Likeliest Means* in August 1659 (YP VII, p. 277).

Just one year before he launched that attack on the regime, Milton was, according to Masson, quite loyal to the Protector. He gives us a vivid picture of Milton: "At no time in the Secretaryship had there been a series of more important letters from Milton's pen than those just inventoried, written for the Protector in the last five months of his life."[13] Robert T. Fallon confirms Masson's view, saying that Milton was ever active and faithful to Cromwell to the last.[14] Especially at the news of the Piedmont Massacre, Cromwell's Protestantism and Milton's sympathy with the Piedmontese came together: "Positively, in reading Milton's dispatches for Cromwell on such subjects as the persecutions of the Voudois and the scheme of a Protestant European League, one hardly knows which is speaking, the secretary or the ruler. Cromwell melts into Milton, and Milton is Cromwell eloquent and Latinyzing."[15] These testimonies may present us with a portrait of the loyalist Milton. But the truth must have been more complex.

Milton's appeal to Cromwell against the Independent ministers' Antichristian plot occurred about the time when they turned themselves into a new ruling body by depriving the Presbyterians of power and by suppressing their onetime revolutionary allies, the Levellers and other radicalist sectaries. The new victor adopted the old ruler's way, forcing a state church with the imposition of tithes and siding with the royalist forces so that the time-honored rights of the propertied class as a whole could be maintained. An apparent religious struggle always involves in it the political, social, and economic ambitions of those who take part in it. The Presbyterians took over not only the prelates' benefices but also the political privileges and economic advantages they had enjoyed. The Independents followed the Presbyterians' pattern when they took power from them.

In the case of the Presbyterians, Milton could safely remove himself from them at the moment he discovered their nature. Though he was once involved with them, he was not doomed to go along with their degeneracy to the end. As for the Independents, however, he was bound to them. An ominous situation had been developing when he accepted the invitation from the new Council of State on March 13, 1649. The climax of the Revolution led by the Independents resulted in the execution of the king and the proclamation of the Republic along with merciless suppression and brutal persecution of the Levellers and other sectaries, who had virtually carried the Revolution to a complete victory of the Parliamentary forces. It was more merciless and brutal than anything that their predecessor Presbyterians had ever attempted, but the pattern of sacrificing the lower class for the victor's interests was the same. It is the way of a ruler regardless of his professed religious principles. Milton must have learned much from these facts, as the sonnetto in 1646 and the twin sonnets in 1652 attest.

One of the first duties Milton was ordered to perform by the Council was to make "some observation" on *The New Chain Discovered*.[16] Lillburne, Overton, Walwyn, and Prince were arrested on the charge of coauthoring it and were sentenced to imprisonment in the Tower on March 28, 1648. There is no convincing evidence that Milton accepted the order. On the other hand, according to Hill, he was not slow to carry out the order issued from the Council on the same day to attack the Irish royalist group.[17] Milton's neglect of the order to reply to *The New Chain* is suggestive of his attitude of discriminating against the Independent leaders' oppressive policy toward the Levellers.

Milton did not seem a mere translator but, to take Don M. Wolfe's phrase, a coworker in the immense variety of duties imposed upon the

Council (YP IV, p. 144). All the duties expected of him, however, seem to have been not necessarily imposing, at least in the judgement of the secretary himself. He was aware of what he should do as secretary. He wrote: "the so called Council of State . . . summoned me, though I was expecting no such event, and desired *to employ my services, especially in connection with foreign affairs*" (YP IV, pp. 627–28, italics mine). His own definition of his business indicates that what was employed was not his whole person but only his service connected with foreign affairs. It suggests that if the Council's order seemed not to accord with his definition he might be excused from it. One such case may have been his negligence of the expected refutation of the Leveller pamphlet.

His position in the revolutionary regime was not that of a humiliating courtier's seat, like the secretaryship Spenser accepted from Grey de Wilton, lord deputy of Ireland, Nor was it the lowly patron-service in which Marvell found himself in the manor house of Lord Fairfax. It seems to have been rather a modern type of intellectual profession. He might reserve to himself the right of selective judgment of what to do as Secretary for Foreign Tongues. When an order happened to match with his dedicated cause, his work was all loyalty and devotion. Masson's admiration for his Latin composition of the state letter to King Gustav in the name of the Protector, mentioned above, is one such happy case. His loyalty to Cromwell, pointed out by Masson and others, is essentially this sort of faithfulness, rooted primarily in the cause of the Revolution and in Cromwell's professed Christian principles, not in his person. In this sense, Milton is a new type of man at the rise of modern society. Thus contrasted with the old outlook on the world, he may be seen as a member of a self-split intelligentsia in a society changing drastically from feudalism to modernity.

At the establishment of the Protectorate his official position was much altered. For instance, his salary was no longer paid from the Council's Contingencies but from His Highness Exchequer of the Lord Protector.[18] This means that he was made more subject to the prestige of Cromwell. Milton was seen, according to a state paper, among the Protector's funeral procession on November 23, 1658,[19] just three months before he was to break silence for the attack on that regime. Faithfulness in the revolutionary cause and a personal admiration for Cromwell must have been commingled, but he seems never to have forsaken a critical detachment from the Protector while he was in active service to him. This double attitude toward Cromwell may best be seen in *The Second Defence of the English People*, published in May 1654, two years after the sonnet addressed to him.

III

We are struck to see that Milton's high-pitched eulogy of Cromwell in this tract is full of undertones. It begins, "Cromwell, we are deserted! You alone remain. On you has fallen the whole burden of our affairs. On you alone they depend" (YP IV, p. 671). Such an expression of admiration is not as open-hearted as it looks. Indeed, when Milton utters, "we are deserted," he must have had good reason to say it. Such pillars of the state as Vane, Bradshaw, Overton, and others had left Cromwell in protest. More precisely, it was he who drove them out of Parliament at the forcible dissolution of the Rump just one year before the publication of this tract. At that time Vane protested saying, "This is not honest, yea, it is against morality and common honesty." Whereupon Cromwell retorted, "O Sir Henry Vane, Sir Henry Vane, the Lord deliver me from Sir Henry Vane!"[20] Cromwell's prompt retort reflects how weighty and dominant was the stature of Vane standing in the way of his ambition. He seems to be exorcizing an annoying imprint of upright and honest Vane out of his obsessed, dark mind.[21] Milton, a close friend of Vane who dedicated his single-minded admiration to him in contrast to his complicated eulogy to Cromwell, analyzed above, would instantly have understood which was honest, his Lord Cromwell or a deserted friend, had he been there.

Another passage may be interpreted in the same way. Milton apparently praises Cromwell for the reason that "the name of King you spurned from your far greater eminence, and rightly so" (YP IV, p. 672). This is also not to be read simply on the literal level. It was public knowledge that Cromwell was forced to give up the crown by the pressure of the army officer group headed by Pride and some of his oldest commanders-in-arms.[22] Since Milton could not have been ignorant of this, why dares he to ignore the fact and fictionalize the story? It seems to have been intentional as it was in the sonnet where, ignoring Cromwell's complicity with the ministers, he urged him not to go along with them. The strategic use of an intensified distance between high praises and cold reality is the key to understanding the truth of the passage.

One more example: "May you then, O Cromwell, increase in your magnanimity, for it becomes you. You, the liberator of your country, the author of liberty, and likewise its guardian and savior, can understand no more distinguished role and none more august" (YP IV, p. 672). Indeed, complete victory of Parliament over the royalist force could not have been achieved without the leadership of Cromwell. But he would not have gone so far as to execute the king and to establish a Commonwealth unless he had been pushed and supported by the army agitators, Levellers, and sectaries. The glory of the Republic was mostly grounded upon the sweat and blood of these lower class people, many of whom were expelled and persecuted by Cromwell, as Milton knew well. Thus he knew to what sort of ruler he was really addressing his panegyric. The addressee not only suppressed the people whose republican ideas Milton shared and possibly borrowed from, but also tried by all means to set up a state church with tithes imposed against his own professed principle of the liberty of conscience. This is the same pattern of betrayal Milton found in the Presbyterians' Antichristian nature, but in a more formidable way this time. Therefore, the real meaning underlying this passage may be, "You are not really magnanimous as long as you go on this way. In order to be worth the name of the liberator you should be broad-minded enough to tolerate those who will not follow your narrow-minded policy."

The theme of magnanimity is taken up again at the end of the passage: "In my judgement you can do this in no better way than by admitting those men whom you first cherished as comrades in your toils and dangers to the first share in your counsels" (YP IV, p. 674). Reminding the Protector of his one-time comrades, some of whom left him in protest, Milton boldly asks him to readmit them to the old "first share" in the counsels. Cromwell had been a top member but still an equal among the forty-one others of the Council of State five months before. But at this time the Protectorate Council of State, consisting of only fifteen at the first meeting, though a few members were added later, was not primarily responsible to Parliament but to the Protector. Fallon says, "It becomes known as the Lord Protector's Council and eventually as the Privy Council".[23] In fact, the *Instrument of Government* adopted by Cromwell and his officers on December 16, 1653 states that "the supreme legislative authority of the Commonwealth of England, Scotland, and Ireland . . . shall be and reside in one person, and the people assembled in Parliament: the style of which person shall be the Lord Protector of the Commonwealth of England, Scotland, and Ireland."[24] The statute thus stipulated and its reality as well must have been an agony to Milton the staunch republican. Milton's admonition quoted above virtually repeals the *Instrument* because Oliver's one-man rule was grounded upon it. It is, however, quite dubious that, though admonishing him thus seriously, Milton should have really expected Cromwell to listen to him against the cold reality of the Protectorate regime at that time.

But Milton was not a utopian who stood aloof from the actual process of his times. As the Cromwell sonnet and the passages in *The Second*

Defence show, he is a realist-idealist who tries by all means to find a likely means to alter a depressed situation, even though he knew too well it might fail after all. His realist side may be evidenced by the names of Bradshaw and Robert Overton found in the list of the Protector's fellow counselors-to-be. Both were notorious antiCromwellians and close friends of Milton. Modern scholarship has been active in looking for the daring motive of why he recommended them to Cromwell knowing that it might offend him.[25] Wolfe points out that Bradshaw's relationship to Cromwell was not yet irrevocable at that time and Masson explains that Milton acted as a conciliator between Cromwell and Overton, who had been recalled from Hull for interrogation as to his favoring a republican or Anabaptist revolt among the northern soldiers. The conciliation was successful and Colonel Overton went back to Scotland three months after the publication of the tract, this time promoted to major-general, second in command to Monck. The incident tells us that Milton's knowledge was exact and practical, even to the level of personal relations, and that his apparently idealistic advice to Cromwell was not ungrounded but based on solid information.

More significant than this explicit mentioning of names is Milton's complete reservation regarding the name of Sir Henry Vane. His name ought to have been the first and most remarkable one on the list in the light of his important role and reputation in the glorious course of the Revolution and Milton's sincere trust in him. Again Wolfe's insight into the matter is valuable. "Vane's name is such a striking omission in Milton's list of noble republicans that no sophisticated reader would have overlooked its significance (YP IV, p. 264). Milton, the experienced secretary of the Lord Protector's Council, must have known well what sort of break existed between Cromwell and Vane, and therefore withdrew the name from the list. But the idealist Milton revolted. Instead of mentioning Vane by name, Milton rendered him, to quote Wolfe, "ever present" throughout the passage by strongly advocating liberty of conscience, which would remind anyone and most surely Cromwell of Vane.

Milton gives his final advice to Cromwell: "I would have you leave the church to the church and shrewdly relieve yourself and the government of half your burden (one that is at the same time completely alien to you)" (YP IV, p. 678). This was the point he mistakenly expected Cromwell to learn from Vane, as the twin sonnets clearly show. Yet he dared to suggest again that Cromwell should devise a way to sever state from church, which few but Vane knew how to do. The phrase "relieve yourself and the government of half your burden" deliberately reminds Cromwell of the earlier reference to "the whole burden of our affairs fallen upon you." The lesson of the contrast seems unrelentingly directed to the bearer of an undue amount of burden. While thus apparently advising Cromwell, Milton may have been aware that his efforts would again be futile. Despite Milton's entreaty in the sonnet, Cromwell never slackened his hand in forcing conscience. The Committee for the Propagation of the Gospel had started the Triers system for the interests of the Independents on March 20, 1654. But Milton dared to do what he was convinced was right for the cause of the Reformation-Revolution. And his efforts proved to be utterly fruitless again.

It must have been saddening to Milton that he could be truly faithful to the cause of liberty of conscience only through such a twisted and veiled criticism of the Lord Protector he was obliged to serve. He continued to work for the regime most assiduously despite all such frustrations as Cromwell's inimical relationship with Milton's admired republican friends, his setting up the Ejectors system in August 1654, adopting the Humble Petition and Advice in May 1657, and his abrupt dissolution of the so-called Protector's Parliament, this time with a protest by Major-General Charles Fleetwood, whose name Milton listed first in the counseling body for Cromwell in *The Second Defence.*

At the end of the tract Milton compares himself to an epic poet: "I have borne witness, I might almost say I have erected a monument that will not soon pass away, to those deeds that were illustrious, that were glorious, that were almost beyond any praise, and if I have done nothing else, I have surely redeemed my pledge" (YP IV, p. 685). Throughout the passage there runs a triumphant and satisfied note in his voice. Though it was ordered by the Council of State to refute *Regii Sanguinis Clamor,* Milton devoted himself wholly to *The Second Defence.* This is another testimony to the happy realization of his own defined service to the government: "As for me, whatever the issue, I have bestowed my services by no means grudgingly nor, I hope, in vain, where I judged that they would be most useful to the state" (YP IV, p. 684).

Herbert Grierson saw in the closing part of the tract Milton's feeling that he had in a way fulfilled his first plan for an epic on the exploits of the English people and statesmen.[26] He may be right as far as Milton's earlier professed plan of a British historical theme is concerned. The fulfillment of the theme in prose may have freed him from the earlier pledge to go further to the more sublime subject of an epic. Yet there remains some lingering question which will not wholly admit Grierson's view. In the final part Milton seems more anxious about drawing the reader's attention to posterity's judgment of the regime than celebrating the fulfillment of his pledge. He says that he spoke according to an epic rule of "not the whole life of the hero . . . but . . . one event of his life." By "the whole life" he means the entire course of the Revolution. He goes on, "The rest I omit . . . If after such brave deeds you ignobly fail, if you do aught unworthy of yourselves, be sure that posterity will speak out and pass judgment" (YP IV, pp. 684–85). By "the rest" must be meant what the Protectorate is expected to do "after such brave deeds" of the revolutionary people. Milton was most concerned about this unfinished part of the Revolution throughout the eulogy-admonition section aimed toward Cromwell and the English people. What he really meant by referring to the epic device of *in medias res* is that the epic hero — that is, the English people — has not completed his heroic exploit yet, and has the rest to accomplish if he wishes to be counted worthy of the name of hero. Milton warns them, "the foundations were soundly laid, the beginnings, in fact more than the beginnings, were splendid, but posterity will look in vain, not without a certain distress, for those who were to complete the work, who were to put the pediment in place" (YP IV, p. 685). This remark carries the same warning that Milton expressed to Cromwell in an earlier part: "Finally, honour yourself, so that, having achieved that liberty in pursuit of which you endured so many hardships and encountered so many perils, you may not permit it to be violated by yourself or in any degree diminished by others" (YP IV, p. 673).

Now we can see that the fulfillment of the earlier epic plan in *The Second Defence* must have been not a full-hearted matter of celebration as Grierson suggested. Rather, it may mean that the completion of the tract did not give Milton a fresh start toward a new epic with an entirely different theme. It seems that his strong awareness of the unfinished Revolution must have driven him on to pursue, as the subject of an epic, the problem that he had encountered but could not effectually grapple with, that is, the struggle with the Antichrist who tempted Presbyterians, Independent leaders, Cromwell, and the English people to nullify the achievements of the Revolution at each peak of their power.

Milton's concluding words sound the more saddening against the fact that his apprehensions expressed in the tract were soon to come true: "Yet there was not wanting one who could rightly counsel, encourage, and inspire, who could honour both the noble deeds and those who had done them, and make both deeds and doers illustrious with praises that will never die" (YP IV, p. 685–686). "One" obviously refers to the author of the tract himself. Yes, there remained Milton the counsellor, encourager, and inspirer, the panegyrist of the glories of the Revolution. But it is he who was most worried about which way his master and his fellow English people would go.

IV

Sonnet XIX seems a witness to Milton's dilemma. The date of composition has not been exactly determined but it has usually been placed between 1652 and 1655.[27] This covers the period from Cromwell's ascendancy, confirmed at the victory of Worcester, to the stable stage of the Protectorate. During that period there took place such events as Milton's total blindness (probably on February 28, 1652),[28] encounters with "new foes" in his Independent camp, the dissolution of the Rump, the establishment of the Protectorate, the setting up of a virtual state church by the systems of the Triers and Ejectors in 1654, and the grant to Milton of a £288 annual salary from His Highness Exchequer of Oliver Cromwell on April 17, 1655.

The main trend of the sonnet's interpretation has been triggered by the title "On his Blindness" which was not found in the original 1673 edition. Indeed the loss of his sight must have been of grave concern to Milton, but a poetical representation of darkness may have referred more to the poet's depressing experiences, both internal and external:

> When I consider how my light is spent,
> Ere half my days, in this dark world and wide.

By "this dark world and wide" is meant not only the poet's internal world of crisis but also this fallen world in which both his physical and spiritual light were spent. Darkness and sinfulness were an interchangeable cliché in the religious writings of these days.[29]

The dark-sinful world in which his light is spent is actually the Protectorate regime, to which Milton devoted himself wholly. Indeed, he suffered from the Antichristian powers of the prelates, the king, Presbyterians and Independent leaders. He could indict each of them as an Antichristian foe, external to himself. But he cannot separate himself from the Protectorate, a far more formidable Antichristian power, because he has chosen to work for it. No other power can defend the achieved glories of the Revolution against the overwhelming tide of the royalist forces. He must have found himself totally helpless and groping for a way to serve his maker. He cries,

> And that one Talent which is death to hide,
> Lodg'd with me useless, though my Soul more bent
> To serve therewith my Maker.

So far the sonnet has expressed a crisis of the self, yet this crisis was not brought about by his own actions. Such despair as blindness and the

Antichristian nature of the Protectorate may have assaulted him most bitterly, but they came from without. What is really fatal is that he is tempted to doubt the ways of God. The sonnet discloses this temptation at lines 7–8, the central point of the fourteen-line form:

> Doth God exact day-labour, light deni'd,
> I fondly ask; But patience to prevent
> That murmur, soon replies.

The crisis passes in a moment as Patience intervenes for him. But in the actual world similar crises must have attacked him as often as the dark world made him despair. *The Christian Doctrine* provides a gloss on this kind of sin: "Opposed to this [patience] is impatience toward God, a sin which even the saints are sometimes tempted to commit" (YP VI, p. 663). The utterance "Doth God exact . . . ?" is this category of sin. Thus would such a regenerate person as Milton be tempted in this dark world. Especially in light of his life principle of sallying out to meet an adversary, he may sometimes have experienced the sin of impatience toward God. He once said, "we bring not innocence into the world, we bring impurity much rather" (YP III, p. 515). He continues: "that which purifies us is triall, and triall is by what is contrary" (ibid.). The sonnet is a valid witness to the principle of man's purification by trial.

The sonnet reveals that temptation comes not directly but through an internal weakness such as blindness or a sense of powerlessness. Though the poet is thus tempted, he is immune from actual commitment of the sin. Personified Patience — that is, a regenerate part of him — promptly protects him, saying "who best / Bear his mild yoke, they serve him best / . . . They also serve who only stand and wait." While thus standing and waiting deep in his meditative mind, the blind Milton must have performed various duties for the sake of the Commonwealth. His experience of man's vulnerability to temptation may have been one he kept in mind as a contributive motif for the scene of temptation in *Paradise Lost*, where Eve's and Adam's inward propensity to be tempted is the decisive moment of man's Fall.

It was as late as August 1659, one year after the death of Cromwell and one year before the Restoration, that Milton finally and totally shattered the image of Cromwell by referring to the six years of his rule as a "short but scandalous night" in *The Likeliest Means* (YP VII, p. 274). The epithet "scandalous" seems a highly deliberate choice of word. "Scandal" originally meant a snare for an enemy, or a cause of moral stumbling. A derivative meaning was perplexity of conscience, occasioned by the conduct of one who is looked up to as an example (*OED*). This seems to be the meaning Milton intended for the word.

The perplexity of his conscience during the Protectorate was occasioned by the Antichristian conduct of the Protector he looked up to as an exemplary Christian warrior. Indeed, as the original meaning of the word signifies, he stumbled on the Protector's scandalous conduct, which he had believed to be a consolidating basis of the Revolution. His trust in Cromwell turned out to be a snare by which he was trapped in the night of a single man's rule, the last thing the true republican Milton would submit to. That is precisely "dark world and wide" in which the blind Milton's total being was spent, and which tempted him to commit the sin of impatience toward God.

This phrase from *The Likeliest Means* suggests that he was once benighted in this dark world. He must have been unavoidably snared into this night by his belief in an active life in this world in which he could know good by evil. No one can be free from this sort of temptation crisis as long as one sallies out into the fallen world. And there was no solution to this enigma except in the myth of Genesis. It should be remembered that at this time in 1658 Milton had most probably started *Paradise Lost.* That the epic's central theme is the temptation and Fall of man is suggestive of how substantially Milton's ectypal temptation experiences contributed to the working out of an epical representation of the archetypal pattern of the Genesis story.

V

So far Milton's personal sufferings in the course of the Revolution have been traced for a possible material cause of the epic. In order to be of universal scope, however, an epic will require a more far-reaching dimension of experiences open to historical and national perspectives. Yes, Cromwell was not his only stumbling block.

Milton was not wholly freed from the top political and military groups even after his hearty celebration of what he called a dawning from the Protectorate's scandalous night. On May 13, 1659, the leading republican officers led by Lambert and Desborough presented to the restored Rump *The Humble Petition and Address of the Officers,* urging them to set up a new parliament. The gist of the fifteen articles of the *Petition* was to maintain a commonwealth without a single person, kingship, or house of lords. The fifteenth article proposed to set up "a Representative body of the People, consisting of a House succeedingly chosen by the People . . . and of a select Senate, Co-ordinate in Power, of able and faithful persons, eminent for Godliness, and such as continue adhering to this Cause" (YP VII, p. 72). The proposed senate was, according to Austin Woolrich, intended to restrain the house of commons. In contrast to the house, which was to be annually elected, life membership was planned in the senate, as implied in the phrase "such as continue adhering to this Cause." The reason the officers stipulated these provisions for the senate, says Woolrich, was as "a safeguard against the army being treated by any future Parliament as the Long Parliament had tried to treat it in 1647, the Rump in 1653, and Richard's Parliament in recent weeks" (YP VII, p. 72). The senate was to be an ultimate state power to curb the house for the sake of the army. Although the officers learned much from the unhappy period of Cromwell, and thus provided the ban on a single man's rule, they did not finally trust Parliament.

Milton, who had stood for Cromwell and the army and supported them at each of the parliamentary dissolutions, remained sober about the officers' move this time. Around the period when the Rump, which was groaning on its deathbed, was managing to win a small victory over the officers in September–October 1659, he stood for Parliament and criticized the officers' ambition in A Letter to a Friend: "How grievous will it then be, how infamous to the true religion which [we] professe, how dishonourable to the Name of God, that his fear & the power of his knowledge in an Army professing to be his, should not work that obedience, that fidelity to their supreme Magistrates, that levied them, & payed them" (YP VII, p. 327). This seems to suggest Milton's loyalty to Parliament. Indeed, he had once accepted the supremacy of Parliament, and dedicated the three divorce tracts and Areopagitica to the Long Parliament. He lauded the Rump "for the deliverance of thir Countrie, endu'd with fortitude and Heroick vertue" (YP III, p. 191). He must have been sincere in what he said about Parliament. However, since the ascendency of Cromwell, he had acted not for Parliament but for Cromwell and the army against his pledge of faithfulness to Parliament.[30]

This seems a fundamental dilemma which the realist Milton could not resolve in the actual arena. The same sort of distrust of Parliament appears again in the midst of his severe attack on the army officers' ambition over Parliament: "the 1st thing to be found out with all speed, without which no common wealth can subsist, must be a senate or generall Councill of State in whome must be the power 1st to preserve the publick peace" (YP VII, p. 329). It should be pointed out that "the 1st thing to be found out with all speed" signifies Milton's resolute intention to dissuade the Rump leaders from listening to the officers' proposal for a new election. Instead, he proposes "a senate or general Councill of State" based upon the restored Rump. He says, "This must be either the parlament readmitted to sitt, or a councell of State, allowed of by the Army since they only now have the power" (YP VII, p. 329). Again we see the realist Milton who prefers the fait accompli. In the power struggle among the military and political leaders after the forced resignation of Richard Cromwell, Milton saw nothing effective to meet the approaching threats of the royalist forces but the united front of Parliamentary power and the top military group: "That which I conceive only able to ciment & unite for ever the Army either to the parlament recall'd, or this chosen councell, must be mutuall league & oath private or publick not to desert one another till death" (YP VII, p. 329). Such a united power of life membership of the top groups would become an arbitrary dictatorial rule; And as the Aschan allusion to Lambert in this *Letter* suggests (YP VII, pp. 328–29), Milton never trusted some of the leading officers.[31] Yet he seemed to prefer a Council of State to Parliament for a proposed union with the army leaders, which would have made the united body more limited, with a tendency to be more dictatorial.

Then why dared he to propose such a risky design of government against his professed principle of the supremacy of Parliament? An answer should be sought in the confusion of the post-Protectorate period: "Being now in Anarchy without counselling & governing power & the Army I suppose finding themselves insufficient to discharge at once both military & civill offices" (YP VII, p. 329). He feared that the situation might be moving too rapidly to talk about the form of tomorrow's government: "And whether the civill government be an annuall democracy or a perpetual Aristocracy, is too nice a consideration for the extremities wherein wee are & the hazard of our safety from a common enemie, gaping at present to devour us" (YP VII, p. 331).

Against this common enemy of the royalist forces, the realist-strategist Milton's whole energy was concentrated to rally all the powers available for this given situation. Since the Antichrist was "gaping at present to devour us," any radical change in the present governing body should not be attempted. This must be why his proposal of a limited reorganization of the government was grounded upon a determined avoidance of a new election. At the conclusion he warns again of the imminent danger of the common enemy: "But unless these things which I have above propos'd one way or other be 1st settled, in my fear, which god avert, we instantly ruine; or at best become the servants of one or other single person, the secret author & fomenter of all these disturbances" (YP VII, p. 332). In this passage we can see Milton's deepest dilemma. His fear is directed at what he calls "the secret author and fomenter of all these disturbances." That is the Antichrist who puts on the mask of an English monarch, whose power was magic enough to tempt the minds of many people into all these disturbances. These people would call back the son of Charles I to the throne if they had a chance of voting for a new Parliament. Thus what Milton actually feared most was the voice of the people. This must be the fundamental reason Milton abhorred a popular election throughout the entire course of the Revolution and went so far as to justify each forcible dissolution of Parliament, serving the Protector, only to be disillusioned in the end.

Wolfe reminds us of the tremendous power of the king, which continued to overshadow the Commonwealth throughout the Revolution till it really devoured the Commonwealth: "The magic of the King's name, to the average illiterate rustic as well as to the aristocrat forfeiting a part of his wealth to the inexorable new republic, was a reality no glorious victories of Cromwell could dispel" (YP IV, p. 185). This was the popular sentiment in 1653 when the triumphant Cromwell dissolved the Rump and set up the Protectorate. The sentiment was more threatening in the autumn of 1659, when the restored Rump was dying under the demand for reentry by the purged Presbyterians, whose royalized nature Milton had exposed as Antichristian early in the Revolution. The situation at the time he wrote the *Letter* was moving far more to the advantage of the royalist forces. The reason he dared to propose an extremely limited minority rule of the existing political and military powers must be sought in his last desperate determination to resist the imminent danger of the approaching Antichristian forces. However, this drove him into further alienation from the English people, in whose name he had worked hard throughout the Revolution.

In Milton's last tract, the second edition of *The Readie and Easie Way* in April 1660, he seems to have overcome the dilemma. The motto prefacing the tract, "We have advised Sulla himself, advise we now the people," reveals Milton's final disillusion about military rule. He had dedicated earlier writings to the Long Parliament, but this was the first time he turned directly to the people.

Did he really come down to meet the people this time? The answer is still no. In this tract he proposed the same sort of self-contained, oligarchic, grand council and flat denial of a general election as he had expressed in the *Letter* half a year before. He is now even more resolutely oligarchic, proposing to centralize power in a grand council of life membership with no particular mention of Parliament, because the situation had decidedly swung toward the royalist forces in only a few months. The secluded Presbyterians were readmitted to Parliament on February 21, 1660, and they nullified the voters' qualification rule, fixed by the Rump three days before, which had aimed chiefly to exclude advocates of a single man and those related to Papists.[32] This aggravating situation was not limited to the top political level but spread to a general sentiment. Pepys's diary at this time, cited by Woolrich, describes how exuberantly London citizens were preparing to welcome General Monck marching from Scotland, who was known to be pledged to the restoration of the monarchy (YP VII, p. 175).

Such an irresistible, popular tide of Antichristian power drove Milton to stick to a more rigid oligarchic rule. He says, "The happiness of a nation must needs be firmest and certainest in a full and free Councel of thir own electing" (YP VII, p. 427). Woolrich's comment is to the point: "Yet it is just on the score of the people's right to elect their government, and remove those who offend them, that Milton's own proposals are most vulnerable" (YP VII, p. 180). Yes, he most fatally stumbled on this score of the English people to whom he wished to dedicate himself. In reality, however, the people who were neglected and denied by him the right to vote retaliated on April 25, 1660, by electing those he most dreaded to sit in Parliament.

This is the destiny of reprisal the realist-strategist Milton was compelled to bear. This must have been the most deep-rooted and enigmatic experience he suffered throughout the entire course of the abortive Revolution. It would have remained an insoluble and intractable element in Milton's scheme of the Providential universe, if the Hebraic-Christian myth of Satan-serpent's temptation and the Fall of man had not been reactivated to transmute the experience of his revolutionary failure into a major element of the epic. Behind the temptation and Fall in *Paradise Lost* lies the revolutionary Milton who had succumbed to the guile of the Antichrist.

VI

So far we have observed Milton the occasional sonneteer and writer of the tractates who worked for the Revolution and experienced its glories and disgraces. This is not the whole picture of Milton. While he was undergoing these experiences, the epic poet must have been internalizing them. We cannot trace the exact process, since no evidence remains. But it will be possible at least to attempt to build an outline of his poetics and to approximate how he transmuted his experiences into poetry.

Milton's personal suffering from the abuses the Presbyterians hurled at his tracts on true marital love and liberty of expression spewed forth in anger in the sonnetto of 1648 examined above, one of the earliest testimonies that he experienced the old ally's betrayal as a new appearance of Antichrist. He internalized his grief and disillusionment in a motif of Christian wrath and patterned them in a universal figure of Antichrist. The internal patterning of experience into a Christian framework seems to be Milton's principle of making poetry.

He expressed an embryonic idea of this in *The Reason of Church*

Government in February 1642. Discussing the fundamentals necessary to make poetry, he says: "but by devout prayer to that eternal Spirit . . . to this must be added industrious and select reading, steady observation, insight into all seemly and generous arts and affairs" (YP I, pp. 820–21). The devout prayer to the eternal Spirit is placed before the three other disciplines. By that Spirit is meant, according to Maurice Kelley, both Milton's muse and a personification of the various attributes of God the Father (YP I, p. 821, fn 144). Milton himself says that the Spirit is one "who can enrich all utterance and knowledge, and sends out his Seraphim with the hallow'd fire of his Alter to touch and purify the lips of whom he pleases" (YP I, p. 821). The idea of the Seraphim as enrichers of the poor mind was first shaped in the figure of the Attendant Spirit in the *Masque* seven and a half years before the tract. He is apparently a kind of Socratic daemon who comes from heaven down to earth for those few people who "by due steps aspire / To lay their just hands on that golden key" (12–13). He leads the benighted Brothers to save a kidnapped Lady from the tempter Comus. As a dramatic character he defends the innocent children of the noble family within the world of poetry. At the same time he represents the guiding principle of the poem's theme, that is, the saving of this world from evil power by enriching the enfeebled mind of man. The action of the character in the poetic world and the principle of redeeming the actual world are inseparably embodied in the figure of the Attendant Spirit.

The Seraphim whom the eternal Spirit sends from heaven in *The Reason of Church Government* is a more definitely specified agent of making poetry, developed from the quasi-Platonic daemon in the *Masque* who is sent by Jove from the starry threshold of his court (1–2). In the tract, however, Milton lays emphasis not upon the Spirit *per se* but upon devout prayer to him. One's active devotion is the first thing required for the Spirit to send his Seraphim "to touch and purify the lips of whom he pleases," for what pleases the Spirit is devout prayer. To this Milton adds "industrious and select reading, steady observation, insight into all seemly and generous arts and affairs," each of which requires as much positive effort as the first requisite of prayer to the Spirit. Milton's poetics is above all a discipline of the self in the midst of the fallen world. The devout prayer works to organize all the efforts of the self, processing such exterior and alien materials as classical learning and experiential knowledge of the world into a pattern of Christian meaning. While it requires the self's most active working in various fields, Milton's poetics strictly controls any self-centered elements and aims to build a solid figural body of Christian truth.

The idea of poetic composition is expressed in more elaborate form in *Apology for Smectymnuus* in April 1642: "And long it was not after, when I was confirm'd in this opinion, that he who would not be frustrated of his hope to write well hereafter in laudable things, ought himselfe to bee a true Poem, that is a composition, and patterne of the best and honourablest things" (YP I, p. 890). Before writing a poem, one must prepare an internal composition, which Milton identifies with the composer's self and defines as "a patterne of the best and honourablest things," clearly requiring the purification of self-centered elements.

Milton seems to have had in mind first the Christian belief and practice of *imitatio Christi*, and next the Aristotelian concept of poetry as a probable or necessary imitation of an ideal thing. In this sense of an ennobled composition of the self, Milton's poetics may be called an expression of a personality, but the personality is not understood as one's given character nor as the self-split man Christopher Hill and not a few critics have tried to see in Milton.

Having established the basic concept of a self-concentrated but self-negating poetics, Milton continues, "he [who would not be frustrated of his hope to write well] would not presume to sing high praises of heroick men, or famous Cities, unless he have in himselfe the experience and practice of all that which is praiseworthy" (YP I, p. 890). Milton's examples of true poets are Dante and Petrarch, who composed within themselves a true poem of the self out of their love for Beatrice and Laura. The literary figures of Beatrice and Laura are understood in Milton's poetics as an externalized form of this internally composed self-poem.

The late medieval poets set up the fair sex as the pattern of the best and most honorable things. Milton, a legitimate son of the Reformation, raised for it a vision of a New Jerusalem to be founded upon his native soil. Only for the sake of its realization dared he to oust himself from the Church of England, hurry back from a continental tour, and plunge himself into the turmoils of the Revolution to the point of losing his sight.

It should be remembered that Milton's poetics was elaborated along with the idea of the didactic function of poetry. He places poetry at the ultimate stage of his ideal school curriculum in *Of Education*, written two years after *Apology*. He says, "To which [Rhetoric] Poetry would be made subsequent, or rather precedent, as being less suttle and fine, but more simple, sensuous and passionate" (YP II, p. 403). This equivocal passage is best explained by Rajan: "Poetry is subsequent to rhetoric in the educational scheme. It is precedent in its value, its intrinsic dignity."[33] In both senses, poetry is the summation of the knowledge of all the fields which a youth must learn for future, noble life in the real world.

This carefully stratified learning culminating in poetry will train pupils "to be able writers and composers in every excellent matter, when they shall be thus frought with an universal insight into things" (YP II, p. 406).

The sonnetto and sonnets discussed above are brief examples of how Milton transfigured limited experiences into a universal struggle with the Antichrist. The composition of an epic will require time for a vast amount of experiential knowledge to mature into a true poem. The *propria persona* of *Paradise Lost* confesses, "Since first this subject for heroic song / Pleased me long choosing and beginning late" (IX, 25–26). It was a long way from the Lady in the *Masque*, who is easily kidnapped but hardly tempted, to Eve in the epic, who is trapped with small difficulty and quickly self-tempted to fall. The universal insight into things which Milton derived from his revolutionary experiences must be responsible for this pessimistic and realistic understanding of man.

VII

Milton resumed and probably completed the remaining Books V and VI of the *History of Britain* and set out for the inviting frontier of *Christian Doctrine* around the year 1655. He continued to work on it, according to Kelley, until as late as but not later than the early years of the Restoration.[34] While involved in a desperate revolutionary reality, he was working on abiding problems of history and theology, suggesting that he saw the Revolution not only with the realist-strategist's eye but with a more detached and comprehensive eye as well. This perspective is summed up in his letter to Henry Oldenburgh on December 20, 1659: "For I fear, as you do, lest to the lately united enemies of religion and liberty we shall, in the midst of civil dissensions or rather insanities, seem to vulnerable, though actually they will not have inflicted a greater wound on religion than we have long been doing by our crimes" (YP VIII, p. 515). Milton understood the civil discords not merely as an external event to be criticized but as a self-involved, fatal matter, blaming the madness of the situation on nobody but "we." He had finally accepted all the disappointing events not as simply reproachable phenomena of others' ambition and avarice but above all as a sinful matter of "our crimes." This suggests that Milton internalized his sufferings over the revolutionary failure in a Christian framework of confession. In the motto to *The Readie and Easie Way*, Milton stated his wish to advise the people rather than Sulla. This wish came to a full realization in *Christian Doctrine*, dedicated to "All the Churches of Christ and All in any part of the world who confess the Christian Faith, Peace, Knowledge of the Truth, and eternal Salvation in God the Father and in our Lord Jesus

Christ" (YP VI, p. 118). Though *Christian Doctrine* is a detailed interpretation of the passages cited from the Bible, it is not intended to be a theological survey for the sake of theology. Milton says, "I should show that I had been concerned not for religion but for life's well-being." Its primary aim is "to wipe away those two repulsive afflictions, tyranny and superstition, from human life and the human mind" (YP VI, pp. 118, 384). Its purpose is not fundamentally different from that of his revolutionary tracts, that is, the liberty of conscience from any forcers without and within man. Thus the seemingly separate categories of political activity and theological speculation are related to each other in Milton's central concern for man's well-being in this world.

The concept of Adam becomes meaningful in this unified context of theology and politics because the revolutionary leaders and Milton himself experienced a crisis of temptation, and many of them, including Cromwell, were tempted to fall. Milton says, "For Adam, the parent and head of all men, either stood or fell as a representative of the whole human race" (YP VI, p. 384): "Our first parents implanted it [original sin] in us . . . even those who were born of regenerate parents, for although faith removes each man's personal guilt, it does not altogether root out the vice which dwells within us" (YP VI, p. 389). This truth is repeatedly confirmed by the degeneration of Cromwell and other leaders of the Revolution. They were tempted to fall by a fraud of the Antichrist just as Adam was by the concealed hand of Satan. Accordingly, Milton specifically calls Adam "the parent and head of men."

Milton says about the process of sin originating in the Fall of Adam: "This sin was instigated first by the devil. . . . Secondly it was instigated by man's own inconstant nature, which meant that he, like the devil before him *did not stand firm in the truth*" (YP VI, pp. 382–383). This is grounded upon the Genesis story and St. John's interpretation of it (John viii:44). But at the same time it confirms the experiential tests Milton underwent in his involvement in the actual temptation crises of the revolutionary leaders. He must have seen how the second process of temptation took place in each case of the degenerated people. He himself once stood at the verge of a crisis and found no other way out but to side with the military powers whose nature he knew too well. This may color his special mention of the instigation of sin by man's inconstant nature: "he . . . did not stand firm in the truth."

The extant outlines for a tragedy show that Milton had considered temptation as a central theme for poetry from about 1629–31.[35] The theme had been cherished throughout the revolutionary years, during which he had experienced the irresistible power of the Antichrist that tempted

Presbyterians, Independent ministers, and military leaders including Cromwell. Though we do not know when Milton changed his plans from tragedy to epic, a technical problem which seems to have caused the change may be followed up. In the tragic plans entitled "Paradise Lost" a tempter serpent is not specified to appear on stage. He is merely listed among the characters in the first plan, and is missing in the second and the third (YP VIII, p. 588). It seems that in the tragedy the temptation scene is not to be actually performed on stage. The tempter appears in the fourth plan entitled "Adam unparadiz'd." A stage direction says, "here again may appear Lucifer relating, & insulting in what he had don to the destruction of man. man next and Eve having by this time bin seduc't by the serpent appeares confusedly cover'd with leaves" (YP VIII, p. 560). This reappearing tempter in the fourth plan does not perform any action on stage either. The temptation is only to be narrated by the tempter Lucifer.

Paying attention to the serpent's absence from stage in each of the tragic plans, Allan H. Gilbert conjectures,

If he did not reappear in the fifth plan, Milton may have felt that omission of the crucial scene was ruinous, and therefore have abandoned the tragedy. It may be, however, that in the last plan the serpent did again come on the stage. If so, Milton's feeling against an animal actor may have been among the reasons that led him to abandon tragedy for epic, in which the disguised Tempter could play his part with dignity.[36]

This seems convincing as far as the technical problem of dramaturgy is concerned, but a more decisive factor may have worked in Milton to change the form. Lucifer and the serpent that were separately listed in the tragic plans were understood as one body of a serpent-Satan in the history of Christian exegesis. In *Christian Doctrine* Milton adopted this established view of the Tempter, and preferred the name of Satan to that of Lucifer for the chief of the bad angels. He fused in Satan all the distinctive functions for which he had been labeled variously as enemy, old serpent, tempter or destroyer (YP VI, p. 350). The change of the antagonist from Lucifer to Satan seems crucial. It should not be delimited to a mere issue of nomenclature. It could give the temptation scene tremendous momentum with a unified figure of the Hebraic serpent and the Christian archfiend Satan, whose contemporary reappearances as the Antichrist Milton was actually experiencing. The tragic plans were written early in the Revolution, when Milton was innocently working with the "reformer" Presbyterians. His radical change of the antagonist must have been closely related to his own sufferings from the Antichrist, whose original substance, as Milton knew well from Revelation, was Satan.

The activity of the Antichrist was put into historical perspective in the epistle to *Christian Doctrine:* "The process of restoring religion to something of its pure original state, after it had been defiled with impurities from more than thirteen hundred years, dates from the beginning of the last century" (YP VI, p. 117). Milton's confidence in a final victory over the Antichrist is remarkable, given the cold reality after 1652 in which his trust in the revolutionary regime was collapsing. Apparently he understood the English Revolution as a historical hope of liberation from the Antichristian domination of the world, and was aware of being himself engaged in a continuous battle with the Antichrist whose doomed destruction was prophesied in Revelation.

Milton does not merely process the biblical materials for the sake of their theological interest. Rather, his statement reflects a long process of his actual experiences with the living powers of the devil. He was keenly aware that Satan was really working behind historical appearances of the Antichrist. It seems that, having substantialized the concept of Satan with his own experiences, Milton felt impelled to deal with the theme of temptation, not as an offstage episode in a tragedy, but as the vividly detailed, central scene of the epic.

VIII

Throughout the entire scene of temptation in *Paradise Lost,* Milton stresses Satan's constant and complete victory over the perfect images of God. We are struck to see that every condition in the Garden is prepared for man to be tempted and fall. Eve happened to be left alone of her own accord far from the sight of Adam as Satan was most pleased to observe (IX, 421 ff, 479 ff). It is almost noon, which prepares for natural hunger and thirst in her (739–40). The fruit of the tree of knowledge really smells savoury, as Satan had told her (579, 740–41), and may be plucked with her outstretched arm, as he had told her (590, 781). Above all she is so completely innocent as not to suspect any shadow of evil in the serpent-Satan. And finally, Adam has already pledged himself to be inseparable from her, and behaves at the crisis as he pledged.

Milton thus presented the prototypal world of Eden as vulnerable to evil and the perfect image of God as susceptible to the devil. Since he believed, as seen in *Doctrine,* that Edenic man was our original parent whose sin we necessarily inherited, he understood the epic scene not as sheer imagination but as a mimetic representation of the ultimate reality behind all the succeeding historical events of the fallen world. He had actively committed himself to one of those historical events, the contemporary English Revolution, believing it to be not merely a human power struggle but a final battle with the Antichrist so that the eternal

Spirit might realize the ultimate truth on English soil. Primeval time, present, and future are united in the typological progress of God's realization of the truth. The organic correlation of archetype and ectype connects the suprahistorical Edenic world with the poet's experiences in history.

Although Satan can metamorphose himself into any shape he pleases, as he did before into a vulture, a cormorant, a lion, a tiger, and a toad, he appears to Eve disguised as a natural serpent (413, 494–95). As far as the plot is concerned, his choice results from a devilish sense that the temptation of man will require the utmost caution and demand such a complete disguise that the devil may not betray himself at any surprise, as happened with his toad transformation (IV, 810 ff). This perfect disguise is intended by Satan particularly for the deception of man, just as, in later history, the Antichrist was to appear as Papist, Prelate, the King, and so on. Like Satan, the various embodiments of Antichrist took a completely deceptive form, appearing as amiable benefactors to man and thus insinuating themselves into his inconstant nature.

The figure of a serpent-disguised Satan is a faithful representation of the original event of temptation, which Milton believed really took place in no other way. A serpent-Satan reveals the essential nature of the devil as fraud, whose Antichristian ectypes he experienced in the sudden degeneration of reformers and revolutionaries at the peak of their glory.

In contrast to Eve, Adam was tempted and fell with no sight of the Tempter at all, justifying himself in a soliloquy, just as Eve resorted to soliloquy for justification of her own evil desire and deed (679 ff). He is following her course. He is willing to fall from the beginning with no battle with the devil, though he knows better than Eve about the enemy as "Some cursed fraud" (904) and as "that false worm" (1065).

The cause of Adam's self-destruction is his preference for human affection over divine decree, "The link of nature" (914). It is true that Milton constructed the scene on the basis of the Genesis story and St. Paul's interpretation: "Adam was not deceived by the devil" (I Tim. ii, 14). Within these biblical frameworks, Milton's invention is outstanding in the figuration of Adam as instigated to sin by his own inconstant nature. As long as Adam stands on man-centered ground, there is no way out for him but to fall with the Temptress.

The figure of Adam is an archetype which Milton seems to have constructed with the belief that ectypal cases of self-instigated sin were to appear in the course of history. He must have thought that he encountered many such cases in the Revolution. It should, however, be pointed out that a literary figure and actual instances are by no means analogical to Milton. Their relation is like that of a scientific law and its natural occurrences. The actual event and its ultimate truth are in a typological relationship. Milton's literary figure was constructed from the original myth of temptation on the one hand, and on the other from the actual events he understood to be in such a relation to it. A particular emphasis on experience as a discipline for making poetry is made more clearly meaningful in this essential affinity between the suprahistorical reality and its phenomenal aspects in the fallen world.

The point is not that each or some cases of such experiences contributed some feature of the temptation scene. This is the way of speculative analogy, by which we were more than once told that Cromwell, Charles I, Shaftesbury, or an unconscious part of Milton was a model of Satan. Milton's way is more firmly based on the archetypal Genesis myth, which worked on him to transfigure each experiential phenomenon into what we might call a *Gestalt* reservoir of his poetic mind. External experiences must be internalized through a typological imagination into a significative value that can enrich the self of a poet. This must be the reason Milton mentioned first "devout prayer to that eternal Spirit" as an indispensable term for making poetry, for a typological imagination is not an esthetic or epistemological discipline in the modern sense, but an insight into a universal truth which could be revealed to him only through devout prayer to that Spirit. This is the way the self is enriched to be himself "a true Poem." The radical transfiguration of experiential materials is a cardinal element of his devout prayer to the Spirit. He must have prayed for a positive salvational way out of the despairing suffering inflicted by his trusted allies' Antichristian betrayals. They were all tempted by power and wealth and fell with no die-hard battle with the disguised enemy, just as Eve was trapped by a serpent, and self-temptingly fell. This is the way Milton transfigured immediate, confused despair into a Christian archetype, in which there appeared the definite contour of a final hope.

What particularizes the case of Adam is that his fall, though self-conscious, "seemed remediless" (919). The experience of the realist-strategist Milton, who committed himself irrevocably to a worldly power, illustrates this motif of apparent inevitability. *The Second Defence*, with its encomium and concealed criticism of Oliver Cromwell disclosed how "remedilessly" he was involved in the Protectorate regime. Despite all the discouraging facts, he did not leave Cromwell as his friends protestingly did.

He believed that the Cromwellian power was the only stronghold for the glorious achievements of the Revolution. At the same time he saw it as a most cunning Antichristian forcer of conscience. The dilemma of having to serve this worldly power vexed him. Even after he seemed to be liberated from that power by labeling it "a short but scandalous night," he was again trapped into relying, for the defence of the Revolution, on a military power he did not trust. He was finally defeated by that tide of the English people who, he believed, were deceived by the disguised Antichrist as innocently as Eve had been beguiled by the serpent-disguised Satan.

In contrast with these people and Eve, Milton was aware that he was tempted by some hidden enemy, just as Adam had found himself trapped knowingly by some hidden enemy, just as Adam had found himself trapped knowingly but remedilessly by what he himself called "some cursed form." These various phenomena of temptation and fall might be categorized into a type of Eve and a type of Adam. This may be one reason the scene of temptation in *Paradise Lost* is divided into two parts, illustrating stupidly innocent falling in the case of Eve and tragically self-conscious complicity in the case of Adam.

Such a dark figuration of the perfect image of God is indeed a deduction from the Genesis story. But at the same time it is grounded upon conclusions Milton drew from the temptation crises of regenerate persons, including himself, and from what he perceived as actual instances of the fall of many once-trustworthy people. The epic conjoins experience and theology in a mature presentation and judgment of man's inconstant nature.

Aichi University of Education, Japan

NOTES

1. Christopher Hill, *Milton and the English Revolution* (London, 1977), p. 4.

2. Robert T. Fallon made the same sort of approach in his essay "Milton's Epics and the Spanish War: Toward a Poetics of Experience," *Milton Studies*, XV, ed. James D. Simmonds (Pittsburgh, 1981), pp. 3–28. Let me say that Hill and Fallon have set out on a new promising direction of Milton scholarship.

3. *The Complete Prose Works of John Milton*, ed. Don M. Wolfe et al. (New Haven, 1953–82), vol. VI, p. 195. Hereafter cited as YP.

4. All quotations from Milton's poems are from *John Milton: Complete Poems and Major Prose*, ed. Merritt Y. Hughes (New York, 1957).

5. See Christopher Hill, *Antichrist in Seventeenth-Century England* (Oxford, 1971), p. 4.

6. S. R. Gardiner, ed., *The Constitutional Documents of the Puritan Revolution, 1625–1660* (Oxford, 1968), p. 140.

7. See E. A. J. Honigman, ed., *Milton's Sonnets* (London, 1966), p. 147.

8. David Masson, *The Life of John Milton* (Gloucester, Mass., 1965), vol. IV, p. 567.

9. Honigman, *Milton's Sonnets*, p. 149.

10. Masson, *Life*, IV, 394.

11. Maurice Ashley, ed., *Cromwell* (Englewood Cliffs, N.J., 1969), p. 36.

12. See William R. Parker, *Milton* (Oxford, 1968), vol. II, p. 1065.

13. Masson, *Life*, V, 397.

14. Robert T. Fallon, "Filling the Gaps: New Perspective on Mr. Secretary Milton," *Milton Studies*, XII, ed. James D. Simmonds (Pittsburgh, 1979), p. 190.

15. Masson, *Life*, V, 398.

16. Ibid., IV, 87.

17. Hill, *Milton and the English Revolution*, p. 102.

18. Fallon, "Filling the Gaps," pp. 186–87.

19. J. Milton French, ed., *The Life Records of John Milton* (Staten Island, N.Y., 1966), vol. V, p. 243.

20. Masson, *Life*, V, 412.

21. For the inveterate hostility between Cromwell and Vane see Masson, *Life*, IV, 407–08.

22. Christopher Hill, *God's Englishman: Oliver Cromwell and the English Revolution* (New York, 1970), p. 181.

23. Fallon, "Filling the Gaps," p. 181.

24. Gardiner, *Constitutional Documents*, p. 405.

25. Masson, *Life*, IV, 605–08; Parker, *Milton*, I, 440; Wolfe, YP IV, pp. 261–64.

26. Herbert Grierson, *Milton and Wordsworth: Poets and Prophets* (London, 1960), pp. 72–79.

27. See James Dales's entry in *Milton Encyclopedia*, ed. William B. Hunter, Jr. (Lewisburg, Pa., 1980), vol. VIII, p. 27.

28. French, *Life Records*, III, 197.

29. Honigman, *Milton's Sonnets*, p. 174.

30. For Milton's complicated attitude toward Parliament see Don M. Wolfe, *Milton in the Puritan Revolution* (London, 1941), chap. 10.

31. See Woolrich's n. 25, YP VII, p. 328.

32. See Woolrich's n. 112, YP VII, p. 431.

33. B. Rajan, "Simple, Sensuous and Passionate," *RES*, XXI (1945), rpt. in *Milton in Modern Essays in Criticism*, ed. A. E. Barker (Oxford, 1965), p. 8.

34. Maurice Kelley. *This Great Argument* (Magnolia, Mass., 1962), p. 23.

35. See John M. Steadman's commentary in YP VIII, p. 539 ff.

36. Allan H. Gilbert, *On the Composition of "Paradise Lost"* (New York, 1966), pp. 22–23.

THE LIMITS OF ALLEGORY:
TEXTUAL EXPANSION OF NARCISSUS
IN *PARADISE LOST*

Kenneth J. Knoespel

M ILTON'S ELABORATION of Ovidian stories in *Paradise Lost* cannot be properly understood by recourse to moral *exempla* or allegory alone. The reason for this is quite simply that Milton approached Ovid as an equal and not as a poet whose work needed to be opened by an external code provided by medieval or Renaissance commentary. Milton's silent imitation of the Narcissus story supplies an important example of this. Discussion of the story, however, has remained unnecessarily restricted to Eve's creation account. While imitation of Ovid's fable is concentrated in the pool scene, detail from the fable is also used to fashion Satan and Adam. More particularly Ovid's narrative provides components that psychologically animate Milton's characters. As a consequence the fable transcends its traditional setting of love psychology and becomes a means for describing human perception and its limitations. At the same time Ovid's fable helps Milton create a mental life for his characters. In the broadest sense, Milton transforms the fable from a narrative about love to a narrative about understanding.

Study of Milton's use of Narcissus has remained limited to Eve because scholars continue to approach the fable from the vantage point of Renaissance allegory. Since Addison, critics have wondered about a moral in Eve's creation account and have sought out commentaries and handbooks to locate its precise meaning. The inadequacy of such an approach is found in the proliferation of discussions which appeal to external meaning.[1] The fable, however, always evokes more meaning than any single meaning supplied from the outside. In the Renaissance, fables were not simply reduced to a single meaning but were primarily used to teach Latin. Imitation of Latin style, not simple repetition of traditional meaning, was the pedagogical goal.[2] The careful attention given to vocabulary, syntax, and figures of speech in Renaissance commentaries should caution us from moving too quickly from perceived allusion to meaning, for in so doing we may replace the actual text with an imaginary one. Not surprisingly, what we recall today when we think of Nar-

79

cissus — usually a figure suspended before his image — is a simplified version of the fable. To trust such mental reconstruction of the plot is to risk giving meaning to a recalled narrative rather than to detail in Milton's text.

Milton gives special meaning to the narrator's intervention in the Latin story, but critics continue to base discussions on a comparison of Eve and the figure before his image. By stressing deception rather than warning, critics transform the fable into a passive rather than active narrative. Eve's weakness, rather than the divine source of correction, is stressed. The source of warning in *Paradise Lost* finally alerts us to the most substantial alteration Milton makes in Ovid's fable. While Ovid ironically stressed the role of understanding in regard to individual perception, Milton shows through Satan and Adam as well as Eve that understanding and correction can never come from reliance on individual perception alone but must come from guidance.

Milton first brings Ovid's fable into the poem in the allegory of Sin and Death. Here the association of Satan and Narcissus is not unusual because the pride of Satan and Narcissus was commonly observed in commentaries. But Milton does not simply accept traditional meaning. By dramatizing Satan's intellective pride, he psychologizes self-love and prepares for the psychological setting of Eve's creation scene. Here careful adaptation of the fable describes the limits of perception and interpretation. This scene too, rather than being restricted to Eve, anticipates Milton's subsequent elaboration of Adam's own problematic response to divine guidance.

I

For Milton's seventeenth-century reader the fall of Satan was a grave warning against pride. Pride jars the hierarchy established by God, and the pride of Satan is declared early in the work:

> hee it was, whose guile
> Stirr'd up with Envy and Revenge, deceiv'd
> The Mother of Mankind; what time his Pride
> Had cast him out from Heav'n, with all his Host
> Of Rebel Angels, by whose aid aspiring
> To set himself in Glory above his Peers,
> He trusted to have equall'd the most High.　　　(I, 34–40)[3]

A long history of commentary sought to identify the source of Satan's pride. Augustine located its source in introspection and attraction to knowledge Satan believed his own. The intellective account of Satan's corruption is repeated by Richard Hooker in *Ecclesiastical Polity* and remains such a commonplace that it is even used by Donne in a wedding sermon. Ovidian commentaries as early as the *Ovide moralisé* added to this commentary by associating Satan's pride with the vanity of Narcissus.[4] In the seventeenth century George Sandys concludes his commentary on Ovid's fable with a stern warning: "A fearfull example we have of the danger of selfe-love in the fall of the Angells; who intermitting the beatificall vision, by reflecting upon themselves, and admiring their own excellency, forgot their dependence upon their creator."[5] Moral commentary like Sandys's assumed that *exempla* made abstractions more accessible. Within such an interpretive setting it is the moral, not the story's detail, which is given attention. This is not the case in Milton's poem. While use of Narcissus certainly may be read against the background of commentary, it goes beyond such simple relations and becomes itself a further textual elaboration of the fable.

Milton never draws an explicit relation between Satan and Narcissus because he does not need to. This had been done by a long tradition of commentary. Sin's comments also evoke Ovid's fable.

> I pleas'd, and with attractive graces won
> The most averse, thee chiefly, who full oft
> Thyself in me thy perfect image viewing,
> Becam'st enamor'd, and such joy thou took'st
> With me in secret, that my womb conceived
> A growing burden.   (II, 762–67)

"Thyself in me thy perfect image viewing / Becam'st enamor'd" invites us to think of Narcissus. Here, as later in Eve's creation account, syntax supports the reflective phenomena being described. Words such as "pleas'd," "full oft," "image," "attractive graces" also anticipate vocabulary later used to describe Eve. Portrayed as an allegory, Satan's family history conveys his own mental past and amplifies the psychological detail of Ovid's fable. Milton is really not interested in imitating the plot but in internalizing a configuration represented in the fable. Knowledge in Ovid's story pertains to the comprehension of physical phenomena that may lead to deception. Without understanding that one's own visual image may be reflected by a smooth surface, Narcissus drinks at a pool and falls in love with the image he sees. Recognition that the image is his own fulfills Tiresias' prophecy — he knows himself and must die. While Narcissus literally falls in love with an extension of his physical image, we understand through Milton's allegory that Satan's love pertains to *thought* itself.

Milton's allegory makes sophisticated use of the phenomena described in Ovid's fable. Like Narcissus, Satan is at first unaware of the deceptive nature of self-love. Unlike Narcissus, however, who is warned by an unheard narrator, Satan is warned by his own physical symptoms: "sudden miserable pain" (II, 752), diminished sight, dizziness — all of which make it evident that self-reflection disrupts normal faculties. The symptoms herald illness and become elaborated through Milton's evocation of another myth. Emerging as an "armed Goddess" (II, 757) from Satan's head, Sin reveals herself as a strident idea and evokes the cerebral birth of Tritonian Pallas in Hesiod's *Theogony* (924–26). Like the Greek goddess who instigated war between the Titans, Sin becomes a figure who threatens to draw Satan and other angels into mental idolatry.[6]

Sin disturbs the celestial onlookers as soon as she is realized. At the sudden appearance of this fantastical shape they not only jump back in fear and amazement but speak. This sudden invention of speech stresses the unusual nature of the event they witness, for language is used to define, and thereby control that which has not been experienced before. (The threat posed by Sin is conveyed even more directly by the Hebrew word for Sin, *pesha*, which literally means rebellion.)[7] By identifying Sin as a warning "Sign" (II, 760), Milton further emphasizes Sin's birth as a linguistic event. Unable to recognize the "Sign" before him, Satan demonstrates the extent of his deformation. The fact that Milton places questions about language and meaning in an allegory enforces the importance of interpretation. Not only Satan but the reader too is suddenly reminded of his role as interpreter. Further on this interpretive motif will coincide even further with Milton's adaption of Ovid's fable.

The appearance of Satan's mental image in Heaven signals that a transgression has been committed. Permanent destruction occurs, however, only as Satan falls in love with his conception. Like Narcissus, who enjoys his image apart from Theban society, Satan must separate himself from his heavenly colleagues and enjoy his mental image in secret. Bearing the heavenly likeness of her progenitor, Sin functions as a mirror image, not, however, a reflected image but more like an ever present twin inciting Satan to rebel against his fixed position in heavenly society. Only later is Satan forced to recognize the extent of his deformation. When discovered by the angels sent to guard Paradise, Satan cannot be recognized because his shape is so marred. Like Sin, his appearance is associated with flames, and the angels stand back in amazement at the image that suddenly appears before them. As he taunts the angels into recognizing him, we learn that he still has not recognized himself.

> Know ye not then said Satan fill'd with scorn,
> Know ye not mee? ye knew me once no mate
> For you, there sitting where ye durst not soar;
> Not to know mee argues yourselves unknown.   (IV, 827–30)

Accused of not knowing themselves, the angels reverse the charge. Their words hold a mirror in which he may see himself.

> Think not, revolted Spirit, thy shape the same,
> Or undiminisht brightness, to be known
> As when thou stood'st in Heav'n upright and pure;
> That Glory then when thou no more wast good,
> Departed from thee, and thou resembl'st now
> Thy sin and place of doom obscure and foul.   (IV, 835–40)

Even when forced to recognize his present deformed shape Satan continues to be attracted to the idea he conceived of himself in Heaven. Like Narcissus, who continues gazing expectantly at his shape in Hades (504–05),[8] Satan continues to love his false image in Hell. Turned away from God and facing his own image, Satan suffers a fate that Christian tradition compared to Narcissus. Through the allegorical account of Sin's conception, Milton expands the meaning of Narcissus to include the deceptive nature of thought itself.

II

When Patrick Hume comes to Milton's imitation of Narcissus in the pool scene, he remarks that here Milton "has litt upon something so new and strange."[9] These new and strange qualities, however, remain acceptable because they do not appear unnatural. Actually Milton's invention makes both Eve *and* Narcissus appear more natural. Eve is hardly a developed character in Genesis, and the Narcissus of Ovid's fable fascinates but is never literally regarded as a real person. By drawing them together, Milton makes both stand forth in ways previously unknown. This is accomplished through detailed imitation of Ovid's Latin, not through recourse to a single moral. The selective interplay between the remembered fable and the present text animates Eve and gives her a psychology. This would have been particularly strong for the seventeenth-century reader, whose familiarity with Ovidian vocabulary, syntax, and meter was as great as our knowledge of multiplication tables. He could not condemn her because she had done nothing wrong. The potential moral given to Narcissus does not converge with Eve until later. Thus detail from the fable simultaneously provides Eve with mental capacity and introduces a potential interpretation.

Before looking at the pool scene we must recognize that it is part of a larger Ovidian setting. Eden invites comparison with Narcissus' own Theban landscape.[10] Both are pristine, unpopulated territories which become settings for early history. Landscapes in Ovid are often sensuous settings for potential violence, and this is true of Eden as well. The natural settings in Ovid are never simple backdrops because humans so often quite literally become part of them. Eden too suggests the potential for change.

As Milton describes Eden and Satan at the beginning of Book IV, his vocabulary shows him extending his descriptive study of Satan, whose very presence brings heightened concern with the deceptive qualities of faces and smooth surfaces. He seeks to hide the depression that accompanies his fallen state. The narrator points to his "borrow'd visage" (IV, 116) and compares his mind to heavenly minds.

> For heav'nly minds from such distempers foul
> Are ever clear. Whereof hee soon aware,
> Each perturbation smooth'd with outward calm,
> Artificer of fraud; and was the first
> That practis'd falsehood under saintly show.   (IV, 118–22)

"Distemper" and "perturbation" even suggest that Milton is carrying out a medical analysis of Satan. Borrowed faces, counterfeiting, and words such as clear, smooth, calm, anticipate the lake which will deceive Eve. The "woody Theatre" of trees (IV, 141) and the reference to "Landskip" (IV, 153) suggest that we are viewing a masquelike stage setting that only waits for the placement of Adam and Eve. The scene is similar to the landscapes of Renaissance pastoral poetry with their enchanted fountains and streams. The fluid landscape of Paradise grows before our eyes, allowing us to hear and see the scene that was the setting for Eve's creation.

> Another side, umbrageous Grots and Caves
> Of Cool recess, o'er which the mantling Vine
> Lays forth her purple Grape, and gently creeps
> Luxuriant; meanwhile murmuring waters fall
> Down the slope hills, disperst, or in a Lake,
> That to the fringed Bank with Myrtle crown'd,
> Her crystal mirror holds, unite their streams.   (IV, 257–63)

The scene conveys a hypnotic attraction. The personification of the water holding a "crystal mirror" anticipates the very physical quality that soon confuses Eve.

Although both Eve and Narcissus approach the pool innocently, they

do so for different reasons. Narcissus is attracted to the spring by the
beauty of the setting and by thirst from hunting (413–14). "A murmuring sound" (435) draws Eve's attention to the spring. Milton transforms
Ovid's personification of Echo back into a natural phenomenon. Just as
Narcissus is immediately attracted to the sound of an answering voice,
Eve is drawn by aural stimulation. She approaches the spring as if it will
help her identify both herself and the place she is in. Because Eve approaches the pool with an expectation that is not present in Ovid, she
is consequently aware of more than her own image when she first looks
into the lake. She has a desire for knowledge not found in Narcissus. At
first the water appears as another sky. When she suddenly sees a figure
before her in the water her reaction, like the angels at the sudden appearance of Sin, is one of surprise: "I started back" (462). Pleased that
another figure appears in this vacant landscape, Eve quickly looks back
into the lake. The syntax of lines 460–65 conveys the interaction of Eve
and her reflection.

> As I bent down to look, just opposite,
> A Shape within the wat'ry gleam appear'd
> Bending to look on me, I started back,
> It started back, but pleas'd I soon return'd
> Pleas'd it returned as soon with answering looks
> Of sympathy and love.   (460–65)

Her reactions are mirrored syntactically: "I started back / It started back,"
"pleased I soon return'd / Pleas'd it returned." In lines 464–65 Milton
describes Eve's own sympathetic response to the image through description of the reflection. Here too references to "answering looks" conflate
the visual and aural phenomena and alert one to the absence of any
vocal response.

Ovid too emphasizes Narcissus' interaction with his reflection
through syntax: "se cupit inprudens et, qui probat, ipse probatur, /
dumque petit, petitur, pariterque accendit et ardet" ("Unwittingly he
desires himself; he praises, and is himself what he praises; and while he
seeks, is sought; equally he kindles love and burns with love" (425–26).
The sequence of active and passive forms (probat and probatur, petit
and petitur) even obscures the difference between subject and object.
Narcissus, like Eve, is attracted by the correspondence between his own
actions and the behavior of the figure before him.

In both stories a sequence of interaction between subject and figure
precedes a turning point. For Narcissus interaction with his image leads
to destructive self-recognition:

quisquis es, huc exi! quid me, puer unice, fallis
quove petitus abis? certe nec forma nec aetas
est mea, quam fugias, et amarunt me quoque nymphae
spem mihi nescio quam vultu promittis amico,
eumque ego porrexi tibi bracchia, porrigis ultro,
cum risi, adrides; lacrimas quoque saepe notavi
me lacrimante tuas; nutu quoque signa remittis
et, quantum motu formosi suspicor oris,
verba refers aures non pervenientia nostras!
iste ego sum: sensi, nec me mea fallit imago.   (454–63)

[Whoever you are, come forth hither! Why, O peerless youth, do you elude me? or whither do you go when I strive to reach you? Surely my form and age are not such that you should shun them, and me too the nymphs have loved. Some ground for hope you offer with your friendly looks, and when I have stretched out my arms to you, you stretch yours too. When I have smiled, you smile back; and I have often seen tears, when I weep, on your cheeks. My becks you answer with your nod; and, as I suspect from the movement of your sweet lips, you answer my words as well, but words which do not reach my ears. — Oh, I am he! I have felt it, I know now my own image.]

Narcissus' recognition is the product of deductive reasoning. He begins to list the ways the other figure is compatible to him in an attempt to understand why it continues to elude him. His own figure is beautiful; it has attracted Echo and others; why should it not attract the person before him? The figure responds by stretching out his arms when Narcissus tries to reach him; it smiles, it cries, it moves as Narcissus does; it even appears to speak but its words do not reach his ears. Suddenly Narcissus recognizes himself. Precisely the inability to hear the figure leads Narcissus to the realization that the voiceless figure is a reflection of himself. Even in self-recognition, however, Narcissus cannot separate himself from his image. And this, of course, is the paradox at the center of Ovid's story.

The absence of self-recognition that accompanies Eve's interplay with the figure before her is the major component that distinguishes the two narratives. Significantly here too sound becomes a turning point. It is not, however, the absence but the presence of a voice which makes the crucial difference. A heavenly voice interrupts Eve's pantomime before the reflection and leads her from the deceptive image.

> What thou seest,
> What there thou seest fair Creature is thyself,
> With thee it came and goes: but follow me,
> And I will bring thee where no shadow stays

> Thy coming, and thy soft imbraces, hee
> Whose image thou art, him thou shalt enjoy
> Inseparably thine, to him shalt bear
> Multitudes like thyself, and thence be call'd
> Mother of human Race.   (IV, 467–75)

Although Eve is distinguished from Narcissus, the text remains informed by the fable because the warning voice is linked to Ovid's narrative on a structural level that is often overlooked. In the midst of recounting the confusion of Narcissus, the narrator interrupts, warning his character as if he can no longer separate himself from the story he is telling:

> credule quid frustra simulacra fugacia captas?
> quod petis, est nusquam; quod amas, advertere, perdes!
> ista repercussae, quam cernis, imaginis umbra est:
> nil habet ista sui; tecum venitque manetque;
> tecum discedete, si tu discedere possis!   (432–36)

[O fondly foolish boy, why vainly seek to clasp a fleeting image? What you seek is nowhere; but turn yourself away, and the object of your love will be no more. That which you behold is but the shadow of a reflected form and has no substance of its own. With you it comes, with you it stays, and it will go with you — if you can go.]

The narrator's warning is ironic not only because Narcissus' acts now fit the earlier prophecy but because as a figure in a story he cannot hear the narrator's voice. A different situation appears in Milton's text because comprehension is possible. Eve is not ironically divorced from the warning voice. Yet even though she comes under its spell she does not immediately understand. God's intervention too is far more than an elementary lesson in physics. It is a prophecy that gives Eve an identity and her creation purpose.[11] Quite literally she is the image of Adam and with him will conceive images sufficient to fill the earth. Unlike Narcissus, whom Ovid compares to a marble statue (419), Eve herself is to become a creator. She must fulfill what her name in Hebrew means (*Hawwah* — life),[12] a meaning implicit in what the voice has told her. In contrast to the figure of Sin, who bears a progeny of fear and distortion, Eve is to bear a race that remains close to God. Like the voice of Gabriel that brings fruitful tidings to Mary, the voice of God brings fertility to Eve.

Because the future of mankind depends on Eve's engagement with Adam, her reluctance to accept him attains significance. For a short time the voice of God has complete control over her. "What could I do, / But follow straight, invisibly thus lead?" (IV, 475–76). But then the voice relinquishes its spellbinding force. It is only a momentary intervention, a celestial push whose momentum terrestrial reason must sustain. Eve's behavior suggests that the immediate sensual phenomena, not reason, control her behavior. The memory of the "smooth wat'ry image," a sensual visual image, controls her actions, not the invisible instruction offered by the voice. She follows the voice

> Till I espi'd thee, fair indeed and tall,
> Under a Platan; yet methought less fair,
> Less winning soft, less amiably mild,
> Than that smooth wat'ry image; back I turned.   (IV, 477–80)

Turning to her own fair image, Eve displays a propensity to vanity that Christian tradition had long associated with women and the Mother of Mankind.[13] Yet while a warning concerning feminine vanity is certainly present here, greater importance is given to heeding God's word. Like Satan, Eve must respond to God's warning. For Satan such warning comes in the painful conception of Sin — a sign which must be understood. For Eve it comes in the presence of God's voice which must be obeyed, for the moment Eve is turned toward the "smooth wat'ry image," she shows that her mind is drawn by the image she believes would bring most pleasure. Unable to comprehend the instructive voice of God, she turns away from reason and toward an image associated with distortion and death.[14]

The danger of Eve's behavior is only hinted at before she is once again drawn from her reflection, this time by an earthly voice accompanied by physical gesture.

> Thou following cri'd'st aloud, Return fair Eve,
> Whom fli'st thou? whom thou fli'st, of him thou art
> His flesh, his bone; to give thee being I lent
> Out of my side to thee, nearest my heart
> Substantial Life, to have thee by my side
> Henceforth an individual solace dear;
> Part of my Soul I seek thee, and thee claim
> My other half; with that thy gentle hand
> Seiz'd mine, I yielded, and from that time see
> How beauty is excell'd by manly grace
> And wisdom, which alone is truly fair.   (IV, 481–91)

Unable to comprehend God's invisible presence, Eve is physically drawn to Adam whose wisdom should guide and direct her behavior. As Eve concludes the account of her creation she tells how she was separated from the deceitful image that held such fascination for her. Her actions, however, have suggested that she bears the weakness of a feminine psychology. At the same time they silently warn of the destruction and barren consequences that would follow should she become self-reliant.

Yet even though Milton's imitation of Narcissus appears to fade as she turns away from her image toward Adam, the dilemma posed by Ovid's story remains. Just as Eve begins to return to her image, Adam calls out for her. No one to my knowledge has pointed to the similarity between Adam's words to Eve and Narcissus' plea to his image when it suddenly disappears in the water before him.

> Dixit et ad faciem rediit male sanus eandem
> et lacrimis turbavit aquas, obscuraque moto
> reddita forma lacu est; quam cum vidisset abire,
> "quo refugis? remane nec me, crudelis, amantem
> desere!" clamavit. (474–78)

[He spoke and, half distraught, turned again to the same image. His tears ruffled the water, and dimly the image came back from the troubled pool. As he saw it thus depart, he cried; "Oh, whither do you flee? Stay here, and desert not him who loves thee, cruel one!]

At the very point in Milton's text at which discussion of Narcissus usually stops, it actually continues. The progression of the Ovidian fable does not depend on a recreation of Ovid's plot but comes from questions of perception and comprehension raised by the fable.

III

To understand why Milton compares Adam to Narcissus, it is necessary to consider Adam's own memory of Eve's creation and his desire for a partner. By presenting arguments to God about the unnatural quality of life without human companionship, Adam exemplifies his capacity for reasonable judgment. This exercise tests — and displays — his ability to reason and demonstrates that through reason he bears God's image within himself. The unspoken conclusion of his amicable debate with God is that his divine, intellectual capacity should permit him to deal reasonably with the "other self" that God has intended to create for him all along. Here too Milton implies that reason is a faculty best exercised with another: it is not a private but a public occupation.

Since Adam's capacity for reasonable discourse is identified as having the utmost importance by God himself, its rapid dissolution bears a major implication. Even while suspended in the trance, Adam's "likeness" overwhelms him. Not surprisingly, Eve's creation scene recalls Sin's ominous birth. Sense and emotion, not reason, govern his perception of the image that appears before him. With a single glance the rest of God's creation is diminished: "That what seem'd fair in all the World, seem'd now / Mean, or in her summ'd up" (VIII, 472–73). When Adam awakes, his excitement indicates that his identity is already bound to the shape that was formed from his own. "I wak'd / To find her, or for ever to deplore / Her loss" (VIII, 478–80). His mental image of her must become materialized.

Adam's remembrance of Eve's first moments in Paradise gives us a significantly edited version of what we have already learned from Eve. The heavenly voice, not the "smooth wat'ry image," is recalled. Milton, however, does not permit us to forget the visual phenomena, because Adam idealizes her very form. When she approaches he is spellbound.

> I now see
> Bone of my Bone, Flesh of my Flesh, my Self
> Before me.   (VII, 494–96)

Likeness, not difference, becomes the more important. This is not surprising, for having conceived her as a reflection of himself, Adam cannot imagine her different from himself. Consequently he misrepresents what has taken place. "Virgin Modesty" (VIII, 501), not attraction to a "wat'ry image," caused Eve to turn away from him and "pleaded reason" (VIII, 510) gained her return. But neither modesty nor reason pervades the scene. What appears as modesty is desire for an illusion; what Adam recalls as reason is an emotional appeal reminiscent of Narcissus' own plea to his disturbed image.

Attracted to Eve as a corporeal image of himself, Adam is unable to fix his attention on the godlike image he bears within himself. Reason is disoriented in Eve's presence. Even though Adam has a conceptual awareness that differences exist between himself and Eve, it remains passive and unarticulated.

> For well I understand in the prime end
> Of Nature her th' inferior, in the mind
> And inward Faculties, which most excel,
> In outward also her resembling less
> His Image who made both, and less expressing
> The character of that Dominion given
> O'er other Creatures; Yet when I approach
> Her loveliness, so absolute she seems
> And in herself complete, so well to know
> Her own, that what she wills to do or say,
> Seems wisest, virtuousest, discreetest, best;
> All higher knowledge in her presence falls
> Degraded; Wisdom in discourse with her
> Loses, discount'nanc't, and like folly shows.   (VIII, 540–53)

The speech recreates the configuration implicit in Eve's creation account. In each case attraction to a beautiful image establishes the necessity for choice. Here, as earlier, the passage shows rational choice impeded by emotion. In Eve's presence reason appears like folly. The parallel is carried even further when we recognize that Raphael's warning recalls, indeed repeats, God's warning to Eve. "For what admirs't thou, what transports thee? / An outside" (VIII, 567–70). Here substance and syntax recall God's warning to Eve: "What thou seest, / What there thou seest, fair creature, is thy self" (IV, 467–68). Both in turn invoke Ovid's Latin: "quod petis, ut nusquam, quod amas avertere perdes!" ("What you seek is nowhere; but turn yourself away, and the object of your love will be no more"), (433).

Adam's response to Raphael's warning shows a weakness in his understanding. Because he is unable to comprehend its significance, he argues against it.

> Neither her out-side form'd so fair, nor aught
> In procreation common to all kinds
> (Though higher of the genial Bed by far,
> And with mysterious reverence I deem)
> So much delights me as those graceful acts,
> Those thousand decencies that daily flow
> From all her words and actions, mixed with Love
> And sweet compliance, which declare unfeign'd
> Union of Mind, or in us both one Soul;
> Harmony to behold in wedded pair
> More grateful than harmonious sound to the ear.
>
> (VIII, 596–606)

As he seeks to clarify his position, Adam actually displays the confusion that Raphael's discourse sought to correct. It is not Eve's beautiful form itself which poses the greatest threat but Adam's satisfaction with her presence. He cannot make the necessary distinction between himself and his "other self." When he should experience difference, he finds "unfeign'd / Union of Mind" and harmony that is "more grateful than harmonious sound to the ear."

While the comparison of mental harmony to sound is hardly unusual, it does stress the personal nature of perception. Like the perception of sound, the judgment of one's relation to another person is subjective. The attention given to sound also invites us to recall the motif of aural deception present in the fable. Sound, even more than optical imagery, can be deceptive and requires interpretation. Actually, within the religious setting of *Paradise Lost*, sound — as a medium of speech — is intimately related to vision.[15] Indeed, scenes that appear dominated by visual phenomena actually turn out to emphasize aural phenomena. Satan is warned by Sin, a figure who signifies rebellion. Eve is warned by a voice which draws her from a visual image. Adam listens and must understand. Of course the combination of visual and aural detail is found in Ovid's fable. But while such intersection is supported by the fable, it must ultimately depend on the ways metaphors of sound and vision intersect. The scriptural uses of mirror metaphors are the foremost examples of such intersection within a Christian context and I will return to them below.

Considered in a setting that invites comparison with Ovid's fable, the passage alerts us to Adam's subjective perception in other ways as well. While Adam's perception may be "unfeigned" according to himself, the reader's knowledge of the substantial differences which do exist entail, as it were, the validity of Adam's assertion. He simply is not conscious of his own limitation. There is a discrepancy between his subjective comprehension and the more objective vantage point created by the text. This discrepancy is expressed by Adam's selective recollection of details from Eve's creation account and his own emotional attraction to her. While Adam understands, he does not understand completely. This becomes even more evident in the most elaborate example of guidance in the poem.

Adam's response to Raphael's epic narrative of the War in Heaven suggests that he does not comprehend the exemplary history sufficiently to apply it to himself. At the conclusion of the history, the narrator stresses that Adam has been given an *exemplum* from which he should learn.

> Say, Goddess, what ensu'd when Raphael
> The affable Archangel, had forewarn'd
> Adam, by dire example, to beware
> Apostasy, by what befell in Heaven
> To those Apostates, lest the like befall
> In Paradise to Adam or his Race.   (VII, 41–45)

What ensues is not quite as simple as critics have thought, for the simile used to describe Adam's reaction further complements the progression of references to Narcissus.

> as one whose drought,
> Yet scarce allayed, still eyes the current stream
> Whose liquid murmur heard new thirst excites.   (VII, 66–68)

The comparison invites varied interpretations. Initially it invites us to think of Adam longing for expanded revelation and invokes similar comparisons of divine guidance and refreshing water in the Bible (Rev. xxii, 1). But the figure also invokes an Ovidian description.

> dumque sitim sedare cupit, sitis altera crevit,
> dumque bibit, visae correptus imagine formae
> spem sine corpore amat, corpus putat esse, quod
> umbra est. (415–17)

[While he seeks to slake his thirst another thirst springs up, and while he drinks he is smitten by the sight of the beautiful form he sees. He loves an unsubstantial hope and thinks that substance which is only shadow.]

Internal detail also draws the passage into an Ovidian configuration, for it recalls the "murmuring sound" that first attracted Eve to the lake. Here, however, the "liquid murmur" is a figure of speech which leads to aural not visual phenomena. Not surprisingly, hearing is stressed frequently in surrounding passages. When he urges Raphael to continue, Adam observes that what he has heard has caused "full wonder in our ears, / Far differing from this World" (VII, 70–72). At the end of Raphael's higher discourse, hearing is again referred to in a passage which invites comparison with Ovid's fable.

> So Charming left his voice that he a while
> Thought him still speaking, still stood fixed to hear;
> Then, as new wak't, thus gratefully repli'd
> What thanks sufficient, or what recompense
> Equal have I to render thee, Divine
> Historian, who thus largely hast allay'd
> The thirst I had of knowledge. (VIII, 1–8)

Adam's ringing ears once more call attention to the preceding revelation of higher wisdom and prepare for more common discourse. The addition of these lines to the 1667 edition emphasizes their function as a transition to subsequent exchanges on cosmology and physics. But the special attention given to aural phenomena once more raises the problem of interpretation. Momentarily suspended in anticipation of additional sound, Adam invites comparison with Narcissus' suspension before visual phenomena. At the same time that the passage alerts one to revelation of higher knowledge, it also questions human capacity to comprehend divine guidance. For this reason the passage complements the pool scene. The charming effect of Raphael's exemplary discourse on Adam corresponds to the spellbinding force of God's voice on Eve: "what could I do, / But follow straight, invisibly thus led?" The passages resonate in other ways as well. While Eve is fixed expectantly before a visual illusion, Adam remains momentarily fixed in anticipation of more sound.

Each is also described as waking. Eve literally awakes to misperception and correction. Adam figuratively awakes in a setting pervaded by the need for interpretation.

Even though Adam looks into the mirror of heavenly doctrine repeatedly, he cannot adequately apply its meaning to himself. Because he cannot distinguish himself from Eve, he reflects her inferior and finally distorted image. When she tastes the forbidden fruit he follows her actions.

> I with thee have fixt my Lot,
> Certain to undergo like doom; if Death
> Consort with thee, Death is to mee as Life;
> So forcible within my heart I feel
> The Bond of Nature draw me to my own,
> My own in thee, for what thou art is mine. (IX, 952–57)

Just as Ovidian detail accompanies Milton's account of their first meeting, it now also accompanies the account of their mutual degeneration. As Adam testifies that his fate is joined with Eve's his words once more recall Narcissus: "hic, quid diligitur, vellem diuturnior esset; / nunc duo concordes anima moriemur in una" ("I would he that is loved might live longer; but as it is we two shall die together in one breath") (471–73). Here too we are reminded of the earlier depiction of Satan. Just as Satan's godlike image came to bear the distortion first seen in Sin, Adam's godlike image is marred when he shapes his actions after Eve. For both Satan and Adam a capacity to participate freely in godlike wisdom is disrupted by self-conceived, goddesslike figures that have sinister births.

We have been considering the way Milton uses detail from Ovid to create an atmosphere of limited comprehension. Satan, Eve, and Adam are animated with detail that helps convey their response to mental, visual, and aural phenomena. Now a distinction already made must be repeated. Milton's use of the fable is not confined to sensual deception but emphasizes, above all, interpretation. In particular it is the narrator's intervention, not Narcissus' suspension before his image, which deserves most attention. The iconographic representation of Narcissus in Renaissance painting, sculpture, and emblem books has less importance for the poem than Milton's own inventive application of the fable to narrative. The passive image of the deceived Narcissus forever captured by his reflection is augmented by a far more active image of warning which is continually present in Milton's narrative. The fact that the warnings themselves are not completely understood show that Milton actually uses the fable to raise questions about interpretation.

Emphasis on interpretation does not depend entirely on Ovid's fable.

It also relies on Christian epistemology and is encouraged by the meta-phoric use of mirrors in scripture.[16] The material mirror that destroys Narcissus is balanced by God's word identified in the New Testament as a corrective mirror. Passages such as 1 Corinthians xiii, 12 provided commentators with a mirror expressive of man's limited vision when he sought to fathom God. When he looked at the scriptures, heard them read, or considered God's creation, man's vision was limited like his sight when he peered into a metal mirror. Just as faith was required if man were to correct himself after the indistinct image in the mirror, faith was required when one sought to make out God's presence. When attention was fixed faithfully on God's word, guidance and correction would shine forth and lead toward a fuller realization of God's image. When atten-tion was focused only on the material mirror, all that appeared was self-reflection and knowledge which distorts the observer's relation to the creator. A distinction between these two mirrors stands behind Milton's use of Ovid's story.

The mirror metaphors used in scripture stress that understanding requires faith. As we know, Protestant emphasis on personal faith could lead to inspired understanding as well as doubt about the certainty of one's perception.[17] But understanding, whether inspired or the result of a rational process, is only one step toward shaping a godlike image. Only active response to God's guidance reveals our understanding.

But be ye doers of the word and not hearers only, deceiving your own selves. For if any be a hearer of the word, and not a doer, he is like a man beholding his natu-ral face in a mirror. For he beholdeth himself, and goeth his way, and immediately forgetteth what manner of man he was. But whosoever looked into the perfect law of liberty, and continueth in it, he being not a forgetful hearer but a doer of the work, this man shall be blessed in his deed. (James i, 22–25)

Milton's adaption of Ovid's fable must finally be viewed within such a scriptural setting. Once again it is the narrator's intervention in Ovid's text which deserves special attention. While it conveys an ironic warn-ing, it also concludes with a challenge to action complementary to the scriptural admonition: "si tu discedere possis!" (436). Even in Ovid's story comprehension is not enough. The image requires interpretation which in turn demands action.

IV

Milton's use of the Narcissus fable is not confined to Eve. Rather than being used as an *exemplum* or a story to be moralized, the fable provides narrative detail for the characterization of Satan, Eve, and Adam. In each case amplification of Ovidian detail contributes to the portrayal of psychology or the internal senses. The *Metamorphoses* had long been regarded as a collection of personal histories that could also function as a manual for psychology. Milton's use of Narcissus shows us that he does not regard Ovid's text (or more specifically the meanings given to the fable through commentary) as an end but a beginning of meanings. At the beginning of this essay I indicated that impetus for such amplification comes in part from school exercises. Another factor which deserves more study may be mentioned. When the adaption of Narcissus is compared with the Latin text, it is apparent that Milton has ignored all fantastic detail in the fable. Mythological elements such as Liriope, Cephisus, and Tiresias are omitted, and, unlike Ovid's personification of Echo, Milton's references to Echo direct attention to natural phenomena. Actually the detail that he does use is amplified to appear even more believable. This suggests that seventeenth-century interest in demythologizing classical fable informs Milton's approach to Ovid.[18] Thus while Milton's textual imitation carries an implicit criticism of allegory it comes from euhemerism rather than any interpretive innovation. By assuming that all fable recounts the action of actual figures, euhemerism not only provides an alternative to allegorical criticism but urges the psychological amplification of ancient fable.

Milton's use of Ovid witnesses to the changing perception of Ovid in the seventeenth century. This is not sufficiently recognized. While fables were approached through moral allegory and provided models for the depiction of mythological matter in the first half of the century, they become matter for witty and often bawdy jokes by the end of the century. At the same time, however, they also begin to provide details useful in the portrayal of mental life. Recent work shows how Ovid supplies psychological detail for characters in Restoration drama.[19] Ovid's *Heroides* supplies both models and matter for psychological characterization in early epistolary novels. Thus even though allegory becomes a less popular mode of interpretation and composition, interest in Ovid continues and even expands. In the broadest sense, Milton's use of Narcissus in *Paradise Lost* is part of the shifting perception of Ovid in the seventeenth century.

Georgia Institute of Technology

NOTES

This study has gained much from discussions with my friend and colleague Richard J. DuRocher, *Milton and Ovid* (Ithaca, 1985). Anyone working with Ovid and Milton must also happily acknowledge Louis L. Martz, *Poet of Exile: A Study of Milton's Poetry* (New Haven, 1980).

1. Addison was the first to wonder publicly "whether some moral is not couch'd under this place." Joseph Addison, *The Works: Complete in Three Volumes* (New York, 1837), vol. II, p. 20 (Spectator No. 325, Thursday, March 13, 1711–12). A summary of critical approaches to this passage is found in Stanley E. Fish, *Surprised by Sin: The Reader in "Paradise Lost"* (London, 1967), pp. 216–19. See also Albert W. Fields, "Milton and Self-Knowledge," *PMLA*, LXXXIII (1968), 392–96; Fredson Bowers, "Adam, Eve, and the Fall in *Paradise Lost*," *PMLA*, LXXXIV (1969), 264–73; Jonathan H. Collett, "Milton's Use of Classical Myth," *PMLA*, LXXXV (1970), 88–96; Northrop Frye, "The Revelation to Eve," in *"Paradise Lost": A Tercentenary Tribute*, ed. Balachandra Rajan (Toronto, 1969), 18–47; Lee A. Jacobus, "Self-Knowledge in *Paradise Lost*: Conscience and Contemplation," *Milton Studies*, III, ed. James D. Simmonds (Pittsburgh, 1971), pp. 103–18.

2. See D. L. Clark's still useful *Milton at St. Paul's School* (New York, 1948) and the more recent study by John R. Mulder, *The Temple of the Mind: Education and Literary Taste in Seventeenth-Century England* (New York, 1969).

3. All quotations are from *John Milton: Complete Poems and Major Prose*, ed. Merritt Y. Hughes (New York, 1957), hereafter cited in the text by book and line number.

4. See D. C. Allen, "Milton's Eve and the Evening Angels," *MLN*, LXXV (1960), 108–09; John Freccero, "Dante and the Neutral Angels," *The Romanic Review*, LI (1960), 3–14; Augustine, *De Genesi ad Litteram* (IV, 24), *PL* XXXIV, p. 313. *Pat L* and *Pat G* will refer to *Patrologia series latina*, 221 volumes, and *Patrologia series graeca*, 161 volumes, ed. Jacques Paul Migne (Paris, 1844–1900); Richard Hooker, *Ecclesiastical Polity*, ed. Ronald Bayne (New York, 1907; rpt. 1925), vol. I, pp. 163–64; John Donne, *Sermons*, ed. G. R. Potter and E. M. Simpson (Berkeley and Los Angeles, 1953–62), vol. III, sermon 11, p. 254. At the end of the Narcissus commentary in the *Ovide moralisé* (3.1875–76), the reader is reminded that "Par orgueil cheïrent jadis / Li fol angle de Paradis." Quoted in Louise Vinge, *The Narcissus Theme in Western Literature up to the Early Nineteenth Century* (Lund, 1967), p. 94.

5. *Ovid's Metamorphosis Englished, Mythologized and Represented in Figures by George Sandys* (Oxford, 1632), p. 106.

6. The early Church Fathers emphasize that idolatry could take place in the mind. In *De Idololatria* Tertullian observes that "enim et sine iddolo idololatria fiat" ("idolatry may take place even without idolatrous images") (*Pat L* I, col. 740). He further suggests that language is the means by which idolatry enters the mind. "Meminisse debemus etiam in verbis quoque idololatriae incursum; praecavendum" ("We must remember that idolatry enters our minds even in words and take precaution") (col. 768). The conceptual idolatry Milton portrays in Satan should be placed within such a theological tradition.

7. *The Encyclopedia of the Jewish Religion*, ed. R. J. Zwi Werblowsky and Geoffrey Wigoder (New York, 1966), p. 361.

8. All references are to Ovid's *Metamorphoses*, 2 vols., Loeb Edition (New York, 1921), vol. I, Book III, 339–510. It is cited by line number in the text.

9. Patrick Hume, *Annotations on Milton's Paradise Lost . . .* (London, 1695), p. 150.

10. See Hugh Parry, "Ovid's Metamorphoses: Violence in a Pastoral Landscape," *Transactions and Proceedings of the American Philological Society*, XCV (1964), 168–82; the major study of Ovid's use of natural setting is Charles Segal, *Landscape in Ovid's Metamorphoses: A Study in the Transformation of a Literary Symbol*, Hermes Zeitshrift für Klassische Philologie, Einzelschriften 23 (Wiesbaden, 1969).

11. Examination of sixteenth-century Ovidian commentary suggests that the voice of God may also be a symbolic manifestation of the Echo motif. In the sixteenth century

Echo was regarded as a symbol for God's spirit. An example of such a reading is found in Alexander Farra's *Settenario* (Venice, 1571), p. 224: "L'Echo inamorata di Narciso significa esso divino spirito discendente alla illustratione dell'animo nostro" ("Echo, enamored in Narcissus, signifies the holy spirit descending to illuminate our minds"). A similar interpretation is found in Robert Estienne (Stephanus), *Dictionarium historicum, ac poeticum* (Lyons, 1579), no pagination: "Echo, Nympha, nullo oculo visa, & a pane, pastorum deo, mirum in modu adamata: quae quidem physice coeli harmoniam significare dicitur, solis amica, tanquam domini, & moderatioris omnium corporum coelestium ex quibus ipsa componitur, atque teperatur" ("Echo, a nymph who remains invisible; a nymph loved in wondrous manner by Pan, the god of shepherds; a nymph who is even said to signify in a physical sense celestial harmony; friend of the sun, the lord, the ruler of all celestial bodies of which she herself is composed, and lovingly warmed"). For a thorough study of Echo see Friedrich Wieseler, *Narkissos: Eine Kunstmythologische Abhandlung* (Göttingen, 1856); for a more recent commentary on Echo in Milton see John Hollander, *The Figure of Echo* (Berkeley and Los Angeles, 1981).

12. *Encyclopedia of Religion and Ethics*, ed. James Hastings (New York, 1912), p. 607.

13. Discussion of feminine vanity appears often in the writing of the Church Fathers. Their discourses were often directed toward women recently converted to Christianity. Because Christianity required faith in the unseen, any behavior that exaggerated the appearance of the body required censorship. Mirrors are repeatedly condemned. Near the beginning of his treatise *De cultu feminarum*, Tertullian explains that the fallen angels first invented mirrors and then used them to corrupt women (*Pat L* I, p. 1420). Tertullian ironically observes that the mirror would have reminded Eve of her destructive vanity: "si jam et speculo tantum mentiri liceret: et haec Eva concupisset de paradiso expulsa, jam mortua, opinor!" ("If the mirror had been able to deceive so much, I think Eve would have desired to be expelled, already dead from Paradise"), (col. 1419). In his treatise *Paedagogus*, Clement of Alexandria specifies that Narcissus is an *exemplum* of the destructive nature of mirrors: "neque enim (ut est in Graecorum fabulis) formoso Narcisso recte successit, quod suae fuerit contemplator imaginis. Quod si Moyses praecipit hominibus nullam facere imaginem, quae Deum arte repraesentet: quomodo hae recte fecerint mulieres, quae fallaci personae fictione suas per reverationem imitantur imagines?" ("Neither was the beautiful Narcissus [as the Greek fable says] successful in contemplating his own image. But if Moses admonished men not to make any images which represented God through artifice, how can women justify making up images of themselves to be adored by others?"), (*Pat G* VIII, col. 571).

14. As Eve wavers between Adam and the "wat'ry image," she recalls Lot's wife. Reference to Sodom in the Trinity MS suggests that Lot and his wife were not far removed from Milton's mind (*John Milton's Complete Poetical Works: Reproduced in Photographic Facsimile*, ed. Harris F. Fletcher, vol. II, *The First Edition of "Paradise Lost"* [Urbana, 1945], pp. 18, 26).

15. For careful consideration of the relation between vision and language, see Joseph A. Wittreich, Jr., *Visionary Poetics: Milton and His Legacy* (San Marino, Cal., 1979); also helpful is Michael Lieb, *The Poetics of the Holy: A Reading of "Paradise Lost"* (Chapel Hill, 1981).

16. For detailed study of the occurrence of mirrors and their metaphoric use in classical Greek and Latin literature see Norbert Hugedé, *La Metaphor du miroir dans les Épitres de Sainte Paul aux Corinthiens* (Paris, 1957).

17. For careful discussion of Protestant hermeneutics see Georgia B. Christopher, *Milton and the Science of the Saints* (Princeton, 1983).

18. The ways Milton's poem surpasses allegory have been discussed in detail by Michael Murrin, "The Language of Milton's Heaven," in *The Allegorical Epic: Essays in Its Rise and Decline* (Chicago, 1980), pp. 153–71. Murrin does not, however, consider the function of euhemerism in Milton's poem.

19. In the "Preface to Ovid's Epistles," Dryden portrays Ovid as a kind of court wit; *The Poetical Works of John Dryden*, ed. George R. Noyes (Boston, 1909; rpt. 1950), pp. 88–92. In Restoration drama Ovid becomes a model for the comic portrayal of erotic love. These comments are indebted to Anthony Manousos, "Love's Slave Declassé: Ovidian Comedy in the Early Eighteenth Century," a paper presented at the MLA Convention, 1981. See also Harriet Hawkins, *Likeness of Truth in Elizabethan and Restoration Drama* (Oxford, 1972), pp. 790–97.

SATAN, SIN, AND DEATH:
A MOSAIC TRIO IN *PARADISE LOST*

Samuel S. Stollman

T HE STRANGE interlude in *Paradise Lost* of Satan, Sin, and Death (II, 629–889, 1024–33; and X, 229–409) has, for the incongruities of its elements, been deemed "a blemish on the poem and an external encrustation."[1] Cumulative interpretations, sources, and analogues, while explicating facets of the scenes, leave the reader with the returning question: granted that these episodes are, to cite some of the commentary, an allegory of lust, parodies of the Trinity and of the myth of Athena, classical allusions to Hesiod and Ovid, hexameral traditions, biblical "reminiscences," "cosmic history," "a domestic farce," an imitation of Spenser, and combinations of these, what is their unifying principle?[2]

Of course, we may regard the scenario as a mosaic of diverse elements, following Roland M. Frye, who, remarking on the visual traditions behind Milton's conceptualization of the "Infernal Trinity," offers that Milton "conveys in poetry an understanding of the demonic which for complexity and balance is beyond the possibilities of any single work of visual art."[3] Or we may apply Ide and Wittreich's comment regarding Milton's last poems that "each [is] a generic chaos harmonized."[4] Nevertheless, that very complexity of elements, atypicality of genre, and apparent absence of a comprehensive informing principle tempt us to conclude with John Broadbent that "Sin and Death don't function consistently in *PL*" and "therefore to regard them as embodiments of concerns which have not been fully integrated into the poem" (p. 46).

My thesis, however, is that, integrated or not, the personifications of Sin and Death and their encounters with Satan act out one of Milton's major doctrines, namely, his (and that of a "startling spectrum" of his contemporaries)[5] antinomian view of the Mosaic Law and of the Law's impediment to the attainment of Christian liberty. Recurringly in the tracts and especially in *Christian Doctrine*, Milton maintains that the *summum bonum* is Christian liberty, attainable only by the believer's renunciation of the codified form of the Mosaic Law which, according to Paul, is associated with servitude, sin, and death.[6] The supersession of "Judaic bondage" by Christian liberty is a doctrine so crucial to Milton's thought and so widely held in the Puritan Revolution that we expect the antinomy of the "twofold Scripture" not only to be promulgated in *Paradise Lost* (as it is in XII, 280–314) but also to be dramatized in the Adversary's undertaking to prevent man—both Jew and unregenerate Christian—from achieving enfranchisement from the Law and immunity from its consequences.

For these doctrinal and dramatic considerations, as well as others I shall detail, I am led to conclude that, whatever other allusions and correlatives Milton has brought together here, he has included Paul's warning in Romans of the consequences of perpetuating the Mosaic Law. The three—Satan, Sin, and Death—form a Mosaic trio. Satan, in this configuration, is delineated as a perverse, parodic Moses figure, enacting the type of Moses and the Mosaic Law, with Sin and Death, in their caricature of the Mosaic Law, establishing Satan in his role of typing the Law. In his "mirror activities"—to use Shawcross's phrase—Satan enacts the Mosaic roles of liberator, mediator, and lawgiver.[7] Sin and Death, in turn, reinforce the charade: in their incestuous ties to Satan as a Moses figure, Sin and Death call to mind Milton's view in *Christian Doctrine* that they are engendered by the Mosaic Law.

The trio, then, may be read not only as a parody of Moses but also, given Milton's use of typology, as the dramatization of Satan's exploitation of the types of Moses and the Law. In Satan's scheme the type of Moses which foreshadows Jesus and the type of the Law which prefigures the Gospel are reduced to carnal denotations. In effect, Satan arrogates his perverted notion of the type of Moses in order to liberate his cohorts, and exploits the "works" of Sin and Death to lead man to damnation and thus to subvert God's plan. While the infernal trio are a parody of the Trinity, they are also a parodic typological enactment of Moses and the Mosaic Law.

As I shall document in the following pages, most of the elements of my thesis have already been proposed. That Moses is an essential persona in *Paradise Lost* has been demonstrated. That Milton employs a typological perspective in the epic, including his treatment of Moses, has also been shown. That Milton presents Satan distorting and exploiting the types has been asserted. That the Mosaic Law and Moses as the representative of that Law are major types is enunciated in the epic itself. And that Sin and Death are engendered by the Mosaic Law is posited in *Christian Doctrine*. What is new in my thesis is my application of these data to the Satanic trio.

I

Moses' role in *Paradise Lost* begins with the narrator's invocation to the "Shepherd, who first taught the chosen Seed" (I, 8) and continues in some twenty-five allusions. "In *Paradise Lost*," Norman Flinker writes, "the narrator, Abdiel, Satan, the Son and Adam all speak lines that have reminded various editors and critics of Moses."[8] Among these is Jason R. Rosenblatt, who, in "The Mosaic Voice in *Paradise Lost*," defends the presence of the "Mosaic tradition" in the epic: "Moses," he writes, "is the single historical figure who spans the abyss between perfection and sin — unique and inimitable as a result of his communion with God, yet somehow like us in our sinfulness."[9]

Moses' uniqueness, according to Flinker, includes his typological role: "In both *Paradise Lost* and *Paradise Regained* . . . Moses represents one stage in a typological development from Adam to Christ. Milton refers to Moses from this overall Christian perspective, in order to help point the way towards man's ultimate spiritual salvation" (p. 168). While descrying "*two* distinct Moses traditions — the neo-Platonic and the typological — [that] help to define Milton's epic voice," Rosenblatt finds the typological more determinative: "When the Fall of Man is evoked, the epic narrator exploits a complex typological conception of Moses as at once a symbol of Old Testament obscurity and a mediator who leads to Christ" (p. 207).

Attempting to abort this typological development is Satan. According to William G. Madsen, Satan is included in Milton's typological "mode of discourse," except that "Satan is usually a dogged literalist, and his characteristic habit of mind and language is one of reduction."[10] Similarly, Barbara K. Lewalski, analyzing Satan's role in *Paradise Regained*, explains that Satan is engaged in typological warfare with Jesus: "Satan's temptation strategy will . . . begin from the types: he will endeavor to cause Christ to regress from his present state of understanding — to accept inferior types in place of those he has already seized upon — or else to identify himself with the major types in their literal signification and thereby fail to achieve the spiritual understanding and fulfillment of the types which is his peculiar mission."[11]

John R. Mulder, in his analysis of Satan's "obsession" with "temples and mountains" in Books I and V of *Paradise Lost*, offers a somewhat different interpretation of Satan's "strategy" but one that is nevertheless typological: "Satan and his host see God's method but have no knowledge of His purpose. They observe His types but do not know that these are only His foreshadowings. They mistake a type or figure for His reality, which they are driven to destroy."[12] What is noteworthy in these comments is that the three typologists agree that Satan is involved in the types — aware of them and eager to exploit them for his purposes.

While Milton invokes Moses typologically to foreshadow Jesus, he also identifies Moses with the Law, again as a type, foreshadowing the Gospel. Both Moses and the Law, expropriated here by Satan and his aides, are seen by Christian typologists as "Highly belov'd" but nevertheless imperfect. Thus, Milton writes in *Christian Doctrine:* "The imperfection of the law was made apparent in the person of Moses himself. For Moses, who was the type of the law, could not lead the children of Israel into the land of Canaan, that is, into eternal rest. But an entrance was granted to them under Joshua, that is, Jesus" (YP VI, p. 519).

The typological role of Moses as Lawgiver is also foretold by Michael in *Paradise Lost:*

> And therefore shall not *Moses*, though of God
> Highly belov'd, being but the Minister
> Of Law, his people into *Canaan* lead;
> But *Joshua* whom the Gentiles *Jesus* call,
> His Name and Office bearing, who shall quell
> The adversary Serpent, and bring back
> Through the world's wilderness long wander'd man
> Safe to eternal Paradise of rest.   (XII, 307–14)

Milton also types Moses as Mediator, again foreshadowing Jesus:

> But the voice of God
> To mortal ear is dreadful; they [the Jews] beseech
> That *Moses* might report to them his will,
> And terror cease; he grants what they besought,
> Instructed that to God is no access
> Without Mediator, whose high Office now
> *Moses* in figure bears, to introduce
> One greater.   (XII, 235–42)

As noted earlier, in addition to treating Moses as a type, Milton views the Mosaic Law as a type. The Law — ceremonial, civil, and moral — is totally abrogated to make way for the Gospel and Christian liberty:

THE MOSAIC LAW WAS A WRITTEN CODE, CONSISTING OF MANY STIPULATIONS, AND INTENDED FOR THE ISRAELITES ALONE. IT HELD A PROMISE OF LIFE FOR THE OBEDIENT AND A CURSE FOR THE DISOBEDIENT. ITS AIM WAS TO MAKE THE ISRAELITES HAVE A RECOURSE TO THE RIGHTEOUSNESS OF THE PROMISED CHRIST, THROUGH A RECOGNITION OF MANKIND'S, AND THEREFORE OF THEIR OWN DEPRAVITY. ITS AIM, ALSO, WAS THAT ALL

WE OTHER NATIONS SHOULD AFTERWARDS BE EDUCATED FROM THIS ELEMENTARY, CHILD-
ISH AND SERVILE DISCIPLINE TO THE ADULT STATURE OF A NEW CREATURE, AND TO A
MANLY FREEDOM UNDER THE GOSPEL, WORTHY OF GOD'S SONS. Heb. ix. 8, etc. as above.
(*CD*, YP VI, p. 517)

Elaborating this doctrine, Milton continues:

AND A CURSE FOR THE etc. Deut. xxvii. 26: *cursed who does not fulfil the words of
this law, by obeying it;* Gal. iii. 10: *all those who are of the works of the law are
under a curse, for it is written, Cursed is everyone. . . .*

   DEPRAVITY . . . Rom. iii. 20: *through the law comes the knowledge of sin,* and
iv. 15: *the law brings anger,* and v. 20: *the law was introduced so that transgression should be plentiful, but when transgression became plentiful grace was much
more plentiful,* and vii. 5: *when we were in the flesh and desires for sins which existed through the law, worked in our members to bring forth fruit to death,* and
vii. 7–9: *I did not know sin except through the law . . . : but sin, seizing its opportunity by means of that commandment, brought about in me . . . ,* and 12, 13: *the
law itself is holy, and that commandment is holy and just and good. Was, then, a
good thing the death of me? God forbid. It was sin that killed me, and thus it appeared to me in its true colors, because it made death from something good, and
thus sin was made altogether sinful, through that commandment;* Gal. iii. 19: *why,
then, the law? It was added because of transgressions, until that seed should come
to whom the promise was made.* (Pp. 518–19)

Further Milton writes: "II Cor. iii. 6: *the letter kills:* that is to say,
the letter of the law . . . *kills,* in that it does not promise life" (p. 519).

In Chapter XXVII, collating the New Testament verses treating the
abolition of the Law, Milton cites Paul's description of the Law as con-
sanguineous with Sin and Death:

   First, . . . the law is abolished above all because it is a law of works, and in
order that it may give place to a law of grace. . . .

   2. *the law brings anger: for where there is no law there is no transgression,*
iv. 15. It is no single part of the law, but the whole law which causes anger [in Merritt Y. Hughes's edition the translation is "wrath"]. . . . [A]s anger and grace are
incompatible, it follows that the law and the gospel are incompatible too. . . .

   5. . . . the whole law . . . is a law of sin and of death. It is a law of sin
because it stimulates sin, and of death because it produces death and is opposed to
the law of the spirit of life. But it is this same complete law which is abolished:
Rom. viii. 2: *the law of the spirit of life which is in Christ Jesus, has freed me from
the law of sin and of death.*

   6. It was certainly not merely the ceremonial law through which the desires
of sins flourished in our members to bring forth fruit to death, Rom. vii. . . .

   7. All believers should undoubtedly be considered righteous, since they are
justified by God through faith. But Paul distinctly says that there is no law for the

righteous. . . . Now justification is beyond the scope . . . of the whole Mosaic law. . . .

In addition, this law not only cannot justify, it disturbs believers and makes them waver. It even tempts God, if we try to fulfil it. It contains no promise, in fact it breaks and puts an end to all promises — of inheritance, of adoption, of grace itself and even of the spirit. What is more, it makes us accursed. (Pp. 528–30)

The followers of the Law are not only cursed but the progeny of the Devil:

John viii. 43: *you cannot hear my word*, that is, since you would not when you could, you are now unable. You are unable not through any decree of God but because of your own obstinate and habitual incredulity or, at any rate, because of your pride, which stops your ears, or, finally, as the next verse puts it, *because you are of your father, the Devil, and want to perform your fathers desires*. Again, viii. 46: *if I speak the truth, why do you not believe me?* Christ himself answers for them, viii. 47: *you do not hear because you are not of God*. What does *you are not of God* mean? Does it mean "you are not elect"? No, indeed it is synonymous with "you are of the Devil," viii, 44, that is, you follow the Devil rather than God. (Pp. 200–01)

In sum, *Christian Doctrine* catechizes as follows: the Law was "holy and just and good," but Sin "made death from something good"; "the desires for sins which existed through the law, worked in our members to bring forth fruit to death"; the Law "puts an end to all promises"; the Mosaic Law is a type to be fulfilled in the Gospel; and those who adhere to the Law and reject the Gospel are followers of the Devil.

The antinomian view of the Mosaic Law is also presented in *Paradise Lost*. "The Law that is against thee" (*PL* XII, 416) is questioned by Adam, who adopts the Pauline premise:

> This yet I apprehend not, why to those
> Among whom God will deign to dwell on Earth
> So many and so various Laws are giv'n;
> So many Laws argue so many sins
> Among them; how can God with such reside? (XII, 280–84)

To which Michael replies:

> Doubt not but that sin
> Will reign among them, as of thee begot;
> And therefore was Law given them to evince
> Thir natural pravity, by stirring up
> Sin against Law to fight; that when they see
> Law can discover sin, but not remove,

Save by those shadowy expiations weak,
                 . . . they may conclude
Some blood more precious must be paid for Man,
Just for unjust, that in such righteousness
To them by Faith imputed, they may find
Justification towards God, and peace
Of Conscience, which the Law by Ceremonies
Cannot appease, nor Man the moral part
Perform, and not performing cannot live.
So Law appears imperfet, and but giv'n
With purpose to resign them in full time
Up to a better Cov'nant, disciplin'd
From shadowy Types to Truth, from Flesh to Spirit,
From imposition of strict Laws, to free
Acceptance of large Grace, from servile fear
To filial, works of Law to works of Faith.   (XII, 285–306)

These verses are a succinct statement of Milton's view of the Law in *Christian Doctrine* and support Madsen's observation that "most of Milton's references to typology appear in the context of the opposition between the carnal Law and the spiritual Gospel" (p. 49). It is clear that Milton regards the Law as a type of the Gospel; that is, that the Law's purpose is to lead the Jews (and all men) to the Gospel's "better Cov'nant."

It should also be clear that it is Satan's design that this purpose not be realized. If, indeed, Satan is engaged in typological warfare with Jesus, it follows that Satan will exploit the type of Moses as Liberator-Mediator-Lawgiver in a perverse, literal, and carnal application — to liberate his cohorts and to destroy man.

The thesis, which I have found helpful in elucidating at least thirty passages in Books II and X, contributes especially to our understanding of the following cruxes: Satan's "leadership" role; the motif of the "flames"; the transformation of Sin from "fair" to foul; certain aspects of the incestuous relationship of Satan and Sin; the nature of Sin's brood of monsters; references to God's "wrath"; the construction of the bridge from Hell to Earth; and Satan's charge to Sin and Death to "go and be strong." In these and several other contexts the Mosaic-trio thesis is strikingly helpful — in illuminating features of the passages that are obscure, and in uniting, in a narrative sequence, "concerns which have not been fully integrated into the poem."[13] In the remaining passages the Mosaic-trio design is no less discernible than the configuration of an "infernal trinity" or James's allegory of lust. The Mosaic-trio thesis encompasses more elements that are doctrinal and topical than do other explications of the text.

II

The motif of Satan as Moses-Liberator appears in Book II of *Paradise Lost* with "I abroad / Through all the Coasts of dark destruction seek / Deliverance for us all" (463–65).

Satan's Mosaic role is then broadened to include Moses as Lawgiver. This dimension is introduced in the description of Satan's "thoughts inflam'd of highest design" (630) and of the Gates "impal'd with circling fire, / Yet unconsum'd" (647–48), a parodic typing of the first revelation to Moses in the burning bush: "And the angel of the Lord appeared unto him in a flame of fire out of the midst of a bush; and he looked, and, behold, the bush was not consumed" (Exod. iii, 2; see also xix, 18 and xx, 15).

"Impal'd with circling fire" also recalls the metaphor in *Reason of Church-Government:* "And thus we find . . . that the rules of Church-discipline are not only commanded, but hedg'd about with such a terrible *impalement* [my emphasis] of commands as he that will break through wilfully to violate the least of them, must hazard the wounding of his conscience even to death" (YP I, p. 760).

Milton's description of Sin as "fair" (*PL* II, 650), Sin's description of herself as "shining heav'n'ly fair" (757), the poet's later description of Sin as Satan's "fair / Enchanting Daughter" (X, 352–53), and Satan's address to his "Fair Daughter" (X, 384) are contrasted with "But [Sin] ended foul in many a scaly fold / Voluminous and vast" (II, 651–52) and "Now . . . so foul, once deem'd so fair / In Heav'n" (748–49). While the reader is not surprised at Satan's inverted esthetic and moral judgments, how is he to understand Sin's earlier comeliness?

In the Mosaic-trio context the transformation can be explained in terms of Paul's views of Sin and the Law: "Sin indeed," he says, "was in the world before the law was given, but sin is not counted where there is not law" (Rom. v, 13). This view, that Sin was ontologically prior to the Law but dormant and innocuous, and hence initially and relatively "fair," helps explain Milton's presentation of Sin as once having been comely.

"But [Sin] ended foul in many a scaly fold / Voluminous and vast" (651–52), using imagery from Hesiod, continues the allegory of the Law and its nature to proliferate. The wordplay in "voluminous," meaning "coiled like a scroll," suggests the glosses of the Church Fathers: "Who is ignorant of the foul errors, the ridiculous wresting of Scripture, the Heresies, the vanities thick sown through the *volums* [my italics] of *Justin Martyr, Clemens, Origen, Tertullian* and others of eldest time?" (*Of Reformation,* YP I, pp. 551–52).

The nature of Sin's and Satan's offspring is significant: they are not similar to their mother or father but are of the genus *canis* as in *An Apology* where Milton attacks the Prelates: "No marvell if the people turne beasts, when their Teachers themselves as *Isaiah* calls them, *Are dumbe and greedy dogs that can never have enough, ignorant, blind, and cannot understand . . . while they all look their own way every one for his gaine from his quarter*" (YP I, p. 932). The progeny of Satan and Sin, the "Hell Hounds" with "wide *Cerberean* mouths" (II, 654–55) as in Ovid, call to mind Milton's prelatical bestiary who keep "a sorcerous doctrine of formalities . . . [which] transforme them out of Christian men into *Iudaizing* beasts," with further echoes of the early *Comus* (*An Apology*, YP I, p. 932). Similarly, Milton uses "wolf" imagery in describing the clerics who distort Scripture to exploit their flocks:

> Wolves shall succeed for teachers, grievous Wolves,
> Who all the sacred mysteries of Heav'n
> To thir own vile advantages shall turn
> Of lucre and ambition, and the truth
> With superstitions and traditions taint,
> Left only in those written Records pure,
> Though not but by the Spirit understood.   (XII, 508–14)

These are the false teachers alluded to by Milton in his early poetry: "the grim Wolf" of *Lycidas* and the "hireling Wolves" of the *Sonnet to Cromwell*.

As the canine imagery continues with the point that the Hell Hounds "would creep, / If aught disturb'd thir noise, into her womb" (II, 656–57), we are mystified by the allegory. I suggest that Milton is depicting the church "Judaizers" who, when accused of advocating "superstitions and traditions," "take refuge" in the institution of the Mosaic Law. The motif continues some lines below, when Sin laments: "my womb conceiv'd / A growing burden" (766–67), allegorizing the proliferation of the Law, from Adam's "sole Command" (III, 94) to the Jews' Mosaic Law and, later, to the church's "superstitions and traditions" (XII, 512).

Sin reveals her offspring, "These yelling Monsters" (II, 795), who surround her and are, in a Mosaic context, the "law[s] of sin" (*CD*, YP VI, p. 529) that are "hourly conceiv'd / And hourly born, with sorrow infinite" (796–97), and "terrors" (801), so "That rest or intermission none I find" (802). The imagery recalls not only Spenser's "Error" (*FQ* I, i, 14, 15) but also Paul's dismissal of the Mosaic Law and Milton's condemnation of the multiplication of ecclesiastical laws. For Milton, the Christian's grievous "error" is to endorse "Mosaic bondage."

Death's arraignment of Satan as he "Who first broke peace in Heav'n and Faith, till then / Unbrok'n" (690–91), is, in a Mosaic context, not only a condemnation of Satan *qua* Satan, but also an ironic accusation of Satan in his perversely typological role as Lawgiver, and thus the empowerer of Sin ("thou us impow'r'd / To fortify thus far, and overlay / With this portentous Bridge the dark Abyss" [X, 369–71]). Satan broke Faith not only as rebel but also as advocate of the Law — and, consequently, of Sin.

The verses relating Satan's drawing "after him . . . Heav'n's Sons" (II, 692), now "outcast from God" (694), and "Hell-doom'd" (697), refer on the most literal level to the rebel angels in their postlapsarian state; but at the same time they are strongly evocative, in a Mosaic context (as well as in the context of Milton's use of archetypes), of the "Chosen People" who, according to Milton's doctrine, incurred the wrath of the Deity for adhering to the Law.[14]

"To execute / Whate'er his wrath, which he calls Justice" (732–33) recalls the Law which works "wrath" or "anger" because it "cannot justify." This connection has been noted by Rosenblatt:

In *Christian Doctrine*, opposing the Covenant of Grace to the Mosaic Law, Milton quotes . . . Romans iv, 15 ("the law worketh wrath") and v, 20 ("moreover the law entered, that the offence might abound; but where sin abounded, grace did much more abound") (CM, XVI, 107). Similarly, in *Paradise Lost*, wrath is used as a virtual synonym of Law ("over wrath grace shall abound," XII, 478): and this meaning is not absent from God's reply to the Son, whom he addresses as "the only peace / Found out for mankind under wrath" (III, 274–75). (Pp. 223–24)

Sin's prediction that God's "wrath . . . one day will destroy ye both [Satan and Death]" (II, 734), which parallels Michael's reading of the future in Book XII, 429–31, refers, in the equation of "wrath," "Justice," and the "Law," to Milton's typological "evolution" of the Law in Jesus "fulfilling . . . the Law of God, impos'd / On penalty of death," satisfying "high Justice," "Both by obedience and by love" (XII, 396–403).

Sin's disclosure to Satan: "dim thine eyes, and dizzy swum / In darkness, while thy head flames thick and fast / Threw forth" (II, 753–55); and "Out of thy head I sprung" (758), while alluding to the imagery of Hesiod, parodies the Theophany and Revelation: "Now mount Sinai was altogether on smoke, because the Lord descended upon it in fire" (Exod. xix, 18; see also Deut. iv, 36, v, 19–23).[15] Milton's association of the Law with Sin is further delineated in Sin's observations that she herself is "Likest to . . . [Satan] in shape and count'nance bright" (756), that she is his "perfect image" (764), and that they are in "secret harmony" (X, 358). We have here a clear parody of John x, 30: "I and the Father are one," but at the same time, in the Mosaic overlay, the rationale for Sin's identification with Satan. "Count'nance bright," while not excluding allusions such as Satan's Luciferian origins, may be a parody of Moses' appearance after the Revelation: "And when Aaron and all the children of Israel saw Moses, behold, the skin of his face sent forth beams" (Exod. xxxiv, 29–30).

Sin's relating that "Familiar grown / I pleas'd" (II, 761–62) is an attempt to answer the Pauline question of the adherence of the Jews (and "Judaizers") to the Mosaic Law despite the onerousness of the Law. "The subtle Fiend his lore / Soon learn'd" (815–16) refers to Satan's discovery of the type of the Law with its attributes of Sin and Death, and to his perception that he might exploit them for his purposes. Satan's recollection "of dalliance had with . . . [Sin] in Heav'n, and joys / Then sweet" (819–20) alludes once again to Paul's formulation of the genesis of the Law, Sin, and Death; and that Sin did not become deadly until the Law was proclaimed. Satan's reference to his and Sin's "dire change / Befall'n us unforeseen" (820–21) denotes not only their fall into Hell but also their transformation brought about by the Law.

Satan's assurance, "I come no enemy, but to set free / From out this dark and dismal house of pain" (822–23), parodies Moses' comforting words to the Israelites in the Egyptian house of bondage. Saying that he will "soon return, / And bring ye to the place where Thou [Sin] and Death / Shall dwell at ease" (839–41), Satan continues the parody of Moses the Liberator undertaking to lead his people to the Promised Land (Deut. xii, 9), but of course it is Satan promising to free Sin and Death to "be fed and fill'd / Immeasurably" (843–44), with an echo of Moses' promise to Israel of a land of plenty.

Sin's admission that she is "forbidden to unlock / These Adamantine Gates" (852–53) refers to the Law, in "forbidden," which she proceeds to violate. Her address to Satan, "thou my Author" (864), and her honorific "Satan our great Author" (X, 236) suggest a written or engraved record, which a parody of the Mosaic Law readily supplies. "Whom should I obey / But thee, whom follow?" (II, 865–66) parodies the "author" of the Law. And her expectation, "thou wilt bring me soon / To that new world of light and bliss . . . where I shall reign / At thy right hand voluptuous" (866–69) again combines a parody of the Trinity in the latter phrase with a parody of Moses the Liberator in the former.

Sin taking "the fatal Key, / Sad instrument of all our woe" (871–72) may symbolize the "curse" of the Law, according to *Christian Doctrine*. "Then in the key-hole turns / Th' intricate wards, and every Bolt and Bar / . . . with ease / Unfastens" (876–79) would then suggest the complexities and commandments of the Law and the "ease" with which Sin defies them. "Harsh Thunder" (882) and "smoke and ruddy flame" (889) again allude to the Revelation: "And all the people perceived the thunderings, and the lightnings, and the voice of the horn and the mountain smoking" (Exod. xx, 15); "and the smoke thereof ascended as the smoke of a furnace, and the whole mount quaked greatly" (Exod. xix, 18).

"She op'n'd, but to shut / Excell'd her power" (II, 883–84) recalls Paul's "Now justification is beyond the scope . . . of the whole Mosaic Law" (CD, YP VI, p. 529). That is, Sin, identified incestuously with Satan and Death, and thus treated by Milton as the fruit of the Mosaic Law, opens the gates of Hell to man: "If it had not been for the law, I [Paul] should not have known sin. I should not have known what it is to covet if the law had not said, 'Ye shall not covet'" (Rom. vii, 7). But the Law (with its attribute of Sin) cannot save, that is, cannot "shut" the gates of Hell. As Milton writes in *Christian Doctrine*, "there is no law for the righteous"; "they are justified by God through faith." The law "contains no promise, in fact it breaks and puts an end to all promises — of inheritance, of adoption, of grace itself and even of the spirit. What is more, it makes us accursed" (p. 530).

"That with extended wings a Banner'd Host / Under spread Ensigns marching might pass through" (885–86), though referring to Satan's hosts, calls to mind Moses leading the children of Israel, in tribal formation, through the wilderness of Sinai: "So they pitched by their standards, and so they set forward" (Num. ii, 34).

In the next sequence Satan has gone ahead, alone. In the Satan-Moses correspondence we have the allusion to Moses, the Mediator, by himself ascending the mountain of Sinai to receive the Law. "Sin and Death amain / Following his track, such was the will of Heav'n, / Pav'd after him a broad and beat'n way" (II, 1024–26). From the Pauline perspective, Sin and Death would follow immediately upon the giving of the Law, with the "will of Heav'n" referring to the ultimate "aim" of the Law (CD, YP VI, p. 517) and to its "purpose" (PL XII, 301). The "broad and beat'n way" evokes parodically not only the New Testament dictum: "Enter by the narrow gate; for the gate is wide and the way is easy, that leads to destruction, and those who enter by it are many" (Matt. vii, 13),[16] but also the "Way" of the Law in the Hebrew Bible, e.g., "Ye shall *walk* in all the *way* [emphasis added] which the Lord your God hath commanded you, that you may live, and that it may be well with you" (Deut. v, 30; see also viii, 6, x, 12, xi, 22).

The "Way," in Hebrew, *Halachah*, meaning the "way to walk," embraces both the Written and the Oral Law and would have been current in Jesus' time. While John's citation of Jesus' "I am the way" (xiv, 6) is, according to scholars,[17] Jesus' repudiation of the "Way" of the Law, the term "Way" is in one instance used by Paul in its Judaic sense: "But this I admit to you, that according to the Way, which they call a sect [the name for the early Christians who still observed the Law], I worship the God of our fathers, believing everything laid down by the law or written in the prophets" (Acts xxiv, 14). The "broad and beat'n way," then, may also refer to the Way of the Law.

The association of the "Way" with the works of the Law is further intimated in the Causeway's traffic, "by which the Spirits perverse / With easy intercourse pass to and fro / To tempt or punish mortals" (II, 1030–32), recalling Paul's description of the Law's (read: the "Way's") function to "tempt or punish" man. "Except whom / God and good Angels guard by special grace" (1032–33) recalls "Behold, I send an angel before thee, to keep thee by the way, and to bring thee into the place which I have prepared" (Exod. xxiii, 20). It also continues the Mosaic motif in Milton's doctrine that some are saved "although they believed or believe in God alone":

the ultimate object of faith is not Christ, the Mediator, but God the Father. . . . So it does not seem surprising that there are a lot of Jews, and Gentiles too, who are saved although they believed or believe in God alone, either because they lived before Christ or because, even though they have lived after him, he has not been revealed to them. . . . Thus those illustrious men who lived under the law, Abel, Enoch, Noah etc., are honoured with an attestation of their true faith, although it is stated that they believed only in God. (*CD*, YP VI, p. 475)

The Causeway, described now as "a Monument / Of merit high to all th' infernal Host" (X, 258–59), parodies Mt. Sinai and those who follow the Law. That the "way" alludes to the works of the Law is strengthened by the equation of "way" and "Monument . . . high," which evokes the mountain of the Law. "Of merit high to all th' infernal Host" is a parody of the Law and of the "Hosts of Israel" (Num. ii). The "Way" is then compared to that built by Xerxes who "the Liberty of *Greece* to yoke . . . over *Hellespont* / Bridging his way, *Europe* with *Asia* join'd" (306–10). There is a touch of humor in *Hellespont* (Hell's Pontifice). But what is of relevance to my thesis is the simile that associates the "Bridge" with the servitude of Greece. The Law, which is the archetype of the "Bridge," is everywhere equated by Milton with "bondage."

"Now had they brought the work by wondrous Art / Pontifical, a ridge of pendent Rock" (312–13), to completion, "this new wondrous Pontifice, unhop't" (348). The "ridge of pendent rock" evokes not only

Peter but also Sinai and the "tablet of the law." "Unhop't" may be read as "without hope," a Miltonic joke with reference to the Law. While Rajan has noted that "there is no precedent for the incident [the building of the Pontifice] in the literature of the Temptation," Trefman and Sims have identified the Pontifice with the Catholic church.[18] The identification does not provide a "precedent"; the Mosaic Law, however, does. The association of the Mosaic Law with the Pontifice as "works" and servitude gives the incident a precedent in Christian doctrine. According to Paul and Milton the Mosaic Law (the Pontifice) "tempts" God to punish man.

"At sight / Of that stupendous Bridge his joy increas'd" (350–51). One can almost hear in "stupendous" Milton's derision as well as anger, for Satan will use the "Judaic" traditions (Catholic and Anglican) to doom man. The various terms in Book X referring to the "Way" are literalistic reductions of the type of the Law: "path" (256), "Monument of merit" (258–59), "Bridge" (301), "passage broad" (304), "ridge of pendent Rock" (313), "Pontifice" (348), "magnific deeds" (354), "Trophies" (355), "glorious Work" (391), "Road" (394), and "Causey" (415).

Sin praises Satan: "O Parent, these are thy magnific deeds, / Thy Trophies, which thou view'st as not thine own, / Thou art thir Author and prime Architect" (354–56). Deeds are characteristic of the Law. Though not created by Satan-Moses, the "Way," the Law, becomes Satan's instrument; and "this new wondrous Pontifice, unhop't" (348), in inviting traffic, becomes his achievement. Sin exclaims, "Thou hast achiev'd our liberty" (368), typing the forthcoming "exodus" of Sin and Death from Hell to Earth. But, of course, in their perverted world, their "liberty" will derive from man's bondage.

"Thine now is all this World, thy virtue hath won / What thy hands builded not, thy Wisdom gain'd / With odds what War hath lost, and fully aveng'd / Our foil in Heav'n" (372–75). In my reading, Satan, as Mediator-Lawgiver, is exploiting the type of the Law rather than creating the Law. Thus, "thy Virtue hath won / What thy hands builded not" refers not only to the efforts of Sin and Death but also, ironically, to the Law created by God for His purposes. The parodic mode of discourse continues with Satan being credited with "Virtue" and "Wisdom." Satan acknowledges "this glorious Work" (391), recalling the "pomp and glory" of the ceremonial Law as well as the entire Mosaic Law as a Law of Works. The parodic typology continues in Satan bidding Sin and Death to embark on their mission to destroy man: "Him first make sure your thrall, and lastly kill" (402), recalling the "bondage" and "curse" Paul and Milton associate with those living under the Law.

Satan parts from Sin and Death with "go and be strong" (409), which

Sims reads as a "reminiscence" of the charge of Moses to Israel (Deut. xi, 8) and of God to Joshua (Josh. i, 6, 9), but "reversed in purpose and [which] becomes in Satan's mouth, a charge of Sin and Death to possess the earth" (p. 166). The echo is clear but we must not overlook the charge by Moses to Israel and by God to Joshua, *to observe the Mosaic Law:* "therefore shall ye keep all the commandments which I command you this day, that you may be strong" (Deut. xi, 8); and "Only be strong and very courageous, and observe to do according to all the Law which Moses My servant commanded thee . . . that thou mayest prosper wherever thou goest" (Josh. i, 7).

Once the crucial episodes are read as parodying the types of Moses and the Mosaic Law, even the patently mythological coda in Book II, 890–1024, derived from Hesiod, with its personification of Chaos and Night, is a continuation of the Mosaic theme. Satan's journey through Chaos and Night recalls the wandering of the Israelites (here represented by Satan) in the wilderness on the way to the Promised Land, with a reminiscence of the expedition of the Spies, and Moses' request of Edom (Num. xx, 21) and the Emorites (Num. xxi, 22) to pass through their lands: "I come no Spy, / With purpose to explore or disturb / The secrets of your Realm, but by constraint / Wand'ring this darksome Desert . . . I seek / What readiest path leads where your gloomy bounds / Confine with Heav'n" (II, 970–77). Satan's report to his followers upon completing his mission (X, 460–503) parodies Moses' "Farewell Discourse" to the Israelites, in Deuteronomy.

III

The case for a Mosaic-trio reading is to be made not only from implications in the sequences themselves but also from Milton's imagery, vehicle and tenor, in at least one of his tracts. In *Doctrine and Discipline of Divorce* (1644) Milton identifies Satan and his kin with the traditions and prohibitions of the Anglican church:

The greatest *burden* in the world is superstition, not only of *ceremonies* in the church but of *imaginary* and *scarecrow sins* at home. What greater weakening, what more subtle *strategem* against our *Christian warfare*, when besides the *gross body* of real transgressions to *encounter*, we shall be terrified by a vain and *shadowy menacing* of faults that are not? When things indifferent shall be set to overfront us under the *banners of sin*, what wonder if we be routed, and by this *art* of our *adversary*, fall into the *subjection* of worst and *deadliest* offenses. (YP II, p. 699; my italics)

This passage, which is an attack on the proliferation of ecclesiastical law, seems to adumbrate the Satanic trio in the later epic. What is personified in *Paradise Lost* is found in metaphor here: the personae of Satan, Sin, and Death, their dramatic meeting and subsequent collaboration are strikingly evoked. From this passage it would appear that the concept of an infernal Mosaic trio, despite the problem of the decorum of the passages in *Paradise Lost*, was not an "external encrustation" on Milton's thought or imagination. The Mosaic trio is suggested in the "gross body of real transgressions"—the tablet of the Law—as well as in the human traditions of "imaginary and scarecrow sins" which are the offspring of a Law-centered mentality. Both the Mosaic Law and human traditions are now—upon the abrogation of the Law, Milton argues—supported only by the adversary.

In this passage, Milton's imagery is reminiscent of that in Books II and X, "Burden" echoing Sin's "growing burden" (II, 767), and "imaginary and scarecrow sins" recalling the two "shapes" sitting at Hell's gates as well as Sin's brood of monsters. "The gross body of real transgressions to encounter" parallels the "dark Encounter" (II, 718) of Satan and Death. "Shadowy menacing" harks back to "shadow seem'd" (II, 669) and "Phantasm" (II, 743). "The banners of sin" echoes a "Banner'd Host" (II, 885). "Subtle strategem" recalls the device of Sin and Death—the "portentous Bridge"—to lead man down to Hell. "This art of our adversary" is reminiscent of the "wondrous Art / Pontifical" (X, 312–13) and calls to mind Satan's "calumnious Art" of sophistry (V, 770), which Milton associates with a Pharisaic church.

The entire tenor of the extended metaphor is that the Laws are "deadliest offenses." The imagery of the prose delineates the motif that I have attempted to demonstrate in the Satan, Sin, and Death passages of Books II and X.

IV

The Mosaic-trio interpretation not only unifies the episodes themselves but is integrated with the epic as a whole. In *Paradise Lost* Milton juxtaposes personae and concepts: Satan and Jesus, servitude and liberty, the Law and the Gospel. If the Law is "spiritualized" and "fulfilled" by Jesus in Books III and XII, where and how does Satan "carnalize" the Law and negate its purpose? Books II and X, with the Satanic trio, answer these questions. In Book II Satan is the Mosaic Liberator, Mediator, and Lawgiver; in Book III Jesus is the antitype of all these. In Books II and X the carnal type of the Law is dramatized; in Book XII Michael expounds the spiritual antitype of the Gospel. In Books II and X Satan and his helpers prepare to utilize the Law to destroy man; in Book XII the Law's antitype promises to destroy Satan, Sin, and Death.

Rajan has noted the "symmetries of disposition" of Books II and X, which "are joined by the presence of Sin and Death."[19] That symmetry is to be found not only in the placement of Sin and Death but also in their function. Book II, preceding the Fall, recounts the initiation of the "Way," and Book X, anticipating the "fall" of Israel and the Judaized church, narrates the implementation of that project.

Reading the episodes typologically reveals additional architectonic features of the epic. Rajan, again, citing the work of James Whaler, describes Milton's technique in the "Xerxes" simile (*PL* X, 307–10) as "anticipatory usage," in that "the doom awaiting the infernal pair [Sin and Death] is the same . . . as the disaster which befell the Persian expedition."[20] My typological reading of Books II and X has Satan, Sin, and Death, in effect, foreshadowing the Fall of Adam, foretold in Book III, and the "fall" of Israel and the unreformed church, related in Book XII. The typological framework of these episodes makes them "anticipatory" as well as "symmetrical."

If these episodes are "anticipatory" and "symmetrical," why are they not also unambiguously "typological"? It may very well be, however, that these scenes were more connotative to the seventeenth-century reader than they are to us. After all, not only Milton but many of his contemporaries were engaged in defining the perimeters of Christian liberty derived from the abrogation of the Mosaic Law. In such a doctrinally conscious environment readers of Milton's Satan, Sin, and Death passages would have discerned an antinomian allegory in Milton's multiplex allusions. While the Mosaic-trio reading is perhaps novel to us, it is useful to keep in mind Christopher Hill's observation regarding seventeenth-century readers: "Not being able to say certain things directly Milton would expect his readers — at least the fit readers, however few — to be alert to hints, to allusions for which we have to strain our ears to-day, to analogies, to perhapses."[21]

There are, then, sufficient grounds — thematic, doctrinal, structural, and topical — to warrant a reading of the episodes as a parodic typing of Moses and the Mosaic Law. The Mosaic-trio thesis widens the compass of Milton's "typological view of history," which, according to Mulder, "enabled . . . [him] to arrange all the details of *Paradise Lost* into one pattern" (p. 159, n. 6). Above all, the presence of a Mosaic motif in the Satan, Sin, and Death passages extends the venue of one of Milton's major tenets — that the Law is bondage and, in its codified form, the instrument of Satan.

Samuel Johnson deemed the episodes an "unskilful allegory [which] appears . . . one of the greatest faults of the poem; and to this there was

no temptation, but the author's opinion of its beauty."[22] Milton's temptation, as I see it, was his desire to dramatize the deleterious role of the
Mosaic Law in the history of the church, and in his own time, from the
perspective of Pauline Christianity. In caricaturing the Mosaic Law in
the bizarre personifications of Satan, Sin, and Death, Milton had no com-
punction, as he attests in *Reason of Church-Government:* "the imperfect and obscure institution of the law the apostles themselves doubt not
ofttimes to vilify" (YP I, p. 647). For the Christian poet of that polemi-
cal century, the correspondence of Satan, Moses, and Mosaic Law was
a typical doctrinal temptation.

University of Windsor
Windsor, Ontario

NOTES

1. Merritt Y. Hughes, ed. *John Milton: Complete Poems and Major Prose* (New
York, 1957), p. 177. I have used this edition for the quotations from Milton's poetry.

2. For a collation of views, particularly sources and analogues, see Hughes, *Complete Poems*, pp. 177–78 and notes to pp. 247–53 et passim; John Carey and Alastair Fowler,
eds., *The Poems of John Milton* (London, 1968), pp. 538–48 et passim; John Broadbent,
ed., *John Milton: "Paradise Lost," Books I–II* (Cambridge, 1972), pp. 44–46; E. M. W.
Tillyard, "The Causeway from Hell to the World in the Tenth Book of *Paradise Lost*,"
SP, XXXVIII (1941), 266–70; John M. Patrick, "Milton, Phineas Fletcher, Spenser, and
Ovid — Sin at Hell's Gates," *N&Q*, CCI (1956), 384–86; John M. Steadman, "Milton and
St. Basil: The Genesis of Sin and Death," *MLN*, LXXIII (1958), 83–84; idem, "Grosseteste
on the Genealogy of Sin and Death," *N&Q*, CCII (1959), 367–68; idem, "Tradition and
Innovation in Milton's 'Sin': The Problem of Literary Indebtedness," *PQ*, XXXIX (1960),
93–103; Robert B. White, Jr., "Milton's Allegory of Sin and Death: A Comment on Back-
grounds," *MP*, LXX (1973), 337–41; Charles Martindale, "The Epic of Ideas: Lucan's *De
Bello civili* and *Paradise Lost*," *Comparative Criticism*, III (1981), 133–56.

For the prevailing view that the scenes are allegory with some parody, see Balachandra Rajan, *"Paradise Lost" and the Seventeenth-Century Reader* (1947; rpt. Ann Arbor,
1967), p. 50 et passim; Robert C. Fox, "The Allegory of Sin and Death in *Paradise Lost*,"
MLQ, XXIV (1963), 354–64. For biblical allusions, see James H. Sims, *The Bible in Milton's Epics* (Gainesville, Fla., 1962), pp. 54–59; for the treatment of "cosmic history," see
Philip J. Gallagher, "'Real or Allegoric'; The Ontology of Sin and Death in *Paradise Lost*,"
ELR, VI (1976), 317–35). For the description of the reunion as "a scene of domestic farce,"
see Barbara K. Lewalski, "The Genres of *Paradise Lost*: Literary Genre as a Means of
Accommodation," in *Milton Studies*, XVII, ed. Richard S. Ide and Joseph Wittreich (Pittsburgh, 1983), p. 75.

3. *Milton's Imagery and the Visual Arts* (Princeton, N.J., 1978), p. 124.

4. Ide and Wittreich, "Preface," *Milton Studies*, XVII, p. x.

5. Joan S. Bennett, "'Go': Milton's Antinomianism and the Separation Scene in *Paradise Lost*, Book 9," *PMLA*, XCVIII (1983), 388. Bennett reminds us that the antinomian view of the Mosaic Law was widespread and that Milton "tackled its dramatic, existential implications in all his great poems" (p. 389). For the broad range of antinomianism in Milton's time, see Christopher Hill, *Milton and the English Revolution* (London, 1977).

6. It is the "tablet of the law" that Milton abjures, not the morality of the Law, which is equated with a "secondary law of nature" which is not Judaic but universal — "applicable to all men in their fallen estate, but most clearly perceived by the best nations, in whom it approaches right reason; there is a perfect law of nature, unrecognized by men in their fallen estate, but especially rewritten for the Jews in the Mosaic Law; that perfect law was given by God at the Creation as the natural expression of right reason and the eternal law" (Arthur E. Barker, *Milton and the Puritan Dilemma* [Toronto, 1942], p. 169). See also Milton's equation of the "moral law," "the law of nature," "the law of nations," and "right reason," in *Doctrine and Discipline of Divorce*, in *Prose Works of John Milton*, ed. Don M. Wolfe et al. (New Haven, 1953–82), II, 292, 306. All prose references will be to this edition and given in the body of the essay as YP. See also an elaboration of the above equation as well as Milton's dichotomization of the Mosaic Law, in my essay, "Milton's Dichotomy of 'Judaism' and 'Hebrasim'," *PMLA*, LXXXIX (1974), 105–12.

7. John Shawcross, "*Paradise Lost* and the Theme of Exodus," *Milton Studies*, II, ed. James D. Simmonds (Pittsburgh, 1970), pp. 6, 25–26, n. 18.

8. "Milton and Moses," Ph.D. diss. New York University, 1973, pp. 127 and 128–54 passim.

9. "The Mosaic Voice in *Paradise Lost*," *Milton Studies*, VII, ed. James D. Simmonds (Pittsburgh, 1975), p. 211.

10. *From Shadowy Types to Truth* (New Haven, 1968), p. 58.

11. *Milton's Brief Epic: The Genre, Meaning, and Art of "Paradise Regained"* (Providence, R.I., 1966), p. 181.

12. *The Temple of the Mind* (New York, 1969), p. 145.

13. Broadbent, *John Milton*, p. 2.

14. There are other suggestions in Milton's works of such an "infernal equation" of the devils and the Jews. The passage from John viii, 43–44, is the most direct statement of such an equation. A possible allusion may be "the advent'rous Bands / With shudd'ring horror pale, and eyes aghast / View'd first thir lamentable lot, and found no rest" (PL II, 615–18), which recalls a passage in *Doctrine and Discipline of Divorce*: "and surely such a Nation [the Jews] seems not to be under the illuminating guidance of Gods law, but under the horrible doom rather of such as despise the Gospel" (YP II, p. 290).

15. These lines certainly recall the myth of the birth of Athena from the head of Jove and therefore are a "parody of orthodox theology," according to Arlene Hughes, but at the same time they parody the revelation of the Mosaic Law (Merritt Y. Hughes, *Complete Poems*, p. 252, n. 869).

16. Robert Graves and Joshua Podro, *The Nazarene Gospel Restored* (Garden City, N.Y., 1954), p. 307, regard this verse as an inversion of a rabbinic teaching: "The *Midrash* on *Canticles*" v. 2. 2. runs:

God said unto Israel: 'Open unto Me an opening for repentance, and though it be as strait as the needle's eye, yet will I open the door widely that wagons and chariots may enter and pass.'

"This seems to be the very *Midrash* misquoted in *Matthew* vii. 13–14 and *Luke* xiii. 24. The prophets used the word 'highway' to symbolize the way of repentance, not that of damnation: it is so used in *Jeremiah* xxxi. 21."

17. "In *John* xiv. 6, Jesus is made to declare himself the Way, the Truth, and the Life; but 'I' has been characteristically substituted for 'the Law'" (ibid., p. 643). Graves and Podro "restore" the text as follows: "Jesus answered and said: 'Nay, but whither I go ye know, and the way ye know. For the Law is the way, and the truth, and the life'" (p. 646). See *The Encyclopaedia of Religion and Ethics*, vol. III, ed. James Hastings et al. (New York, 1928), p. 574. Discussing the Way as used in Acts xxiv, 14, "the way which they called a sect," the editors add: "Weiszacker (*Apostolic Age*, Eng. trans. 1895, ii, 262) and others quote as a parallel the Talmudic *Halakhoth*, literally 'walks,' as a parallel especially to 1 Co 417 ('my ways in Christ' . . .); but these are special rules of conduct, not a single great way of life."

18. Rajan, *Seventeenth-Century Reader*, p. 50; Simon Trefman, "A Note on the Bridge of Chaos in *Paradise Lost* and Matthew XVI. 18–19," *Seventeenth-Century News*, XX (1963), Item 204; Sims, *The Bible*, pp. 58–59.

19. Rajan, "*Paradise Lost* and the Balance of Structures," *UTQ*, XLI (Spring 1972), 222.

20. Rajan, *Seventeenth-Century Reader*, p. 124.

21. *Milton and the English Revolution*, p. 405.

22. *Samuel Johnson: Rasselas, Poems and Selected Prose*, ed. Bertrand H. Bronson (New York, 1952), p. 466.

REPENTANCE IN *PARADISE LOST*

Golda Werman

I N B o o k X of *Paradise Lost* Milton presents an unusual, even audacious picture of Adam and Eve's fall: instead of lingering on their guilt or lashing out in anger and indignation at the transgressors who defiled mankind forever, responses one would expect in a Puritan epic on man's original sin, the poet portrays in tender detail the young sinners' painful struggle to regain God's grace, and this before they have learned of Christ and his saving mission. Other Christian hexameral writers eschewed the complex subject of repentance in the pre-Christian Adam and Eve.[1] Even Genesis has nothing to say on this subject, though repentance is often mentioned in other parts of the Bible. Milton, who followed Genesis and the hexameral works closely in many details of his poem, ignored their silence on this subject. He makes Adam and Eve's repentance a major theme in the epic and devotes some of his most moving lines to the young sinners' self-motivated efforts to be accepted once again into God's favor.

Milton rejected the orthodox Calvinist view of man as a wretchedly sinful creature, totally depraved and so vitiated by the effects of original sin that he can have no part in his own salvation. Calvin taught that God, knowing that man would fall, decided before all time and without respect to man's works, who is to be saved and who is to be eternally damned. In *Paradise Lost* Adam and Eve are not completely stripped of their pristine heroic stature after their sin; they retain the spiritual strength to seek salvation, based on the exercise of free will. Milton focuses on the fallen couple's struggle to regain God's favor instead of on their shame and guilt. He finds no compelling biblical reason to give up on man, despite his fall to temptation, and insists that man plays an effective part in his own salvation. In this the poet goes beyond Arminian belief and approaches Erasmus, who reasoned, in his celebrated debate on free will with Luther, that God's offer of grace sufficient for salvation is based on man's efforts to atone.[2]

Paradoxically, Milton's views are also close to the Jewish midrashic ideas on repentance; the ancient rabbinic biblical commentaries known as Midrash can serve to elucidate *Paradise Lost*. The Rabbis believed, as did Milton, that despite man's sinful nature he maintains the divine

121

spark which is expressed in the freedom of the will. This freedom to choose makes man responsible for his own actions, repentance included. Adam and Eve are treated as types of penitent sinners in the apocryphal *Book of Adam and Eve* (9; 27), in the Babylonian Talmud (Eruvin 18b; Avodah Zarah 8a), and in the Midrash *Avot de-Rabbi Nathan.* In *Pirkei de-Rabbi Eliezer*, an eighth-century Midrash which Milton used, most probably in the 1644 Latin translation by the Dutch Arminian Willem Vorstius, Adam is portrayed as a sorrowful penitent, praying for the removal of his sin, who is forgiven by a merciful God.[3] Adam's repentance serves as a paradigm for all future generations whose atonement will be accepted by the Creator. Milton's Adam and Eve likewise retain their spiritual freedom to choose between good and evil, even after they disobeyed God; they remain capable of participating in their own salvation.

This is not to suggest that Milton was in any sense a Judeophile simply because he agreed with the Rabbis that the Bible taught that God endowed man with both free will and repentance; nor did the congruence of his thought with that of the midrashists result from a deliberate choice in the direction of the Judaizing sects so prevalent in his age. Rather, his individualistic approach to spiritual problems often led him to scriptural interpretations which were remarkably similar to those found in the midrashic literature. He avoided the explications of the Protestant sectaries in favor of his own independent and rational approach to the Bible; he fervently avowed free will; he had a predilection for Old Testament themes; and he read the Bible in Hebrew, without the emendations which appeared in the English and Latin translations. Like the midrashists, Milton turned and turned the scriptural text to derive every possible meaning from it; like them he believed that the Bible contained all the truths necessary for life and that they could be recovered with dedicated effort and learned application.

Milton's unorthodox ideas on salvation, based on his careful and dedicated reading of the Bible, are found in his controversial theological work, the *Christian Doctrine.* In *Paradise Lost* he transforms these midrashiclike insights into a poetic form in which the ambiguity allowed for an uncensorious religious interpretation. *Paradise Lost* was published twice in Milton's lifetime and enjoyed a wide readership throughout the world after his death; the heretical material in the epic became obvious to most readers only after the *Christian Doctrine* was published in 1825.

Milton outlines the orthodox pattern of repentance in the *Christian Doctrine:* "Repentance is the gift of God by virtue of which the regenerate man, seeing with sorrow that he has offended God by his sins, detests and avoids them and, through a sense of the divine mercy, turns to God with all humility, and is eager in his heart to follow what is right."[4] The steps on the way to penitence are: "recognition of sin, contrition, confession, abandonment of evil and conversion to good" (p. 468). In *Paradise Lost* Adam and Eve follow this conventional progression.

However, Milton introduces a large measure of free will into the penitential process, and in this he differed radically from the orthodox Protestant dogma of his day. Reformed theology affirmed Augustine's conviction that because of Adam and Eve's sin all men forfeited their free will. Salvation is entirely of God; even the faith by which man accepts God's grace, won through Christ's merit, is a divine gift. Those who receive the gift of saving faith are the elect, Augustine teaches. Furthermore, God's grace is irresistible. It is given to those who have been chosen by the Creator before the beginning of time and for no reason that man can fathom: God's "judgments are inscrutable and . . . [his] ways past finding out."[5]

Calvin went beyond Augustine in declaring that God chooses, without regard to man's merit, not only those who are elected to salvation but also those who are predestined to eternal reprobation. Even the fall was predetermined, Calvin declares: "In the hidden counsel of God it was determined that Adam should fall from the unimpaired condition of his nature, and by his defection should involve all his posterity in sentence of eternal death."[6] Because of his sinful nature, inherited through Adam, man has been justly deprived of free will and is bound over to God in miserable servitude.

Luther agreed that man has no free will in matters that pertain to God: "there we do not choose, we do not do anything; but we are chosen, we are equipped, we are born again, we accept."[7] The Protestant doctrine of grace demanded that man, who is a worthless sinner, be helpless in the hands of his Creator, on whom he solely depends for grace. Luther rejected Erasmus' opinion that human free will can effectively apply itself to salvation or turn away from those matters; only God has free will, Luther argues, and it is nothing less than blasphemy to apply this divine quality to sinning man.[8]

Zwingli, Bucer, and other Protestant theologians agreed with Luther and Calvin that man's sinful condition made it impossible for him to contribute anything to his own salvation; only sovereign grace can achieve salvation. According to Luther, God works both good and evil in man according to his nature; all that happens with respect to salvation, however, comes to man from mere necessity. To illustrate this Luther invokes Augustine: man's will is like a beast standing between two riders. If God rides, it wills and goes where God wills. If Satan rides, it wills and goes where Satan wills. Nor can the beast choose to which rider he will go, but the riders fight to decide who shall hold.[9]

The denial of free will in man's salvation is at the center of seventeenth-century orthodox Protestantism; the doctrine of grace required that God be everything, man be nothing. Even the belief that man can come to a knowledge of God through his own reason, as taught in natural theology or scholasticism, was considered sacrilegious because it makes the apprehension of the Creator man's achievement rather than the gift of God. Erasmus' contention, that since God is kindness itself no man need despair of his pardon, infuriated Luther; he finds these words Christless and "chillier than ice." Erasmus is impious and perverted in asserting that there is strength within man to repent, that there is such a thing as striving with all one's strength, that God has mercy which we can call upon, and that God is by nature just and kind.[10] We can come to God only through Christ; only he can save us. To claim that piety is possible without Christ, to profess that God can be whole-heartedly served without Christ, is sacrilege to Luther; every Jew or Gentile who knows nothing of Christ could make the same claim.[11] It is, in short, un-Christian.

Seventeenth-century Puritan sermonizers preached the same lesson; man is helpless in his own salvation. Remorse is not repentance; neither is suffering. Only a personal commitment to Christ can lead to repentance, Thomas Hooker declared in his widely read guidebook, *The Soule's Humiliation*.[12] When Adam sinned he lost the ability to seek God's favor unaided; sinning man must therefore freely implant his soul in Jesus, for Christ alone can atone for sinners. Thomas Taylor, in *The Practice of Repentance*, extended man's inability to achieve repentance without Christ to include the unfallen state as well: "Adam in innocency knew it [repentance] not," how much less when his nature became corrupt through sin.[13] The orthodox reformed position on atonement is summed up by William Perkins in *The Nature and Practice of Repentance:* "noone can hate sin unless he be sanctified, and he that is sanctified is justified; and he that is justified must needs have that faithe which unites him to Christ, and makes him bone of his bone, and flesh of his flesh."[14] Salvation is unthinkable without the personal spiritual knowledge of Christ, the Savior.

Puritan lecturers preached the urgency of committing one's soul to Christ, on whom all salvation depends.[15] Puritan diaries expound with morbid introspection the details of the often slippery progress of the soul's abandonment to Jesus.[16] Books such as Arthur Dent's *The Plaine Mans Pathway to Heaven* (1601) charted the signs of salvation for Puritans, for whom soteriology was the major point of life. It was one of the few books that John Bunyan read, a tribute to its popularity; another was Luther's *Commentarie upon the Epistle of S.Paul to the Galathians*, which taught him that there is no damnation to those who are in Christ Jesus.[17] Since in Calvinism faith is the result of election and not its cause, as it is in Arminianism, people searched themselves endlessly for signs indicating the degree to which they had been enabled to surrender their souls to Jesus. The Westminster Confession enunciated the Calvinist creed (1645–1647): only through a deep and abiding faith in Christ's redeeming sacrifice can man escape his sinful condition, for he is too depraved as a consequence of original sin to have any part in his own salvation.

In Milton's theodicy God granted man the gift of free will, based on his correct use of reason; Adam explains this to Eve before their fateful parting in Book IX of the epic: "God left free the Will, for what obeys / Reason is free."[18] In the *Christian Doctrine* Milton asserts that man decides, of his own free will, whether to accept or to reject God's universal offer of grace sufficient for salvation (p. 192);[19] "none but such [as reject my grace] from mercy I exclude" declares God to the Son in *Paradise Lost* (III, 202).

Luther and Calvin feared that making God's will dependent on man's actions changed the order of nature by subordinating God's will, which is the first cause, to man's will, which is the second cause. Milton does not agree: "God's will is no less the first cause of everything if he decrees that certain things shall depend upon the will of man, than if he had decreed to make all things inevitable" (*CD*, pp. 163–64). God's decision to save man "entails the action of a will which he himself has freed and a belief which he himself demands from men. If this condition is left in the power of men who are free to act, it is absolutely in keeping with justice and does not detract at all from the importance of divine grace. . . . God does not . . . depend upon the will of man, but accomplishes his own will, and in doing so has willed that in the love and worship of God, and thus in their own salvation, men should always use their free will. If we do not, whatever worship or love we men offer to God is worthless and of no account" (*CD*, p. 189). He repeats the same idea in *Paradise Lost*, when God explains to the Son that he would have no pleasure from obedience not freely offered, from allegiance that "serv'd necessity, / Not mee" (III, 110–11).

Therefore, Milton reasons, all men who turn their hearts to God of their own will and in all sincerity, will be saved through God's grace and in his justice: "God, to show the glory of his long-suffering and justice, excludes no man from the way of penitence and eternal salvation, unless that man has continued to reject and despise the offer of grace, and of grace sufficient for salvation" (*CD*, p. 194).

In Milton's view of Christian doctrine, it follows that no one is predestined to either election or reprobation without regard to justice. Calvin's predestined reprobation has no basis in Scripture whatsoever, Milton states, since reprobation is rescinded by repentance, and repentance is available to all who sincerely seek it. "If you repent, you will not perish" is the lesson God teaches, according to Milton's reading of Scripture. Milton's proof texts are, among others: "When the wicked man turns away from the wickedness that he has committed and does that which is lawful and right, he shall save his soul alive" (Ezek. xviii, 27); and, "If that nation against whom I have pronounced turn from their evil, I will repent of the evil that I thought to do unto them" (Jer. xviii, 8). A free-willed repentance, Milton argues, based on God's merciful offer of grace, is a basic tenet of Christianity (*CD*, p. 192).

Predestined election, Milton explains, is simply a reward for a select few whom God has chosen above the rest because he foresaw that they would persevere in the faith, as the God of *Paradise Lost* explains (III, 183–84). God's election is based on justice. His foreknowledge imposes no necessity on man's absolutely unimpaired freedom in matters of faith. If God interfered in any way with man's free choice in spiritual matters, "then liberty will be an empty word, and will have to be banished utterly not only from religion but also from morality and even from indifferent matters" (*CD*, p. 164).

Neither was the Protestant belief in justification *sola fide*, solely by faith in Christ, congenial to Milton's thinking. Faith comes from "a true knowledge of God, though this may at first be imperfect" (*CD*, p. 476); its source is in the individual will. It is not a matter of the intellect, of having been informed, but of the will, in deciding to accept Christ. To Milton "implicit faith, which blindly accepts and so believes, is not real faith at all" (*CD*, p. 472). Faith requires works, and in offering works of faith man again participates in his own salvation. Milton, in this way, dismisses the Calvinist position that man is a mere puppet whose salvation or reprobation was determined by God before all time, and who is therefore helpless in his own salvation. Nor does he agree with Luther's emendation of Paul's "a man is justified by faith without the deeds of the law" (Rom. iii, 28) to "a man is justified by faith alone." Milton's text is James ii, 24: "you see now that it is by doing something good, and not only by believing that a man is justified." The law is abrogated, agrees Milton, but not the substance of the law which is the "love of God and of our neighbor" (*CD*, p. 532). The faith which justifies us is a living faith, not a dead one, "and the only living faith is a faith which acts" (*CD*, p. 490). Milton repeats this credo several times in *Paradise Lost* (XI, 256–57; XII, 427).

Milton further believes that the redemption which Christ paid in his perfect sacrifice is sufficient for all mankind and that everyone is called to share in the grace which his redemption bought. Even those who have not been initiated into the knowledge of Christ and have not implanted their souls in Jesus but "believed only in God the Father" are included in God's universal offer of salvation. In Milton's view of Christianity, "the ultimate object of faith is not Christ the Mediator, but God the Father," a belief he derives from the selected evidence of the New Testament: not John vi, 29, "you must believe in the one he has sent," and not Romans x, 9, "if your lips confess that Jesus is Lord and if you believe in your heart that God raised him from the dead, then you will be saved"; but John xii, 44, "Jesus declared publicly, whoever believes in me believes not in me but in the one who sent me," and Hebrews vii, 25, "his power to save is utterly certain . . . for all who come to God through him" (*CD*, pp. 474–75).

The poet rejected Luther's portrait of Adam as the exemplar of sinful man's helplessness and futility, despairing and impotent because he does not yet have the saving knowledge of Christ:

When there is no promise of forgiveness of sins and no faith, the sinner cannot act otherwise. If God had said: "Adam, you have sinned; but I shall forgive you your sin," then with the utmost loathing Adam would have humbly and frankly acknowledged his sin. But because the hope for the forgiveness of his sins is not yet available, he feels and sees nothing except death itself because of his transgression of the command. . . . Man cannot do otherwise when no hope of forgiveness and promise of grace is available. Because death is unbearable for human nature, it begets despair and blasphemy.[20]

Milton's Adam does repent before he has the saving knowledge of Christ, and Eve, his snare and helpmeet, atones along with him — and this on their own volition, with a mighty effort of the will.

In *Paradise Lost* Adam and Eve sin in Book IX, they atone in Book X, and Adam feels that his prayer "was heard with favor" and that God has accepted his atonement early in Book XI, line 153. Yet Adam does not learn of Christ's role in man's redemption until late in Book XII. So movingly has Milton portrayed Adam and Eve in the process of working out their redemption that many critics feel that the epic is complete at the end of Book X, before Adam has been educated as a Christian and has accepted Christ, the Savior.[21] Milton does not deny the need for a profound faith in Christ; on the contrary, he asserts this creed. But in his passionate advocacy of unrestricted free will and the individual's responsibility for his own moral life, even including atonement, he emphasizes and dramatizes the role of choice in the developing personalities and characters of Adam and Eve; the role of Jesus in man's salvation is given much less detailed attention.[22]

The poet evinces a sympathetic understanding for his naive heroes who are required, in the process of making decisions, to face choices for which they have no precedent, to weigh and to decide, to choose the good in preference to the bad. They are so young and inexperienced; they have so much to learn, so many things to try. The poet's belief in the doctrine of free will makes him patient with his heroes' faulty choices for they can only learn to choose correctly by testing at least some of the possibilities available to them. It appears difficult for Milton to condemn these innocents too harshly when their world abounds with so many possibilities for evil.

Milton's emphasis on free will in repentance, as expressed in the epic, corresponds to the Jewish model of Adam and Eve's repentance based on the individual's exercise of free will, as it is presented in the midrashic commentaries on the Bible. It may well have been his passionate belief in free will, which he shared with the Rabbis, which first drew him to Midrash and induced Milton to use midrashic material in *Paradise Lost;* the use of Midrash in the epic has been documented for over half a century.[23] Adam's penitence, as depicted in the poem, is remarkably like the rabbinic portrait of the first man as a repentant sinner who is redeemed through suffering and remorse, often with the help of Eve. Repentance in the Midrash is a corollary to free will: God, who in his providence granted man the freedom to choose, also provided him with repentance as a corrective to the errors which inevitably result from the dynamics of free choice.

The poet's belief in free will also embraced the conviction that the human spirit has the strength to overcome the consequences of wrong choosing through penitence. That God excludes no one from penitence and salvation except those who choose not to be saved is repeatedly stated in both the *Christian Doctrine* and in *Paradise Lost,* where God informs the Son: "To Prayer, repentance, and obedience due, / Though but endeavor'd with sincere intent, / Mine ear shall not be slow, mine eye not shut" (III, 191–93). This same view is a cornerstone of rabbinic thought; God accepts the atonement of every sinner if it is freely offered and sincere. In one medieval Midrash God proclaims: "If your sins are as high as heaven, even to the seventh heaven and even to the throne of glory, and you repent, I will receive you" (*Pesikta Rabbati* 185a). Free will for Milton as for the midrashists implies an ongoing testing of the world and must allow for the possibility of repentance for choices wrongly made.

Like many Protestants of his age Milton used midrashic material which had been translated by Christian Hebraists. I have already shown that for many narrative and structural details of *Paradise Lost* Milton made use of the late Palestinian Midrash, *Pirkei de-Rabbi Eliezer*, which was translated into Latin in 1644. He undoubtedly used other contemporary Protestant translations of midrashic material, too; they had become standard texts for seventeenth-century theologians.[24] Having relinquished the Catholic exegetical traditions, and having no traditions of their own, Protestants turned to the ancient Jewish biblical explications which might help them in their aim of establishing a theocracy based on the biblical model.

Preachers and writers of the seventeenth century cited these secondary sources extensively and punctuated their sermons with rabbinic quotations derived from them. Since sermons were a popular form of edification and entertainment, and were well attended, Jewish midrashic literature became widely disseminated. Midrash was in the air. It is therefore impossible to know whether Milton unconsciously absorbed midrashic ideas which appealed to him, whether he deliberately went directly to the translated material for biblical interpretations, or whether in his own unconventional reading of the Bible he independently came to some of the same conclusions. It is significant, however, that in developing the theme of Adam and Eve's repentance Milton chose a subject which was almost never touched by Protestant writers on the fall of man, but which the ancient midrashists dealt with at length.

There is nothing in Genesis to suggest that Adam and Eve repented for their sin: the biblical account depicts the archetypal sinners and emphasizes man's fall from grace. But neither does the story deny Adam's repentance. The midrashists view Adam as archetypal man, confronted by choices, wrestling with his *yezer ha-ra* (inclination to evil), falling to temptation and making the unfortunate choice for which he is punished, losing Eden for himself and for all mankind. But as the Rabbis who wrote the Midrash understand it, man is not lost to hope. God, who gave man the gift of free choice, also provided him with the remedy for the bad choices to which his propensity for evil often drives him.

A return to God is always possible for the sincerely contrite sinner, say the Rabbis. The very word for repentance in Hebrew, *teshuvah*, from the root *shuv* (return), signifies the motion of the sinner who, by an effort of will, turns from evil and returns to God. The Old Testament is clear on the sinful character of men, "For there is not a just man upon earth that doeth good and sinneth not" (Eccles. vii, 20); but it also holds out the promise of God's pardon, "Let the wicked forsake his way, and the unrighteous man his thoughts and let him return unto the Lord, and he will have mercy upon him; and to our God, for he will abundantly pardon" (Isa. lv, 7).

This idea is extended and developed by the Rabbis. The Midrash proclaims that even if the sinner repents only one day, or according to some versions one hour before his death, God will accept him: "'Repent one day before your death,' Rabbi Eliezer exhorted. They asked him, 'Does one know on what day he will die?' He replied, 'Then all the more reason that he repent today lest he die tomorrow; thus all his life is spent in repentance'" (TB Shabbat 153a). The centrality of repentance in Jewish theology is expressed in a midrash which assigns to atonement a role in God's original plan: "Adam was created from the dust of the place where the Temple was to rise for the atonement of man's sins" (Genesis Rabbah 14.8).

Several midrashic works characterize Adam and Eve as prototypes of repenting sinners. Adam is regarded as a righteous patriarch and his penance is described in the talmudic tractates TB Eruvin 18b, TB Avodah Zarah 18a, and in the extra-canonical minor talmudic tractate *Avot de-Rabbi Nathan*. In *Pirkei de-Rabbi Eliezer* (XX.147), Adam prays to God: "'Sovereign of all worlds! Remove, I pray Thee, my sins from me and accept my repentance, that all the generations will learn that repentance is a reality.' What did the Holy One, blessed be He, do? He put forth His right hand, and accepted his repentance, and took away from him his sin." The *Apocalypse of Moses* (IX, 1–3), an apocryphal work dealing with the lives of Adam and Eve, contains a moving passage, similar to the one in Book X of *Paradise Lost* in which Eve offers to sacrifice herself for Adam: "And Adam sighed greatly and said, 'What shall I do; I am in great distress.' And Eve also cried and said to Adam, 'My master, rise, give me half of your ills and I shall bear them because this thing did come from me; because of me did you come to trouble.'" And the angel comes to her and says: "'Rise, Eve, from your repentance.'"[25]

Rabbi Meir explicates the biblical verse, "And Adam lived a hundred and thirty years, and begot a son in his own likeness, after his own image" (Gen. v, 3), as follows: "Adam was a great saint. When he saw that death was ordained as a punishment for his sin he spent 130 years in fasting, severed relations with his wife, and wore fig leaves on his body" (TB Eruvin 18a). However, the Rabbis stress that though Adam first brought sin into the world, his responsibility for the death of others is limited; each man dies because of his own iniquities: "Thus all holy men are brought before God, death having been decreed upon them. They are not pardoned until they behold the Divine Presence. First they reprove Adam, saying to Him, 'Thou hast brought death upon us.' And Adam answers them, 'I am responsible for but one sin, but among you there is not a single one that does not bear many sins'" (*Tanḥuma*, Ḥukkat 16). Furthermore, despite his sin Adam receives the promise of a blessed life in the next world. The Midrash Genesis Rabbah 31.7 states: "He was sent out of the Garden of Eden in this world, but not in the world to come."

Milton subscribes to the orthodox Christian view that all men sinned in Adam and Eve. In the *Christian Doctrine* he declares:

Anyone who examines this sin carefully will admit, and rightly, that it was a most atrocious offence, and that it broke every part of the law. For what fault is there which man did not commit in committing this sin? He was to be condemned both for trusting Satan and for not trusting God; he was faithless, ungrateful, disobedient, greedy, uxorious; she, negligent of her husband's welfare; both of them committed theft, robbery with violence, murder against their children; each was sacrilegious and deceitful, cunningly aspiring to divinity although thoroughly unworthy of it, proud and arrogant. (Pp. 383–84)

But Milton considerably mitigates the rigor of his condemnation by observing, as the Rabbis had, that God created Adam and Eve with a certain predisposition to sin and that this quality is a "depravity which all human minds have in common" (*CD*, p. 389). He bases his views on the following Old Testament texts, among others: Genesis vi, 5, "And God saw that the wickedness of man was great in the earth and that every imagination of the thoughts of his heart was only evil continually"; Genesis viii, 21, "And the Lord said in his heart, I will not again curse the ground any more for man's sake, for the imagination of man's heart is evil from his youth"; and Jeremiah xvii, 9, "The heart is deceitful above all things, and desperately wicked." Milton concludes that Adam and Eve were guilty of "evil desire" (*CD*, p. 388), and that all their progeny inherited this trait.

The words "evil desire" to describe man's proclivity for evil is close to the midrashic designation of the *yeẓer ha-ra* (inclination to evil) to account for the human condition described in the biblical passages which Milton quotes. According to the Rabbis, every person is born with the *yeẓer ha-ra;* he also has in him the seed of the *yeẓer ha-tov* (the inclination to good) which, however, develops only later with the growth of reason. The adult then has a dual nature consisting of the *yeẓer ha-tov*, which prompts him to obey God and to deal well with his fellow men, and the *yezer ha-ra*, which tempts him to yield to lust and to disobey God. Man's dual nature, say the midrashists, is a sign of God's beneficence: it endows man with the dignity of freedom by enabling and obliging him to choose between the good and evil in himself. Milton concurs. The God of *Paradise Lost* asserts emphatically that he equipped man with all that was necessary to prevail against evil: "I made him just and right, / Sufficient to have stood"; but he also gave man faults, which left him "free to fall" (III, 98–99). As in midrashic commentary, the God of *Paradise Lost* gave man the freedom to choose the good and evil in himself through reason: "Reason also is choice" (III, 108).

Furthermore, the *yezer ha-ra* has a good purpose in God's plan, the Rabbis stress. Referring to the biblical verse in Genesis i, 31, "And God saw everything that he had made, and, behold, it was very good," the Rabbis ask, "Can the *yezer ha-ra* be considered very good?" (Genesis Rabbah 9.7). They answer that were it not for the *yezer ha-ra* man would not marry, nor beget children, nor build a house, nor engage in commerce. The *yezer ha-ra* is the source of energy which makes man competitive and willing to strive and labor in a world that is fraught with dangerous temptations. It provides the spark which inspires man to build and create. In the *Areopagitica* Milton asks much the same question and arrives at a conclusion which is similar to that of the ancient midrashists: "Wherefore did he create passions within us, pleasures round about us, but that these rightly tempered are the very ingredients of virtue? . . . This justifies the high providence of God, who, though he command us temperance, justice, continence, yet pours out before us, even to a profuseness all desirable things, and gives us minds that can wander beyond all limit and satiety."[26] Milton agrees with the midrashists that the freedom to determine his own behavior impels man into a position of constant inner struggle with temptation; given his propensity for evil, some of his choices will inevitably lead him into errors. And, like the midrashists, Milton provides for the reversibility of failure by repentance. God "excludes no man from the way of penitence and eternal salvation" (*CD*, p. 194).

The conviction that man's sins might be revoked through penitence prompts Milton to focus on the totality of Adam's human qualities, both good and bad, rather than on his sinfulness alone. Like the midrashists, the poet is concerned with Adam as archetypal man rather than as archetypal sinner; he portrays the father of mankind as psychologically believable, complex, activated by the contradictory forces which exist in us all, good, yet fallible. For both Milton and the Rabbis the provision for Adam's successful penitence is an inherent theological consequence of free will: if man is made vulnerable to failure, he also has available to him the possibility of ameliorating, even reversing the fault.

By separating the action into two arenas, heaven and earth, Milton combines Christ's atonement for Adam and Eve with the fallen couple's self-motivated and mutually engendered repentance based on their effective exercise of free will. In heaven the Son, charged by the Father with the task of descending to earth to judge Adam and Eve, repeats an earlier promise (III, 236–42) to sacrifice himself for man "When time shall be" (X, 74). Thus God has been told of the Son's offer and the reader has been informed, but the young sinners on earth remain unaware of the Savior's promise as they struggle on their own to find the way to repentance.

The portrayal of Adam and Eve's recovery in Book X demonstrates Milton's trust in the ability of the young sinners to return to God through a mighty effort of the will. He shows them striving for self-understanding, which leads them to a comprehension of how to make godly choices. Their penitence is not based on abandoning themselves to Christ, since they know nothing as yet of the Savior's sacrificial mission for man. Instead of depending on Jesus to be their intermediary in heaven and to help them on earth, they rely on each other for support and inspiration. Milton asserts the centrality of Christ's sacrifice as a prerequisite for redemption, but he has the affirmation of Christ's role take place in heaven, unknown to the sinners in Eden at the time that they strengthen each other in their struggle back to God.

In the epic, Adam's initial response to his sin is extreme, in line with the orthodox Protestant view of original sin. He is in total despair, both for himself and for his progeny. He can see no way out: "in mee all / Posterity stands curst" (X, 817–18), and "from me what can proceed, / But all corrupt, both Mind and Will deprav'd" (X, 824–25). And he is fiercely angry, with himself, "the source and spring / Of all corruption" (X, 832–33), with God, for creating "terms too hard" (X, 751), and with Eve, "false / And hateful" (X, 868–69). He questions God's wisdom both for creating him, "Did I request thee, Maker, from my Clay / To mould me Man"? (X, 743–44), and for creating Eve, "this fair defect / Of Nature" (X, 891–92). With all the power of his superior intelligence he tries to find a way out of his predicament, but the sum of his reasoning leads him back, always, to despondent hopelessness. Adam quickly grasps the ultimate consequences of his actions and is angered and paralyzed by the starkness of his vision. Eve, too, is deeply sorrowful, but she is humble and contrite. Though less intelligent than Adam, she has a richer and sounder emotional nature which enables her to respond to the situation with a measure of balance and to seek out possibilities for the ameliora- tion of the sin. Her first impulse is to beg Adam for forgiveness. With "Tears that ceas'd not flowing" (X, 910) she throws herself at Adam's feet and implores him, her "only strength and stay" (X, 921), not to aban- don her. The power of her emotional plea reawakens Adam's love for her and brings him to his senses; moved by her plea for his help, "his anger all he lost" (X, 945).

Eve intuitively grasps the possibility for recovery and understands that the first step in the process is the restoration of the love they felt for each other before they sinned. She asks for peace between them for the short time they have left to live, "scarce one short hour perhaps" (X, 924). Adam acquiesces to her entreaty for peace, adding that in love they may "light'n / Each other's burden" (X, 960–61); their lives will be longer than Eve thinks, he reasons, since they did not die immediately after sin- ning. Eve offers a second suggestion: she will pray to God at "the place of judgment" (X, 932) and ask him to allow her to bear the sins of both. Adam is not convinced; if prayers were efficacious he would speed to the place of judgment, pray louder than Eve, ask to bear the fault himself.

Until this point in the process of recovery Eve has used her intuitive good sense and has taken the lead, resolutely insisting that they repair their relationship; Adam has followed, in love and cooperation. There is peace between them and Adam has reflected on Eve's suggestion for prayer. These were necessary steps, without which there would have been no progress. Sound intuition has given the necessary impetus to their first steps out of despair. However, with Eve's next and last recommendation of suicide, "Destruction with destruction to destroy" (X, 1006), Milton asseverates the limits of intuition, the feminine quality, and sets the stage for right reason, the masculine, higher element in the process of correct choosing. Strengthened by Eve's love, Adam takes control of the situa- tion; with his more profound intelligence he elaborates on her sugges- tions and deepens the moral significance of their actions. Each provides the other with necessary help and support and this enables the sinning pair to muster the strength with which to overcome despair. Their re- turn to God has begun.

Adam is not willing to accept simple solutions to complicated prob- lems; he rejects Eve's suggestion of suicide, which would prevent the birth of the "woeful Race" (X, 984) that must follow them. Reasoning that God would not allow himself to be cheated of the punishment due to him, that he would in fact be even further provoked by the new sin of self-destruction, Adam turns his "more attentive mind" (X, 1011) to positive resolutions of their plight. Only alive, he reasons, can they serve God. Bringing children into the world will give their lives meaning through fulfilling his decree that Eve's "Seed shall bruise / The Serpent's head" (X, 1031–32). Adam's reasoning further leads him to the conviction that God's punishment is just, and bearable. Eve's childbirth pains will soon be forgotten in the joy of motherhood; his own labors will be a blessing: "Idleness had been worse" (X, 1055). Through reason he understands that God is a merciful Father, "pitying while he judg'd" (X, 1059).

This line of deduction leads Adam to hope that God will not abandon them; they can trust in his providence and he will teach them how to cope in the harsh world. It therefore follows, Adam concludes, that God will accept their penitential prayers: "Undoubtedly he will relent and turn / From his displeasure" (X, 1093–94). Right reason, a necessary adjunct to free will, leads to hope when properly used.

When Adam feels the return of God's grace early in Book XI, he knows nothing of Christ as Savior. He knows only what Raphael had told him during the narration of the war in heaven: that God has appointed the Son "Head" (V, 606), that all the angels must bow to him and "confess him Lord" (V, 608), that he is God's appointed through whom God's will is fulfilled (VI, 729), that he is the Messiah (V, 664), and that he is the "rightful King" (V, 818). Raphael describes the Son as an omnipotence, loyal to God, who must be worshiped by the other angels and who alone has the power to end the war in heaven — a type of epic hero. He never informs Adam of Christ's sacrifice. Even after Adam's fall, when the Son presents himself as God's messenger, sent to relay the judgment, Milton eschews a ready opportunity to have him reveal himself as the Redeemer. He clothes Adam and Eve with animal skins, which can be interpreted as a salvific gesture, but the Son informs Adam and Eve only of the punishments recorded in the Bible; he remains silent on the hope for salvation through him.

The recovery scene in Book X movingly dramatizes the spiritual struggle of the young sinners from despair to hope through mutual help, and has the ring of truth. Much less convincing is Adam's cry of *O felix culpa* late in Book XII (469–478) when he learns about Christ and his saving mission. Unlike the rich description of the Paradise in which Adam and Eve lived together, and which they lost together, the eternal Paradise after death and the inner Paradise which they will individually inherit through Christ's sacrifice are never fully dramatized but merely talked about.

Nor is Christ's saving mission dramatized. Milton concentrates on the human arena in which Adam and Eve act out the spectacle of free choosing in the struggle to repent. What many would expect to be the high point of a Christian epic pales in comparison with former scenes; Adam's education into Christ and his acceptance of the Savior in Books XI and XII are rather woodenly rendered.

Milton has never been able to muster his full artistry when describing the Christ who died for man's sins. Early in his life he attempted a poem on the crucifixion, *The Passion*, but could not complete it; in a note affixed to the poem he explains that he found the subject "above the years he had when he wrote it, and nothing satisfied with what was begun, left it unfinished." Yet he published the unfinished piece in the first volume of poems in 1645, and again in the 1673 volume, obviously as a statement of his recognition of the centrality of this subject in his religious doctrine. Nonetheless, his inability to finish the poem and to handle the theme properly speak for themselves, suggesting a dichotomy between his intellectual and his emotional responses to the subject. Even late in life when he wrote his final poetic statement on the meaning of the life of Jesus, *Paradise Regained*, Milton chose to focus on the temptation rather than on the crucifixion.

There is another important point of contact between *Paradise Lost* and midrashic thinking. The Rabbis teach that the repentant sinner reaches a higher spiritual level than the wholly righteous man who has never sinned (TB Berakhot 34b). In *Paradise Lost* the Son expresses a similar idea while watching the remorseful Adam and Eve pray humbly for forgiveness. Addressing the Father, whose prevenient grace has made their repentance possible, he declares:

> See Father, what first fruits on Earth are sprung
> From thy implanted Grace in Man, these Sighs
> And Prayers, which in this Golden Censer, mixt
> With Incense, I thy Priest before thee bring,
> Fruits of more pleasing savor from thy seed
> Sown with contrition in his heart, than those
> Which his own hand manuring all the Trees
> Of Paradise could have produc't, ere fall'n
> From innocence.   (XI, 22–30)

Milton and the Rabbis have the same reverential esteem for the repentant sinner's tearful prayers, which they see as the most sincere form of worship. Only the torments of contrition enable man to reach the inner depths where God's image manifest in man can still be found and from which man can summon, through God's grace, the means for prayer that is most meaningful and therefore most acceptable to God. This apprehension is unavailable to the unfallen.

Milton's method in depicting Adam's repentance is based on a conception of free will which requires man to be responsible for his own actions, even including repentance. In keeping Adam and Eve unaware of the Son's offer of sacrifice throughout their successful struggle to repent, Milton suggests that man must find the strength and will within himself to seek redemption. In Book XI, line 3, the reader is told that God's "prevenient Grace" had made their repentance possible, but this explanation is provided only after we have seen Adam and Eve strive and persevere on their own, without apparent heavenly help. When Adam learns of Christ's saving mission at the end of Book XII, it is very late in his religious development.

Jewish midrashic commentary can serve as a useful gloss to *Paradise Lost*, for Milton and the midrashists have the same insight into man and his dilemma: confronted with two basic impulses, for good and for evil, man is charged to choose between them by exercising free will through the use of reason. This is a feature of the human condition, before and after the fall. The possibility for error is always present, but so is its corollary, repentance. Free will, for Milton and the midrashists, implies an ongoing testing of the world and must allow for the possibility of repentance for choices wrongly made. Milton agrees with the Rabbis that even Adam and Eve, the prototypal sinners, recovered some of their God-endowed nobility through their self-directed penitence, a view which their shared belief in the dignity of human nature and the justice of God to men makes inevitable.

Tel Aviv University

NOTES

1. See, for the rare exceptions, John E. Parish, "Pre-Miltonic Representations of Adam as a Christian," *Rice Institute Pamphlets*, XL, 3 (October 1953), 1–24, who discusses, among other works, Heinrich Bullinger's treatise *Der Alt Glaub*, which depicts a penitent Adam.

2. Martin Luther, *On the Bondage of the Will: De Servo Arbitrio* (1525), *The Reply to Erasmus*, trans. J. I. Packer and O. R. Johnston (Cambridge, 1957; rpt. 1973), cites Erasmus' arguments before replying to them. Arminian belief was declared heretical at the Synod of Dort (1618–1619); Erasmus was a confirmed Catholic to his death.

3. See my article, "Midrash in *Paradise Lost: Capitula Rabbi Elieser*," in *Milton Studies*, XVIII, ed. James D. Simmonds (Pittsburgh, 1983), pp. 145–71. The term Midrash applies to the rabbinic method of biblical interpretation as well as to the ancient exegetical literature as a whole. The scholars who wrote the ancient midrashic literature are called Rabbis or Sages.

4. *CD*, p. 466. All quotations from Milton's *Christian Doctrine* are taken from the *Complete Prose Works of John Milton*, ed. Don M. Wolfe et al. (New Haven, 1953–1982). It appears in vol. VI, ed. Maurice Kelley (1973), hereafter cited parenthetically in the text.

5. Maurice Kelley, Introduction, YP VI, p. 76, citing *De Dono Perseverantiae*, (428), 35.

6. John Calvin, *Articles Concerning Predestination*, in the *Library of Christian Classics*, ed. John Baillie (1953), XXII, 179, cited by C. A. Patrides, *Milton and the Christian Tradition* (Oxford, 1966), p. 192.

7. Martin Luther, *Works: Lectures on Genesis 1–5*, ed. Jaroslav Pelikan (St. Louis, 1958), p. 155.

8. Luther, *On the Bondage of the Will*, p. 141.

9. Ibid., pp. 103–04.

10. Ibid., p. 75.

11. Ibid., p. 74.

12. Thomas Hooker, *The Soule's Humiliation* (London, 1640), p. 15.

13. Thomas Taylor, *The Practice of Repentance* (London, 1635), p. 18.

14. William Perkins, *Two Treatises* (London, 1632), p. 2.

15. See Paul S. Seaver, *The Puritan Lectureships: The Politics of Religious Dissent, 1560–1662* (Stanford, 1970), for an account of the importance of sermons to the Puritans.

16. Vavasor Powell, *Spiritual Experiences of Sundry Beleevers*, 2d ed. (London, 1653); Henry Jessey, *The Exceeding Riches of Grace Advanced By the Spirit of Grace, In an Empty Nothing Creature*, 6th ed. (London, 1652); Jane Turner, *Choice Experiences of the Kind Dealings of God Before, In, and After Conversion* (London, 1653), are but three of many such confessions. For a more complete list see William York Tindall, *John Bunyan, Mechanick Preacher* (Ann Arbor: University Microfilms, 1967).

17. John Bunyan, *Grace Abounding*, ed. John Brown (Cambridge, 1907), pp. 10, 41. Luther's work was printed in English (London, 1635). Dent's work was in its eighteenth edition when Bunyan read it.

18. John Milton, *Complete Poems and Major Prose*, ed. Merritt Y. Hughes (New York, 1957), pp. 351–52.

19. This is in accord with Arminian doctrine which teaches that man is free to accept or to reject God's universal offer of divine grace sufficient for salvation. See Dennis Danielson, "Milton's Arminianism and *Paradise Lost*," *Milton Studies*, XII, ed. James D. Simmonds (Pittsburgh, 1978), pp. 47–73.

20. Luther, *Lectures on Genesis 1–5*, p. 240. But in another context Luther says that Adam apprehended the future advent of the Messiah *sola fide* and was saved; cited by Patrides, *Milton and the Christian Tradition*, p. 127, from Luther's *Works*, XLV.203. Patrides also quotes the Swiss theologian, Rudolph Gwalter, who called Adam "a christian man" for recognizing Genesis iii, 15 as the protevangelium.

21. John Dryden, *Essays*, ed. W. P. Ker (New York, 1961), vol. I, p. 268, found the scriptural passages in Books XI and XII tedious and would have preferred the epic without them; Joseph Addison, Spectator Paper 363, is bored with the final two books, complaining that Milton pays too little attention to the art; C. S. Lewis, *A Preface to "Paradise Lost"* (London, 1942), is also dissatisfied with the end of the epic, declaring it an "untransmuted lump of futurity"; M. M. Mahood, *Poetry and Humanism* (New Haven, 1950), p. 186, states that "the verse flags dismally in the final two books"; Kenneth Muir, *John Milton* (London, 1955), p. 160, agrees that Books XI and XII are "poetically on a much lower level than the rest"; William Madsen, *Three Studies in the Renaissance* (New

Haven, 1958), p. 270, writes that the drama of the epic ends in Book X; and J. B. Broadbent, *Some Graver Subject* (London, 1960), p. 267, describes Books XI and XII as a didactic sermon.

22. E. M. W. Tillyard, *Milton* (London, 1930), p. 279, verbalizing a conviction held implicitly by many readers of *Paradise Lost*, wrote: "Milton had no profound belief in the incarnate Christ. He happened to believe in the idea of spiritual regeneration. . . . He would like to believe that man, once created and set in his surroundings, has it in him to work out unaided his own salvation. But such a belief was so utterly incompatible with Christianity that it was out of the question for Milton to admit — even to himself."

23. Among the scholars who have dealt with Milton's use of Midrash are: Harris F. Fletcher, *Milton's Semitic Studies* (Chicago, 1926) and *Milton's Rabbinic Readings* (Urbana, 1930); Edward C. Baldwin, "Some Extra-Biblical Semitic Influences Upon Milton's Story of the Fall of Man," *JEGP*, XXVIII (1929), 366–401; Harold Fisch, "Hebraic Style and Motifs in *Paradise Lost*," in *Language and Style in Milton*, ed. Ronald D. Emma and John Shawcross (New York, 1967), pp. 30–64; Jason Rosenblatt, "A Revaluation of Milton's Indebtedness to Hebraica in *Paradise Lost*," (Ph.D. diss., Brown University, 1969).

24. Among these works are Johannes Buxtorf's *Lexicon Chaldaicum Talmudicum* (1640), which contains learned articles on rabbinic subjects; Christopher Cartwright's *Mellificum Hebraicum* (1649), which glosses the Old and New Testaments with exegetical and homiletical midrashim; and John Lightfoot's *Horae Hebraicae et Talmudicae* (1658–1674), which glosses the New Testament with extracts from the Mishnah, the Talmud, Rashi, the Tosafot, and Maimonides.

25. According to R. H. Charles, *The Pseudepigrapha* (Oxford, 1913; rpt. 1969), p. 124, the medieval Latin manuscript of the *Apocalypse of Moses* had an extensive circulation in the fourteenth, fifteenth, and sixteenth centuries in England.

26. *The Student's Milton*, ed. Frank Allen Patterson (New York, 1961), p. 733.

COVENANT AND THE "CROWNE OF LIFE": A FIGURAL TAPESTRY IN *PARADISE LOST*

Patricia Elizabeth Davis

I N T H E tenth chapter of Book I of *The Christian Doctrine,* Milton celebrates the once dynamic communion between God and Adam, arguing that since Adam "was by nature good and holy and was naturally disposed to do right," God was reluctant to bind him "by the requirements of any covenant to something which he would do of his own accord."[1] With the Fall, of course, Adam forfeited this easy reciprocity with God, forcing his descendants to pursue divine grace with "shadowy expiations weak" (*PL* XII, 291).[2] But in the exegetical tradition Milton inherited as a seventeenth-century Protestant, "the spring of divine mercy" follows hard upon "the winter of divine wrath,"[3] and the typological echoes in *Paradise Lost* encourage Milton's readers to turn their fallen vision "Up to a better Cov'nant . . . From shadowy Types to Truth, from Flesh to Spirit" (*PL* XII, 302–03). Milton's epic contains one image cluster which is particularly resonant typologically, although it has never been fully explored in studies of *Paradise Lost.* Embracing the "covenant of grace" realized in Christ's Passion, Milton laces his descriptions of Heaven, Eden, and earth after the Fall with types of Christ's immutable crown of thorns, a type in turn of the "crowne of life" that symbolizes heavenly joy and immortality in Revelation ii, 10.[4] This imagery progressively assimilates man's experience in a fallen world into the unity and perfection of God's eternal plan: interwoven with the archetypal crown are flowers that by tradition both symbolize man's degeneration and foreshadow his redemption through Christ. Moreover, every time Milton's protagonists literally or figuratively bind on or cast away one of these garland-crowns, they symbolically prefigure Christ's "divine drama of salvation" *and* affirm their own capacity to make immediate covenant with God.[5] Milton's typology thus invites his readers to see the covenant relationship between God and man (the relationship that gives shape to the biblical narrative) continuing in their own history — a notion theologians would later call "progressive revelation."[6] As Georgia Christopher explains, Milton transcends the "onward temporal thrust of the typological perspective," making the narrative of *Paradise Lost* "intimately topical."[7]

Milton first prefigures the "divine drama of salvation" in Book III of *Paradise Lost*, where, in a scenario loosely derived from Revelation iv, 2–4, he portrays an angelic host casting garland-crowns before the throne of God. According to St. John, the throne "was to loke upon, like unto a jasper stone, and a sardine, & there was a rainbow rounde about the throne in sight like to an emeraude." But for Milton, God's essential light is pure, figuratively crowning Him "through a cloud / Drawn round about . . . like a radiant Shrine, / Dark with excessive bright" (III, 378–80). Therefore, Milton's symbol of man's aspiring spiritual purity is initially colorless: interwoven with the enduring gold of the angelic crowns is the "vegetable Gold" (IV, 220) of the "Immortal Amarant,"

> a Flow'r which once
> In Paradise, fast by the Tree of Life
> Began to bloom, but soon for man's offense
> To Heav'n remov'd where first it grew, there grows,
> And flow'rs aloft shading the Fount of Life.   (III, 353–57)

The Amaranth is an apt symbol of humanity in its pure and sinless state: as Roland M. Frye notes, Milton drew the symbolic significance of the flower from "the unfading or *amaranton* inheritance or crown promised to the faithful Christian in 1 Peter 1:4."[8] Don Cameron Allen, citing Milton's debt to the *Paedogogus* of Clement of Alexandria, describes it as an immaculate flower "beyond the things of earth," having "neither color nor form." An emblem of "the essential light of God and the infused light by which his creatures shine," Milton's Amaranth suggests that man in his prelapsarian state is an emanation of the "Fountain of Light" that is the "Author of all being" (*PL* III, 374–75).[9] Adam, then, is the "bright consummate flow'r" that is to be "by gradual scale sublim'd" until he can become part of the angelic host that clusters around the "full blaze" of God's throne (V, 481, 483; III, 378).

But the miniature drama enacted in Milton's Heaven celebrates the Son's offer to redeem Adam after the Fall, an offer that requires the Son to plunge himself into the spiritual obscurity of a fallen world. To symbolize his self-immolation, the multitude of angels surrounding God's throne cast down their crowns "With solemn Adoration," and figuratively put on a new immortality by binding "thir resplendent locks inwreath'd with beams" with the Amaranth, now saturated with color (III, 351, 361). For Milton, color is not a manifestation of evil, but a sign of the creature's distance from his Creator, so this interweaving of pure and refracted light represents the Son's immersion in mortality while he still retains "the effulgence of [God's] Glory . . . Transfus'd" (III, 388–89). It is meet, then, that in striking the celestial pavement, the angelic crowns break the pure, unobscured ray of God's light into an array of colors reminiscent of St. John's rainbow, "impurpling" Heaven's surface with "Celestial Roses" (III, 362–64). Suddenly the immaculate and immortal Amaranth is fused with a flower symbolic of human passion and mortality, yet transformed into an emblem of salvation by Christ's sacrifice. As Milton's contemporary William Parks suggests in his commentary on the Song of Songs, "the often effusion of [Christ's] blood was the better coloring of this Rose" (the Rose of Sharon).[10] Jonathan Edwards is even more explicit: "Roses grow upon briars," he observes, "which is to signify that all temporal sweets are mixt with bitter. But . . . that pure happiness, the crown of glory, is to be come at in no other way than by bearing Christ's cross, by a life of mortification, self-denial, and labour, and bearing all things for Christ. The rose, that is chief of all flowers, is the last thing that comes out. The briary, prickly, bush grows before that; the end and crown of all is the beautifull and fragrant rose."[11]

In one brief but provocative scene, then, Milton uses the imagistic "pressure" of light and color,[12] the paradox of an immutable flower, and the eternal "crowne of life" inwreathed with emblems of mortality to portray Adam's regeneration through Christ. Even more significantly, he creates a typological matrix for the flower symbolism that abounds in prelapsarian Eden, reappearing in the "flow'ry verge" of the rainbow given as a sign of covenant to Noah (XI, 881) and, ultimately, in Christ's crown of thorns — the earthly crown of roses resurrected as an "incorruptible crowne of glorie" (1 Pet. v, 4). With this delicate manipulation of imagery, Milton follows and enriches the popular tradition of figural exegesis, a tradition carried to its height in works such as Thomas Hayne's *General View of the Holy Scriptures*. Comparing Christ with Adam, Hayne comes to a crisp conclusion: "Adam: was debarred of the Tree of Life; Christ *is* the true Tree of Life." Later, he declares that "Noah is another Adam" — but with a crucial distinction: "Adam: Had the Tree of Life in Paradise, for a seale of *conservation;* Noah: Had a rainbow as a covenant of *preservation.*"[13]

Conservation to preservation, preservation to regeneration: in Book IV of *Paradise Lost*, the seeds of both the Fall and the new covenant germinate in the imagery with which Milton describes Adam and Eve's "blissful bower" in Paradise,

> a place
> Chos'n by the sovran Planter, when he fram'd
> All things to man's delightful use.   (IV, 690–92)

The bower symbolizes Adam and Eve's mutual love, a love Adam describes as "the Crown of all our bliss" (IV, 728) and attributes to the pure and infinite goodness of God. Yet purity is not a quality of the "shady Lodge" that shelters Adam and Eve. The bower filters the pure rays of the sun through a voluptuous "mosaic" of "Flowers, Garlands, and sweet-smelling Herbs" and a roof of "thickest covert" and "inwoven shade" (720, 700, 709, 693). Moreover, roses rear "high thir flourisht heads" between its verdant walls (698–99), parodying the colorless Amaranth which "flow'rs aloft" in Heaven. Finally, within the bower, Adam and Eve

> lull'd by Nightingales imbracing slept,
> And on thir naked limbs the flow'ry roof
> Show'r'd Roses, which the Morn repair'd.   (IV, 771–73)

This showering descent of roses is a visual echo of the symbolic gesture performed before the throne of God in Book III, and therefore prefigures both the Fall and the "Morn" that will "repair" man's spirit — the morning of Christ's nativity. But the promise of redemption woven into this figural tapestry is not put into relief until Milton has laid a seductive backdrop for Eve's fall.

Eve is a rose, "with perfect beauty adorn'd" (IV, 634), for as Henry Hawkins explains in his *Partheneia Sacra*, the rose is an emblem that can effectively represent only Eve or the Virgin Mary: "The Rose is the Imperial Queene of Flowers, which al doe homage to, as to their Princesse, she being the glorie and delight of that Monarchie. . . . It is the chiefest grace of spouses on their Nuptial dayes, and the Bride wil as soone forget her fillet as her *Rose*. . . . In a word, the *Rose* for beautie is a *Rose*, for sweetnes a *Rose*, and for al the graces possible in flowers, a *verie Rose*; the quintessence of beautie, sweets, and graces, al at once, and al as epitomized in the name of ROSE."[14] Eve is the touchstone of beauty in Paradise just as the rose is superlative among flowers. Unfortunately, "thornie Eva" (as Hawkins terms her) forfeits her right to association with the emblem when she heeds Satan's cozening words:

> I turn'd my thoughts, and with capacious mind
> Consider'd all things visible in Heav'n,
> Or Earth, or Middle, all things fair and good;
> But all that fair and good in thy Divine
> Semblance, and in *thy Beauty's heavenly Ray*
> United I beheld.   (IX, 603–08; italics mine)

Aspiring to Godhead, Eve envisions her own beauty as the pure ray of God's light. Lifting her veil of innocence, however, she finds not God's white radiance, but the dark cast of shame. "Defac't, deflow'r'd, and . . . to Death devote," Eve is unable to see "those heav'nly shapes," which "dazzle now this earthly, with thir blaze / Insufferably bright" (IX, 901, 1082–84).

The scene of Eve's temptation and fall captures her at the peak of her beauty, surrounded and figuratively crowned by a blaze of vivid, glowing color. She stands

> Veil'd in a Cloud of Fragrance . . .
> Half spi'd, so thick the Roses bushing round
> About her glow'd.   (IX, 425–27)

"Half spi'd" and enveloped by "thick-wov'n Arborets and Flow'rs" (IX, 437), Eve prefigures the "wat'ry Cloud" bound by the "flow'ry verge" of the rainbow given as a symbol of covenant to Noah. But Eve in her original innocence is not bound by an indissoluble covenant: she is the "fairest unsupported Flow'r" (IX, 432) among the garland of colorful blossoms she upstays "with Myrtle band" (431), and her "Flow'ry Plat" (456) cannot protect her spiritual purity.[15] As Adam sadly learns in Book XI,

> God áttributes to place
> No sanctity, if none be thither brought
> By Men who there frequent, or therein dwell.   (836–38)

In her "Spring of Roses intermixt / With Myrtle" (IX, 218–19), Eve tragically finds "what to redress," casting away her veil of innocence for the "vain Covering" of mortality (IX, 1113). For Karl Wentersdorf, the rose and the myrtle, because of their association with Venus, symbolize "the moral dangers implied in [Eve's] work plan," dangers to which she readily succumbs without the guidance of Adam.[16] Milton concentrates the impact of her fall in a parodic reenactment of the divine drama in Heaven. Again, the motif of the garland-crown is central; but instead of calling up man's spiritual aspirations, it symbolizes Adam's uxoriousness. Waiting impatiently for Eve's return from her divided labors, he weaves

> Of choicest Flow'rs a Garland to adorn
> Her Tresses, and her rural labors crown.   (IX, 840–41)

Discovering the "fatal Trespass" (889), he

> Astonied stood and Blank, while horror chill
> Ran through his veins, and all his joints relax'd;
> From his slack hand the Garland wreath'd for *Eve*
> Down dropp'd, and all the faded Roses shed.   (890–93)

Before Milton redirects his imagery "Up to a better Cov'nant," he uses it to reveal the tragedy of Eve's apostasy and its implications for mankind.

But as both Patrides and Christopher have observed, the story of Adam and Eve as it is presented in *Paradise Lost* "adumbrates the whole course of salvation history."[17] Woven into the symbolic fabric of Adam and Eve's "blissful bower" are means of regreening the garland of faded roses, and of affirming God's willingness to "intermix" his covenant "in the woman's seed renew'd" (XI, 115–16). Indeed, in the larger figural context of *Paradise Lost*, the myrtle that binds Eve's drooping flower children evolves, like the Amaranth before it, into a symbol of God's silent covenant with man, a mild restraint on the graceful but overreaching flower in his spiritual garden. Satan, then, is not as clever as he thinks when he leads Eve "Beyond a row of Myrtles" to taste of the Tree of Life (IX, 627). The myrtle is an evergreen, and as an eighteenth-century emblem book explains, an "Emblem of real worth, whose gloomiest hour / Transcends the blaze of pomp, excels the pride of pow'r"; for it "disperses a sweet fragrance round about it, and though it produces no various coloured flowers to glitter in the sunbeams, yet it always preserves Nature's own hue, and flourishing an ever-green through the year, is admired for its constancy."[18] In Greek folklore, that "constancy" is magnified into immortality and the promise of resurrection.[19] In the Old Testament, the myrtle signifies the promise and bounty of God, who plants it in the wilderness for the children of Israel (Isa. xli, 19). And in traditional figural exegesis, it symbolizes and prefigures Christ's resurrection (and man's spiritual redemption), as Calvin illustrates in his 1609 commentary on this prophetic passage from Isaiah 55: "For thornes, there shall grow firre trees: for nettles, shall grow the mirrhe tree; and it shall bee to the Lord for a name, and for an everlasting signe that shall not bee taken away." Contending that "these things indeed appertaine to Christs kingdome, and therefore ought to be spiritually understood," Calvin reads the verse as a firm declaration of "our redemption," for Christ "therewithall takes away whatsoever thing might hurt or hinder the same: nay, he turnes it wholly the contrarie way, that out of every evil we might draw some good."[20] In *Paradise Lost*, Christ is the "better coloring" of the rose and the sturdier fiber of the myrtle with which it is bound.

Still another symbol of renewal interlaces the verdant walls of Adam and Eve's shelter. On the one hand, the "*Iris* all hues" (IV, 698) foreshadows the Fall, resonating against the "Tents of various hue" inhabited by the "Bevy of fair Women" who tempt and deceive Lamech's sons in Book XI (556 ff). Yet in the larger figural context of the poem it anticipates the covenant of grace and the advent of Christ, for it is interwoven, like the myrtle, with the rose, and as Henry Hawkins suggests, is a type of the radiant and refulgent *Bow of Heaven* . . . the Triumphal Arch of the heavenlie *Numens*. . . . And for the *Camelion* of the ayre, she doubtles used no other pattern then it, to coppie forth the great varietie of coulours she assumes. This prodigie of Nature . . . is indeed the faire and goodlie mirrour of the heavenlie Intelligences themselves. . . . If the Angels would lay aside their wings, and goe afoot, I doe not think, they could have a better way to descend by, and ascend again, then by this Causway, passed al with jewels heer and there, and where not, al strewed with tapistries; the Turkie ones are nothing like; nor those of Barbarie come neere them; while those the mothes wil eate, and time destroy their coulours, and fade; but these, wil last til al be quite worne out.[21]

By the conclusion of *Paradise Lost,* Milton's iris imagery has come full circle, blossoming from the "shadowy Type" of "Iris all hues" into the semicircular "Causway" of covenant, Noah's rainbow. The rainbow, in turn, is a type of the superlative crown of glory whose colors time cannot destroy — the new, unfading immortality that every just man will wear when Christ descends again. As Milton makes even more explicit in his *Ode on the Morning of Christ's Nativity,*

> Yea, Truth and Justice then
> Will down return to men,
>   Th'enameled *Arras* of the Rainbow wearing,
> And Mercy set between,
> Thron'd in Celestial sheen,
>   With radiant feet the tissued clouds down steering.   (141–46)

As the arch-typologist Samuel Mather confirms (citing Isaiah liv, 9 and Revelation x, 1 as proof), Noah's rainbow is more than an emblematic fleshing-out of the iris: it prefigures "Christ the Angel of the Covenant," who "is described, as having a *Rainbow upon his Head*."[22] It is a type of the regenerative garland-crown of "Celestial Roses" described in Book III of *Paradise Lost,* for like the Amaranth that binds the "resplendent locks" of God's angelic host, the "color'd streaks" of the rainbow symbolically bind God's distended brow, "Lest it again dissolve and show'r the Earth" (XI, 879, 883). Witness Michael's injunction to Adam in Book XI of *Paradise Lost:*

> Yet doubt not but in Valley and in Plain
> God is as here, and will be found alike
> Present, and of his presence many a sign
> Still following thee, *still compassing thee round*
> With goodness and paternal Love, his Face
> Express, and of his steps the track Divine. (349–54; italics mine)

Michael himself arrives in a blaze of glory that prefigures Christ's Incarnation and schools Adam in the language and imagery of accommodation. Observing the angel's descent, Adam wonders

> why in the East
> Darkness ere Day's mid-course, and Morning light
> More orient in yon Western Cloud that draws
> O'er the blue Firmament a radiant white,
> And slow descends, with something heav'nly fraught. (XI, 203–07)

As "the heav'nly Bands" of Michael's immaculate train emerge from "a Sky of Jasper," Adam discovers that "carnal fear" has "dimm'd" his eye, and that his vision (like Eve's before him) is obscured to the "pure Ethereal stream" of God's "Eternal coeternal beam" (XI, 208–12; III, 2, 7). Therefore Michael approaches Adam

> Not in his shape Celestial, but as Man
> Clad to meet Man; over his lucid Arms
> A military Vest of purple flow'd
> Livelier than *Melibaean*, or the grain
> Of *Sarra*, worn by Kings and Heroes old
> In time of truce; *Iris* had dipt the woof.   (XI, 239–44)

It is no accident that Michael's rainbow raiment borrows its emblematic significance from the iris, or that Adam later describes Noah's rainbow as a "flow'ry verge," "Conspicuous with three listed colors gay, / Betok'ning peace from God, and Cov'nant new" (XI, 881, 866–67). As the first interpreter of God's word, Adam has learned to discipline his fallen vision "Up to a better Cov'nant." As Adam's heirs, we, too, are encouraged to become creative exegetes: Milton's masterful transformations of the archetypal symbol of immortality, Revelation's "crowne of life," celebrate the internal scripture of the human spirit, where the "divine drama" of Christ's Passion and resurrection can find eternal expression.

University of Alabama, Huntsville

NOTES

1. *Complete Prose Works of John Milton*, ed. Don M. Wolfe et al. (New Haven, 1953–82), vol. vi, p. 352.

2. All citations of Milton's poetry are from *Complete Poems and Major Prose*, ed. Merritt Y. Hughes (Indianapolis, 1957).

3. C. A. Patrides, *Milton and the Christian Tradition* (Hamden, Conn., 1977),

p. 130. Among other critics who have examined Milton's response to figural tradition are William S. Madsen, *From Shadowy Types to Truth: Studies in Milton's Symbolism* (New Haven, 1965); Barbara K. Lewalski, *Milton's Brief Epic: The Genre, Meaning, and Art of "Paradise Regained"* (Providence, R.I., 1966); and Georgia B. Christopher, *Milton and the Science of the Saints* (Princeton, 1982).

4. The "covenant of grace" is discussed in Book I of Milton's *Christian Doctrine.* For evidence of the figural value attributed to Revelation's "crowne of life," see Psalm xxi, 3: "For thou didest prevent him with liberal blessings, & didest set a crowne of pure golde upon his head." The Geneva Bible glosses this psalm typologically, anticipating Milton's transformation of his celestial crowns into eschatological symbols: "David in the persone of the people praiseth God for the victorie, attributing it to God and not to the strength of man. Where in the holie Gost directeth the faithful to Christ who is the perfection of the kingdome." (Unless otherwise indicated, all biblical quotations are from the Geneva Bible.)

5. Madsen, *From Shadowy Types*, p. 99.

6. Hans W. Frei, *The Eclipse of Biblical Narrative: A Study in Eighteenth and Nineteenth Century Hermeneutics* (New Haven, 1974), p. 172.

7. Christopher, *Science of the Saints*, pp. 142–43.

8. Roland M. Frye, *Milton's Imagery and the Visual Arts: Iconographic Tradition in the Epic Poem* (Princeton, 1978), p. 186. Frye insists that we appreciate the Amaranth as a real flower "famous, among gardeners as well as theologians, for its remarkably long life" and "the persistence of its blossoms" — qualities that enhance its symbolic significance in Milton's Heaven.

9. Don Cameron Allen, *The Harmonious Vision: Studies in Milton's Poetry* (Baltimore, 1954), pp. 98–99, and "Milton's Amarant," *MLN*, LXXII (April 1957), 256–58.

10. William Parks, *The Rose and the Lily* (London, 1639), p. 14. The Amaranth was known to Milton's contemporaries as "love-lies-bleeding," its purplish color suggesting both eros and immortality. See Karl P. Wentersdorf, "The Thematic Significance of the Flower Catalogue in Milton's *Lycidas*," *ELH*, XLVII (Fall 1980), 509–10.

11. Jonathan Edwards, *Images or Shadows of Divine Things*, ed. Perry Miller (New Haven, 1948), p. 43.

12. Allen, *Harmonious Vision*, 96.

13. Thomas Hayne, *The General View of the Holy Scriptures: or, The Times, Places, and Persons of the Holy Scriptures*, 2d ed. (London, 1640), pp. 28, 60. The distinction between conservation and preservation is subtle but important: Adam's amelioration necessitates the "conservation" or proper use of spiritual resources inherent in his nature. Noah, as one of Adam's descendants, must depend on God's grace to help him preserve the vestiges of truth his race has not yet forfeited.

14. Henry Hawkins, *Partheneia Sacra, or the Mysterious and Delicious Garden of the Sacred Parthenes*, ed. John Horden (1633; facsimile rpt. Menston, Yorkshire, 1971), pp. 17–18.

15. Both the *OED* and Merritt Hughes gloss "plat" as "plot"; but a "plat" can also be "a contexture of interlaced hair, straw, etc.," or a plait (*OED*). This meaning accords nicely with the interlaced garland imagery that runs throughout the scene of Eve's temptation.

16. Karl P. Wentersdorf, "*Paradise Lost* IX: The Garden and the Flowered Couch," *MQ*, XIII (1979), 136.

17. Christopher, *Science of the Saints*, p. 146. See also Patrides, *Premises and Motifs in Renaissance Thought and Literature* (Princeton, 1982), pp. 99–101.

18. [John H. Wynne], *Choice Emblems, Natural, Historical, Fabulous, Moral and Divine, for the Improvement and Pastime of Youth* (London, 1772), pp. 181–82.

19. See *Funk and Wagnalls Standard Dictionary of Folklore, Mythology, and Legend*, ed. Maria Leach (New York, 1972), p. 776. The myrtle is an appropriate symbol of the new dispensation: in popular figural exegesis, Adam was allowed to take it with him when he left Eden, where it was the chief scented tree.

20. John Calvin, *A Commentary Upon the Prophecies of Isaiah*, trans. Clement Cotton (London, 1609), p. 575. This rendering of Isaiah lv, 13 is Calvin's, and differs in spelling and punctuation from the 1583 Geneva Bible.

21. Hawkins, *Partheneia Sacra*, pp. 92–93. In Christian iconography, the iris is also a symbol of the Virgin Mary. See Wentersdorf, "*Paradise Lost* IX," p. 135.

22. Samuel Mather, *The Figures and Types of the Old Testament*, 2d ed., 1705 (New York, 1969), p. 27.

"MANY *MILTONS* IN THIS ONE MAN": MARVELL'S MOWER POEMS AND *PARADISE LOST*

Carol Gilbertson

G EOFFREY HARTMAN writes that in the Mower sequence of *Upon Appleton House*, the mower — who inadvertently "massacre[s]" a bird along with the grass — "discovers that 'All flesh is grass' by moving through its converse, 'All grass is flesh.'"[1] Marvell's quick mind apparently delighted in such literalization of borrowed image, which Hartman calls the "proleptic use of metaphor." In the Mower poems Marvell extends the implications of the *Appleton House* literalization: if all grass is flesh, the Mower metaphorically mows down flesh when he performs his daily chore; when, distracted by rejected love, he slashes his own ankle with his scythe, he literally cuts down flesh as well. Elaine Hoffman Baruch refers to a quotation from Marvell's contemporary Samuel Pecke (1659) — "Time devours Things; his Sithe our Legs will hit" — and then comments on Marvell's literalization of the same traditional metaphor: "The mower's scythe literally hits Damon in the leg. Trope becomes reality."[2] In fact, not only does Marvell's Mower act out Death's role, but he also consciously identifies with that personified figure when he contemplates his wound and reminds himself that "Death thou art a Mower too" (*Damon*, 88).[3]

E. W. Tayler, carefully avoiding the simple equations of allegory, argues that in the Mower poems the "organization of the action and the relationship of the Mower to Nature are in themselves expressive of the Fall," and the "reader has been led to consider a pastoral love complaint in relation to an event in scriptural history."[4] In other words, besides literalizing particular conventional metaphors, the Mower poems "literalize" the general notion of the Fall. The Mower — a Marvellian substitute for the traditional contemplative shepherd of pastoral — iconically acts out the scriptural event of the Fall in his language, his self-destructive mowing, and his realization of a lost harmony between nature and mind. This pervasive suggestion of the Fall (apparent although Marvell "does not even use terms ambiguously suggestive of scriptural events"[5]) rises partly from the general subtext of Scripture and from some of Marvell's

151

many other sources, but it gains special resonance from his debts to the great Christian literary work of his time: John Milton's *Paradise Lost.* By literalizing the epic's metaphors, reenacting its pastoral similes, and echoing its language, Marvell's Mower poems recall its psychological situations and explore its theological issues, and the Mower Damon, while both a realistic rustic and a conventional pastoral figure, is also an icon of Death and a type of fallen human. Like Milton's Satan (as a precursor of fallen human) he longs for a lost wholeness, and like Adam and Eve he brings on his own fall and wanders lost in a wilderness of sin.[6]

II

Many readers of Marvell's poems assume Milton in the background as a powerful contemporary who shared with Marvell the pastoral and Christian heritage of the Renaissance. Some critics have briefly discussed the more specific influence of Milton's 1645 *Poems* on Marvell's lyrics, and some connections between their prose works are obvious. Recent studies argue an even closer literary and political relationship between them.[7] But no one has considered the interesting possibility that in the Mower poems Marvell is deeply indebted to Milton's ambitious epic.

Accepting this influence involves revising the traditional conjectures about the composition dates of both poets' poems. Many scholars have argued that Marvell wrote most of his lyric poems in 1650–53, during his stay at the Fairfax estate, even though they were not published until the posthumous folio in 1681. *Paradise Lost* was first published in 1667, though critics have generally assumed that Milton began composing his epic around 1660.

But much scholarship already questions the assumption that Marvell wrote all his lyric poetry in this early period. Most critics now agree that *The Garden* and *The Mower against Gardens* present literary gardens rather than real descriptions of the Fairfax estate. Some critics question the division of Marvell's writing career into two chronological phases — lyrical and political — and some of these argue that many of the lyric poems could well have been composed in the later 1650s and even 1660s.[8]

Exactly when Milton wrote *Paradise Lost* is just as controversial. J. Milton French calls the dating of the epic "a sea of uncertainties and arguments." John Aubrey says Milton had finished writing the epic in 1663, and we know that the poet gave what was probably a complete manuscript to Thomas Ellwood in 1665. Most of the early biographers imply that the project took Milton many years, a theory which Allan H. Gilbert's modern study corroborates. Both the earliest, anonymous biographer and Anthony à Wood suggest that Milton began composition around 1655. Milton's nephew Edward Phillips, who says he "had the perusal of [the epic] from the very beginning," mentions that the parcels of poetry he saw were "Written by whatever hand came next," suggesting that Milton had dictated the lines, which often needed "Correction as to the Orthography and Pointing." French thinks that some particular lines Phillips says he saw could have been composed as early as 1642, the same year Milton first wrote of his plans for an important literary project.[9] In 1940 Grant McColley argued convincingly that Milton probably began the epic in earnest as early as 1652–53, after his blindness had become nearly total but before he had hired a regular amanuensis in 1657 (thus Phillips's "whatever hand came next") and when he had a brief respite from pamphlet writing and official obligations (between 1651 and 1654). More recently, John T. Shawcross has concluded that "intermittent composition seems probable from 1640 through around 1655, with more undivided attention paid to the poem from around 1655–1658 and 1661 through 1665." It is even possible that Marvell transcribed some of the lines dictated by the blind poet, since Milton's 1652/3 letter to Bradshaw recommending Marvell for political appointment presupposes an established relationship that we know developed into a long-standing friendship.[10]

Milton valued Marvell's opinion of *Paradise Lost* enough to have him write the commendatory poem for its 1674 edition. It is generally assumed that Marvell composed *On Mr. Milton's "Paradise lost"* some time after the publication of the first edition in 1667, and that the opening lines refer to Marvell's first reading of the epic in that form. But these lines could just as plausibly be describing Milton in the early 1650s after his blindness, showing Marvell his "Design" for a future poem or some early drafts, so that the "slender Book" would refer to Milton's early plans for a tragedy, his outline for the poem, or even a few completed books, rather than the first edition. Marvell's language suggests a long acquaintance with the poem from the beginning, in snatches or in stages (cf. Phillips's reference to parcels of "Ten, Twenty, or Thirty Verses at a Time"):[11] Marvell structures lines 1–30 as his sequential reaction to the poem, the language suggesting an incomplete work ("Design," "Argument," "Intent," "Project"), and uses the conditional future tense ("would ruine," "should find," "would explain") when he speaks of his earlier fears about Milton's possible failure. Marvell writes that in the end, when he saw the whole poem (which could have been some time before 1667), he was finally able to proclaim it an overwhelming success, the "Majesty" of Milton's completed work.

My suggestions for re-dating could be argued in much more detail. Here I want only to assume the reasonable possibility that Marvell listened to Milton recite parts of his epic, or that he read it in manuscript (or even in its first edition) before or while he wrote the Mower poems. The other possibility, that the blind Milton heard Marvell's Mower poems while working on his epic, seems a less likely explanation for the connections I discuss below, since Marvell's poems do not appear to have circulated much in manuscript before their 1681 publication.[12] Even if Marvell had read Milton his poems — as their relationship certainly would allow — it seems more likely that the younger and lesser known poet and political figure would be influenced by the older, more respected poet and public figure rather than vice versa.

Marvell is perhaps the best known borrower and synthesizer of all Renaissance lyric poets. While Milton completely assimilates his sources, Marvell is notorious for transforming ideas, tropes, and language from his predecessors and contemporaries in strikingly original ways. Because such debts are difficult to establish, critics have often argued only for specific verbal echoes. B. Rajan, in introducing *The Presence of Milton*, warns against searching for the Miltonic presence only in such "verbal remembrance," which is "too often treated as local rather than contextual, as emulation diminishing into mimicry."[13] Though Marvell's poems contain some striking verbal echoes of Milton, they are always part of a larger contextual indebtedness. Mnay of the borrowings have a particularly visual dimension: Milton's picture of the fallen world stretches across these poems as backdrop, and Marvell's mental eye catches and holds Milton's momentary images of fallen humankind.

III

Milton's Adam and Eve are portrayed as pastoral reapers whose divinely appointed daily task includes to "Lop" and "prune," "to tend Plant, Herb, and Flow'r" (IX, 210, 206), and to reap nature's resulting bounty (V, 318–401).[14] Their job is to hold back the teeming "Luxuriant" growth (IV, 260; this is the Mower's word for the rich spring growth he resents in *The Mower's Song*), which is also called "Luxurious" growth (IX, 209, the same word the Mower uses earlier to condemn human artifice in *The Mower against Gardens*). When Adam awaits Eve's return from her morning work, unaware of the cosmic result of her fruit-picking, he weaves a floral garland

> to adorn
> Her tresses, and her rural labors crown,
> As reapers oft are wont thir Harvest Queen.   (IX, 840–42)

The simile both glorifies Adam's simple celebratory action and diminishes Adam and Eve to rustic peasants, to "uncouth Swain" (*Lycidas* 186) and country maid. Through this elevation and diminution, the simile universalizes Adam and Eve and their actions: Adam celebrating Eve's "rural labors" is like a Damon presenting gifts to Juliana.[15]

Milton's pastoral similes cumulatively glow in the reader's mind as a small world, set apart from the narrative and yet forming an essential part of the poem's cosmic world. Anachronistic excursions into classical and contemporary rustic life, these similes both contract and expand the central story's cosmic dimensions, some creating ominous overtones in the context of the Fall, which occurs in the most nearly perfect pastoral world. When these pastoral similes are recalled collectively, Adam and Eve can be seen as part of the pastoral world inhabited by the "reapers" (IX, 842), the "belated Peasant" (I, 783), "th'amaz'd Night-wanderer" (IX, 640), and the "Laborer" (XII, 631–32). Geoffrey Hartman discusses Milton's similes as a central part of Milton's "counterplot" — Milton's intention to show "God's foreknowledge of the creation's triumph," his "omnipotent" and "divine imperturbability" despite the errors of "man's free will." Several of the similes show a pastoral figure as pensive observer, "reflecting a mind balanced on the critical pivot": in *Paradise Lost* the "center around which and to which all actions turn is whether man can stand though free to fall, whether man and the world can survive their autonomy."[16]

Tayler's central argument about the Mower poems is that "Marvell sees the Fall primarily as a change that occurred in the mind of man, . . . in the way man looks at or thinks about Nature"; the Mower is thus a pivotal figure similar to those Hartman discusses in Milton's similes — a fallen human with a "'double . . . Mind', one that possesses both the Mower's capacity for the harmony of the 'true survey' and the alienation of the 'bloody . . . stroke'; for Innocence and Vice; for Nature and Art."[17] Since mowing is a human act of shaping nature, the creation of an artifice which in this case becomes inadvertently self-destructive, the Mower emblematically represents what Christian writers have seen as the central earthly paradox — the unknowable limits on the seemingly unlimited human imagination. It is precisely that uncertainty about limits that Milton's Serpent exploits in persuading Eve to pick and eat the fruit; Adam's identification with her causes him to mirror that act. Just as Marvell's self-mown Mower cuts down flesh as he harvests his crop, Milton's Adam and Eve bring death to the world as they harvest the Garden's fruit. In both cases the fallen imagination includes self-delusion.

In making his central figure a mower rather than a reaper or pruner like Adam and Eve, Marvell makes more explicit and emblematic the potentially destructive relationship of fallen humans to nature. Both poets share a central metaphor, which represents fallen human nature through deluded love, seen in Adam and Eve's lustful mistrust after the Fall and in Damon's imagined Juliana and her love: obsessive desire, blindness to the beloved's true appearance and reality, frustrated sexuality, and painful loss. But Marvell's Mower is an unrequited lover who is both dignified and comic in his attempts to impress. The wit of these short lyrics, along with their sometimes oafish protagonist, distance them from Milton's long epic, which — despite lighter moments — is a mostly earnest portrayal of spiritual chasms and heights. But George M. Puttenham emphasized the serious purpose of even crude pastoral: "vnder the vaile of homely persons, and in rude speeches to insinuate and glaunce at greater matters." And Marvell himself argues that he often writes "betwixt jest and earnest":[18] the Mower poems play out a religious myth in the simple life of a realistic rural character, much as the Second Shepherds' Play comically reenacts the Nativity. The blundering Mower is nearly laughable but mostly sympathetic; he is also an iconic figure who enacts in a limited, rural realm the psychological and moral tensions of the entire mortal world, much as do the rustic figures of Milton's pastoral similes. In fact, the Mower seriocomically reenacts the postlapsarian scenes prophesied in these similes, many of which focus on sin's effects on the human mind: self-deception, delusion, and narcissism.

IV

Though the echoes of *Paradise Lost* are much sharper in the other three Mower poems, *The Mower against Gardens* contains some notable parallels with Milton's epic. (I consider the poems here in their folio order.) If he is borrowing from Milton in *The Mower against Gardens*, Marvell seems to be toying with the kind of "random" allusion Tayler sees in many of Marvell's pastoral poems, rather than making any consistent reference;[19] his attitude toward the Mower as supposed innocent is not as clear as in the other Mower poems, since here the Mower condemns the world for its hubristic tampering, and later the Mower's hubris destroys him.

The Mower's abhorrence of the Gardener's horticultural concoctions has precedent in Milton's description of Eden as a place which "nice Art" has not touched (IV, 239–43) and in Michael's denunciation of the human "Arts" that hubristically "polish life" (XI, 609–12). The Mower's condemnation of society's gardens is a catalogue of scriptural and pastoral prohibitions, many also referred to in *Paradise Lost*, including *luxuria*, the squaring of nature, and the mingling of kinds. The Mower argues that the "Forbidden mixtures" in the garden produce "uncertain and adult'rate fruit" which "Might put the Palate in dispute" (22, 25–26). In *Paradise Lost,* unfallen Eve plans her menu for Raphael "so contriv'd as not to mix / Tastes" (V, 334–35); later Milton plays on the literal and figurative meanings of *taste:* lustful fallen Adam looks at Eve and calls her "now . . . exact of taste," "Since to each meaning savor we apply, / And Palate call judicious" (IX, 1017, 1019–20). The Mower's description of the "sweet Fields" where "The *Gods* themselves with us do dwell" (40) echoes Milton's description of the pristine Earth before the creation of humans, which "Seem'd like to Heav'n, a seat where Gods might dwell" (VII, 329; cf. Eden as the "Fit haunt of Gods," XI, 271).

In Milton's simile describing Satan's first view of Eve, the Archfiend, who dwells in the artificial city of Pandemonium, is reduced to a stifled urbanite encountering the fresh countryside, which in the narrative is the Garden of Eden (IX, 445–54). Marvell reverses the scene: rather than the experienced city-dweller meeting the virgin nymph, the Mower is the innocent shocked by his encounter with metaphorical fallen women, nature's flowers, which have become the painted floral harlots of the domesticated garden. The seduction of virgin flowers as a metaphor of the Fall has iconographic parallels in *Paradise Lost.* Satan sees Eve as the "fairest unsupported Flow'r" (IX, 432), which exudes "graceful Innocence" (IX, 459; the Mower's rural nature dispenses "A wild and fragrant Innocence," 33–34). Adam refers to fallen Eve as a corrupted flower: "Defac't, deflow'r'd, and now to Death devote" (IX, 901).[20]

Satan's and the Mower's situations are certainly not identical, yet they have similar ironic dimensions. Satan-Serpent is hardly the casually touring city-dweller of the simile, delighting in the innocence of a country nymph: though he is taken with Eve's purity, we have already been told that his real pleasure is that he has found Eve alone and therefore vulnerable (IX, 421–24, 457). Dean R. Baldwin points out that Marvell's pun in "Mower," which also means "One who makes mouths; a jester, a mocker" (*OED*), helps to determine our ironic interpretation of the Mower's argument.[21] Since by definition a mower must alter nature to earn his livelihood, the Mower's simplistic and self-righteous judgment of other humans who manipulate nature rings false.

V

In Marvell's second Mower poem, *Damon the Mower,* this character's self-confident railing of the previous poem is gone, since his supposedly innocent paradisal world has been replaced by its cruel parody; his beloved Juliana has rejected him, and Damon now sees only scorching summer and parched fields. Here he sings a traditional pastoral complaint mourning the misery that unrequited love brings, a misery nostalgically contrasted with the Edenic Golden Age gone by, when nature (without human love) was without tension.

Now Damon is more clearly the image of the fallen human who lives in self-delusion. Blinded by the self-importance love brings, Damon places himself, as do Milton's angels, at the center of a universe in which he is only a small, insignificant part. He parades his oddly inappropriate gifts to Juliana, glorifies his former status as a darling of nature, boasts of his wealth as a mower, and praises his physical appearance. His defensive self-glorification further corroborates the self-delusion that the speaker of the frame poem has already pointed to when he said that the external world only "*seem[ed]* to paint / The Scene more fit for his complaint" (3–4; emphasis mine).

That self-delusion is imagistically portrayed here in Damon's boast about the distorted self-reflection he sees in the curved mirror of his scythe. Marvell has deftly altered the pastoral convention of self-admiration in having Damon use the tool of his trade as his mirror. Damon literally sees himself "through a glass, darkly";[22] not only must he look at the distorting curved metal in just the "right" way, but the scythe renders him not his reflection, but his "Picture done" (58–59). Fallen human looks into his own crooked tool — the instrument with which he carries out sin's curse of labor, the bends and curves of his distorting postlapsarian imagination — in order to see and proudly judge himself fit, beautiful, and righteous.

Damon's portrayal of himself as the fairies' honoree (61–64) has a visual source in Milton's simile in Book I comparing the fallen angels to "Faery Elves" observed by a Peasant. Milton portrays the near comic disparity between the self-proclaimed grandeur and the progressively less grand description of the fallen angels, who are the epic's imagistic precursors of fallen humans; Marvell shows the comic distance between the boasts of Damon, who is archetypal fallen human, and his pathetic revealed self. At the end of a chain of similes to describe the visual effect of the apparent diminution of the formerly grand angels, Milton finally compares them to

> Faery Elves,
> Whose midnight Revels, by a Forest side
> Or Fountain some belated Peasant sees,
> Or dreams he sees, while over-head the Moon
> Sits Arbitress, and nearer to the Earth

> Wheels her pale course; they on thir mirth and dance
> Intent, with jocund Music charm his ear;
> At once with joy and fear his heart rebounds.   (I, 781–88)

Though "in thir own dimensions" the fallen angels see themselves as "A thousand Demi-Gods," they in perspective seem more like "smallest forms" (793, 796, 789), hordes of diminutive dwarfs or pygmies. As if to collapse our cosmic perspective, the simile reduces them to a band of tiny fairy elves observed from human height by an ordinary peasant; then suddenly, by pulling back so that we can view the moon wheeling overhead, Milton again enlarges the scene to cosmic dimensions, diminishing the self-aggrandizing angels to charming little supernatural playthings. Yet not quite. Milton wants to diminish the angels but not to erase completely their dramatic potential, or to forget their evil power. The human peasant feels both "joy and fear." Like the simultaneously powerful and impotent fallen angels, fairies in English folk tradition were both terrifying and enchanting supernatural beings who influenced mortals' affairs for good or evil.[23]

In his discussion of this simile as part of Milton's "counterplot," Hartman argues that the focus shifts from the elves to the Peasant as observer, representing "the individual's naive and autonomous power of discrimination." The wheeling moon "Sits Arbitress," the image of what Hartman calls an "uncertain" and "changeable," but also "imperturbably transcendant discrimination," watching the delusion of a mortal by diminutive yet insidious immortals, watching what can also be seen as self-delusion, with the fairies as products of a hopeful imagination.[24]

In *Damon* Marvell has recreated Milton's scene with his own peasant-observer. Damon proudly croons:

> The deathless Fairyes take me oft
> To lead them in their Danses soft;
> And, when I tune my self to sing,
> About me they contract their Ring.   (61–64)

Here too, the rustic observer is deluded and charmed, and nature is arbiter between the human being and his thoughts; the Mower will eventually come to see his self-delusion through the changes in the natural world, a distorted vision evident when he compares his face reflected in his scythe to the thin new moon's reflection of the sun's brilliant sphere. Just as in Milton's simile, the reality of nature sits outside Damon's created scene of himself and his adoring fairies, not judging but pulling him toward his eventual realization of the terrifying power of the human imagination. Both the Peasant's emotions ("joy and fear") are implicitly

Damon's too: he is boasting of his former joy in his communion with nature, yet the "deathless" fairies contracting their ring sound more like captors moving in on their potential prisoner than like celebratory playmates.[25]

Hartman cites another simile as part of the counterplot, the image of the "careful Plowman," who "doubting stands / Lest on the threshing floor his hopeful sheaves / Prove chaff" (IV, 983–85), which occurs when the "Angelic Squadron" captures Satan squatting "like a Toad" at Eve's ear (IV, 977, 800). The Plowman is another fallen human, like the earlier Peasant an observer whose internal conflict makes us question the reliability of human thought: the Plowman doubts even as he hopes for his harvest. The real dramatic conflict of the simile, as of the epic, lies in the human mind:

The fate of the world lies between Gabriel and Satan, but also between the wind and the ripe ears, but also between man and his thoughts.[26]

The "mooned horns" which the angels sharpen (IV, 978) appear at first to refer to their spears and then are compared to bending ears of wheat. Like Damon's scythe, which cuts down the grass, these spears can either destroy or reap the grain. Human thoughts can be either spear or shield, chaff or harvest, destruction or creation.

Damon's language suggests this paradox. Because he complains as he mows, the imaginative act is linked with the act of mowing, "Joyning [his] Labour to [his] Pain" (68). His scythe is sharp like his sorrow (7), and as he scythes, he sighs and sings (67–72).[27] His scythe produces the hay crop and, he claims, "discovers" the ground it mows (51–52) and later creates a "Heraldry" of grass (*Song*, 27), but at the same time destroys the blades of grass ("Depopulating all the Ground," 74) and mows Damon down. So his mowing (moaning) and scything (sighing) are linked with the creative or destructive human imagination. He is the Mower and the grass: as he thinks, he mows, and vice versa; so as he mows (discovers, complains, sighs) the grass (flesh, self), he creates his fallen vision of himself and his love, while simultaneously destroying his own flesh.[28]

The Fall in Milton is circular: the disobedience, a conscious act of pride, causes the knowledge, itself sinful and in turn engendering pride. Humans are their own destruction. The circularity of sin — the confusion of tempter and tempted, destroyer and destroyed — resounds through Milton's epic. The fallen angels "enthrall themselves" (III, 125), "Self-tempted, self-deprav'd" (III, 130). Satan "like a devilish Engine back recoils / Upon himself" (IV, 17–18). Adam sees that "all from mee / Shall with a fierce reflux on mee redound" (X, 738–39), "On mee . . . as the source and spring / Of all corruption" (X, 832–33). Marvell takes this central concept of the circularity of sin — and the visual image of it in Milton's Serpent curling back upon itself — and translates it to another icon of circularity, the self-mown Mower: "By his own Sythe, the Mower mown" (*Damon*, 80).

For Damon, the recurring process of cutting down the grass and his own flesh is a Dantean symbolic retribution: "still my Grief is where it was" (70). Destroying his flesh only renews his pain, which grows again like the grass, continuing the endless cycle: "But, when the Iron blunter grows, / Sighing I whet my Sythe and Woes" (71–72 — cf. *L'Allegro*, 66: "And the Mower whets his scythe"). Though this poem's pastoral setting and its rustic figure are distinctively Marvell's, both the atmosphere and the act play upon associations with Milton's portrayal of the human Fall, so it is not surprising that Marvell should have used language that echoes Milton's. After Eve plucks and eats the fruit,

> Earth felt the wound, and Nature from her seat
> *Sighing* through all her Works gave *signs* of *woe*,
> That all was lost.   (IX, 782–84; emphases mine)

The similarities — both auditory and thematic — between Marvell's line 72 and Milton's line 783 are striking: both open with the participle "Sighing," repeat its long *i* sound in a near-pun ("signs" in Milton, "Sythe" in Marvell), and end with the word "woe." In both Milton and Marvell the Fall has brought pain to nature and misery to humans. Earth's cosmic "wound" in Milton (IX, 782) is Damon's literal "Wound" (84) and his unhealable metaphorical "Wound," his incessant "Pain" and "Grief" (68, 70). Milton's passage occurs just as Eve "pluck'd" the fruit with her "*rash* hand" (780–81; emphasis mine), and "Earth" feels the wound; Marvell's passage occurs just as the Mower slashes "by *careless* chance" "Each stroke between the *Earth* and Root" (75–77; emphases mine). Both cut themselves off from their sources in God and nature. Eve brings on her fall and the Fall of all humankind, ironically thinking the fruit the "*Cure* of all" (766); Damon falls down on the grass, and for him "no *Cure* is found" (85). Eve brings death to the world, while postlapsarian Damon recognizes that "Death thou art a Mower too" (88).[29]

He who asserted his pride and defied his death falls victim to both pride and death:

> The edged Stele by careless chance
> Did into his own Ankle glance;
> And there among the Grass fell down,
> By his own Sythe, the Mower mown.   (77–80)

The puns on "Sythe" and "glance" suggest much more than an acciden-tal slashing of flesh. The "scorching beams" from Juliana's eyes (24) have wounded Damon metaphorically and now literally with the "glance" of Damon's scythe (86). In a similar way in *Paradise Lost* the tempting "charm of Beauty's powerful *glance*" (VIII, 533) turns to fallen Adam's lustful "*glance* or toy / Of amorous intent" (IX, 1034–35); later Adam's "Curse aslope" metaphorically "*Glanc'd*" on the ground to signify his sentence of forced agricultural labor (X, 1053–54; all emphases mine). In Marvell the human curse becomes the literal glance of Damon's in-strument of postlapsarian labor, performed close to the ground ("between the Earth and Root," 76), the metaphorical steely glance of unrequited love, and the glance of Damon's deluded vision of himself in his scythe-mirror.

In God's declaration of Adam's curse (X, 201–08), Milton uses nearly verbatim the language of Genesis iii, 17–19, which Damon's predicament imagistically recalls. Just as sin in *Paradise Lost* brought forth "Thorns" and "Thistles" (X, 203), Damon claims that he might have continued mowing happily "Had not Love here his Thistles sow'd" (66). The con-junction in *Damon* of hard agricultural labor, pain, and sweat that the sun no longer licks off (as it did for both Damon before Juliana, 45–46, and Adam before the Fall, VIII, 253–56)[30] echoes Adam's curse, to "Till / The Ground" and reap "th'Herb of the Field" (XI, 97–98; X, 204), to suffer "sweat impos'd" (XI, 172). Damon sees his daily activity of com-plaining while he mows as "Joyning my Labour to my Pain" (68). For humankind, the link of hard labor — the "irksome toil" Adam speaks of (IX, 242) — with the pain of sin is the epitome of God's curse.

Though Damon cuts himself down and metaphorically dies "by Loves despight" (82), death does not literally come to him. His minor wound can be staunched and sealed with country herbs. He merely in-creases his misery in love and life, wishing for death as the final cure for his unhealable wound: "'Tis death alone that this must do" (87). Fallen Adam moans that he "overlive[s]" and asks why he is "mockt with death, and length'n'd out / To deathless pain" (X, 773–75); he is chagrined to realize, as Damon must, that "Death be not one stroke, . . . but endless misery" (X, 809–10).

VI

Marvell further explores postlapsarian self-delusion in *The Mower to the Glo-worms*. Damon's defiant boasts have modulated now to mourn-ful self-recognition. It is a cool, damp, late summer night; the mild, false light of autumn's foolish fires has displaced the "scorching beams" Juli-

ana gave off in the heart of summer. In *Damon,* the Mower kept up fruitful activity while his thoughts wandered, but here even his body wanders while his mind roves in the abyss of his confused thoughts, guided
every which way by delusive hopes and fears.

The nocturnal scene of Marvell's *Glo-worms* imagistically recalls the
simile Milton uses to characterize the Serpent's temptation of Eve as he
leads her to the Forbidden Tree. When Satan-Serpent makes his argument, he literalizes Milton's metaphor of tangled deception, twining and
intertwining and making "intricate seem straight" (IX, 631–33). Milton
compares this optical illusion to the delusive cosmological phenomenon
of the *ignis fatuus,* or will-o'-th'-wisp:

> Hope elevates, and joy
> Bright'ns his Crest, as when a wand'ring Fire,
> Compact of unctuous vapor, which the Night
> Condenses, and the cold invirons round,
> Kindl'd through agitation to a Flame,
> Which oft, they say, some evil Spirit attends,
> Hovering and blazing with delusive Light,
> Misleads th'amaz'd Night-wanderer from his way
> To Bogs and Mires, and oft through Pond or Pool,
> There swallow'd up and lost, from succor far.
> So glister'd the dire Snake, and into fraud
> Led *Eve* our credulous Mother, to the Tree
> Of prohibition, root of all our woe.   (IX, 633–45)

The simile begins as an abstract metaphorical statement on hope
and joy, though the larger context makes clear — and lines 643–44 following the simile make explicit — that the Snake is the misleader and Eve
the misled (in line 614 she is referred to as "amaz'd unwary," paralleling
the "amaz'd Night-wanderer" of the simile). Yet Eve is joyously hopeful
in her delusion that she will raise her station as much as the Serpent seems
to have elevated his powers of reason and speech. So Milton is comparing the will-o'-th'-wisp to the Serpent as misleader, but more importantly,
to the self-delusive heightening of one's own hopes and joys. In this sense,
Eve tempts herself.

This ambiguous mixture of deception and self-delusion, seen earlier
in the "belated Peasant" simile, is the Mower's mental world in *Glo-
worms,* metaphorically portrayed in his loss of way in murky night. The
Mower moves toward recognition of his own delusion and moves us to
see that the foolish fire is metaphorical — his created love for Juliana,
which has so crazed him that he has lost all aim in life. The Mower addresses the glowworms,

> whose officious Flame
> To wandring Mowers shows the way,
> That in the Night have lost their aim,
> And after foolish Fires do stray.   (9–11)

The visual resemblance to Milton's simile is clear, but Marvell's passage also contains striking verbal and thematic echoes: Milton's "*Night-wanderer*" misled "from his *way*" parallels Marvell's "*wandring* Mowers" "in the *Night*," who are supposedly shown "the *way*" by the glowworms after they have "lost their *aim*" (all emphases mine); in both cases, the disorientation caused by following foolish fires seems irremediable ("swallow'd up and lost, from succor far"; "so displac'd / That I shall never find my home").[31]

Milton uses a similar image of the end of *Paradise Lost*, again to portray postlapsarian mental and spiritual confusion. When Adam and Eve are being cast out of the Garden,

> The Cherubim descended; on the ground
> Gliding meteorous, as Ev'ning Mist
> Ris'n from a River o'er the marish glides,
> And gathers ground fast at the Laborer's heel
> Homeward returning.   (XII, 628–32)

In all three passages—Milton's two similes and Marvell's *Gloworms*—a postlapsarian rustic figure sets out toward home, guided (or misguided) by a luminous mist. The Laborer is chased "Homeward" by the mist at his back, while in contrast the Mower and the Night-wanderer follow the foolish fire, finding themselves totally lost. Marvell's Mower is misled by an *ignis fatuus* (his blinding vision of Juliana's love) away from his secure "home" of symbiotic communion with nature, and toward a postlapsarian wilderness of self-delusion. In both Milton's similes, the simultaneous comparison and contrast of the simile's small scene with the contextual narrative adds a tense poignancy to the story. Eve and the Night-wanderer both are led toward specious destinations: Eve is misled by the Serpent literally toward the forbidden tree and sin's wilderness and thus metaphorically away from Edenic harmony; the Night-wanderer is misled by the *ignis fatuus* away from home and toward a more physical disorientation. In the Laborer simile, the first couple—as punishment for their sin—is being driven away from their home in Eden by divinely sent cherubim, while the Laborer moves deliberately toward his home and safety, his action ironically contrasting with their movement toward the metaphorical wilderness of sin and their literal new home in the non-Edenic postlapsarian world. The verbal parallels between the three passages make the similarities between all these post-lapsarian rustic figures even more notable. Earlier, fallen Adam could "find no *way*, from deep to deeper plung'd" (X, 844). Now, like the "*wandring*" Mower who has "lost" the "*way*" and cannot find his "home," and like the Night-*wanderer* who is misled "from his *way*" and completely "lost," Adam and Eve take "thir solitary *way*" with "*wand'ring* steps and slow" and do not know "where to choose / Thir place of rest" (all emphases mine).[32]

VII

The final Mower poem, *The Mower's Song*, begins with the character's clear, direct statement of his forced realization: his mind is no longer one with its natural environment. While he pines with sorrow, the grass, in seeming defiance, is lush and green. Now he has a glimmer of recognition that he has always experienced the schism of mind and nature: one reality, his mind, looked at another reality, the greenness of the grass, and in it "Did see its Hopes as in a Glass" (3–4). Just as Adam and Eve's "inward State of Mind," which had been "calm Region once," is "toss't and turbulent" after the Fall (IX, 1125–26), the Mower's mind, which had been "once the true survey" of gay springtime meadows, is now "displac'd" (*Glo-worms*, 15) and "double" (*Gardens*, 9).

Damon's refrain demonstrates his perception of the mind-nature separation: "When *Juliana* came, and She / What I do to the Grass, does to my Thoughts and Me." Unrequited love is only the catalyst for the Mower's realization of his true condition: now his earlier, perceived dissociation of mind and nature has become the dissociation of his own sensibility. The Mower's "I," which cuts down the grass, is metaphorically his scythe and synecdochically his mind or thoughts, which cut down his flesh ("Me").

In a passage that follows closely after the simile comparing Adam to a reaper, Milton presents Adam in a similar state of dissociation:

> Great joy he promis'd to his thoughts, and new
> Solace in her return, so long delay'd;
> Yet oft his heart, divine of something ill,
> Misgave him; hee the falt'ring measure felt.   (IX, 843–46)

The Mower's dissociation of "my thoughts and me" re-creates fallen Adam's predicament, presaged in the above passage in the separation of "he" and "his thoughts," and "his heart" and "him," which is linked with the ominous "return" of his beloved just as the Mower's dissociation is linked to Juliana's coming. The Mower's refrain ritualistically captures a past dramatic moment and holds it in time as an eternally relived painful realization in the fallen world. In Milton's passage, the pathos results from our tense anticipation, knowing what will happen, in contrast with unfallen Adam's prescient fear. In both cases, the displaced blame is part of the fallen self-delusion. Just as Adam later recognizes his mutuality with Eve's destructive act in the Fall, seen in his prophecy "And mee with thee hath ruin'd" (IX, 906), the fallen Mower's refrain equates his and Juliana's acts of destructive mowing.

The Mower's recognition of his lost communion with nature resembles Satan's recognition, when he first sees Eden's beauty, of the loss of his "sweet interchange" with the natural world, the "Pleasures" he sees causing "Torment within" (IX, 115, 120–21) and "bitter memory / Of what he was" (IV, 24–25). Like Satan, who "with pain of longing pines" when he first sees Adam and Eve (IV, 511), who looked at Eve's goodness and "pin'd / His loss" (IV, 848–49), the Mower "pine[s]" (7) at the sight of gay spring meadows (his earlier vision, in *The Mower against Gardens,* of virginal nature and his own innocence). Satan seeks "others to make such / As I" (IX, 127–28), to make Adam "Companion of his woe" (IV, 907); the Mower resolves that his former "Companions" (26), the meadows, like him will fall. The Mower wills that everything "Will in one common Ruine fall," Satan "that destruction wide may range" (IX, 134). The Mower's pathetic revenge on "all" in his little meadow is microcosmically emblematic of Satan's more far-reaching revenge, the Mower's "common Ruine" a burlesque re-creation of the continuing "hideous ruin" of original sin (I, 46), "ruin upon ruin" (II, 995), "misery . . . join'd / In equal ruin" (I, 90–91).

The Mower wishes for death "as the inevitable end to consciousness" and to the misery that Juliana has brought.[33] Adam, suffering guilt and shame after his Fall, peruses his "doom" — "That dust I am, and shall to dust return" (X, 770). Since in Marvell's chain of literalized metaphors all grass is flesh and all flesh is dust, the metaphorical equivalences would allow the Mower as archetypal fallen human to say: "That grass I am, and shall to grass return." Yet the Mower in *Song* no longer wants to end it all. While Adam fears an immortality that would be a living death (X, 786–88), this Mower intends the grass to be his "Heraldry" (27), the monument to adorn his tomb and to immortalize him. Though the Mower hopes to equalize everything in his universal act of destruction, creating a kind of mock communion with his estranged nature, he instead alienates himself from natural things by the human creation he has "wrought" (20). The Mower does end the seeming immortality of the grass, but he simultaneously transforms the natural process into artistic stasis — the artificial, immortal creation of his heraldry, his visions, his poetry. And yet the paradox of the Mower mown is in the grass image too: the grass will continue to sprout, ripen, and wither as a permanent heraldry of both death and regeneration.

VIII

Though the Mower poems seem to project a grim view of sin without grace, Marvell's prose and his other religious lyrics suggest that this is not his total vision.[34] *The Coronet,* closely related in imagery to both the Mower poems and *Paradise Lost,* is a believer's prayer for divine redemption in the face of human inadequacy. But C. A. Patrides may be right that Marvell would "much rather sit and sing, then whet and comb his silver wings," rather than prepare for "longer flight.[35] In the Mower poems the inevitable bleakness of the Mower's earthly reality is one appropriate response to the human focus of *Paradise Lost,* repeatedly underlined by the similes. Milton's similes "seldom invoke the Passion as a direct fulfillment of the Fall," as Linda Gregerson writes; "they rather invoke . . . the time between the Fall and the Incarnation, the time between the comings of Christ, times when the Fall is enacted again and again."[36] Michael prophesies to Adam Christ's future redemption of mankind and the resulting victory over death and stresses that the Christian life brings "A paradise within thee, happier far" than the lost geographical Eden (XII, 587). But the inspiring image for Marvell's Mower poems is Milton's final scene: a solitary couple hesitantly stepping out into the bleak, cold world of time and death.

Unlike Adam and Eve, the Mower is unguided and has only delusive rather than divine hope, yet his fall is still somewhat happy. The Mower's relationship to death makes the poems possible and interesting, just as the act of sin gives Adam and Eve their pathos and *Paradise Lost* its reason for being. In one sense, the Mower's grass-cutting is harmless and even charming, and as postlapsarian humans ourselves we sympathize with his growing realization of the self-conscious mind's powers and limitations. In his pastoral similes, Milton too presents an ambivalent picture of the postlapsarian world of both joy and fear, hope and doubt: what to fallen Adam and Eve seems a future of desolate wandering in an abysmal wilderness is to the postlapsarian Laborer both the drudgery of work and the pleasant security of home. By transposing images, phrases, and scenes from Milton's epic to a playful yet profound pastoral context, Marvell both dramatizes the dire effects of the first sin and nudges us to an appreciation of the mortality that allows for poetry. Like Adam and Eve, the Mower is both grass and flesh, life and death, creator and destroyer. He is icon but also pathetic and sympathetic fallen human being, whose postlapsarian delusion leads him to choose death over salvation, but whose mortality gives birth to art.

Emphasizing the complex relationship of the Mower poems to Milton's *Paradise Lost* risks the distortion of Marvell's independent poetic achievement. *On Mr. Milton's Paradise lost* shows that Marvell was himself aware of the problem of imitation, influence, and independence. Kenneth Gross argues that Marvell's chief aim was "To commend and echo Milton . . . , and yet keep imaginative space open for himself," firmly justifying Milton's choice of blank verse (45–54), but refusing "to concede his own God-given right to rhyme."[37] In effectively echoing Milton's blank verse epic in his rhymed Mower poems, Marvell illustrates his own argument. Perhaps he is commenting on his own literary habits when he mockingly says that those who imitate Milton will only "detect their Ignorance or Theft"; writing that "none will dare" (25), he who so clearly dares may be joking with a knowing Milton. In the Mower poems Marvell reduced "sacred Truths" to what could be called "Fable and old Song" (8). But he recognized the power of a religious vision dramatically transposed from Scripture to epic, and in filtering *Paradise Lost* through the genre of pastoral lyric, Marvell achieved yet another illuminating transformation.

Luther College

NOTES

1. Geoffrey Hartman, "Marvell, St. Paul, and the Body of Hope," *ELH*, XXXI, no. 2 (1964), 188.

2. Elaine Hoffman Baruch, "Themes and Counterthemes in 'Damon the Mower,'" *CL*, XXVI (Summer 1974), 256.

3. All references to Marvell's poems are to *The Poems and Letters of Andrew Marvell*, ed. H. M. Margoliouth, 3d. ed. rev. Pierre Legouis with E. E. Duncan-Jones (Oxford, 1971).

4. E. W. Tayler, "Marvell's Garden of the Mind," in *Nature and Art in Renaissance Literature* (1964), rpt. in *Marvell: Modern Judgements*, ed. Michael Wilding (London, 1969), p. 262.

5. Ibid.

6. Damon and Adam are compared by K. W. Gransden, "Time, Guilt and Pleasure: A Note on Marvell's Nostalgia," *Ariel*, I, no. 2 (April 1970), 94–95; Hartman, "Marvell, St. Paul," p. 193; Barbara Everett, "Marvell's 'The Mower's Song,'" *Critical Quarterly*, IV, no. 3 (1962), 220. *Damon* is a near anagram of *Adam*, both names including — even in their etymological forms — the morpheme *dam*. Except in the Septuagint, *Adam* is used

biblically as a title meaning "the man," rather than as a name; see Madeleine S. Miller and M. Lane Miller, *Harper's Bible Dictionary*, 8th ed. (New York, 1973), p. 6. The name *Damon* is so common in pastoral as to be more representative than particular. One etymological meaning of *Adam* is "the one made" or "the maker" (Donald Attwater, comp., *Names and Name-Days* [London, 1939], p. 1); *Damon* has a somewhat similar meaning in its origins in the Greek *damaö*, meaning "the tamed" or "one who tames" (Eric Partridge, *Name This Child: A Dictionary of Modern British and American Given or Christian Names*, 3d ed. [London, 1936], p. 85; and Evelyn Wells, *A Treasury of Names* [New York, 1946], p. 207).

7. See Christopher Hill, "Milton and Marvell," in *Approaches to Marvell: The York Tercentenary Lectures*, ed. C. A. Patrides (London, 1978), p. 22; Michael Craze, *The Life and Lyrics of Andrew Marvell* (New York, 1979), pp. 55–56; Richard Leigh, *The Transproser Rehears'd* (1673), who concluded that "There are many *Miltons* in this one Man" (quoted in Joseph Anthony Wittreich, Jr., "Perplexing the Explanation: Marvell's 'On Mr. Milton's Paradise lost,'" in *Approaches to Marvell*, p. 284); Joseph H. Summers, *The Heirs of Donne and Jonson* (London, 1970), p. 133. Judith Scherer Herz offers the most comprehensive argument for a longstanding relationship of borrowing and counter-borrowing, with Marvell sometimes using Milton's metaphors "while working with quite different thematic concerns and artistic problems" ("Milton and Marvell: The Poet as Fit Reader," *MLQ*, XXXIX, no. 3 [1978], 239–63).

8. See, for example, L. N. Wall, "Some Notes on Marvell's Sources," *N & Q*, n.s. IV, no. 4 (1957), 172–73; Pierre Legouis, "Floral Horologes," *N & Q*, n.s. XVI, no. 5 (1969), 193–94; Karl Josef Höltgen, "Floral Horologes Prior to Marvell's 'Garden,'" *N & Q*, n.s. XVI, no. 10 (1969), 381–82; Hannah Disinger Demaray, "The Literary Gardens of Andrew Marvell and John Milton," in *Gardens and Culture: Eight Studies in History and Aesthetics*, ed. Hannah Disinger Demaray (Beirut, 1969), pp. 115–42; John Dixon Hunt, "'Loose Nature' and the 'Garden Square': The Gardenist Background for Marvell's Poetry," in *Approaches to Marvell*, pp. 331–52; Tayler, "Marvell's Garden of the Mind," pp. 250, 271; Lawrence W. Hyman, *Andrew Marvell* (New York, 1964), p. 105; George DeF. Lord, ed. *Andrew Marvell: The Complete Poetry* (New York, 1968), pp. x–xi; Summers, *Heirs of Donne*, p. 162; Isabel MacCaffrey, "Some Notes on Marvell's Poetry, Suggested by a Reading of His Prose," *MP*, LXI, no. 4 (1964), 261–69; Kitty Datta, "Marvell's Prose and Poetry: More Notes," *MP*, LXIII, no. 4 (1966), 319–21; E. E. Duncan-Jones, "Marvell: A Great Master of Words," Warton Lecture of English Poetry, *Proceedings of the British Academy*, LXI (1975), 275n.; R. I. V. Hodge, "Marvell's Fairfax Poems: Some Considerations Concerning Dates," *MP*, LXXI, no. 4 (1974), 347–55.

9. See J. Milton French, *The Life Records of John Milton* (1949; rpt. New York, 1966), Vol. IV, p. 191; John Aubrey, "Minutes of the Life of Mr. John Milton," in *The Early Lives of Milton*, ed. Helen Darbishire (1932; rpt. New York, 1965), p. 13; William Riley Parker, *Milton: A Biography* (Oxford, 1968), Vol. I, pp. 597–98; Allan H. Gilbert, *On the Composition of "Paradise Lost"* (Chapel Hill, 1947); John Phillips, "The Life of Mr. John Milton," in *Early Lives*, pp. 28–29; Anthony à Wood, from *Fasti Oxonienses* (1691), in *Early Lives*, pp. 45–46; Edward Phillips, in *Early Lives*, p. 73; French, *Life Records*, II, 50–51 (the lines Phillips quotes are what is now *PL* IV, 32–41); *The Reason of Church Government*, in *Complete Prose Works of John Milton*, ed. Don M. Wolfe et al. (New Haven 1953–82), Vol. I, pp. 812–13, 820–21.

10. Grant McColley, *"Paradise Lost": An Account of Its Growth and Major Origins* (Chicago, 1940), p. 303; John T. Shawcross, *With Mortal Voice: The Creation of "Paradise Lost"* (Lexington, 1982), pp. 174–76. Much evidence points to Marvell's "over twenty

years of discipleship and friendship" with Milton (Hill, "Milton and Marvell," pp. 5–8, 17), including correspondence, possible collaboration, mutual friendships, overlapping political responsibilities, and shared religious and political beliefs; see French, *Life Records*, I, 405, III, 305–06; Parker, *Milton*, II, 964; David Masson, *The Life of John Milton* (1881–94; rev. ed. Gloucester, Mass., 1965), Vol. IV, pp. 624–25, V, 402, 572, VI, 200, 453; E. E. Duncan-Jones, *Times Literary Supplement*, 2 December 1949, p. 791, 13 January 1950, p. 25, 31 July 1953, p. 493, 20 June 1958, p. 345; W. Arthur Turner, "Milton, Marvell and 'Dradon' at Cromwell's Funeral," *PQ*, XXVIII, no. 2 (1949), 320–23. Marvell helped to save Milton from a death sentence, defended him in print, and "us'd to frequent him the oftenest of any body" (John Toland, "The Life of John Milton" [1698], in *Early Lives*, p. 175); see Aubrey, *Early Lives*, p. 7; Edward Phillips, *Early Lives*, p. 74. Marvell promised Aubrey he would write notes for a biography of Milton for which Aubrey left blank the page facing Marvell's biography; see French, V, 234; Hilton Kelliher, comp., *Andrew Marvell: Poet and Politician, 1621–78*, Catalogue of British Library Tercentenary Exhibition (London, 1978), p. 95. Some even wonder if Marvell could have been the earliest, anonymous biographer (French, V, 276–78; Pierre Legouis, *André Marvell* [Paris, 1928], p. 232).

11. *Early Lives*, p. 73.

12. Most of Marvell's occasional poems appeared in his lifetime. Of the lyric poems, only *A Dialogue between Thyrsis and Dorinda* — the authorship of which is questionable — appeared in several manuscripts, printed versions, and musical settings before its appearance in the folio in 1681. It does not appear in *Eng. poet. d. 49* (Elizabeth Story Donno, ed., *Andrew Marvell: The Complete Poems* [Middlesex, Eng., 1972], p. 221). Kelliher, *Andrew Marvell*, p. 50, has pointed out the existence of a manuscript of *A Dialogue Between the Resolved Soul, and Created Pleasure*, found by Samuel Pepys in 1678, and a copy of *To his Coy Mistress* from c. 1675, but until there is further evidence of other manuscripts, we must assume that not many copies of Marvell's lyric poems circulated in his lifetime.

13. *Milton Studies*, XI, ed. B. Rajan (Pittsburgh, 1978), pp. xiii–xiv.

14. All references to Milton's works are to *Complete Poems and Major Prose*, ed. Merritt Y. Hughes (New York, 1957).

15. For a discussion of "magnifying and diminishing similes" in *PL*, see Hartman, "Milton's Counterplot," *ELH*, XXV, no. 1 (1958), 1–12. Muriel Bradbrook, "Marvell and Rural Solitude," *RES*, XVII (1941), 46; H. M. Richmond, "'Rural Lyricism': A Renaissance Mutation of the Pastoral," *CL*, XVI, no. 3 (1964), 193–210; and David Kalstone, "Marvell and the Fictions of Pastoral," *ELR*, IV, no. 1 (1974), 175, 187, all have written about Marvell's and Milton's similar use of the pastoral tradition. For discussion of the independent world of Milton's similes, see Patricia Parker, "Eve, Evening, and the Labor of Reading in *Paradise Lost*," *ELR*, IX, no. 2 (1979), 338; Christopher Grose, *Milton's Epic Process: "Paradise Lost" and its Miltonic Background* (New Haven, 1973), pp. 168–69; Stanley Fish, *Surprised by Sin* (Berkeley, 1967), p. 313.

16. Hartman, "Milton's Counterplot," pp. 3, 5, 10–11.

17. Tayler, "Marvell's Garden of the Mind," pp. 263–65.

18. George M. Puttenham, *The Arte of English Poesie*, ed. G. D. Willcock and Alice Walker (Cambridge, 1936), quoted in ibid., p. 251; Marvell, *The Rehearsal Transpros'd*, in *The Complete Works in Verse and Prose of Andrew Marvell*, ed. Alexander B. Grosart (London, 1868–75), Vol. III, p. 295, quoted in Datta, "Marvell's Prose," p. 319.

19. Tayler, "Marvell's Garden of the Mind," p. 255.

20. Hartman, "Marvell, St. Paul," p. 193, compares the Miltonic images of both

Proserpine and Eve as the "gatherer gathered" to Marvell's "Mower mown," citing *PL* IV, 268 ff. (first noticed by F. R. Leavis) and IX, 426 ff.

21. Dean R. Baldwin, "Marvell's 'Mower Poems,'" *Explicator*, XXXV, no. 3 (1977), 25–26.

22. A. M. Cinquemani refers to this passage from 1 Corinthians xiii, 12 in discussing Eve's prelapsarian narcissism in Book IV ("Milton's *Paradise Lost* IV, 460–473," *Explicator*, XXX, no. 7 [1972], 56); Hartman calls line 4 of *The Mower's Song* "a commonplace reference" to this biblical passage ("Marvell, St. Paul," p. 182n). Just as Eve's narcissistic pride leads to her fall (see Cleanth Brooks, "Eve's Awakening," in *Essays in Honor of Walter Clyde Currey* [1954], quoted in A. Bartlett Giamatti, *The Earthly Paradise and the Renaissance Epic* [Princeton, 1966], p. 316n.; William G. Madsen, *From Shadowy Types to Truth: Studies in Milton's Symbolism* [New Haven, 1968], pp. 68–69), Damon enacts the self-destructiveness of narcissism when his scythe-mirror mows him down (see Gransden, "Time, Guilt," p. 95).

23. Ernest W. Baughman, ed., *Type and Motif Index of the Folktales of England and North America*, Indiana University Folklore Series No. 20 (The Hague, 1966); Stith Thompson, ed., *Motif-Index of Folk Literature* (Bloomington, 1956).

24. Hartman, "Milton's Counterplot," pp. 3, 10.

25. See Kenneth Gross, "'Pardon Me, Mighty Poet': Versions of the Bard in Marvell's 'On Mr. Milton's *Paradise Lost*,'" *Milton Studies*, XVI, ed. James D. Simmonds (Pittsburgh, 1982), 81, 89–90, on the interesting parallels between Milton's language in this simile and Marvell's language in "On Mr. Milton's Paradise Lost."

26. Ibid., pp. 11–12.

27. Donald M. Friedman notes the pun, citing the *OED*'s variant spelling of *sithe* for *sigh*: *Marvell's Pastoral Art* (London, 1970), p. 145, n. 54. Both *scythe* and *sigh* had the earlier variant spellings *sithe* and *sythe*, and all forms were pronounced similarly. See E. J. Dobson, *English Pronunciation 1500–1700*, 2d ed. (Oxford, 1968), vol. I, pp. 181–82, 370; II, 942–44. The 1681 folio uses the *gh* spelling for *sighing* in line 72, but uses two spellings for *scythe*: "sythe" (7, 69, 72, 75, 80) and "sithe" (51, 58). It is likely that in "By his own Sythe, the Mower mown" (80), Marvell was punning, "By his own sigh, the Mower moans."

28. Marvell may also be responding to traditional iconography here. Erwin Panofsky shows that Father Time acts "either as a Destroyer, or as a Revealer, or as a universal and inexorable power which through the cycle of procreation and destruction causes what may be called a cosmic continuity": *Studies in Iconology: Humanistic Themes in the Art of the Renaissance* (1939; rpt. New York, 1967), pp. 82–91.

29. Both Milton and Marvell use the conventional imagery of Death, pictured in traditional iconography with a scythe slung over one shoulder. From the early eleventh century, both Time and Death were iconographically portrayed with a scythe or sickle (Panofsky, *Studies in Iconology*, pp. 77, 82–83). In *Paradise Lost* after the Fall, Sin offers her ravenous son Death "whatever thing / The Scythe of Time mows down," to "devour unspar'd" (X, 605–06).

30. Gransden, "Time, Guilt," p. 95.

31. Though the Mower presents the glowworms as kind and generous lights which guide humans lost in the night, the image's two quite different connotations in the Renaissance (see Kitty Scoular [Datta], *Natural Magic: Studies in the Presentation of Nature in English Poetry from Spenser to Marvell* [Oxford, 1965], pp. 103–08) make the Mower's trust in them ironic. The glowworm could be a warm, jewel-like guide through the cold darkness, but was most often a symbol of illusion and deceit: its heat was nonexistent,

its light unpredictable; by day it was a mere black bug; and its appearance marked the coming of nature's death at autumn. So the glowworm of Marvell's poem can be seen as another *ignis fatuus* of sorts, the Mower misled by his notion of the glowworms as much as Eve is misled by Satan as glittering worm. See also Don Parry Norford, "Marvell and the Arts of Contemplation and Action," *ELH*, XLI, no. 1 (1974), 64n.

32. See Milton's similar language of wandering in PL II, 522–27, 558–61, 614–22.

33. Friedman, *Marvell's Pastoral Art*, p. 140.

34. Bruce King, *Marvell's Allegorical Poetry* (New York, 1977), p. 139, argues that Marvell's allegory in the Mower poems can be taken in either a "bad" sense, "as pertaining to the Fall and the results of sin," or in a "good" sense, "seeing in the natural world signs of Christian hope." Though Marvell's presentation is ambivalent and some of King's allegorical readings are plausible, King's final optimistic interpretation distorts the narrative and rhetorical direction of the series. As Hartman argues, "Marvell evokes no sustained image of Eden, only the tastings and testings of hope by the individual mind" ("Marvell, St. Paul," p. 193).

35. C. A. Patrides, "'Till prepared for longer flight': The Sublunar Poetry of Andrew Marvell," in *Approaches to Marvell*, p. 52.

36. Linda Gregerson, "The Limbs of Truth: Milton's Use of Simile in *Paradise Lost*," *Milton Studies*, XIV, ed. James D. Simmonds (Pittsburgh, 1980), p. 139.

37. Gross, pp. 78, 93. Wittreich, "Perplexing the Explanation," pp. 287–88, Herz, "Milton and Marvell," p. 244, and Gross, pp. 77–78, 81, all demonstrate that the poem is indebted to the epic it salutes: it "emblematizes" the epic (Wittreich), echoing language, structure, "dramatic stances, metaphors, key words," and "larger systems of value" (Gross) from *PL*.

THE KENOTIC EXPERIENCE
OF *SAMSON AGONISTES*

Darryl Tippens

E ARLY IN his career as a Christian poet, the youthful Milton exuberantly sounded the trumpet, thinking he was ushering in the glorious reign of God's saints. But to his surprise the people failed him. They
not only did not respond, they rejected and humiliated him. Beside the
public rejection of his call, several private disasters accumulated in the
poet's life. What had started as a clear race of glory turned into a bitter
shame. How could he explain this turn of events? Where was he to turn?
As usual, he turned to Scripture. Did not the Bible in fact predict Milton's very experience? Isn't the journey of the saint always by way of
the Valley of Humiliation? In rereading Philippians ii, 5–11, the *carmen
Christi* or Hymn to Christ, Milton found his answer. Here was the interpretive key, the paradox of grace, to which he would appeal again and
again. In this text the Protestant poet found *kenosis,* a theme richly elaborated in the Christian tradition and a major influence in Western thought
from the Church Fathers to contemporary process theologians. Apparently derived from Hellenistic myths but transformed by Old Testament
suffering servant theology and St. Paul's Gospel, kenosis proved to be
the very pattern of reality which would give shape to Milton's art and
meaning to his life.

A few critics have mentioned the theme in Milton, most notably
Barbara Lewalski, John Shawcross, Mary Christopher Pecheux and Michael Lieb. Lewalski has found kenosis to be "of central importance" in
Paradise Regained where the Son is " made incarnate by a true *kenosis*
or emptying out of these divine attributes, so that he might regain them
again 'through the teaching of the Father.'" Shawcross has detected a
kind of "fraudulent kenosis" in which Satan's self-imbruting parodies
Christ's incarnation, and Mother Pecheux suggests the importance of
kenosis in her comparison of the ironically parallel descents of Christ and
Satan. Lieb, in a particularly enlightening essay, has shown kenosis to
be of major importance to Milton: "Like the Church Fathers, Milton views
kenosis as the Son's preincarnate act of emptying himself of his godhead
to take upon himself the nature of man." According to Lieb this motif

173

transcends the dogmatic concerns of *Christian Doctrine* and ultimately shapes the theme of the antiprelatical tracts, the two epics and the minor poems; kenosis is integral to Milton's conduct as a writer.[1]

As these scholars have observed, Milton was both aware of scriptural and patristic teachings on the subject, and he made significant use of them, though surprisingly little has been said of the matter. Only Lieb has argued the importance of the theme in the minor poems and the epics, yet even he has missed the profound importance of the theme in *Samson Agonistes*. An analysis of the tragedy in light of the kenotic tradition proves how central that theme is. The language, imagery, and idea of kenosis reside at the heart of Samson's experience (and presumably Milton's too). Furthermore, a recognition of the play's kenotic thought offers some assistance in meeting a number of vexing questions in *Samson* criticism: How is the play structured? Is it Christian, Hellenic, or Hebraic in spirit? How does *Samson* fit into the poet's artistic development? In what sense is the work tragic? And, if the work is the final one, how does it complete Milton's agenda as England's greatest Christian poet?

I

Before examining Milton's poetry, one must dissociate kenosis from its purely modern sense and discover the sense which applies in Milton's art; one must also see the idea as both theological statement and, more importantly, as an ethical or philosophical structure, a way of looking at the world of experience.[2]

The modern doctrine of kenosis states that Christ "by His Incarnation divested Himself of His divine attributes of omniscience and omnipotence, so that in His incarnate life the Divine Person is revealed and solely revealed through human consciousness."[3] In this definition the divine nature is so limited in Christ's earthly life that, practically speaking, he ceases to be divine. This demythologized nontrinitarian approach is not, however, the only theory of kenosis.

The more traditional view, which prevailed until the mid-nineteenth century, emphasized the humiliation and abasement experienced by Christ in his incarnation, rather than the loss of divine power or nature. Milton, like the Church Fathers and the Reformed writers Grotius and Zanchius, views the kenosis as the profound and saving act in Christ's renunciation of glory, his descent to a world of suffering and humiliation followed by an exaltation to immense glory. In Milton's view, Christ "descended." Though he had "received all these things from the Father, and was in the form of God," Milton writes in *Christian Doctrine*, "he did not reckon it robbery to be equal with God."[4] In his descent the Son underwent a radical emptying, exinanition or kenosis (κενόω, to make empty, to deprive of content or possession).[5] For Milton, not only Christ's death, but the whole life of incarnation was an act of kenosis: "His humiliation means that Christ, as . . . God-man, submitted himself voluntarily, both in life and in death, to the divine justice, in order to suffer all the things which were necessary to our redemption" (YP VI, p. 438). Like most Christian writers, Milton perceived the kenotic experience as a parabolic journey of descents and ascents. The downward movement of humiliation, following St. Paul's hymn, is matched by an upward movement: "Christ's humiliation is followed by his exaltation. By this it is meant that Christ having triumphed over death and laid aside the form of a servant, was raised to immortality and to the highest glory by God the father, for our good" (YP VI, pp. 440–41). A number of elements, here so briefly stated, become immensely significant in Milton's poetry: the divine hero who dwells in glory in a state of perfection or blessedness; the descent to servant status; the process of emptying; the life of humiliation, the death which is paradoxically triumphant, and finally the ascent to a state of superior glory. Variations of this kenotic plot appear as early as the nativity ode, last through the epics and the tragedy, and apply in varying degrees to the Son of God, Adam, Eve, Satan (ironically), and especially Samson.

For Milton, as for most Protestant readers of his century, the humiliation of Christ was more than a theological abstraction or a scholastic theory of atonement. Christ underwent the curriculum of suffering and death to provide man, in the words of the Puritan divine Henry Airay, "a most cleere pattern unto us."[6] Milton concurs with this typological view: "The second aim of the whole mediatorial ministry is to shape us in Christ's image, both Christ emptied of glory and Christ exalted. Rom. viii. 29: 'to be shaped in the image of his son'" (YP VI, p. 450). Similarly, Luther viewed Christ as "the Head, the Firstborn, the Archetype, and the Image among many brethren."[7]

Kenosis, then, is important both because it gives us a clue to Milton's view of the Son's nature in the epics, but much more because it points to a universal pattern given to the elect. According to the Authorized Version gloss to the Philippian hymn, St. Paul "sets before his Christian readers a most perfit example of all modestie and sweete conversation, Christ Jesus, whom we ought to follow with all our might."[8] The kenotic parabola of abasement and exaltation belongs to all. Henry Airay writes that Christ's example proves that "the high-way to be exalted into glory is to decke our selves inwardly with lowliness of minde."[9] Indeed, kenosis is the map of everyone's experience. We are all "children of God" destined to make the journey of the exile. Milton is clear on this point: "We are shaped in the image of Christ emptied of glory" (YP VI, p. 451). Christ is the kenotic sufferer *par excellence*, but his experience was to be infinitely replicated throughout time.

Very importantly, this timeless emblem worked both forward and backward. For those living after Christ, the pattern was a "prodigy of example" and a "great lesson" to Bishop Jeremy Taylor.[10] To Calvin, Paul "shews what a pattern of humility has been presented before us in Christ."[11] Augustine made the point even more explicit: "See, O man, what God has become for you. Take to heart the lessons of his great humility. . . . You, though you were only man, wished to be God; and you were lost. He, though he was God, wished to be man that he might find what had been lost. Human pride pressed you down so that divine humility alone could lift you up."[12] Such themes pervade Milton's last great poems. For the Reformed reader with a spiritual eye, the stories of Adam, Eve, the Son of God and Samson are universally significant. The kenotic pattern of their lives is the ground of true experience, a timeless way of comprehending existence.

Milton's heroes must encounter and read correctly, like all true believers, the "true experience" of kenosis. They must go beyond merely encountering the experience (for many unfaithful experience a kind of pseudo kenosis — Satan, Dalila, the Philistines, etc.) and actually come to interpret the meaning of their descents properly.[13] They must learn to be shaped in Christ's kenotic image and move beyond vainglory and the selfish cycle of blame into a higher world of exinanition.[14]

Although the kenotic motif is pervasive in the epics, I shall only briefly allude to them in order to focus on Milton's most interesting kenotic drama (which I take to be the poet's last work), *Samson Agonistes*, the work which most clearly illustrates the human, earthly application of the paradigm. Samson is the most fully human of the last great characters — lacking the prelapsarian privileges of Adam and Eve, as well as the divine perspectives of Satan and the Son of God. For Samson, Paradise can only be a memory or dream. He stands very close to his creator as the hero of a *holocaust* (a term redefined by Milton according to the *OED*) who triumphs in the very ashes of a failed life. Samson is perhaps Milton's closest emblem of his own existence.

In order to demonstrate the place of kenosis in the tragedy, the discussion will fall into two parts. First, I shall enumerate the types of kenotic images in the play, images which suggest what is at stake in the drama and which combine to create an understanding of the play's larger purpose. Second, I shall describe the play's "plot" in light of the kenotic theme. Through the cycle of "true experience" Samson submits to the nature of reality and is shaped in the kenotic image. This understanding saves him, though it is an understanding which (apparently) eludes everyone else in the story.

II

Historically, the kenosis was for the Christian interpreter a sublime theme that could only be conveyed through analogy or metaphor. St. Paul, in the Philippian hymn, calls it "an emptying," but inasmuch as the kenosis was considered synonymous with the incarnation, which involved a "putting on" of human flesh as well as a "laying aside of glory," images of divestiture and investiture were frequently associated with kenosis.[15] Many related metaphors were also employed, often inseparably linked. For our purposes, I shall enumerate five categories of kenotic language, all of which appear in Milton's verse. Kenosis may be seen as: (1) impoverishment or emptying, (2) divestiture-investiture, (3) depotentiation, (4) disguise, (5) a vertical progress or a parabolic journey.

Kenosis as an *emptying* or an *impoverishment* is rooted in scriptural language. "That hee being rich," writes St. Paul, "for your sakes became poore, that yee through his povertie might be made rich" (2 Cor. viii, 9). Frequently, in the sermons on the incarnation, the homilist dwelt on the extraordinary impoverishment of Christ in his lowly descent. Bishop Andrewes writes: "But I ask further, 'manifested in the flesh?' what flesh? or how manifested? In what flesh? What! in the pride and beauty of our nature? no; but in the most disgraceful estate of it that might be . . . No; but how? In clouts, in a stable, in a manger . . . Today, in the flesh of a poor babe crying in the cratch, *in medio animalium*."[16] Similarly, Samson is emptied and impoverished, dwelling in rags among the animals. Instead of an invincible warrior, we find him "Eyeless in Gaza at the Mill with slaves" (41) where he grinds "Among the Slaves and Asses [his] comrades / As good for nothing else" (1162–63). He is in moral as well as physical poverty, although Manoa ironically hopes that "God will relent, and quit thee all his debt" (509). When Samson dwells on his prospects, as he does so often, he most fears eking out a life "in poverty, / With sickness and disease" (697). By contrast Dalila is wealthy and richly arrayed. She is "some rich Philistian matron" (722), "vitiated with Gold" (389). Similarly, Harapha and the Philistines personify wealth and richness, as they await God's ironic turnover inherent in the kenosis when he fills the hungry with good things, and the rich he sends empty away (Luke i, 53).

Manoa, who in so many ways performs an ironic imitation of what God is working out,[17] attempts his own kenosis as he tries to impoverish himself in order to "ransom" his son:

> I shall choose
> To live the poorest in my Tribe, than richest,
> And he in that calamitous prison left.
> No, I am fixt not to part hence without him.
> For his redemption all my Patrimony,
> If need be, I am ready to forego
> And quit: not wanting him, I shall want nothing.   (1478–84)

The idea of "emptying" or "pouring out" is also suggested in the Chorus's initial shock at Samson's "diffused" appearance: "O change beyond report, thought or belief! / See how he lies at random, carelessly diffus'd" (117–18). The physical posture implies the spiritual — Samson is depleted.

Secondly, kenosis is a kind of *divestiture* and *investiture*. Bishop Andrewes exploits an honored tradition in saying the incarnation is a putting off of glory and a putting on of "poor clouts."[18] The Hebrew Epistle portrayed the flesh of Christ as a tent or a veil (x, 20) which Milton echoes in his portrait of the Son in *Paradise Regained* "enshrin'd / In fleshly Tabernacle, and human form" (IV, 599–600). Jeremy Taylor writes that Christ appeared "As God, clothed in a robe of glory, at the same instant when you may behold and wonder at his humanity wrapped in cheap and unworthy cradle-bands."[19] Similarly, Milton's *Upon the Circumcision* conveys the traditional imagery:

> he that dwelt above
> High-thron'd in secret bliss, for us frail dust
> Emptied his glory, ev'n to nakedness.

Much more fully Milton develops the language of divestiture in *Paradise Lost* when he merges the language of Philippians ii with the scene in John xiii when Christ "lays aside his garments" (xiii, 4) in order to empty himself in the act of footwashing:

> Then pitying how they stood
> Before him naked to the air, that now
> Must suffer change, disdain'd not to begin
> Thenceforth the form of servant to assume,
> As when he wash'd his servants' feet, so now
> As Father of his Family he clad
> Thir nakedness with Skins of Beasts, or slain,
> Or as the Snake with youthful Coat repaid;
> And thought not much to clothe his Enemies:

> Nor hee thir outward only with the Skins
> Of Beasts, but inward nakedness, much more
> Opprobrious, with his Robe of righteousness
> Arraying cover'd from his Father's sight.   (X, 211–23)

Even more fully in *Samson Agonistes*, Milton creates a rich network of clothing images, in which garments are usually associated with sinfulness and pride, undress or rags with spirituality; yet, like so much of this tragedy, there is no convenient equation, no spiritual key, that assures us of one's spiritual status. It is important to see that Samson as divine hero was formerly clothed with glory, but he now has the attire of a servant: "In slavish habit, ill-fitted weeds / O'erworn and soil'd" (122–23). Samson believes "These rags" are proof of "The base degree" to which he is fallen (414). But of course he is only half right: they do confirm his humiliation, but they also suggest the way to exaltation.

Samson's divestiture is also conveyed through his shorn locks; since Samson was Nazarite, his hair was a sign of his sanctified status, yet Dalila has "shorn the fatal harvest of [his] head" (1024); she "shore" him "Like a tame Wether, all [his] precious fleece" (538). Samson's locks, then, function simultaneously as an outward sign of his covenant with God as well as a memento of his original glory — both of which have been ripped from him. Dalila as Samson's despoiler stands under the same judgment as the false clergy in *Lycidas* who "scramble at the shearer's feast." Robbery and divestiture are cognate notions in kenotic thought, and in the sheep image the two intertwine. Dalila is like the one who enters the sheepfold and robs rather than feeds (John x, 1 ff), in stark contrast to the true hero who "thought it no robbery to be equal to God" (Phil. ii, 6). With this point in mind, Samson's act of robbery/divestiture becomes important: when Samson "like a Robber stripp'dst them [the thirty men] of thir robes" (1188), he performs a prideful inversion of the true kenotic hero who lays aside his garments to assist others.

In the kenotic paradigm there is also a final investiture. The Son lays aside his glory, but he takes on a different garment as well — a fleshly body, an earthly tabernacle, and so forth. And finally he is clothed with an eternal glorious body. So also Samson changes garments. He is dressed in the Philistine's uniform: "In thir state Livery clad" (1616) "as a public servant" (1615). Ironically he appears before the Philistine lords as their servant and retainer, and as their "antic," "mummer," and "mimic" (1325). He comes to play the fool of God in Dagon's theater, disguising God's providential plan. Thus, the language of investiture leads to the idea of disguise.

The incarnation of Christ as a kind of *disguise* or *occultation* pervades the literature on kenosis. According to A. B. Bruce, the Reformers "accepted occultation as an undeniable truth; nay, they gloried in it . . . behind the veil of flesh deity hid itself."[20] Andrewes in his Christmas sermon of 1607 writes: "Well doth the Apostle call it the 'veil of His flesh,' as whereby He was rather obscured than any way set forth; yea eclipsed in all the darkest points of it."[21] According to Bruce:

The standing phrase for the kenosis was *occultatio*, and the favourite illustration the obscuration of the sun by a dense cloud. Zanchius, for example, says: "Under the form of a servant the form of God was so hid that it scarcely appeared any longer to exist, as is also the light of the sun when it is covered by a very dense cloud; for who would not say that the sun had laid aside all his light, and denuded himself of his splendour?"[22]

The theme of *occultatio dei* appealed to the blind poet as well. In *The Passion* he conceived of the incarnation as disguise: "O what a Mask was there, what a disguise!" In *Samson* occultation is an extremely important image. Samson's deity delights in masks. When he is most "unactive deem'd" he breaks forth from the cloud and bolts on the head of the unsuspecting: "Oft he seems to hide his face, / But unexpectedly returns" (1749–50). Samson, too, as the primitive sun figure is a hidden light, a light shining in the darkness yet not seen. The occultation is dual; Samson cannot see himself truly (only at the end is he "With inward eyes illuminated," 1689):

> O dark, dark, dark, amid the blaze of noon,
> Irrecoverably dark, total Eclipse
> Without all hope of day!   (80–82)

But also, the people surrounding him are veiled in clouds of carnal understanding, for they think they see when they do not. The Chorus "sees" Samson lying at random, diffused, and they see his plight (incorrectly) as the failure of his divine calling. Similarly the lords of Philistia come to see the "spectacle" at the temple, where God opens their eyes. Like Gloucester in *King Lear* the people stumbled when they saw. Samson's God is a deity of disguisings.

Manifestation and occultation appear elsewhere in the tragedy — negatively, for example, with Dalila and Harapha. Dalila's clothes reveal her carnal disposition. In stark contrast to the denuded Samson, bare in his rags, Dalila sails forth "bedekt, ornate and gay" (712), like a "fair flower" (729) with "Silk'n veil" (730). Dalila may have good intentions in coming to see her husband, but she hardly seems dressed for the occasion. In fact, after Samson "bares" her guilt (902), she is "Discover'd in the end, till now conceal'd" (998). Her outward ornament places her with the Laudian prelates, not with the humble Savior in mean clouts. Samson and Dalila are poles apart in dress as in spirit.

Milton associates clothing with fallenness, and nakedness with innocence. At the critical moment in *Paradise Lost* when the first couple sins, Milton compares them to Samson and his Philistine woman:

> innocence, that as a veil
> Had shadow'd them from knowing ill, was gone,
> Just confidence, and native righteousness
> And honor from about them, naked left
> To guilty shame: hee [Adam] cover'd, but his Robe
> Uncover'd more. So rose the Danite strong
> Herculean Samson from the Harlot-lap
> Of Philistean Dalilah, and wak'd
> Shorn of his strength, They destitute and bare.   (IX, 1054–62)[23]

The epic simile makes explicit a number of ideas inherent in the tragedy: One's true habit is one's innocence; yet the loss of innocence is paradoxical: it is at once a putting on and a taking off. As they don their fig leaves they stand "destitute and bare."

Depotentiation, a loss of power, is another sense of kenosis found in Reformed literature. This view, in fact, is central to the modern use of the term. Zanchius defined kenosis as "a withholding of divine omnipotence in Christ, supporting his view by a reference to the Ambrosian doctrine of *retractio*.[24] Milton's tragic hero is very much one who has either lost or retracted or concealed (depending on how one views it) his former powers. Has he lost his strength? If so, when exactly was it restored? It is impossible to tell. The important fact is that it is manifested again with shocking force.

Depotentiation, the loss of power, is of course Samson's means to ultimate power; or, viewed from another perspective, it *is* power. God the great iconoclast brings down the rulers of this world through divine weakness. Samson mistakenly had trusted in carnal powers when:

> like a petty God
> I walk'd about admir'd of all and dreaded
> On hostile ground, none daring my affront.   (529–31)

He is then denuded, shorn of his strength and symbolically emasculated:

> At length to lay my head and hallow'd pledge
> Of all my strength in the lascivious lap
> Of a deceitful Concubine who shore me
> Like a tame Wether, all my precious fleece,
> Then turn'd me out ridiculous, despoil'd,
> Shav'n, and disarm'd among my enemies.   (535–40)

In this description Milton manages to suggest depotentiation in multiple images: he is a shorn lamb, a castrated sheep, a despoiled victim (i.e., stripped, robbed, plundered). Samson suggests the suffering servant, Isaiah's passive lamb silent before his shearer. Furthermore, Samson's loss of power is a "feminization" of the hero, which becomes, like all the other kenotic experiences, an entity with dual significance — for the unregenerate Samson "foul effeminancy" is the sure sign of his disgrace, but in fact it is actually God's way. Being "In power of others, never in my own" (78) is the way to true power. To be a "burdenous drone" (567), to be "Effeminently vanquish't" (563) leads to a primary attribute of the Miltonic hero. Initially, Samson least of all understands this truth. He believes "All wickedness is weakness" (834). *Weakness* is an almost unspeakable obscenity which is rivaled only by the word *effeminate*. Ironically, in the close, however, he finds that weakness, turned to God's service, is superior strength: "For my power is made perfect in weaknesse. Very gladly therefore will I rejoyce rather in mine infirmities. . . . for when I am weake then am I strong" (2 Cor. xii, 9–10).[25]

This Pauline principle is the essence of the depotentiated hero, of the suffering servant (who is also blind, Isa. xlii, 19). The servant of Yahweh stands as the passive vicarious victim before God's enemies "like a lamb that is led to the slaughter, and like a sheep that before its shearers is dumb" (Isa. liii, 7).[26] Weakness, rightly interpreted with a spiritual eye, is "no weakness, no contempt, / Dispraise, or blame, nothing but well and fair" (SA 1721–22).

The last great kenotic image is much more than a convenient metaphor. Rather, it is a paradigm of Christian history, a description of God's way of salvation, and an emblem of the pilgrim's progress. Kenosis is, last of all, a *journey* or *progress*, a "dramatic parabola."[27] The divine hero leaves a station of glory, and he descends; he liberates himself or others through his own kenosis; and he ascends to a position of even greater glory. The journey is vertical and is marked by two contrasting tacks, a "race of glory" and a "race of shame" (597), which at times merge and become synonymous. To descend does not merely cause ascent; kenosis does not merely lead to exaltation — they become synonymous entities. To descend is to ascend; to empty oneself is to be exalted. Arnold Stein seemed to be in touch with this curious phenomenon when he described the strange directions of Samson's career: "What shall we call these lines, or is there a name? A Heraclitean way up and way down, where high point and low point are really the same if one has the wit to discover the unexpected by looking for it?"[28]

The kenotic journey is not only vertical, it is timeless and *non se-*

quitur. Kenosis is "out of time," occurring in the dimension of "ritual," thus transcending the "particular historical moments in which they transpire, to become illustrations in time for eternity."[29] And because they are timeless patterns, Boyd Berry and Edward Tayler are correct in saying Samson lacks an Aristotelian middle.[30] The beginning inheres in the end, descent and ascent become one in eternity. Similarly Stanley Fish describes Christian's way in *Pilgrim's Progress* as "an inner commitment of the spirit (a road, as Augustine says, not from place to place, but of the affections), a commitment to the rule of his master, and as long as he walks by *that*, any road he literally walks is *the* way. . . . for you will be in the way only if the way is in you."[31] In other words, the journey from the mill to the theater is not isomorphic with the kenotic journey within. They do touch at critical moments, but they are not identical. It would be convenient to trace Samson's kenotic fall through the first half of the play, his rise in the second. But no such mapping is possible. The play is filled with fallings (debas'd, lowest pitch, descend, fall, flat, droop, stoop, condescend, crestfall'n, depress'd, overthrown) and with risings (top of glory, rousing motions, rising phoenix, dayspring, arise, rise), but the movements are maddeningly mixed. Even in the same moment, in the climactic act, one powerful image (the eagle) strikes downward, while its counterpart (the phoenix) rises — both images convey the same spiritual reality. Down is up; up is down.

If the kenotic parabola is vertical and timeless, the external progress of the plot in some way expresses or comments on the spiritual journey. The literal road is not identical to the spiritual, but they bear a distinct likeness. *Samson Agonistes* is very much a play about movement, about going places. It opens with Samson's urgent need for progress: "A little onward lend thy guiding hand / To these dark steps, a little further on." There are frequent references to walking, journeys, courses, feet, running, steps, and races. Also there are splendid images of movements with suspect value: circlings, enclosure, shipwrecks, tacking, ravelings, transferring, ensnaring, turning out, alluring, entangling, swaying, and drawing awry. Samson is on a pilgrimage, and he faces a series of impediments not unlike those of Bunyan's hero. Samson's great fear (easily understood on the spiritual plane) is cessation of movement. He is afraid to sit idle, to wait, to suffer "sedentary numbness" (571). He feels bound, buried, imprisoned, tied, ensnared, weary, and flat. The movement Samson needs, however, is not an earthly journey but an inner vertical one. The Pauline race proves to be a race within. He discovers the paradox that the greatest action comes in a timeless moment of perfect tranquillity. Ironically, the cessation of movement so feared by the hero is his great moment of triumph. He is "vigorous most / When most unactive deem'd" (1704–05). The description of Samson's destruction of the temple is a most curious and ambiguous blend of intense exertion and quiet passivity. His head is "a while inclin'd";"And eyes fast fixt he stood, as one who pray'd, / Or some great matter in his mind revolv'd." Then of his own accord he tugs and shakes the "massy Pillars" "till down they came" (1635–50). It appears that Samson has finally *acted* heroically. But has he? This action is curiously passive: "This utter'd, straining all his nerves he bow'd" (1646). Milton creates a tantalizing fusion of activity and passivity. Samson strained and he bow'd — not sequentially but simultaneously. That is the nature of the kenotic "act."

The kenotic paradigm, we may summarize, is revealed in the play through a variety of images. Samson was physically and spiritually emptied; he was denuded, shorn, and depotentiated. But he was also disguised, as was his deity. Unknown to his friends, his enemies, and even himself, God was working his will. Samson was on the great pilgrimage, the paradoxical up-and-down vertical progress that appears to lead nowhere, but actually leads to true glory. This is the story of the kenotic hero.

III

Kenotic language and imagery furnish us with a powerful interpretive key to the play, in addition to offering a fruitful link between the tragedy and Milton's other major works, *Paradise Regained* most noticeably. Both *Samson Agonistes* and *Paradise Regained* do read well as companion pieces — two scenes in a diptych portraying the way to glory through exinanition. Both works are extended discussions of the nature of power. In both tragedy and epic one encounters a host of characters (Satan, Dalila, the Philistines, even Manoa and the Chorus) who grossly misunderstand the nature and source of power. Dalila lusts for the "key of strength and safety" (799). Satan extols "coats of mail and military pride" (*PR* III, 312) and envisions the Son of God "on the Throne of David in full glory" (*PR* III, 383). Samson too laments the loss of this worldly power: "in strength / All mortals I excell'd" (522–23).

"What is the way to power?" is the implicit question behind both works. The answer proves so surprising that Satan cannot fathom it, and we may doubt whether anyone in Philistia understands either. The answer is the Gospel principle that one enters the Kingdom "as a child / Helpless" (942–43). Samson must become a child led by a child, or in other terms he must be "the fool, / In power of others" (77–78, cf. 1338). It is a route so utterly strange, few can perceive it. In fact one has to become blind to see it. Both poems reveal the way in which the ordinary sources of greatness must be called into question — whether earthly philosophy, "luggage of war," ambition, or glory in *Paradise Regained* or the external props of strength, eyesight, dignity and freedom in *Samson Agonistes*.

Both poems demonstrate the strange power of "weakness" and the ultimate triumph of the kenotic hero, "By Humiliation and strong Sufferance" (*PR* I, 160). The tragedy concretely demonstrates the idea of kenosis espoused by the Son in his dialogue with Satan. The Son vanquishes his enemy in a transcendent duel of mind and will, and Samson conquers ultimately through the same means. This may seem a strange assertion in view of the tragedy's bloody conclusion, but Milton repeatedly asserts the internal, "spiritual" nature of the hero's contest. The poem is a *psychomachia* of the finest sort in which Samson "some great matter in his mind revolved" (1638). Samson's experience, as one would expect of a kenotic hero, is chiefly inward: he "inward passion felt" (1006). He is illuminated with "inward eyes" (1689). Even the very carnal defeat of the Philistines can be read as an inward triumph:

> He all thir Ammunition
> And feats of War defeats
> With plain Heroic magnitude of mind.   (1277–79)

However, though the Son of God and Samson end up espousing similar positions on the questionable efficacy of earthly power, Samson is not initially like the Son. The early Samson (much like the early Milton we may suppose) accepts most of Satan's assumptions about the means to greatness — through classically heroic action. What was "plausible to the world" (*PR* III, 393) was plausible to Samson also. Only through the kenotic descent does Samson discover the truth that "Luggage of war there shown me, argument / Of human weakness rather than of strength" (*PR* III, 401–02).

By being systematically stripped of his external props, by being turned into a "vain monument of strength" (957), the son of Manoa comes to discover existentially the truth of the Son's words to Satan. Samson stumbles onto the kenotic path through his encounters with a series of tempters who would lure him from the necessary "race of shame."

In the play's opening scenes Samson is manifestly not the kenotic hero. Though he is undergoing a terrible humiliation of sorts, it is more like the humiliation of the defeated rebel angels than Christlike martyrdom. In fact, we see that there are two possible kenotic dramas operating in the tragedy, not one. It is important that kenotic drama implies an analogous "antidrama," the hero of which is variously Satan, Adam, or unredeemed man. At each point the antihero is superficially like, yet radically different from, the true hero, the god-man. Thus, the descent and loss of glory may result from Christlike *humilitas*, or it may be Satan's or Adam's punishment for *superbia*.[32] Samson's uniqueness rests in his capacity to play both roles. For a time he is the grasping-at-glory type, but through the cycle of "true experience" (1756) he abandons the position, embraces his kenotic role fully, and is therefore heroic in the kenotic sense. Thus, Samson is like the regenerated Adam in *Paradise Lost*, but unlike Satan, who cannot interpret his kenosis as other than a "foul descent." Samson's riddle is to make Christian sense of his descent. When that moment occurs, the hero is "regenerated." In fact, once the meaning of his descent dawns on him, it reinterprets all that has transpired as "true experience." He was *always* God's saint, it turns out.

Samson's story concerns the moment of this shift from the Adamic antidrama to the Christlike drama of kenosis. The Hebrew strong man moves from a cycle of blame and doubt characterized by faith in order, reason, talk, and "acts indeed heroic"; he ends up in a transcendent order marked by faith in God (however "irrational" this deity seems), passivity, humility, and silence. The external journey is superficial and almost inconsequential. The high drama within, suggested by Samson's intense mental struggle, is everything. Initially Samson is the contentious questioner of God, as are Manoa and the Chorus. How can a just God humiliate his one true and just champion? Why does God choose a champion of faith only to cast him down? Why does he permit (or even cause) the defeat of his saints?

> Why was my breeding order'd and prescrib'd
> As of a person separate to God,
> Design'd for great exploits; if I must die
> Betray'd, Captiv'd, and both my Eyes put out?   (30–33)

Samson's repeated claims expose many charges: God is cruel and unfair; his ways are unpredictable and illogical; he breaks promises ("Promise was that I / Should Israel from Philistian yoke deliver," 39). This cycle of doubt, one of the most forceful elements of the play, involves nearly everyone and is best seen in the repeated effort to fix blame. Each is gripped by Adamic pride; each acts, in St. Paul's words, "through contention or vaine glorie," not in "meekenesse of minde" esteeming everyone "better then himselfe" (Phil. ii, 3).

The strategy of casting blame deserves greater notice for it links the arguments of the three central episodes. The interminable scrutiny of faults and the minute examination of cause and effect make up a good deal of the discussion. "Who's at fault?" is the riddle. At one point Samson confidently says, "That fault I take not on me, but transfer"(241) — a summary of the deathly cycle of "ravelling" that governs everyone's thinking. When Samson appears to accept blame, it is a thinly disguised shifting of responsibility. Even when he concedes that he is "Sole Author . . . Sole cause" of his misfortune (376), he turns quickly to condemn Dalila in a tour de force of vituperation (379–405). Samson as Adamic antihero cannot escape the endless game of "that-fault-I-take-not-on-me-but-transfer."

Others follow the same strategy. The Chorus and Manoa accept Samson's view of the situation: their hero is humiliated and ruined. He has missed his chance. They too assume that the prophecy has been invalidated, and they can only dream of past glory or some future amelioration. What the Chorus finds in nameless "others" appears in them as well — the temptation to give

> the reins to wand'ring thought
> Regardless of his glory's diminution;
> Till by thir own perplexities involv'd
> They ravel more, still less resolv'd,
> But never find self-satisfying solution.   (302–06)

Like the demons in *Paradise Lost*, the more they dwell on edicts and causes — in short, the more they *think* — the more confused they become. They have predestined themselves to find "no end, in wand'ring mazes lost" (*PL* II, 561). The images of circlings, driving transverse, and drawing awry suggest figuratively what is happening spiritually (*SA* 209, 871, 1041). But Samson proves to be God's kenotic hero; in the course of his descent, he will reject the futile circle for the kenotic path.

With the Harapha episode one detects a new stage in the kenotic pattern. This proud giant, who is scarcely interested in metaphysical debates, seems to offer Samson a real contestant, an opposite the hero can grasp and defeat. But Harapha is not a true opposite; he is rather a mirror image of Samson's former heroic self — vain, boastful, naive, and dependent upon brute strength. This kinsman of Goliath is another incarnation of the kenotic antihero, the personification of Pauline contention and vainglory.[33] Just as he thought he could reason his way clear of moral entanglements, Samson itches for a carnal duel (like Adam and Satan in the epics). The Hebrew champion longs for "Some narrow space enclos'd" (1117), a place where he can justify old wrongs. Yet the Philistine warrior defeats the Hebrew agonist in the cruelest way by refusing any encounter at all. Through this defeat in his quest for some sort of saving action, Samson discovers the very absurdity of external power as an intrinsic value. The spiritual truth of kenosis becomes apparent as Harapha (Samson's alter ego) casts Israel's champion with the host of God's derelicts who have been cut off and delivered up, among slaves and asses, good for nothing:

> Presume not on thy God, whate'er he be
> Thee he regards not, owns not, hath cut off
> Quite from his people, and delivered up
> Into thy Enemies' hand.
> . . . .
> Among the Slaves and Asses thy comrades
> As good for nothing else, no better service
> With those thy boist'rous locks, no worthy match
> For valor to assail, nor by the sword
> Of noble Warrior, so to stain his honor,
> But by the Barber's razor best subdu'd.   (1156–67)

While this attack may be read simply as a typical exchange of hostile words, the *flytings* between heroic combatants, viewed as a hidden statement on kenosis the scurrilous charges are the bitter truth in ways Harapha and the others cannot fathom. Harapha portrays Samson as the great enemy, the pariah dwelling in the hell of isolation from man and God. All the charges are quite true; yet this tragic fact proves to be the hero's triumph. For Samson's growing understanding, these attributes describe the kenotic hero in his emptying. The champion of God is about to become the willing slave *in medio animalium*, the suffering servant "cut off" from his people (Isa. liii, 8).

In the meeting with Harapha, the "hinge of the tragedy,"[34] Samson's turnabout becomes clear. In one sense Dr. Johnson is correct: the reversal is unmotivated. After all, "motivation" is a virtue of the rational world which Samson renounces, and Aristotelian causality is part of the dark infection from which the hero recovers. One might say that the truth dawns on Samson. He sees the truth of his situation, yet the discovery concerns less his own nature than the nature of the divine plan. If this discovery constitutes a recognition scene, it is quite different from those in classical or Shakespearean drama. Samson does not discover his error or *hamartia*, for he has long fathomed the foolish error of his way. His culpability is an incontrovertible fact when the play opens. Rather, Samson's discovery is almost the reverse of classical *anagnorisis*. Instead of uncovering his fatal flaw, Samson learns that the wrong turn has proved, in God's mysterious way, to be the right turn, exactly! When Samson first took the Timnan woman, which appeared to conflict directly with

Mosaic teaching, the author of Judges makes it clear that Samson's faulty choice is providential: "But his father and mother knewe not that it came of the Lord" (Judg. xiv, 4). The Geneva Bible gloss makes the point more explicit: "this was the secret work of the Lord." Milton sees this principle not only in the Samson legend. It is the divine pattern throughout history, the paradox of grace, a shocking truth, too enormous to see, as shocking as finding a god in a manger or on a cross. The application of the kenotic reality is broad. Milton's hero learns that the old heroism is the wrong way, and so his humiliating descent proves to be the divine path after all. This understanding has profound effects on Samson in the scenes which follow.

After the departure of the crestfallen giant, one notices a remarkable change in Samson's spirit. No longer does he try to dissect cause and effect. No longer does he justify or blame. Neither does he trace his sufferings to some sin on his own part or a flaw in God or others. His sufferings simply *are*. Much like Job at the end of his trial, Samson finds a kind of silence to be the only adequate response to the theophany (Job xl, 3–4). His despair seems to have melted as he expresses faith and "Some rousing motions within" (1140, 1171, 1382). Furthermore, he passes into a new kind of ambiguous language that refuses to give away facts. Once more he is God's riddler. Open-ended questions replace declarations, allowing listeners to make their own meaning:

> Have they not Sword-players, and ev'ry sort
> Of Gymnic Artists, Wrestlers, Riders, Runners,
> Jugglers and Dancers, Antics, Mummers, Mimics?   (1323–25)

Similar questions abound: "Myself?" "Can they think me so broken, so debas'd?" "Shall I abuse this / Consecrated gift . . . in place abominable?" (1334–62). Such inquiries are capable of contradictory responses.[35] For Samson's unregenerate auditors, they imply one sort of answer, but for the kenotic hero and the attentive reader, his questions imply something quite different. Samson is not expressing doubt about whether or not he can attend the temple; he is, instead, affirming abasement as the proper posture of the true hero. All Samson's questions, then, may be answered yes and no. He is their fool and he is not. He is to be abased and he is not. The complexity of the final speeches and the final "heroic" act show Milton at his best. Is it suicide or vicarious redemption? Is Samson the active agent or the passive instrument of providence? Is this a story of cruel vengeance, Hellenic tragedy, or a parable of Christian redemption? Conclusions somewhat depend upon whether one can see the implicit operation of kenosis in the protagonist. To those without the circle of faith, he is a pathetic brute or a sad fool; to those within, he is a victorious figure whose deeds are "above heroic."

This story of the kenotic way may be the closest the poet's art ever comes to ritual and mystery. This humiliation and exaltation is for Milton the supremely religious experience, a preeminently private phenomenon, and one not readily dramatized. Ultimately, Milton's idea of kenosis can only be implied, never really seen. Or, if it can be seen, it cannot be located in a single sacerdotal act. This may account for the peculiar absence of cultic ritual and sacrament in so devout a poet as Milton. To Milton, one's whole life is the true sacrament: "Give up your bodies a living sacrifice, holy, acceptable unto God, which is your reasonable serving of God" read St. Paul in Milton's Bible (Rom. xii, 1). Milton's "reasonable serving of God" was the presentation of his whole life as a kenotic performance, which devalues particular rites like the Eucharist or liturgical worship. Milton's sacrament was enacted "in life" and "in death," but not "in church." This kenotic principle may explain the conspicuous absence of ritual in Samson's salvation. Perhaps kenosis makes possible a religion devoid of ecclesiastical form altogether. Is it accidental that the last heroic act among Milton's heroes is the demolition of a temple?

Samson Agonistes, to summarize, demonstrates the idea of kenosis verbalized by the Son in *Paradise Regained*, but, unlike the brief epic, where the hero seems to have an extraordinary grasp of the concept, Samson must acquire through experience the truth that the journey down is the way up. By undergoing the cycle of suffering Samson comes to understand fully the truth of spiritual emptying: that in the extreme point of kenosis "one reaches the supreme height of the self-manifestation of God."[36]

IV

In several respects the kenotic motif provides new and fruitful answers to the old questions about the play's spirit and purpose. Kenotic drama is just one example of a cultural element originating in the ancient Mediterranean world that transcends the conventional labels of "Hebrew," "Greek," and "Christian." When R. C. Jebb first raised the question about the play's "spirit" in 1907, it was thought that such clear distinctions were possible; now we are less sure. Paul Ricoeur has shown the existence of a "Helleno-Hebraic schematization" which calls such a dichotomy into question. Concerning the "existential eruptions" of the consciousness of evil in Western civilization, he writes, "The encounter of the Jewish source with the Greek origin is the fundamental intersection that founds our culture."[37] Several authorities on early Christianity make comparable observations. For example, W. D. Davies asserts that "the traditional convenient dichotomy between Judaism and Hellenism was largely false. In the fusions of the first century the boundaries between these are now seen to have been very fluid."[38] Such insights impinge on our assessment of Milton's work. It is significant that the kenotic paradigm is not uniquely Christian. Although it appears in the earliest Christian liturgies, the paradigm is grounded in Hellenistic myths of descent and ascent of the primal man (the *Urmenschmythos*), and it also bears an equally important kinship to the servant of the Yahweh cycle of Second Isaiah.[39] The kenotic paradigm comes out of an ancient Mediterranean matrix that unites Hellenistic, Hebrew, and Christian traditions. While our particular sense of kenosis is distinctly Christian, we cannot ignore the Jewish and Greek dimensions of the paradigm. Consequently, we find it difficult to call the "spirit" of the play purely Hebrew, Greek, or Christian. An awareness of the kenotic forbids such facile categorizations.

But is the play truly tragic? That is a much more difficult query because it presupposes so much about what constitutes the "tragic." Certainly Milton thought the play tragic, as he makes clear in his introduction to the poem. His argument, never spelled out, would seem to follow these lines: Even if there is some eschatalogical glory for the hero, in earthly existence he knows no such glory. Ascent, joy, and beatitude may compose the final act of the Christian comedy, but the final act cannot cancel the reality of tragic emotion. For this reason Milton considered St. John's Apocalypse a grand tragedy, a kenotic work also concerned with descents into tribulation and ascents to crowns of glory. We inhabit a world marked by exile, abandonment, and the apparent absence of God. Existence requires a radical emptying before any "redemption" is possible. "Deliverance" and "liberty," the drama's themes according to the poem's introduction, do not even prove possible in a human, earthly sense. The hero is "exiled from light." Life is a "captivity" in which the protagonist feels cast off "as never known." For Milton, such a journey through "the land of darkness" is truly tragic. Though one may claim that Manoa and the Chorus celebrate too much in the close for the play to be truly tragic, one must recall that the final lines do not compensate for 1600 lines of darkness (just as Edgar's concluding words hardly compensate for the holocaust in *King Lear*). Furthermore, the final ascent of the kenotic parable is not for *human* eyes.[40] Milton's heroes must make their solitary ways through a dark world fallen on evil days. They *see* no reborn phoenix on the stage — it is only the Chorus's hope. The "overshadowing of the heavenly wings," as the poet called it, can never be seen in this dark world. The fact of resurrection does not cancel the agony of the cross.

Samson Agonistes may indeed be the fullest statement by the Christian poet who endured a world of dark disappointment. In the face of apocalyptic defeat he could mysteriously fathom the divine working and therefore testify to a remnant of meaning. *Samson* is a tragedy, yes, in the common and general sense of the term; but finally it is a tragedy that bursts its bounds, that refuses to be tragedy only, or tragedy comfortable in an old form. It is commonly accepted that at the same moment Milton composed his epics, he was subverting the genre, transforming it and making it new. Similarly *Samson* bears the clear marks of classical tragedy, but the radical Protestant poet found that the old wineskins could not entirely contain the new vision. The result is a play, uniquely Miltonic, truly unlike any other before or since.

The story of a depleted, self-limited, dying God taught Milton to see human existence as profoundly kenotic. Raphael leads us to conceive the analogy:

> What if Earth
> Be but the shadow of Heav'n, and things therein
> Each to other like more than on Earth is thought?
>
> (PL V, 574–76)

Humanity, like the rebellious archangel and the first man, is marked by grasping pride that sends him on a journey into exile. He is the outcast of glory, and only if he rightly interprets his journey can he hope for anything better. Kenosis is the unifying pattern that intimately links the last great poems, for kenotic drama is concerned with the possible ways Satan and his followers, and Adam and his progeny, play out this prescribed drama. Everyone, Milton suggests, must enact a similar drama; but depending on how one interprets it, whether in humble faith or grasping pride, it can either be a "race of glory" or a "race of shame" (597).

Oklahoma Christian College

NOTES

1. Barbara Lewalski, *Milton's Brief Epic* (Providence, 1966), p. 393, n. 69; and "Theme and Action in *Paradise Lost*," in *Milton's Epic Poetry*, ed. C. A. Patrides (Baltimore, 1967), p. 323. John Shawcross, "The Balanced Structure of *Paradise Lost*," *SP*, LXII

(1965), 698–99, Mary Christopher Pecheux, "'O Foul Descent!': Satan and the Serpent Form," *SP*, LXII (1965), 188–96. Michael Lieb, "Milton and Kenotic Christology: Its Literary Bearing," *ELH*, XXXVII (1970), 343, 360. Darryl Tippens, "'Race of Glory, Race of Shame:' Kenotic Thought in *Samson Agonistes, MQ*, XIX (December 1985), pp. 96–100. I am grateful to *MQ* for permission to incorporate some sections of that essay in the present work.

2. For a rewarding historical survey of kenotic thought in both philosophy and theology see Donald G. Dawe, *The Form of a Servant* (Philadelphia, 1963).

3. J. M. Creed, cited in Ralph P. Martin, *Carmen Christi: Philippians ii. 5–11 in Recent Interpretation and in the Setting of Early Christian Worship* (Cambridge, 1967), p. 67.

4. *Complete Prose Works of John Milton*, ed. Don M. Wolfe et al. (New Haven, 1953–82), vol. VI, p. 274. Hereafter referred to as YP.

5. YP VI, pp. 275, 440. See also Lieb, "Kenotic Christology," p. 344, and Pecheux, "'O Foul Descent,'" p. 193. On the definition of κενόω see *Theological Dictionary of the New Testament*, ed. Gerhard Kittel (Grand Rapids, 1964–76), III, p. 661. The idea of kenosis probably antedates the New Testament. Ralph Martin traces the idea of the kenotic descent of the divine hero back to earlier Hellenistic legends (*Carmen Christi*, pp. 76–80), and it appears frequently in classical Greek. Haimon, for example, prophesies Creon's own kenosis by warning him that his kingly pride is a certain sign of emptiness (*Antigone* 709). Cf. *Ajax* 986; *Antigone* 754–57; *The Suppliant Maidens* 660.

6. Henry Airay, *Lectures upon the Whole Epistle of St. Paul to the Philippians*, ed. Christopher Potter (London, 1618), p. 318.

7. *Commentary on the Epistle to the Romans* (Grand Rapids, 1954), p. 116.

8. Authorized Version (London, 1612).

9. *Lectures*, p. 335.

10. Jeremy Taylor, *Life of Our Lord and Saviour* (1649; London, 1941), p. 389.

11. John Calvin, *Commentaries on the Epistles of Paul the Apostle to the Philippians, Colossians and Thessalonians*, ed. and trans. John Pringle (Edinburgh, 1851), p. 54.

12. Augustine, *Sermons for Christmas and Epiphany*, ed. and trans. Thomas C. Lawler, in *Ancient Christian Writers* (New York, 1952), XI pp. 93–94.

13. Very significantly, many characters in Milton's works experience a kenosis, although it is not always a salutary one. For example, Satan in *Paradise Regained* is a kenotic sufferer who is not taught by his experience: "Ejected, emptied, gaz'd unpitied, shunned, / A spectacle of ruin" (I, 414–15). All poetry quotations come from *Complete Poems and Major Prose*, ed. Merritt Y. Hughes (Indianapolis, 1957).

14. The Pauline kenotic hymn is specifically set over against very unchristian behavior: contention and vainglory (Phil. ii, 3). St. Paul exhorts the Christian reader to renounce the Satanic (Adamic) role for the Christian one: "That nothing be done through contention or vaine glory." The Christian is to have "the same mind" that "was even in Christ Jesus" (ii, 5). Samson is caught between these two kenotic roles before he eventually becomes the true kenotic hero.

15. Lieb, "Kenotic Christology," pp. 344–48.

16. Lancelot Andrewes, *Ninety-six Sermons in the Library of Anglo-Catholic Theology*, ed. J. P. Wilson and James Blish (Oxford, 1841), p. 38.

17. Edward W. Tayler, *Milton's Poetry: Its Development in Time* (Pittsburgh, 1979), pp. 111–12.

18. Andrewes, *Sermons*, p. 40.

19. Taylor, *Life of Our Lord*, p. 25.

20. Alex B. Bruce, *The Humiliation of Christ in Its Physical, Ethical, and Official Aspects* (Edinburgh, 1876), p. 151.

21. Andrewes, *Sermons*, p. 38.

22. Bruce, *Humiliation of Christ*, pp. 162–63.

23. Note how Milton weaves various kenotic images into a single line: depotentiation ("shorn of strength"), impoverishment ("destitute"), and divestiture ("bare").

24. Bruce, *Humiliation of Christ*, p. 41.

25. Strength through weakness is a recurrent theme in Milton: "By small / Accomplishing great things, by things deem'd weak / Subverting worldly strong" (*PL* XII, 566–68); "His weakness shall o'ercome Satanic Strength" (*PR* I, 161); "There is a certain road that leads through weakness, as the apostle teaches, to the greatest strength. May I be entirely helpless, provided that in my weakness there may arise all the more powerfully this immortal and more perfect strength" (YP IV, pp. 589–90). Weakness, always an important theme in Milton's career, becomes crucial to the tragedy. The word and its cognates appear more often in the tragedy (fourteen times) than in any other Milton poem.

26. In several respects Samson appears like the Old Testament suffering servant. They are similarly exiles, passive, sorrowful, grief-stricken, shocking in appearance, suffering a vicarious death, judged to be smitten of God, interred with the rich and the wicked.

27. "Dramatic parabola" is Emil Brunner's term (*The Mediator* 1934, pp. 561–63) cited by Martin, *Carmen Christi*, p. 228. Critics of the Pauline hymn have noted the hymn's dramatic structure. It is a "cosmic drama" with hero, antagonist, and an important *peripeteia* in verse 8 (ibid., pp. 74, 228).

28. Arnold Stein, *Heroic Knowledge* (Minneapolis, 1957), p. 153.

29. Albert R. Cirillo, "Time, Light and the Phoenix: The Design of *Samson Agonistes*," in *Calm of Mind*, ed. Joseph A. Wittreich, Jr. (Cleveland, 1971), p. 210.

30. Boyd M. Berry, *Process of Speech: Puritan Religious Writing and Paradise Lost* (Baltimore, 1976), p. 9; Tayler, *Milton's Poetry*, pp. 106–09.

31. Stanley Fish, *Self-Consuming Artifacts: The Experience of Seventeenth-Century Literature* (Los Angeles, 1972), p. 228.

32. Martin, *Carmen Christi*, p. 158.

33. Cf. Henry Airay's contrast of humility and vainglory, *Lectures*, pp. 302–06.

34. Don Cameron Allen, *The Harmonious Vision* (Baltimore, 1954), p. 91.

35. On Samson's ambiguous final speeches see Stanley Fish, "Question and Answer in *Samson Agonistes*," *Critical Quarterly*, II (1969), 237–64.

36. Dawe, *Form of a Servant*, p. 163.

37. Paul Ricoeur, *The Symbolism of Evil* (Boston, 1969), pp. 20, 71–72.

38. Davies, "Paul and the Dead Sea Scrolls: Flesh and Spirit" in *The Scrolls and the New Testament*, ed. Krister Stendahl (New York, 1957), p. 157. See also E. R. Goodenough, *Jewish Symbols in the Greco-Roman Period* (New York, 1953), I, p. 61 ff.; and Martin Hengel, *Judaism and Hellenism* (Philadelphia, 1974).

39. Some scholars stress the origin of the kenotic hymn in the servant poems of Isaiah xl–lv. Others emphasize the origin of the pattern in Greek mythology (Martin, *Carmin Christi*, pp. 76–80, 156).

40. Cf. Calvin's view concerning the last stage of the Christian's pilgrimage (Rom. viii, 30): "glorification is not yet exhibited except in our Head." *Commentaries on the Epistle of Paul to the Romans*, ed. and trans. John Owen (Edinburgh, 1849), p. 320.

"IF THERE BE AUGHT OF PRESAGE": MILTON'S SAMSON AS RIDDLER AND PROPHET

Daniel T. Lochman

S AMSON'S "RECOGNITION" in Milton's dramatic poem has been regarded as pivotal not only to the work's dramatic development, but also to Samson's spiritual regeneration and involvement with the will of God in the enactment of providence. The abruptness of Samson's "rousing motions," which produce "something extraordinary" in his "thoughts," calls attention to the passage, providing a feeling of imminent yet indeterminate change, intimating an approaching denouement. Samson voices his own feelings of anticipation when he predicts his destiny:

> If there be aught of presage in the mind
> This day will be remarkable in my life
> By some great act, or of my days the last.[1]

Ironically, though, Samson's prophetic "presage," as it is stated, turns out to be logically incorrect. Here, as Anthony Low has observed, Samson presents an ironically false set of alternatives.[2] Although the hero seems to have advanced at this point, having departed from his earlier obsession with the past, he is not yet able to connect his destiny to the impending catastrophe. Logically, Samson's attempt at prophecy fails to consider alternatives other than the dual — not mutually exclusive — assertions that *either* the day will be remarkable *or* that it will be his last. He fails to foresee that the day will be *both* remarkable *and* his last. Complicating the passage is the prophetic context of Samson's assertion. His presage seems to remove the statement from the limits of ordinary logic. By its nature, prophecy is a movement beyond the limits, the normal strictures, of the everyday world; it is an excursion into an illogical, unlimited, and often indistinctly perceived future. Samson claims to speak in this supralogical fashion when he offers his cautious conditional ("If there be aught of presage in the mind"), but his claim for prophecy circumscribes a rigid logic. If we are equally rigid in judging the accuracy of the alternatives he proposes, we must conclude that there is no presage in Samson's mind. Yet even if we respond negatively to his conditional — saying that he has no prophetic ability — we will still be incorrect, since, in the catastrophe, we find that both elements of his supposedly mutually exclusive alternatives are correct: he does have "aught" of prophetic ability, but he does not have sufficient "presage" to predict without error his personal future.

The complicated mix of logic and prophecy in this passage, its logical inconsistencies, inaccuracies, and confusion of modes of thought and expression may well be missed by an audience inclined to consider the moment's drama rather than its logic, following the abrupt onset of the hero's "rousing motions." Through the swiftness of Samson's recognition, Milton invites his audience to accept the conditional proposition — to engage in a process of thought rooted in alternatives (either Samson has "presage of the mind" or not) — just as Samson, at the very same place, engages in the construction of obviously faulty alternatives. Yet the audience may miss Milton's redirection of alternative thought processes back upon themselves; they may fail to see that the problems inherent in Samson's dualistic alternatives may apply also to themselves, if they choose to judge Samson as acting freely through choice *or* merely as God's instrument, as a prophet *or* a misguided fool, as a type of Christ *or* of antichrist.[3] Milton's audience, like Samson, must learn to see existence as mixed and ambiguous, irreducible to simple, absolute alternatives.[4] Although the evangelist unambiguously admonishes us to choose for or against God (Matt. xii, 30) — Samson too must choose between "Sun or shade" at the outset — the clarity of that choice does not provide an equally clear means of enacting good or evil in a fallen, unredeemed world.

At the recognition, Samson has already begun to learn the lesson of duality's inadequacy. He has learned to think in more complex ways, no longer seeing himself as either an active agent for deliverance or a failure, either a "faithful Champion" or a sinner, useless to God and his providence. Instead, Samson leaves some room for providential maneuvering; as I have indicated, he prefaces his prophetic alternatives, whose underlying limitations he has not yet escaped, with a conditional, which, at least, allows the possibility that God may have intentions other than those of his own "presageful" thinking. As Kathleen M. Swain observes, Samson's speech "demonstrates a release from monolithic historical fact and from insistence on rationality."[5] Yet Samson cannot fully escape the conundrums created by his patterns of thought. Despite its apparent respect for providence, his conditional is also fraught with difficulty. He still believes that God will grant him either fully accurate prophetic abilities or none at all; he fails to consider that his prophecy may be accurate only in part. Like Satan on the pinnacle at the climax of *Paradise*

Regained, Samson looks for simple absolutes. Because he cannot think of new alternatives, he assumes that there are none and is therefore incorrect. What distinguishes Milton's tragic hero from Christ's adversary is Samson's allowance for ambiguity, his innocent hesitancy in predicting events intimately involved with God's purposes. It is this room for possibility that allows some hope to coincide with — not replace — his despair. In his ironic association of "this day" with something "remarkable" *and* something deadly, he approaches the threshold of prophecy, just as his historical existence is at the threshold of the age of verbal prophecy and providential kingship, to be manifest in the days of Samuel and David.[6] Yet Samson's conscious, verbal, prophetic skills are primitive and limited, predicting only an immediate future. In contrast is the distant foresight of his unwittingly prophetic *act.* The great catastrophe — toward which Samson's recognition points — prefigures God's vengeful destruction of evil, his merciful deliverance of the good at the end of time.

Though much comment has been devoted to Samson's regeneration, his growth in self-awareness, and his transformation to activity from lethargy, his change from a speaker of riddles to a prophet of verbal insight and prophetic act — to a man sometimes capable of clear and right prophecy, sometimes confused by simplistic logical constructs and unable to foresee the complexity of a paradoxical future — has evoked little attention.[7] This study will trace Samson's spiraling progress from a destructive obsession with past promise and present suffering to a unity of present action and providence.

I

Samson's prophetic skill develops in three stages. First, prophecy intrudes into the hero's initial cycle of despair, when Samson transcends his preoccupation with past causes for his present suffering, by considering God's absolute and certain power over evil; second, it becomes a means of joining Samson's personal future to providence, when the hero is provoked to make decisions which will affect his future; and third, his prophecy of victory over personal, national, and religious enemies, inaccurate as it may be in its particulars, provides a link between the hero's future and God's divine plan. In Samson's development as a prophet, the past is subsumed into the present, and the present is projected into the future, so that God's hero learns to preserve the potentiality appropriate to an omnipotent divinity and to avoid the restrictive logic native to merely human, discursive, dialectical thought.

At the outset, Samson's proximity to despair, as well as the cyclical character of his emotional disturbance, rapidly becomes obvious. The connection between Samson's stinging "thoughts" and his reflection upon his past is made explicit in the *prologos:* the "deadly swarm" of thoughts "present" to the hero "what once I was, and what am now" (22). So long as Samson remains locked in this circular, dialectical reflection upon his past promise and present weakness, he can make no psychological advance: his present shame reminds him of his past strength (617–40), and his past glory reminds him of present suffering (23–109).[8] His cure lies in the "redress" of his "ling'ring disease," which seems to "ferment and rage" like "wounds immedicable" (619–20) within the near despairing Samson. The fatal consequence of the disease — its "black mortification"— is apparent to Samson even as he is seemingly locked in its embrace; he has no escape so long as he seeks to explain his present suffering by means of a causal link to the past, ignoring the potential of the future.[9]

In the first 650 lines, from the lamentation in Samson's *prologos* to his lamentation after the second episode, the hero makes little apparent progress. The cyclic consideration of his past in relation to the present and the present in relation to the past serves only to increase the intensity of the stinging thoughts and despair, leading him to single hope in a "speedy death." Yet his movement toward deeper, more malignant despair is balanced by a few hopeful elements: recurring admonitions concerning God's transcendent purposes and power and, especially, Samson's prophecy of God's certain victory over Dagon.

Even in the depths of despair, Samson occasionally recalls — or is led by his companions to recall — God's superior will and virtue. At times, Samson becomes aware of the danger of his despair and its proximity to diffidence, and he is able to caution himself, sometimes with the aid of the Chorus and Manoa, against the self-indulgence implicit in absolute despair. In the *prologos*, Samson nearly complains of God's apparently inaccurate promise, seemingly unjust treatment of his champion. The hero who was to have delivered Israel recovers himself just short of blasphemy:

> Yet stay, let me not rashly call in doubt
> Divine Prediction; what if all foretold
> Had been fulfill'd but through mine own default,
> Whom have I to complain of but myself? (43–46)

Lurking behind Samson's self-deprecation is a dangerous but suppressed alternative — that God's justice may deserve "complaint"; and, as the intensity of his self-deprecation grows, so does his unexpressed questioning of God's goodness, providence, and power. Samson's saving "Yet stay" allows him to consider momentarily the transcendent potentiality of "Divine Prediction," and it allows him to rediscover his own weakness as the principal cause of his misfortune. The restrictive alternatives — either God's promise will be fulfilled in the renewed strength of a delivering Samson or God will arbitrarily abandon his champion — are superseded by the limitless potential of divine "Prediction."

But Samson's recovery from despair through self-administered admonition is only momentary, and it is followed by renewed feelings of despair, shame, and guilt, when he is forced to consider his past from new contexts — as a friend and countryman as well as a son. With the entrance of the Chorus and, later, Manoa, the cycle of despair continues, deepening its obsessive concentration upon the past and present despite the hero's occasional admonitions to consider God's large providence; the despair is even extended outward, touching the newcomers. Until Samson's lamentation at the close of the second episode, the cycle is broken only once, when Samson deviates from it by prophesying God's ultimate triumph. To Manoa's intimation that Samson had brought dishonor to God through "frailty" in his dealings with women and in his "marriage choices," the hero responds with a simple admission of error:

> Father, I do acknowledge and confess
> That I this honor, I this pomp have brought
> To *Dagon*, and advanc'd his praises high
> Among the Heathen round; to God have brought
> Dishonor, obloquy, and op't the mouths
> Of Idolists, and Atheists; have brought scandal
> To *Israel*, diffidence of God, and doubt
> In feeble hearts, propense enough before
> To waver, or fall off and join with Idols.   (448–56)

In this direct admission of guilt, framed in balanced, orderly oppositions which contrast neatly Dagon's "honor" and God's "Dishonor," Samson reveals no subterfuge, no excessive wallowing in self-condemnation, no labored and windy convolution. His simple humility is reminiscent of Eve's, in her admission of guilt to the Son: "The Serpent me beguil'd and I did eat" (*PL* X, 162). This simplicity, devoid of the turbulent syntax, questions, and errant logic of his previous speeches, relieves momentarily the obsession with the past which has impeded his consideration of the present in relation to the future. For a moment, the way to foresight, prophecy, and certitude in God's ultimate victory has been cleared:

> He, be sure,
> Will not connive, or linger, thus provok'd,
> But will arise and his great name assert:

> *Dagon* must stoop, and shall ere long receive
> Such a discomfit, as shall quite despoil him
> Of all these boasted Trophies won on me,
> And with confusion blank his Worshippers.   (465–71)

This frank prediction of God's retributive justice leaps from the text, without metaphor, irony, or other figurative device.[10] It points to a specific truth, with certitude. Yet Samson foresees no role for himself in the enactment of Dagon's "discomfit"; he cannot bridge the gap which divides his self-acknowledged weakness and sinfulness from an awareness of his future involvement with providence. Between the openness and directness of his confession and the confidence of his prophecy, moreover, there intrudes a moment of doubt, signaled by the hero's return to clipped phrases, thought-compressing and incoherence-producing caesurae. Following his open confession, Samson claims that his personal dishonor to God is his "chief affliction, shame and sorrow"—having replaced his initial obsession with blindness (67) and his subsequent shame before the choral tribesmen (187–209). Samson's simple openness wavers, and he returns briefly to the emotional disturbance common since the *prologos*. His sin has become, he says,

> The anguish of my Soul, that suffers not
> Mine eye to harbor sleep, or thoughts to rest.
> This only hope relieves me, that the strife
> With mee hath end; all the contést is now
> 'Twixt God and *Dagon; Dagon* hath presum'd,
> Mee overthrown, to enter lists with God,
> His Deity comparing and preferring
> Before the God of *Abraham*.   (458–65)

Samson is still blind to his personal role in providence and to his personal salvation, even though he reveals some insight into God's incomparable power.[11] He still cannot see that God has not had "end" with him, and his "only hope"—that he may now step passively aside—turns out to be misplaced. He still cannot see that, though "overthrown" now, he will not necessarily remain so: he has not yet cast off the false limits imposed on his thinking by reliance upon dualistic alternatives.

Although the first two episodes offer glimpses of providence, Samson is unable to escape the overwhelming, debilitating despair which is the product of his ruined promise. He is unable to view himself in relation to a broader design. When Manoa gives voice to his paternal concern for Samson's future ("But for thee what shall be done?" 478), the formerly prophetic Samson returns to the defensive shell, the extreme self-condemnation, which he had used to ward off the charges made formerly by the Chorus and Manoa. He seeks to "pay" for and "expiate" his crime through his grinding labor and spiritual despair. He instinctively turns away from Manoa's promise of a life of ease at the household hearth, sensing in that potential future his degradation as a "pitied object," with his "redundant locks" then serving no "purpose" (564–72). At the close of the second episode, however, he can provide no better purpose for his future — only his single wish for "speedy death."

Still, the form of that destructive wish — a prayer — saves Samson from an absolute despair. Prayer implies submission to and acceptance of God's will, even when it seeks "speedy death"; in contrast is the proud, stubborn despair of Satan in *Paradise Lost.* At the close of the second episode Samson teeters on the edge of despair's abyss — using absolutes such as "immedicable" and "remediless" to describe his future. He perceives himself to be "cast . . . off as never known" (641) by the God whom he cannot bring himself to name as the referent of his pronouns ("his," 633, 634, 636; "he," 638). Yet he recovers by offering the "one prayer" that still seems possible: his appeal for death, escape from the evils of the world, a death which constitutes the "close of all . . . miseries, and the balm" (651). Though its subject is self-serving, his prayer implies his humility in relation to the God who is the source of mercy as well as justice; it allows him to recall, though fleetingly, his right relation to God. Samson's "one prayer" invites escape from the cycle of despair implicit in his grinding of himself between the stones of the past and present. It rectifies the exaggeration implicit in Samson's claim that he is the source of all evil, and it reaffirms the limitless set of alternatives open to God, in his omnipotence. In the midst of despair, following his repudiation of his father's vision of the future, Samson must choose between one of the few mutually exclusive alternatives which appear in the work: either he must abandon himself wholly to despair, or he must look as far as possible beyond his present suffering, to his future in union with God's providence. If Samson is ultimately saved in Milton's view — and Milton never explicitly confirms that this postlapsarian hero is (indeed, he even deliberately obfuscates the issue in the confusing, only partially accurate judgments of Samson in the *kommos*) — the spring for his personal salvation resides in the implicit acceptance of God's will exemplified in "this one prayer yet remains": an afterthought which grows out of despair and paradoxically controls it.

Though his prayer might prevent him from falling into absolute hopelessness, Samson is no less despondent; his hope is associated, after all, with a perhaps understandable yet reprehensible impulse for self-destruction. Though the hero has passed his moment of greatest danger, he has not eliminated his proclivity to despair. This is so even as he enters the second stage of his prophetic development — his provocation by external agents to personal involvment in providence. Foreshadowed by Manoa's false promise of a comfortable future at home on the hearth, the prophecies of Samson's tormentors — Dalila and Harapha — are also perceived by the hero as false, and these deceivers provoke Samson to counter their falseness with a view of the future which presupposes a renewed participation in providence. These so-called temptations in fact constitute goads essential to the revivification of Samson's spirit.[12] They do not so much test Samson's "virtue" — he is able to slough off the "Adder's wisdom" and "feign'd shifts" of his tormentors with little trouble — as provoke him to think, culminating, in each case, in blind threats of what he *would* do to his enemies. Ironically, Samson's threats do not accurately predict the future, since they prove sufficient in themselves to drive his enemies away; but they do suggest possibilities for future action, through the potentiality implicit in conditionals and subjunctives. By means of this awakening sense of potentiality, Samson grows in confidence and begins to control his despair: he begins to act to create his own and his people's futures.

In his exchange with Dalila, Samson advances from despair over the past and present to action performed in the present and focused upon the future. He rejects the false prophecy offered by Dalila — a transmutation of that future formerly envisioned by Manoa, with paternal care replaced by uxoriousness and fatherly love by feminine sensuality. Dalila wishes him to live protected,

> At home in leisure and domestic ease,
> Exempt from many a care and chance to which
> Eyesight exposes daily men abroad.   (917–19)

To this comfortable vision, Samson proposes an alternative — one related to his past but anticipatory of the future. The hard consequences of Samson's prior trust argue all too painfully that Dalila's sentimentally persuasive prediction is improbable. He counters her sentimental future with what, given his experience, seems a more probable vision of "perfect thraldom" — subservience to a nagging, hostile wife (938–50). For Samson, the liberty proclaimed by Dalila is illusory, constituting a bondage which would, by contrast, make his present "Gaol" a "house of Liberty." Foresight allows the hero to predict a probable outcome based upon generalized experience; it allows him to project his past into the unrestricted potential of the future, rather than locking it inflexibly in dialectic with an apparently unalterable present. For the first time, Samson becomes aware of the "Liberty" he still holds, despite his bondage, and it is this awareness which allows him to think beyond the limits of the present to the future, as he could not during the previous cycles of despair.

Still, Samson's alternative is not prophetic. At the same time that he begins to consider the future in relation to himself, he continues to couch his predictions in subjunctives which imply logical probability rather than certitude. When provoked sufficiently by the "sorceress," however, he demonstrates through imperatives a prophetic certitude:

> *Bewail* thy falsehood, and the pious works
> It hath brought forth to make thee memorable
> Among illustrious women, faithful wives:
> *Cherish* thy hast'n'd widowhood with the gold
> Of Matrimonial treason: so farewell.   (955–59, my emphasis)

In passing judgment upon his wife, Samson accurately predicts Dalila's fame as an ironic *exemplum* — not of the pious patriot whom she envisions but of the alluring "viper" who leads good men to their foolish destruction, as Milton depicts her in *Paradise Lost* (IX, 1060). Not only are her predictions false, they are also ironic, juxtaposing her predicted fame with her legendary infamy, Samson's poor "lot" with his spectacular triumph. Still, as the swirl of critical controversy regarding her argument attests, Dalila's false prophecy seems plausible and persuasive. Its speaker seems ambitious, boldly nationalistic, and faithfully religious, and her vision seems reasonable as well as pleasant, even in its formulation of the relativism of good and evil.[13] Because of this persuasive appeal, the perception by Samson of her false allegiance — and therefore of her false prophecy — requires his clear, cold recognition of the radical and absolute difference between good and evil, and it assumes his ability to judge among potential alternatives based upon their probability and spiritual allegiance. Though superficially Dalila appears indistinguishable from the Philistine Jael she wishes to become, she incorrectly assumes that good and evil are proximate and interchangeable; she assumes a "doublemouth'd" truth, wherein God and Dagon share an equality which the faithful must always deny (440–41, 465–71, 971–72). As a false prophet, Dalila lacks the right source of inspiration, the intimate impulse for the good, the sense of the absolute, which leads Samson to his fearsome victory.

In his encounter with Harapha, Samson again discovers and denies false prophecy, yet in this case the hero not only negatively punctures inaccuracies but also positively predicts an alternative future. Harapha provokes Samson to engage in heroic boasting—itself a primitive form of prediction. In the first of his boasts to the "tongue-Doughty Giant," Samson confidently foretells the outcome of a potential battle:

> I only with an Oak'n staff *will* meet thee
> And raise such outcries on thy clatter'd Iron,
> Which long *shall* not withhold me from thy head,
> That in a little time, while breath remains thee,
> Thou oft *shalt* wish thyself at Gath to boast
> Again in safety what thou *wouldst* have done
> To Samson, but *shalt* never see Gath more.
>
> (1123–29, my emphasis)

The two conflicting versions of the future—one predicated on the certainty of future verbs and the other on the mere potential of the subjunctive—clearly set off the boldness of the good against the cowardice of evil. Ironically, neither Samson's nor Harapha's predictions can be tested, since the fierceness of Samson's boasts proves sufficient to drive away the "crestfall'n" "Giantship" and the doubtful power he represents. Like the Son's thunderous power before the "impious Foes" in heaven (*PL* VI, 824–43), Samson's merely verbal force is sufficient to put his enemy to flight. Armed with "trust . . . in the living God," Samson easily parries all Harapha's boldest verbal thrusts, affirming the certain power of his God: "thou *shalt* see, or rather to thy sorrow / Soon feel, whose God is strongest, thine or mine" (1154–55, my emphasis). Samson not only predicts the ultimate victory of good over evil, as he had previously with Manoa, but he assumes also that he can play a part in that future victory.

The comedy inherent in Samson's triumphant boasts and Harapha's Gargantuan cowardice obscures the justness of some of the giant's charges. Like Dalila, Harapha is capable of speaking reasonably, at times. Rightly, he warns Samson not to "presume" upon God's continued favor, since his present bondage in "Enemies' hand" seems to be the consequence of sin (1156–67). Rightly too, Harapha questions the legality of Samson's more violent and disturbing acts. Each of the giant's specific indictments—that Samson is a murderer, revolter, and robber (1180)—seems to be applied justly to the fallen hero. Samson's defense forces him to reconsider and justify his past: he must defend it in order to defend God. Hence, even the seemingly less noble of his heroic deeds—the slaying, for instance, of thirty wedding guests at Timnath—take on a certain divine logic, in that they demonstrate the uses made by God of the apparently sinful and unlawful. In this way, the past, which had previously produced despair, is revivified and connected with Samson's providentially determined destiny.

The hero's new and positive use of the past is accompanied by his continuing recognition of false prophecy. Harapha's childishly weak concluding threat—"By *Astaroth*, ere long thou shalt lament / These braveries in Irons loaden on thee" (1242–43) — is simply ignored by Samson, who will never find reason to lament his "braveries." Nor do the threatened "Irons" appear; subsequently, in fact, Samson attains greater liberty when the Officer removes the "links" in order to lead him to the temple (1410). Samson's discernment of Harapha's false prophecy is accompanied by a cultivation of right prophecy. When the Chorus warns Samson that his humbled opponent might seek revenge, Samson correctly foresees that Harapha will not complain to the Philistine lords and asserts his invulnerablitity to pain derived from any potentiality:

> He must allege some cause, and offer'd fight
> Will not dare mention, lest a question rise
> Whether he durst accept the offer or not,
> And that he durst not plain enough appear'd.
> Much more affliction than already felt
> They cannot well impose, nor I sustain;
> If they intend advantage of my labors,
> The work of many hands, which earns my keeping.
>   . . . .
> But come what will, my deadliest foe will prove
> My speediest friend, by death to rid me hence,
> The worst that he can give, to me the best.   (1253–60, 1262–64)

Samson here attributes unfulfilled potentiality not to himself but to his foe — that which Harapha "durst" not do. When he considers himself, Samson speaks with certitude of his physical limits and then speaks prophetically of his own future: his "deadliest foe" *will* prove his "speediest friend," when his death, the calming object of his prayer and single hope, will end his earthly sufferings. Once more, Samson engages in prophecy by ignoring the strictures of rigid alternatives ("But come what will"), recognizing that providence can surmount all eventualities. A similar indifference to alternatives had appeared already when Samson had responded to the Chorus's warnings of Harapha's approach: "Or peace or not, alike to me he comes." Samson here looks beyond the limitations of the *either-or* to the limitless *whatever* when he considers his relationship to God's promise. Yet at this moment Samson has received only an intimation of that relationship; his subsequent turn of thought is still couched in the subjunctive:

> Yet so it may fall out, because thir [the Philistines'] end
> Is hate, not help to me, it may with mine
> Draw thir own ruin who attempt the deed.   (1265–67)

The ambiguity of "it" — which apparently refers to a generalized providence — is amplified by the uncertain auxiliary "may"; yet Samson here, at a stage of becoming rather than being prophetic, avoids the duality of the restricting either-or. Here, the "may," though not fully prophetic, points the way to prophecy by leaving open the potentialities available to God, while answering to the paradox of Samson's prophesied deliverance and an intuition of imminent death.

The new-found boldness within Samson is redirected and qualified, even as his vision of the future comes into clearer focus. When he asserts "I cannot come" (1321), "I will not come" (1332, 1342) to Dagon's temple with the Officer — when he contends such an act would violate God's law and degrade his sense of propriety, through the performance of "indignities" at the "commands" of depraved Philistines — he reveals that he is not yet able to abandon the either-or pattern of dualistic alternatives. Either, he believes, he must go with the Officer and therefore degrade himself and his God or he must refuse boldly and defend his honor and God's: the potentiality which had opened momentarily upon his consideration of joining his fate with the Philistines' commands is lost at his first response to the Officer. Disoriented, Samson's prophetic, future verbs become inaccurate because they once more limit rather than open potentialities — "I will not come."[14] It is as he reflects upon the potential of God's actions — upon the differences between "command" and "constraint" — that he becomes more accurately prophetic. He responds to the Officer's threat ("I am sorry what this stoutness will produce," 1346) with a hedged prediction: "*Perhaps* thou shalt have cause to sorrow indeed" (1347, my emphasis). When the Chorus provokes Samson to consider the consequences of his bold refusal, Samson's prophecy remains hesitant, framed as a question, since he assumes that God would necessarily judge his participation at the Philistines' rites as sinful; again, however, his assumption is based upon dualistic alternatives — either he may obey the command and participate in sin or refuse and remain apart from sin:

> Shall I abuse this Consecrated gift
> Of strength, again returning with my hair
> After my great transgression, so requite
> Favor renew'd, and add a greater sin
> By prostituting holy things to Idols;
> A *Nazarite* in place abominable
> Vaunting my strength, in honor to thir *Dagon?*   (1354–60)

At the threshold of the transition to the third stage in his development as a prophet, Samson's rhetorical question is resolved in a fashion opposite to its intent. Rather than convincing the Chorus of the justness of his refusal to obey the Philistine Lords, Samson challenges the very assumptions which were the basis of his question: Samson's question is transformed from "How can I *abuse* this gift from God by participating in Idol-worship?" to "How can this turn of events be *used* to advance God's providence?" At the moment of this transformed intent, Samson makes a "recognition" which is closely related to the "rousing motions" — he begins to see how he, in the present, can work within God's providence, outside the narrow alternatives of the law, creating the future rather than completing the failures of the past.

As the implications of God's providential transcendence of the law unfold at the moment of recognition, Samson gains insight into the solution of apparently impossible paradoxes — riddles whose solutions now seem more important to him than did that to the riddle he had spoken in his youth. He begins to see how enemies' commands may be obeyed "freely" and in accord with providence. Despite his original hesitancy at "venturing to displease / God for the fear of Man" (1373–74), Samson comes to recognize that God's acts do not necessarily correspond to anticipated alternatives — that Samson himself has presupposed God's jealousy and lack of forgiveness, despite the forgiveness implicit in the strength which returns with his hair. He who can renew the "Consecrated gift / Of strength" in a sinner nearly lapsed in despair can "dispense" with those rules prohibiting one's presence "at Idolatrous Rites."[15] When Samson offers the prophetic yet faulty dilemma with which this study began — either that "this day" will be "remarkable" in his life or his "last" — he at least softens the force of its falseness by an admission of his insufficiency as a prophet: "If there be aught of presage in the mind." Though Samson has learned a fundamental of prophecy — has learned not to restrict God's judgment or providence — he remains incompletely prophetic in word, errant in details. Nevertheless, by this point Samson has turned wholly to the future as the consequence of the present, having set aside in the space of seven hundred lines that former, despairing circularity wherein the past seemed an irreversible genetrix of the present. This reversal, which Milton skillfully effects by means of provocateurs who force Samson to defend rather than punish himself, allows the audience to see the hero again as God's instrument, even if we, like Dalila locked into a world without ready absolutes, have no way of knowing, without revealed insight, that he has been saved. In the last episode — Manoa's return with news of his ostensible "ransom" and the Messenger's revelation of the catastrophe — Milton deliberately emphasizes the blindness of the

Chorus and Manoa, as they speculate wildly about Samson's potential future; and their blindness extends out to the general audience, who, despite knowing the catastrophic result, are left without certitude regarding Samson's salvation.[16]

In his final speeches, the hero's prophetic certitude allows him to look beyond his own misery, permitting him to consider how to address his friends in the Chorus and Philistine enemies. Samson reveals a subtle protectiveness toward the Chorus, thinking of their safety by not wishing them to attend as he prepares to enact "something extraordinary." In his second speech to the Officer, he speaks with ironic duplicity. After Samson's "rousing motions," his thoughts no longer are expressed openly to friend or foe. Although Samson need not have predetermined the catastrophe when he chooses to accompany the Officer, he conceals at least a general conception of his future beneath the irony:

> Masters' commands come with a power resistless
> To such as owe them absolute subjection;
> And for a life who will not change his purpose?   (1404–06)

The transposition of "masters' commands" to *the* Master's commands is an easy one, after his previous decision not to act in "fear of Man."[17] Equally ironic is Samson's last speech to the Philistines, reported to the Chorus and Manoa by the Messenger:

> Hitherto, Lords, what your commands impos'd
> I have perform'd, as reason was, obeying,
> Not without wonder or delight beheld.
> Now of my own accord such other trial
> I mean to show you of my strength, yet greater;
> As with amaze shall strike all who behold.   (1640–45)

Speaking from his "own" accord, Samson predicts his next trick, with heavy irony set upon the puns "strike" and "amaze": the Messenger and Chorus can understand the irony after the fact, as the general audience can at their hearing. In these ironies are embedded the riddles of future action — riddles which can be understood only by certain portions of an audience at certain times: through an enlightened knowledge of previous actions or an inspired revelation of their significance, one can comprehend that the apparent capitulation of the hero in weakness to his enemies is instead a manifestation of wise strength. Though Samson does not prophesy his future acts of destruction to those he intends to destroy, irony permits him to retain a concentration upon the future and his present purpose, sustaining his emergence as a proto-prophet, his learning to speak of the future based upon knowledge of divine purposes. Milton's Samson is given a nascently prophetic voice which, in the hero recorded in Judges, is concealed by riddles and verbal enigmas. Despite its limitations, the prophetic voice of Milton's Samson anticipates the future of prophecy in Scripture, which bears witness to the "Acts" of men like Samson, "In copious Legend, or sweet Lyric Song" (1736–37). As a whole, *Samson Agonistes* records Samson's partially successful attempt to discover prophecy; in this, Samson learns to give voice to the prophecy which his action embodies, in the prefiguring of the deliverance and destruction of the world.

II

John C. Ulreich, Jr., has proposed that *Samson* should be read as a parable, since other figurative readings — allegorical or typological — are not made explicit in Milton's text. He develops his parabolic interpretation in order to argue for the work's prophetic, even apocalyptic structure.[18] As I have indicated, analysis of Samson's character also suggests the central place of prophecy in the development of the hero. Samson develops his prophetic abilities insofar as he abandons alternatives which restrict providence and insofar as he opens himself to an acceptance of limitless potentiality. This development can be traced in Samson's transcendence from a verbal preoccupation with the past — manifest in his riddle — to future-directed, prophetic, and ironic forms of speech. Unlike the Samson in the book of Judges, Milton's Samson must abandon the kind of governance which depends upon the trick of the enigma in order to accept the difficult leadership which is rooted in open act, predicted in word and deed, and anticipating a still more distant future.

The riddling Samson in Judges is of a piece with the legendary strong man at the primitive core of the tale. The mystery of his language is related closely to the nearly magical quality of his strength.[19] The riddle itself refers enigmatically to a youthful test of the legendary hero's strength — his slaying of a lion on his way to the woman in Timnath. When the biblical Samson rediscovers the carcass on his return, he notices that it has become filled with a swarm of bees and their honey. In the original tale, this bizarre event serves as the source of the riddle ("Out of the eater came meat, and out of the strong came swetenes," (Judg. xiv, 14) with which the savage hero provokes thirty Philistine wedding guests.[20] Though the original significance of the riddle remains unknown, the meaning is no doubt rooted in its primitive association of magical gaming and verbal play. Despite its obscurity, commentators, ancient and modern, have long sought to uncover a figurative meaning

for the riddle's mystery.[21] Ulreich attempts to reconstruct Milton's understanding of the riddle, arguing that it signifies the parabolic nature of
the literal tale, as it is developed in Milton's play. According to Ulreich,
Milton developed the following analogies:

"just as the lion which would devour Samson is devoured by him, so Samson, in
seeking to destroy the Philistines, is himself destroyed; and as the death of the eater
produces meat, so the destruction of Samson nourishes his people with the honey
of deliverance."

Ulreich goes on to describe the transformation of the "ancient riddle"
into a "religious paradox," wherein "the primitive fable of Samson the
Destroyer becomes a parable of Deliverance" — a paradox which is latent in the biblical tale and developed by Milton.[22]

   Yet destruction as well as deliverance is implicit in Samson's slaughter of the Philistines; one cannot be separated from the other.[23] In my
view, the riddle represents a primitive substratum of linguistic acuity,
out of which Milton's Samson, though he explicitly disclaims a possession of wisdom, reveals nascent prophetic skills.[24] Just as Samson's character changes from passive despair to active hope, so the hero moves from
the opaque enigma rooted in the past to the beginnings of prophecy, in-
corporating the future into providence, and, ultimately, to catastrophic
act and its emblematic prophecy of apocalyptic destruction and deliverance. Insofar as Samson abandons the gamesmanship implicit in the
riddle and accepts the actuality of prophecy, he begins to involve himself personally in providence and the resolution of his prophesied destiny.
Though Samson must surpass the riddle in order to advance, the play's
audience, unlike Samson, can attribute figurative significance to the
riddle. To Samson, the riddle served as a test of wit, as a means of expressing his dominance, and as a reminder of his youthful strength; yet
the test came to an unfortunate conclusion, since it became linked to his
weakness with women and his apparently sinful abrogation of God's
pledge. To Milton's audience, the riddle suggests a sense of fulfilled promise, through the productive transformation of the "eater" and the "strong"
to "meat" and "honey."[25] More particularly, the figurative sense of the
riddle points to Samson's own fulfilled promise, both as the productive
"meat" which is generated out of his lionlike, consuming strength and
as the prophecy of word and act which is the "sweetness" attendant upon
his death. Ulreich's association of the "eater" in the riddle with Samson
seems deficient, in that the lion is killed by an external agent, whereas
Samson, apparently without the guilt of suicide, dies at his own hands;
moreover, Ulreich's conflation of the riddle's members, so that "the strong"

is comparable to Samson's destruction in the production of sweetness, just as the death of the eater is productive of meat, seems forced. Yet, the riddle Samson has pronounced seems appropriately to predict his role as *both* Destroyer *and* Deliverer. Like Dalila's view of history, the riddle is "Janus-mouth'd" — it speaks simultaneously from Samson's point of view about a glorious though miserable past, completed at the play's beginning, and from the point of view of Milton's audience, as a prefiguring of the hero's tragically fulfilled promise and as an emblematic prophecy of the fulfillment of God's promise at the end of time.[26]

If the riddle prophetically signifies the fulfillment of past potential, it does not therefore imply an absolute abandonment of the past in the transformation to the future. Even though the dead lion becomes "meat," it still conveys its former association with the "eater"; and the "strong" is conjoined with, not replaced by, the sweetness it produces. Rather than an essential, dualistic transformation from Destroyer to Deliverer, the riddle suggests continuity and connection between the Destroyer and the subsequent Deliverer: to paraphrase the riddle: "out of the Destroyer came the Deliverer," just as the "secular" Phoenix rises from the ashes of history. The Destroyer is, therefore, not abandoned but completed as Deliverer: Milton opens rather than constricts potentiality. The riddle thus looks not just back to the lost promise of the past, but forward to Samson's future, which in turn looks forward to the future of all at the apocalypse. Although Samson believes his "days of riddling are past" when he asks the Chorus to explain their nautical metaphor at Harapha's arrival, he is still weaving out the destiny he had unwittingly suggested in his old riddle. Samson does opt for a new prophetic approach — the more open approach instanced first in his prophecy to Manoa, then reinforced by predictions of his own participation in that future, until, facing his enemies, his openness gives way to irony; but the linguistic acuity which had framed the riddle is simply transmuted, not obliterated, when the riddler becomes nascently prophetic. Though in his prose works Milton everywhere disparages the literary form of the riddle as a time-wasting game, the riddle which is given scriptural sanction in the tale of Samson takes on a prophetic character, uniting past and present in a providentially ironic future.[27]

The symbolism of the riddle may have led Milton to connect Samson's verbal play with prophecy, since the concrete symbols of the lion and the honey, though common throughout Scripture, are joined closely at an important point in the Book of Revelation. The symbol of the honey intrudes inversely into the play through Samson's "thoughts," which, at the outset, with the hero locked in the cycle of past and present despair, sting like hornets—creatures devoid of redeeming sweetness. In the play, the "hornets" undergo an implicit metamorphosis, as their repentance-engendering yet dangerous stings finally produce sweet humility and the "single" saving hope of prayer. The association of honey with the pain of wisdom and prophecy is made explicit by Milton in *The Reason of Church Government*, in that same introduction to the Second Book where he relates the biblical works, including the "high and stately Tragedy" of the Apocalypse, to classical genres (CM V, pp. 229–42). There, Milton refers to the tenth chapter of Revelation, where the "Mightie Angel," conventionally glossed as Christ, comes crying "with a Loude voyce, as when a lyon roareth" (x, 3; CM V, pp. 230–31).[28] The image of Christ as a lion, conjoined in Revelation with the imagery of the lamb, is in this chapter associated explicitly with the mixed sweetness and bitterness of prophetic inspiration: the heavenly voice commands John to accept the book held by the Angel and to eat it: "it shal make thy bellie bitter, but it shalbe in thy mouthe as swete as honie." When the prophet has devoured the book, which indeed tastes sweet but makes his "bellie" bitter, the Angel comands him to spew out what he has ingested: "Thou must prophecie againe among the people and nations, and tongues, and to many kings" (x, 9–11). The command to prophesy becomes, for Milton, the whetstone for the double-edged sword of his tongue (Heb. iv, 12; Rev. i, 13, 16; xix, 15, 21), allowing him to justify his verbal defense despite the pain in his "bellie"—that is, the distress he causes and feels from those who rail against the hard truths he must speak. He is like the "ancient prophets" who found that though "divine inspiration" was sweet, "the irksomeness of that truth which they brought was so unpleasant . . . that everywhere they call it a burden" (CM V, p. 230). The bitter stings in the belly of the lion—the bitter thoughts in the mind of the prophet—are made bearable by the sweet certitude of "high valuable wisdom," which Milton in *The Reason of Church Government* defines as the knowledge of "God and his true worship, and what is good and infallibly happy in the state of man's life, what in itself evil and miserable, though vulgarly not so esteemed." It is this wisdom which, according to Milton, the prophet must "dispose" and "employ": it is the "knowledge and illumination which God hath sent him into this world to trade with" (CM V, p. 229). Ultimately, the prophet's mixed pleasure and pain is precisely Samson's, whose internal suffering is manifest in the external, physical symbol of destruction. The buzzing "thoughts" provoke the hero to repentance—to painful self-exploration and condemnation—from which emerges the prophet nascent in word, apocalyptically figurative in deed.

Though Samson's "riddling days are past," Milton's audience can still perceive the riddle's prophetic dimension. For Samson, the riddle represents a part of his past that must be rejected — even at his best he gains only slight insight into his role in providence, and the apocalyptic implications of the riddle are far beyond his capacity: in this latter sense, the riddle is as much an enigma to Samson as to the Philistine audience for whom it was invented.

Ultimately, prophecy connects the past to the present: the choice for Samson is not whether to abandon his past but how to move into the future with confidence and with providential guidance — "venturing all" in unlimited potentiality, striving to avoid restrictive alternatives. Like the people he leads, Samson must look to the future, which leads historically to the Messiah and apocalyptically to the final judgment, performed by the highest judge of Israel. In this historical and personal movement to prophecy, to the future, Samson is neither clearly saved nor damned, despite the hopeful claims made by Manoa and the Chorus in the *kommos*. The certitude manifest in Samson's prophetic act in itself provides no certitude of salvation, since it does not resolve the ambiguity and tension which cloud any judgment of Samson. Though the feeling of providential resolution at the play's close may provide "calm of mind," the fate of Samson as an individual steered by God's providence, yet acting "of my own accord," remains much less certain. The prophet may be a willing instrument of God, but the reward for divine action — prophetic or otherwise — is uncertain, perhaps arbitrary, and Milton leaves considerable uncertainty about the precise outcome of Samson's "impulsion" and "rousing motions" in relation to personal salvation: dragons, eagles, and "secular" birds are at best ambivalent symbols. Despite the ambiguity of the hero's salvation, Samson *has* at the catastrophe ventured all, *has* opted for "Sun or shade," *has* eliminated the need for alternatives by allowing providence to direct the outcome of his actions. This, finally, is sufficient for Samson and, insofar as we can share in a sense of God's just guidance of providence, we too can end with calm, affirming with the Chorus, "All is best, though we oft doubt."

Southwest Texas State University

NOTES

1. *John Milton: Complete Poems and Major Prose*, ed. Merritt Y. Hughes (Indianapolis, 1957) 1387–89. All references to Milton's poetry are to this edition.

2. "Action and Suffering: *Samson Agonistes* and the Irony of Alternatives," *PMLA*, LXXXIV (1969), 514–19, esp. p. 515; Stanley Fish, "Question and Answer in *Samson Agonistes*," *Critical Quarterly*, XI (1969), 254–55. See also Low, *The Blaze of Noon: A Reading of "Samson Agonistes"* (New York, 1974), pp. 80–81; Edward W. Tayler, *Milton's Poetry: Its Development in Time* (Pittsburgh, 1979), pp. 119–20. Mary Ann Radzinowicz, in *Toward "Samson Agonistes"* (Princeton, 1978), p. 106, following Raymond Waddington's "Melancholy Against Melancholy: *Samson Agonistes* as Renaissance Tragedy," in *Calm of Mind: Tercentary Essays on "Paradise Regained" and "Samson Agonistes" in Honor of John S. Diekhoff*, ed. Joseph Wittreich (Cleveland, 1971), pp. 278–80, sees Samson's prophecy as symptomatic of a newly acquired "just measure," "indifference toward his own fate," and "well-tempered spirit"; however, Samson's false logic seems to qualify the fullness of his "just measure" of passion: his reason remains defective, though its defect is no longer of consequence.

3. The dialectic of literary criticism has itself produced many "alternatives," such as the ones represented below: concerning the role of choice or predetermination in Samson's act, see, respectively, John M. Steadman, "'Faithful Champion': The Theological Basis of Milton's Hero of Faith," *Anglia*, LXXVII (1959), 12–28 (rpt. in *Milton: Modern Essays in Criticism*, ed. Arthur E. Barker [New York, 1965], pp. 467–83), and G. A. Wilkes, "The Interpretation of *Samson Agonistes*," *Hunington Library Quarterly*, XXVI (1963), 363–79 (or Fish, "Question and Answer," p. 260); for an important view of the relationship of free will and determinism in Milton, see Dennis Richard Danielson, *Milton's Good God: A Study in Literary Theodicy* (Cambridge, 1982), pp. 131–77; concerning Samson as seer or fool, see William Kerrigan, *The Prophetic Milton* (Charlottesville, N. C., 1974), pp. 214–18, Arnold Stein, *Heroic Knowledge* (Minneapolis, 1957), p. 196, and Joseph Anthony Wittreich, Jr., *Visionary Poetics: Milton's Tradition and His Legacy* (San Marino, Calif., 1979), pp. 202–03; concerning Christian or non-Christian typology, see F. Michael Krouse, *Milton's Samson and the Christian Tradition* (Princeton, 1949), pp. 119–24, T. S. K. Scott-Craig, "Concerning Milton's Samson," *Renaissance News*, V (1952), 45–53, William G. Madsen, *From Shadowy Types to Truth: Studies in Milton's Symbolism* (New Haven, 1968), pp. 181–202, Wittreich, *Visionary Poetics*, pp. 197–99, 200–01, 207, and John T. Shawcross, "The Genres of *Paradise Regain'd* and *Samson Agonistes*: The Wisdom of Their Joint Publication," *Milton Studies*, XVII, ed. Richard S. Ide and Joseph Wittreich (Pittsburgh, 1983), p. 240.

4. Fish, "Question and Answer," p. 260.

5. "The Doubling of the Chorus in *Samson Agonistes*," *Milton Studies*, XX, ed. James D. Simmonds (Pittsburgh, 1984), p. 228.

6. Tayler, *Milton's Poetry*, pp. 119–20.

7. See, however, ibid., p. 110. Tayler insightfuly notes some important conjunctions which go beyond alternatives—"and" replacing "or"—in *Samson*. Tayler notes the insufficiency of logic and reason in Samson's heroic and prophetic act.

8. Radzinowicz, *Toward "Samson,"* pp. 16–28, provides an excellent, thorough reading of the prologue.

9. See Waddington, "Melancholy," pp. 270–72, for a description of the cyclic pattern of Samson's exchange with the Chorus and Manoa; see also John N. Wall, Jr., "The Contrarious Hand of God: *Samson Agonistes* and the Biblical Lament," *Milton Studies*, XII, ed. James D. Simmonds (Pittsburgh, 1978), 126–30. On Samson's need to escape the limited causality of discursive reason, see Fish, "Question and Answer," pp. 244–45.

10. On the significance of this prophecy as a "preliminary climax," see Una Ellis-

Fermor, *The Frontiers of Drama*, 2d ed. (London, 1964), p. 27; Radzinowicz, *Toward "Samson,"* pp. 96–97.

11. Steadman, "'Faithful Champion,'" pp. 472–73.

12. Krouse, *Milton's Samson*, pp. 124–32, applies Elizabeth Pope's "triple equation" of Christ's temptations to the "temptations" of Samson by Dalila, Harapha, and Manoa; but Samson is less endangered by them than by his internal despair.

13. The ambivalent but inevitably damnable nature of Dalila's persuasiveness is a commonplace of *Samson* scholarship; on the relativism she represents, see Virginia R. Mollenkott, "Relativism in *Samson Agonistes*," *SP*, LXVIII (1970), 89–102; Low, *Blaze of Noon*, pp. 150–58. According to Radzinowicz, *Toward "Samson,"* p. 212, "Samson's outward confrontation with Dalila *forces* a renewed inward confrontation of past and present" (my emphasis).

14. A. B. Chambers, in "Wisdom and Fortitude in *Samson Agonistes*," *PMLA*, LXXVIII (1963), 315–20, argues that Samson's refusal "demonstrates that neither fear nor folly can sway him now, that *sapientia et fortitudo* is his" (320). Though Samson does demonstrate bold courage by not "venturing to displease / God for the fear of man," he has not yet learned to venture all for what is felt within. It is this reversal, occasioned by the "rousing motions," which determines his change in purpose. See John C. Ulreich, Jr., "'This Great Deliverer': *Samson Agonistes* as Parable," *MQ*, XIII (1979), 82–83, concerning Samson's choice to obey God rather than fear than fear man; and his "'Beyond the Fifth Act': *Samson Agonistes* as Prophecy," *Milton Studies*, XVII, ed. Richard S. Ide and Joseph Wittreich (Pittsburgh, 1983), pp. 287–88. See Fish, "Question and Answer," p. 255.

15. Low, *Blaze of Noon*, p. 200.

16. Fish, "Question and Answer," pp. 258, 261–62.

17. Ulreich, "'This Great Deliverer,'" p. 82.

18. Ulreich, "'Beyond the Fifth Act,'" pp. 281–318. See also Barbara K. Lewalski, "*Samson Agonistes* and the 'Tragedy' of the Apocalypse," *PMLA*, LXXXV (1970), 1054–61; C. A. Patrides, "'Something Like Prophetic Strain': Apocalyptic Configurations in Milton," *ELN*, XIX (1981–82), 202–06; Wittreich, *Visionary Poetics*, pp. 193–214; Kerrigan, *Prophetic Milton*, pp. 249–58; Northrop Frye, "Agon and Logos: Revolution and Revelation," in *The Prison and the Pinnacle*, ed. Balachandra Rajan (Toronto, 1973), pp. 146–51; Patrides, "Apocalyptic Configurations," pp. 198–99. On the relationship of prophecy to history, see Radzinowicz, *Toward "Samson,"* pp. 87–101; Patrides, "Apocalyptic Configurations," p. 194. For a wise caveat against seeing Revelation as Milton's exclusive model, see idem. p. 207, and Leland Ryken, "*Paradise Lost* and Its Biblical Models," in *Milton and Scriptural Tradition: The Bible into Poetry*, ed. James H. Sims and Leland Ryken (Columbia, Mo., 1984), p. 74.

19. Ulreich, in "Samson's Riddle: Judges 13–16 as Parable," *Cithara*, XVIII (May 1979), 3–28, argues that a Deuteronomic redaction of more primitive versions smoothed out some of the mythic elements' paganisms, but allowed others, like the riddle, to remain (11–17). On the tale as myth, see Giorgio de Santillana and Hertha von Dechend, *Hamlet's Mill: An Essay on Myth and the Frame of Time* (Boston, 1969), pp. 165–78.

20. Throughout, I cite the Geneva Bible, facs. ed. (Madison, Wis., 1969).

21. R. P. apRoberts, "Riddle," in *Princeton Encyclopedia of Poetry and Poetics*, ed. A. Preminger (Princeton, 1974). Ulreich, in "Samson's Riddle," summarizes various hermeneutic approaches to the biblical tale (pp. 5–8).

22. "'This Great Deliverer,'" p. 80.

23. Lewalski, responding to those who find the catastrophe un-Christian in its brutality, overstresses Samson's role as Destroyer, subordinating to it his role as Deliverer: "he is one of a long line of heroes raised up by God to deliver the oppressed peoples and to execute God's wrath upon the wicked, typifying the unleashing of the divine wrath at the end of time" ("*Samson* and the Apocalypse," p. 1061).

24. On Samson's initial association of his fall with a lack of wisdom, see *SA* 52–54 ("O impotence of mind in body strong!"); 206–09 ("Immeasurable strength [people] might behold / In me, of wisdom nothing more than mean"); see also Chambers, "Wisdom and Fortitude," p. 317.

25. C. G. Jung connects this notion of productivity or "fruitfulness" through eating to Christ, memorialized in bread and wine, and to Samson's lion, transformed to meat and honey (*Symbols of Transformation*, trans. R. F. C. Hull [Princeton, 1970], pp. 338–39).

26. Lewalski, "*Samson* and the Apocalypse," p. 1057.

27. Milton disparages riddles in *Pro Populo Anglican Defensio*, III, *The Works of John Milton*, ed. Frank Allen Patterson et al. (New York, 1931–38), VII, p. 187 (hereafter CM), and in *Eikonoklastes*, XXII (V, pp. 256–57; cf. p. 133), but commends Christ's use of riddles for good ends in *The Doctrine and Discipline of Divorce*, XIX (III, pt. ii, p. 497) and *Tetrachordon* (IV, p. 141).

28. The Geneva Bible glosses the "mightie Angel" (x, 1) as "Iesus Christ that came to comfort his Church against the furious assaltes of Satan and Antichrist; so that in all their troubles, the faithful are sure to finde consolacion in him."

THE IRRATIONAL COHERENCE
OF *SAMSON AGONISTES*

William Kerrigan

S O O N E R O R later good interpretations of *Samson Agonistes* encounter a dispute nearly as momentous as the Satan controversy. Do the
two poems published together in 1671 weaken the stature of reason in
Milton's religious vision? Has the poet who wrote of the soul in *Paradise
Lost* that "reason is her being" (V, 487) changed his mind?[1] Or, looking
at it another way, does the heroism depicted in *Paradise Regained* and
Samson Agonistes simply transcend customary rationality? Having studied
as an undergraduate with Yvor Winters, I have some appreciation for
the passions that can be ignited by a threatened demotion in the status
of reason; judging from the criticism they have bequeathed us, Renaissance scholars have traditionally felt that the testimony of the past should
be as uniform as possible on this matter. But one often has the impression that the fervors surrounding the question are outsized. Certain champions of reason seem to assume that, should there come a day when we
would no longer use the word "reason" in its full sovereignty as we sum-
marized the wisdom of Milton and other Renaissance authors, then prose
style would deteriorate, and manners, and chaos would come again, our
jails swelling with devotees of misguided emotion. To fend off this sort
of melodrama it is healthy to remind ourselves that we can go on thinking coherently and acting responsibly without seeing our mentality as
a competitive assembly of "faculties," one of which must reign over the
others, who are then cast as would-be usurpers. The issue before us is
not the fate of civilization but how Milton viewed religious heroism within
a certain picture of the mind. That picture may be said to date from
Plato's internalization of the Greek *polis* in the *Republic*, the major addition thereafter, and indeed the specifically Christian addition, being
Augustine's philosophy of the will.[2] I think Milton celebrated the newer
Christian faculty in his last two works, replacing the conventional alliance between conscience and reason with an alliance, at extraordinary
moments in sacred history, between God and will.

The minority position in Milton studies—in my view, largely
correct—was stated unequivocally by Saurat. After *Paradise Lost*, Mil-

ton "frees himself from dogma; all he keeps of it is God-destiny."[3] The
heroes of *Paradise Regained* and *Samson Agonistes* are guided at their
climactic triumphs by divine prompting—what is called in the final speech
of *Samson* the "unsearchable dispose" of God's "uncontrollable intent."
Will is the faculty of moment in these works, not reason. In *Paradise
Lost* Raphael distinguishes between intuitive intellect, which assents to
a truth present all at once, and discursive reason, which must in delibera-
tion seek out the truth. With the poems of 1671 Milton revises this scheme
in the direction of voluntarism. The heroic will awaits intuitive guidance from "some strong motion" (*PR* I, 290) or "rousing motions":

> I begin to feel
> Some rousing motions in me which dispose
> To something extraordinary my thoughts.   (*SA* 1381–83)

The climax of the drama fully endorses the language of this divine intervention, as "rousing" reappears in the self-delivered Phoenix, "His fiery
virtue rous'd" (1690), and "dispose" is reiterated as God's "unsearchable
dispose." Reason continues to play a role. It protects the waiting, guard-
ing Milton's heroes against the temptation to untimely action. Thus reason, deflating the worldly lures of Satan, gives Christ the patience to wait
and stand; and reason, in the form of a conviction in the justice of his
punishment, puts Samson in the right place at the right time in the right
disposition for God's disposing motions. Milton always wanted a task more
than he wanted knowledge. Even the prophetic poet of *Paradise Lost*
will not rest content with the *visio dei:* he would "see *and tell*" (III, 54;
my emphasis), poetry being conceived of as an act, not just a visionary
knowing; Christ himself, the divine exemplar of this act, turns back to
the Father only to receive the tasks of creation, redemption, and judgment. Insofar as there is an opposition between the inspired action of
the invocations and the elevation of reason in the dialogue between Raphael and Adam, Milton ultimately chooses the way of the invocations,
which in the final poems is projected into the actions of his protagonists.

Douglas Bush leaned in the other direction, though not so decisively
as one might expect. This was not, for him, one literary problem among
others: the issues at stake lay at the foundations of his critical statement,
and more than that, of his identity as a critic. Bush was the first important scholar of Renaissance literature in our language whose work was
dominated by the period concept. Burckhardt had been wrong to insist
on the pagan consequences of the humanist revival of antiquity, and Bush
exhibited this wrongness in his very concept of the period. "Christian
humanism," proclaiming the historical compatibility of faith and human-

istic learning, had as its major content *ratio recta* or "right reason," the belief that knowledge of the good acquired through the patient study of the Bible and classical culture could be, and must be, exemplified in the conduct of life, making the completed person a living embodiment of his knowledge. Bush thought of himself as belonging to and working within the tradition he studied — hence the painful question of the late Milton. Here was the supreme instance of Christian humanism, the bright consummate flower of the entire epoch as Bush had conceived of it, and at the end of his life he was writing about a Christ who repudiates Athenian culture in favor of "light from above" and a self-tormenting giant who goes to the Dagonalia when compelled from within, turning his rage and frustration against his enemies in a violent catharsis seemingly worlds away from the types of heroism born in book-lined studies. If Burckhardt threatened the Renaissance synthesis by exaggerating the unruly development of pagan trends, Milton threatened it by claiming or appearing to claim the self-sufficiency of the Christian God as inward educator.

In 1939 Bush wrote of his personal ordeal over the Athenian temptation in *Paradise Regained*. "When we think of his lifelong devotion to the classical authors who taught him his craft, who inspired alike his love of liberty and his love of discipline, it cannot be other than a painful shock to come upon that violent denunciation of Greek culture in *Paradise Regained*."[4] Bush — and I say this with respect, it being the last infirmity of noble Miltonists — wanted his author to be like himself, but in this case it belonged to the critic's theory that Milton be, like the critic, a Christian humanist. Perhaps, too, the "painful shock" arose, not just from the apparent heterogeneity of Milton's work, but from the uneasy apprehension that if Saurat's volitional "God-destiny" were indeed the regnant value in *Paradise Regained* and *Samson Agonistes*, then one might reassert the unity of Milton's work by qualifying the supposed Christian humanism of *Paradise Lost*. Bush himself stressed the pessimism of its final books. And what of reason in Milton's "great argument"? Must not his rational theodicy break down in the end, since it is impossible to begin with a moral dualism and derive evil without implicating good? Must there not be a higher theodicy of faith — or, to turn a phrase, a "justification by faith"? All the speeches about right reason concern man's prelapsarian condition, and the guiding "Providence" of the final lines does not in any obvious way yoke fallen man to eternal reverence for Greek and Latin culture. "It is painful indeed," Bush acknowledged, "to watch Milton turn and rend some main roots of his being."[5] Although he went on to note that every Christian humanist, if pushed to the limit, would prefer Jerusalem to Athens, which reduced Milton's untraditionality to the tonal quality of his "fervor," the critic's distress seems a remarkable concession to the stand taken by Saurat.

The appeal to the ultimate superiority for Christians of Christianity to antiquity does not really reclaim the Athenian temptation for a Renaissance devoted to Christian humanism. For that superiority normally went without saying, and usually without fervent saying. Milton said it fervently, and howevermuch one emphasizes the classicism of the poem itself, the fact remains that Milton has his incarnate God deny that someone illuminated from above "needs" any other doctrine taught anywhere, "though granted true," and then retort, on the particular matter of Athenian doctrines, "But these are false" (IV, 290–91), among other reasons because Athenians do not know "how man fell / Degraded by himself, on grace depending" (311–12) and therefore, like all proponents of *ratio recta,* "in themselves seek virtue" (314). To make the point unmistakable, Christ goes on to attack reading books as a means to virtue, for you cannot get anywhere with a book unless your judgment is at least its equal, in which case you do not need to read it. Milton was not in the end, and not, in my opinion, in *Paradise Lost,* so submissively admiring of ancient thought as Bush assumed.[6] Elsewhere Christ praises the life of Socrates (III, 96–99), which is often said to count for Christian humanism by qualifying the denunciation of Socratic philosophy. On the contrary, the very disjunction between praiseworthy life and empty thought in the treatment of Socrates cuts *ratio recta* right down the middle. The *ratio* of Socrates is one thing (ignorant), his *recta* another (exemplary).

Other critics have replayed the drama of Bush's "shock." In *Right Reason in the English Renaissance* Robert Hoopes, having told us that "Douglas Bush gave me the subject," declares: "It is always a shock of sorts to readers first coming to Milton to hear the most learned among English poets speak disparagingly of knowledge" — unquestionably so, if these readers have been informed by Bush and Hoopes that "the central meaning of all of Milton's major works is the same: freedom consists in obedience to reason."[7] Hoopes tries to alleviate the shock by feebly suggesting that the condemnation of Athens is but a sequel to *Paradise Lost's* mockery of astronomy, as if we were not dealing with a quantum leap in the suspicion of reason. Bush in the meantime had risen above his old distress. Reworking the 1939 discussion for a concluding chapter in his seventeenth-century volume of the *Oxford History of English Literature,* Bush now proclaimed that "many readers, knowing Milton's lifelong devotion and infinite debt to classical literature and thought, feel a shock when they come upon Christ's repudiation of the philosophy, poetry, and oratory of Greece, which has just received through Satan the poet's beautiful and heart-felt praise. The shock is unwarranted."[8] The palliating arguments had not changed, but Bush had grown so convinced of them that he had ceased to feel the problem. The result, an excellent fable for scholars, is the intellectual syndrome I have termed The Denial of the Most Interesting Crux.[9]

Elements of Bush's Christian humanism have fallen away with the years. For example, few contemporary scholars would agree to his claim that "there is in *Paradise Lost* (as in the whole body of Milton's poetry) very little that is specifically Puritan."[10] The Bush tradition survives, however, though in a less ecumenical form and without much interest in the period concept; in place of "Christian humanism" we now find phrases like "Protestant poetics," where the timeless "poetics" effaces the strong epochal ring of "humanism," and the sectarian precision of "Protestant" undoes the eclectic embrace of "Christian." But the idea of Milton as champion of the good old cause of reason has proved fairly tenacious. It has even been welcomed into influential interpretations of *Samson Agonistes*. For Bush the shocker was *Paradise Regained*. He scarcely bothered to make excuse for the biblical tragedy: the author's pessimism grew with age; he became fixed upon "ultimate things."[11] Until recently the major critics of *Samson* were disentangling its Hebraism from its classicism, exploring its place in the exegetical tradition, and pondering Samuel Johnson's strictures about its missing middle. No one, not even Bush himself, tried to read the drama as a testament to rational Christianity.

To my knowledge, the first important exception is Louis Martz. "Samson's greatness," he proposes, "lies in his rational choice of a God-given opportunity."[12] Martz fleshes out this preposterous characterization of the drama with an expository confidence almost imperial in its disregard of qualifying evidence. This is *Samson Agonistes* as loyal brainchild of *ratio recta*, beheld by a critic wholly unshocked at the disparity between his interpretation and his text. "We note the emphasis on mental action, on reason, and on choice," he writes of Samson's speech to the assembled Philistines, transforming this gloating irony into a compact treatise on Christian humanism:[13]

> "Hitherto, Lords, what your commands impos'd
> I have perform'd, as reason was, obeying,
> Not without wonder or delight beheld.
> Now of my own accord such other trial
> I mean to show you of my strength, yet greater;
> As with amaze shall strike all who behold."   (1640–45)

Deftly and with palpable relish, Samson marks the peripetea in his life and in this tragedy — the moment of his deliverance from long obedience to the Philistine Lords. It is true that he speaks of "reason," meaning his motive for having obeyed the commands of these Lords, which was to destroy them. It is true that he speaks of "my own accord," meaning the unbidden feat he is about to perform. Milton did not offer us puppet heroes. Samson is not a blind slave to divine will. He acts of his "own accord" with God. But did reason get him here? Martz makes no mention of the "rousing motions" that led Samson, like a guiding hand, to this moment of sacred revenge and personal redemption. Throughout the essay he builds a dubious case against the niggling stupidity of the Chorus, trivializing their doubts and sufferings, and tops it off by complaining that their final speech neglects Samson's rationality.[14] Martz has written magnificently of the 1645 *Poems*. After this initial material, however, *The Poet of Exile* is a disappointing book, in large part because the items on its Christian humanist agenda (Ovidian imitation in *Paradise Lost*, ambivalent anticlassicism in *Paradise Regained*, reasonable choice in *Samson Agonistes*) finally do not explain very much in the masterpieces of Milton's artistic comeback.

By far the most ambitious defense of a humanistic *Samson* is Mary Ann Radzinowicz's *Toward Samson Agonistes: The Growth of Milton's Mind*, which attempts a full-scale synthesis of the newly Protestant Milton with the older tradition of Christian rationality. She asserts that Christian liberty, entailing the right to revolt against its suppressors, is "derived from the free following of the spirit of truth and reason in the individual."[15] In this sense Samson's very role as a deliverer makes him a rational man. If that were all there was to it, one would wonder why Samson must obey the Nazarite code, or why God put the strength to secure rational freedom in his hair, and took it away when he said to a woman, "All right, if you must know. The strength to win the freedom to which Israel is rationally entitled is in my hair." "No man who knows ought," Milton grumbled in *The Tenure of Kings and Magistrates*, "can be so stupid to deny that all men naturally were born free."[16] God and free will were true for Milton because they had to be true, because the sense of the world he both derived from and imposed on the Bible demanded they be true, and the way one referred to such bedrock beliefs in the Renaissance was to use words like "naturally" and "reason." To think that these beliefs are in any technical way "derived from" reason is to mistake the force of conviction for philosophical seriousness. Moreover, it requires a good deal of special pleading to discover this exalted vision of rational license in the action of the play. As first Manoa, then

Dalila offer him freedom, Samson twice chooses captivity: until revived by Harapha and struck my rousing motions, he feels altogether severed from the role of deliverer.

"The reasonableness of Samson's 'rouzing motions' is not a seizing of power by an external, even if transcendental, force over a dazzled mind, it is rather an inward prompting to a radical ecumenical faith."[17] With this noble sentiment in mind, Radzinowicz assures us that "when Samson leaves the stage, he goes to do what his will directs in obedience to his reason."[18] I am sure that he does, and so do I when I swing a golf club or walk across the room to put *Toward Samson Agonistes* back on the shelf. If you picture the mind in these terms, you cannot be animated in any other way. "Reason" is in truth a whorish term in the Renaissance lexicon. It can mean mind in general, the logic-making power, the seat of ethical self-determination, or in the contexts of polemic and deep conviction, very little more than "what another would have to possess in order to agree with me." In claiming that Samson "goes to do what his will directs in obedience to his reason," Radzinowicz has shifted ground from the sort of reason, right reason, that counts in this interpretive debate, and might distinguish one reading of the play from another, to the sort of reason without which, in the Renaissance view of man, no one could get up in the morning.

For a time Milton's Samson rationally and heroically refuses to attend the Philistine festivities. To do so would be yet again to break the law, and his defiance, heedless of threats to increase his suffering, has a certain revived grandeur of its own:

> Thou knowst I am an *Ebrew*, therefore tell them,
> Our Law forbids at thir Religious Rites
> My presence; for that cause I cannot come.   (1319–21)

> Besides, how vile, contemptible, ridiculous,
> What act more execrably unclean?   (1361–62)

This stubborn loyalty to the law is the heroism proposed by Samson's reason. He cannot by unaided reason get the idea of destroying the temple because a forbidding law stands between him and toppled pillars. God alone, as the Chorus has rightly said, possesses "full right to exempt / Whom so it pleases him by choice / From National obstriction" (310–12). Samson knows what to do in the theater. He leaves the stage with the scheme in mind, "with inward eyes illuminated." The point is that God put the illumination there.

In theology, voluntarism has traditionally been a great conversation-stopper. The mere contingency of the world, once asserted, leaves noth-

ing else to say. The inscrutability of the divine will drives reason to resignation. But Milton was writing poetry, not theology or philosophy, and
his depiction of the divine will is consequently embedded in a thick weave
of story, myth, and symbol. Only Shakespeare among English poets ex-
ceeds Milton in mastery of the artistic secret of good design. The unerr-
ing feel in Milton's verse for patterned variety, repetition with a difference, the surprising yet apt relationship of beginning to end and whole
to part, is positively uncanny. Edward Le Comte has spent years display-
ing the secret designs interwoven between his many works, a project first
announced in *Yet Once More: Verbal and Psychological Pattern in Milton*, one of the luckiest titles in the history of Milton studies, and Edward Tayler among others has demonstrated that Milton's poetry develops
"in time," in the medium of time, through patterns of anticipation and
fulfillment that make literature of God's typological management of history.[19] In *Paradise Lost* God supplies a newly awakened Eve with the
concept of an image, which involves resemblance and difference: one
needs at least this either to act in Milton's universe or, on the other side
of the text, to read him sensibly. Articulated in the midst of such good
poetic coherence, the will of Milton's God inevitably becomes scrutable,
meaningful. Thus we know in *Paradise Lost* that the prohibition against
the fruit is by theological postulate an arbitrary fiat. The unconditioned
will of God, binding but not itself bound, could have prohibited anything. But as a poet Milton transformed theology: the discussion of eating in Book V and the development from the opening line onward of
a vast network of metaphors extending nourishment into almost every
corner of the epic invites us to apprehend the "good sense," the ontologi-
cal rightness, of the law against eating a fruit.[20]

In *Samson Agonistes*, similarly, the guiding will of an "unsearchable" God can in fact be looked into. God "makes sense" in his ways to
man, and the discipline best equipped to search beyond the barren fiats
of theological voluntarism is literary criticism. A criticism informed by
the Freudian tradition might hope to be especially lucky in this task, for
psychoanalysis shares with voluntarism the assumption that reason is not
sole arbiter in the court of meaning, and has established in its short history an astonishing record at making sense of things otherwise inscrutable.

Lycidas and *Samson* are the most intensely concentrated examples
of the Miltonic virtue of good design. All the major criticism of the tragedy
has contributed to our sense of its architectural elegance. Samson himself touches on one of its coherences when he remarks that God "herein /
Haply had ends beyond my reach to know" (61–62). The "ends" in the
temple may be read "haply" anticipated in the opening speech, though

at this point beyond our reach to know; the dark, dark, dark beginning may be read in retrospect from the blaze of noon, where Samson in sun-clad triumph imaginatively eclipses his earlier degradation. The pressure of the end is felt throughout, as Joseph Summers was the first to note, in the many either/or dichotomies of the drama, all of them destined to collapse into the both/and of the climax, as Samson's capitulation to Dagon becomes the fulfillment of his glorious mission.[21] Aptly, the end of the drama is an octosyllabic sonnet on God's ability to wrest last-minute coherence from doubtful histories.

Much of this pattern-weaving takes place solely in the language of the drama, its figures and its syntax. But Milton creates a biographical pattern as well. The structure of event, the meaning of the drama within the life of its protagonist, proceeds from marriage. Though not a main topic of Christian humanism, marriage is crucial in the late Milton — the mysterious union of sacred history and personal history.

Queried about his notorious taste for the enemy's women, Samson replies:

> The first I saw at Timna, and she pleas'd
> Mee, not my Parents, that I sought to wed,
> The daughter of an Infidel: they knew not
> That what I motion'd was of God; I knew
> From intimate impulse, and therefore urg'd
> The marriage on; that by occasion hence
> I might begin Israel's Deliverance,
> The work to which I was divinely call'd;
> She proving false, the next I took to Wife
> (O that I never had! fond wish too late)
> Was in the Vale of *Sorec, Dalila,*
> That specious monster, my accomplisht snare.
> I thought it lawful from my former act,
> And the same end; still watching to oppress
> *Israel's* oppressors: of what now I suffer
> She was not the prime cause, but I myself,
> Who vanquisht with a peal of words (O weakness!)
> Gave up my fort of silence to a Woman.   (219-36)

The two marriages variously encode with entire drama. Samson's "intimate impulse" proving that "what I motion'd was of God" is, as a privileged and God-given exemption from Hebrew law, the earliest ancestor of the "rousing motions" that prompt him to disobey another law and play at the Dagonalia. The impulse also bears the structure of the tragedy. God urged Samson to disagree with his father in order to take a wife in order to "begin Israel's Deliverance," fulfilling the prophecy of his birth. In the play itself, Samson on the last day of his life relives this early choice by receiving visits from three figures, brought before him in the same sequence of strifes "motion'd" at his marriage—father, wife, Philistine rival.

Milton's account of the episode with the woman of Timna substantially duplicates Judges xiv.[22] He departs from the Bible in having Samson marry Dalila, which serves to confirm a deeper repetition. Although God appears not to have roused him to this second match, Samson felt the power of resemblance: "I thought it lawful from my former act." But this parallel turned out to be more extensive than the husband realized, for the betrayal in his first marriage adumbrated the more catastrophic betrayal in his second:

> This well I knew, nor was at all surpris'd,
> But warn'd by oft experience: did not she
> Of *Timna* at first betray me, and reveal
> The secret wrested from me in her height
> Of Nuptial Love profest, carrying it straight
> To them who had corrupted her, my Spies,
> And Rivals? In this other was there found
> More Faith? who also in her prime of love,
> Spousal embraces, vitiated with Gold,
> Though offer'd only, by the scent conceiv'd
> Her spurious first-born; Treason against me?
> Thrice she assay'd with flattering prayers and sighs,
> And amorous reproaches to win from me
> My capital secret, in what part my strength
> Lay stor'd, in what part summ'd, that she might know:
> Thrice I deluded her, and turn'd to sport
> Her importunity, each time perceiving
> How openly, and with what impudence
> She purpos'd to betray me, and (which was worse
> Than undissembl'd hate) with what contempt
> She sought to make me Traitor to myself;
> Yet the fourth time, when must'ring all her wiles,
> With blandisht parleys, feminine assaults,
> Tongue batteries, she surceas'd not day nor night
> To storm me over-watch't, and wearied out,
> At times when men seek most repose and rest,
> I yielded, and unlock'd her all my heart.   (382–408)

Once again we find the structure of the drama—particularly that part of it not encoded in the Timnan marriage—in Samson's failed temptation at the hands of Dalila. "Thrice" he is visited, and each time preserves his awareness of how these people in their different ways seek "to make me Traitor to myself." He will not be bought from his deserved prison by Manoa, will not be tended as a husband by Dalila, and yet is not so guilty and despairing that he will passively withstand the ridicule of Harapha. When a visitor appears "for the fourth time," Samson is ready to demonstrate that he has at last profited from "oft experience": he will not accompany the messenger. But at this point the four-choice structure of the Dalila temptation is repeated again, in epitome. Samson refuses once ("I cannot come," 1321), twice ("I will not come," 1332), thrice ("I will not come," 1342), then, the rousing motions having intervened, reverses himself on the fourth choice before the fourth visitor: "I am content to go" (1403). No less than his champion, God has secrets. Mysteriously, riddlingly, irrationally, Samson twice relives the pattern of his fall to Dalila on the day of his triumph. "I cannot praise thy marriage choices, Son" (420), says Manoa with good reason. But they are the rough draft of his victory. In the imprudent ways of his marriages, which began with "intimate impulse," lies the dramatic structure through which, at the end, "*Samson* hath quit himself / Like *Samson*" (1709–10).

The drama seems stark, pessimistic, and uncongenial to most readers who approach it from the expectations of Christian humanism. But if we come to *Samson Agonistes* having studied the manifold connections between Milton's poetry and the "true poem" of his life, the impregnation of "marriage choices" with the embryonic structure of the drama seems almost a signature: Milton quitting himself like Milton. Let us underscore yet again the point with which we began the discussion of dramatic structure. The genetic ancestor of the godly motions that rouse Samson freely to break the law was the "intimate impulse" that drew him to the woman of Timna — urged him with divine sanction, in other words, to lose his virginity.

The story of the first time is, of course, a much cherished human anecdote, and as a poet Milton was notably responsive to the force of this particular genesis in the personal mythologies of human beings. Samson tells this story, as we have seen, and in *Paradise Lost* both Adam and Eve narrate their lives from first awakening to the simultaneous loss of virginity at the consummation of their natural marriage. But in the youthful phase (or as one might say in this context, the "Nazarite" phase) of his poetic career Milton mythologized virginity itself, and interestingly enough, Samson is evoked in *Comus*, his conflicted testament to "The sage / And serious doctrine of virginity" (786–87). The Lady has just given voice to "the Sun-clad power of chastity." Refusing to say anything more to her unworthy captor, she predicts the likely effects of complete exposition, evoking Samson triumphant in her last words of the masque:

Yet should I try, the uncontrolled worth
Of this pure cause would kindle my rapt spirits
To such a flame of sacred vehemence,
That dumb things would be mov'd to sympathize,
And the brute Earth would lend her nerves, and shake,
Till all thy magic structures rear'd so high
Were shatter'd into heaps o'er thy false head.   (793–99)

Milton remembered the language of this passage when he came to write directly of Samson's destruction of the temple. "Uncontrolled worth," which suggests that men can determine by merit their own salvation, becomes the voluntarist and Protestant "uncontrollable intent" of God. The "flame of sacred vehemence" reappears in "His fiery virtue rous'd / From under ashes into sudden flame." The shaking of the "brute Earth" anticipates the metaphorical earthquake of the tragedy, "As with the force of winds and waters pent / When Mountains tremble, those two massy Pillars / With horrible convulsion to and fro / He tugg'd, he shook" (1647–50). The striking difference is that the Lady has reasoned herself into a paralysis on the subject of sexuality and is about to become actually paralyzed, whereas "intimate impulse" removed this stumbling-block from the life of Samson. The Lady can wield Samson's ultimate power only by preserving her virginity, whereas Samson himself can get to the temple only by losing his.

In *The Sacred Complex* I argued at length that Milton, in order to purchase the artistic strength of his late masterworks, had to tear down, not the flimsy temple of Comus's magic, but the massy symptom of paralyzing virginity.[23] Both of the poems published in 1671 have rich dimensions of psychological autobiography, exploring the conditions of their own accomplishment. They are companionable self-interpretations in the medium of sacred history, and they halve his life, *Paradise Regained* being, as psychic autobiography, primarily about his youth and *Samson Agonistes* primarily about his maturity and old age. If we take the victory in the temple as in one sense an emblem of Milton's own unexpected and Phoenix-like literary revival, it is possible to discern in the tragic drama several important stages in the long journey from *Comus* to the late works.

The symbiosis of virginity and poetic power had to be severed, and the old prohibition broken, whatever the cost in rancor. Guilt and finitude had to be conceded. Although Milton strenuously denied that his blindness was a divine punishment or a political embarrassment to his party, the inner logic of the creative act dramatized in *Paradise Lost* requires that it be interpreted this way. Because Milton had paid the price

without committing the crime, he could demand his due in inspired revelation of divine secrets, making a debt owed God into a debt God owed
him; *Paradise Lost* acknowledges his guilty blindness in connections between original sin and *gutta serena*.[24] But in *Samson* the guilt of blindness pervades numerous fervent speeches. The hero's unwavering conviction in his own guilt represents his supreme act of moral intelligence,
its reaffirmation preventing him from indicting God, from going home
with Manoa, and from blaming everything on Dalila. Nonetheless, the
guilt with which Samson will "pay on my punishment" (489) feels excessive and obsessional. In an unconscious, Protestant way he is earning
the renewed favor of the rousing motions. For an excess in his guilt, his
conviction of just desert, would imply an excess in his punishment, and
this is exactly what the Chorus declares. God can be hard with his
champions:

> Nor only dost degrade them, or remit
> To life obscur'd, which were a fair dismission,
> But throw'st them lower than thou didst exalt them high.   (687–89)

The unfair difference between "lower" and "high" cries out for theodical
adjustment. It has to be, and is, made up. Like the author of *Paradise
Lost*, Samson completes a private theodicy, winning inspiration by reversing a debt through prevenient guilt.

But what of the rancor? Why did God motion Samson to mate with
his first Judas, laying down an ominous precedent? If Milton had to re-
tract his early investment in virginity to empower the second flowering
of his art, that reversal would seem to entail the intrinsic goodness of
woman, marriage, and family. We find ample evidence of this goodness
in *Paradise Lost*, where Milton and Adam gradually make peace with
Eve, and the final heroic value consists in preserving a marriage on fallen
terms; *Paradise Lost* sanctifies the home, the "place of rest," to which
second Adam returns at the end of *Paradise Regained*, reuniting with
second Eve. In *Samson* the vision of marriage is obviously darker. The
appearance of Dalila prompts the Chorus to a theodical inquiry (1010–
60) that might well have begun "God of our fathers, what is woman?"
Marriage seems a burden to be borne. Why are men charged with godly
purpose given over to lawless and inconstant wives? Manoa at the end
envisions the daughters of the future weeping at Samson's tomb in remorse for their gender. The many critics who have found misogyny here,
and traced it to Milton's disillusionment over Mary Powell, certainly have
a point. Yet marriage and gender undergo some startling metamorphoses in the figurative language of the drama.

Samson is strong on the condition that he be wise in keeping the secret of his strength's location. This link between strength and wisdom is imaged as an internal marriage:

> But thee whose strength, while virtue was her mate   (173)

> Immeasurable strength they might behold
> In me, of wisdom nothing more than mean;
> This with the other should, at least, have pair'd,
> These two proportion'd ill drove me traverse.   (206–09)

His strength was wife to male virtue or wisdom, and precisely as the Chorus has said of real marriages, this one went awry because wisdom, the husband, was weak. Samson suffers from "foul effeminacy" (410). He is now strong only, a female, an emasculated male, a "tame Wether" (538), a "drone" (567): "O impotence of mind, in body strong!" (52). In Milton, too, artistic strength comes in part from an internal woman.[25] This weakness becomes his strength, inasmuch as felt congruence with the will of the Father (from which, and not from reason, revolutionary politics, theological heresies, and inspired poetry really do derive in Milton) activates the feminine identification.

The symbol of this internal marriage, chosen by God himself, who made it both literal and metaphorical, is Samson's unshorn hair — a neatly androgynous "marriage choice," since long hair is a standard gender mark, and may have been partly responsible for Milton's undergraduate nickname, "Lady of Christ's." The strength hung there must be kept away from those who would know and defile its secret location. As we gather from the four assaults of Dalila, the bond of strength and wisdom generates a drama analogous to a woman's preservation of her virginity. Samson's internal marriage represents in this sense spiritual virginity — strength intact, guarded by wisdom. There are clear sexual overtones in passages like this:

> My trust is in the living God who gave me
> At my Nativity this strength, diffus'd
> No less through all my sinews, joints and bones,
> Than thine, while I preserv'd these locks unshorn,
> The pledge of my unviolated vow.   (1140–44)

But the unshorn virginal locks are cut, and Samson loses his maidenhead of hair. If divine impulse urged him to lose his sexual virginity, his own weak virtue forfeited his spiritual virginity. Divine punishments, as readers of Dante know, tend to resemble the very crimes that occasion them, and Samson explicitly connects "grinding" in sexual intercourse with "grinding" in servitude:

> servile mind
> Rewarded well with servile punishment!
> The base degree to which I now am fall'n,
> These rags, this grinding, is not yet so base
> As was my former servitude, ignoble,
> Unmanly.   (412–17)[26]

"Ask for this great Deliverer now, and find him / Eyeless in *Gaza* at the Mill with slaves" (40–41), grinding away in the image of his defilement.

Yet the hair has grown back. There is a second freedom, a new virginity, and a final chance to mate strength with wisdom. The Chorus terms Dalila "unclean, unchaste" (321). The temple of Dagon is a scene of defilement. "What act more execrably unclean?" Samson will be a hero of defiance, a good Nazarite once again. There will be no more of "prostituting holy things to Idols" (1358). Philistia herself is the latest avatar of Samson's unclean and betraying women, and he will resist the fourth visitor, as he should have resisted the fourth onslaught of Dalila. But then, counter to the growing vehemence of this rational heroism, the rousing motions appear, renewing the "intimate impulse" of his first marriage. What must he do with his regained spiritual virginity? Precedent holds: *lose it.* God's ways are various, or might we say contrarious. The wrong thing must be done before the right thing. As Milton designs the irrational coherence of Samson's tragedy, the marriages in their direst consequences — betrayal, blindness, imprisonment, guilt, humiliation — are the strict precondition for his triumph. In the wise vision of this Christian poet, there are a number of excruciating oppositions once the Fall has occurred, such as guilt/innocence, wrong/right, defiled/pure, foolish/wise, weak/strong, woman/man, castrated/potent, forbidden/lawful, in which religious heroes must be or do the first in order to be or do the second. The foreseeing God of Samson, the God of this musky planet Earth, the God, for all his patriarchal severity, of mothers and wives and children, placed this contrary truth at the entrance to the sexual life.

University of Maryland

NOTES

1. All citations from Milton's poetry in this essay use *Complete Poems and Major Prose*, ed. Merritt Y. Hughes (New York, 1957).

2. See the excellent discussion of the history of will in Hannah Arendt, *The Life of the Mind* (New York, 1978), pp. 55–217 (in the second half of the book, which is repaginated).

3. Denis Savrat, *Milton, Man and Thinker* (New York, 1925), p. 237.

4. Douglas Bush, *The Renaissance and English Humanism* (Toronto, 1972), p. 124.

5. Ibid., p. 125.

6. I have expanded on this point in "Milton's Place in Intellectual History: Poetry as Philosophy + ," unpublished essay.

7. Robert Hoopes, *Right Reason in the English Renaissance* (Cambridge, Mass., 1962), pp. vii, 193, 191. Hoopes makes a serious error in assuming that Milton's various passages about "inner light" are simply right reason in metaphor. This assumption would hold for a Nathaniel Culverwell, but not for Milton, who believed in immediate inspiration from above. See Edward Tayler, *Milton's Poetry: Its Development in Time* (Pittsburgh, 1979), p. 261, n. 15.

8. Douglas Bush, *English Literature in the Earlier Seventeenth Century* (Oxford, 1962), p. 398.

9. *The Sacred Complex: On the Psychogenesis of "Paradise Lost"* (Cambridge, Mass., 1983), p. ix.

10. Bush, *English Literature in the Earlier Seventeenth Century*, p. 401.

11. Ibid., p. 394.

12. Martz's "Chorus and Character in *Samson Agonistes*" first appeared in *Milton Studies*, I, ed. James D. Simmonds (Pittsburgh, 1967), pp. 115–35, and with light revision has been reprinted in Martz's *Poet of Exile* (New Haven, 1980), pp. 272–91. The quotation appears in *Poet of Exile*, p. 287.

13. Ibid., p. 287.

14. Ibid., p. 289.

15. Mary Ann Radzinowicz, *Toward Samson Agonistes* (Princeton, 1978), p. 169.

16. *The Complete Prose Works of John Milton*, ed. Don M. Wolfe et al. (New Haven, 1953–1982), vol. III, p. 198.

17. Radzinowicz, *Toward Samson Agonistes*, p. 349.

18. Ibid., p. 61.

19. Edward LeComte, *Yet Once More* (New York, 1953); Tayler, *Milton's Poetry*.

20. *The Sacred Complex*, pp. 254–56.

21. Joseph Summers, "The Movements of the Drama," in *The Lyric and Dramatic Milton*, ed. Joseph Summers (New York, 1965), pp. 157–60; see also Anthony Low, *The Blaze of Noon* (New York, 1974), pp. 62–89.

22. Here I disagree with Philip Gallagher's "The Role of Raphael in *Samson Agonistes*," in *Milton Studies*, XVIII, ed. James D. Simmonds (Pittsburgh, 1983), p. 276, since it seems to me unwieldy to suppose that the biblical Samson does not know that his prompting is from God. I have profited from this article in other ways, especially from its emphasis on Samson's self-indictment.

23. *The Sacred Complex*, pp. 52–56.

24. Ibid., pp. 249–53, 257–59.

25. Ibid., pp. 42, 44, 48–50, 72, 181, 184–86, 188–89.

26. On "grinding" see Edward LeComte, *Milton and Sex* (New York, 1978), p. 113. See also p. 30 for the appearance of this language in the divorce tracts (*Complete Prose Works*, vol. II, p. 258).

THE SCHEMATIC DESIGN
OF THE *SAMSON* MIDDLE

Burton J. Weber

T HE REGENERATION theorists have presented an account of the climax of *Samson Agonistes* which, despite the objections of the providential and revisionist critics, has been widely and rightly admired. The orthodox regeneration theorists, Arnold Stein, Joseph Summers, and Anthony Low, have not presented so definitive an account of the *Samson* middle, however. Summers, for example, describes the dramatic ironies which mark the individual episodes in the center of the play, and provides a description of the whole ("With each episode [Samson] achieves a new position, a new strength, and finds himself in a place he has never been before"),[1] but does not provide a schematic explanation of the movements of the drama, a design to which each of the episodes contributes, and which accounts for their number and order. Such a design has been proposed, however, by allegorical opponents of the regeneration reading. F. Michael Krouse and Patrick Cullen, asserting that Samson is a type of Christ, argue that he is regenerated through trials which parallel the three temptations of Christ in the wilderness.[2] An alternative to their structural proposal, a design compatible with the regeneration reading, lies unnoticed in the alternatives to two of their basic tenets — that the middle of *Samson* consists of three episodes, and that Samson is regenerated through temptation.

The triadic division of the *Samson* middle proposed by the typological critics results from the analogy which they draw between Samson's encounters with his visitors and the temptations of Jesus. The episodes of the play are susceptible of other groupings, however, and Milton's structural cues, his structural parallels and antitheses, indicate what grouping he intends.

A structural parallel exists, first of all, between the Chorus's interview with Samson (115–331) and Manoa's private exchange with him (332–478). The Chorus and Manoa both begin with expressions of dismay at Samson's reversal of fortune: "O change beyond report, thought, or belief!" (115–75), "O miserable change! is this the man, / That invincible Samson" (340–72).[3] Both are comforted by Samson's arguments;

Manoa exclaims, "these words / I as a prophecy receive; for God, / Nothing more certain, will not long defer / To vindicate the glory of his name / Against all competition" (472–76), and the enlightened Chorus express their satisfaction: "Thy words to my remembrance bring / How Succoth and the fort of Penuel / Their great deliverer condemned" (277–89), "Just are the ways of God, / And justifiable to men" (293–325). The fact that at the point of Manoa's proposal of ransom (478ff) the Chorus and Manoa are linked — both try to comfort their comforter — suggests that Samson's opening encounters are parts of a single structural unit, the scenes, so to speak, of a single act.[4] The typological critics follow Hanford in his contention that the play's middle, its "second act," begins with the Manoa episode, but Summers, describing the play's "major action," provides an alternative division: he begins by grouping Samson's encounters with the Chorus and Manoa.[5]

Secondly, the episode with the public officer (1308–444) is set apart by its unique structure, marked, as John Steadman observes, by a *deus ex machina* resolution to matters "strained / Up to the highth" (1348–49). Summers, who lists the officer with Samson's other visitors, fails to indicate where the play's middle ends, though he understands the importance of the episode with the officer.[6] The typological critics, rejecting Hanford's contention that the officer is to be paired with Harapha as a second "instrument of force," mark the close of the *Samson* middle, but, turning to the denouement, they miss the importance of the crisis — the play's "fourth act," so to speak.[7]

Thirdly, structural antitheses suggest that to group the episodes with Dalila and Harapha as the two scenes of act 3 (732–1075, 1076–307) is not a mere critical expedient of the kind scorned by Steadman;[8] the grouping reflects a structural relationship. Dalila and Harapha are paired, by way of antithesis, with the Chorus and Manoa, the two visitors of act 2. Harapha upon his entrance contrasts himself with the Chorus: "I come not, Samson, to condole thy chance, / As these perhaps, yet wish it had not been, / Though for no friendly intent" (1076–78). The analogy between Manoa's offer and that of Dalila, used by the typologists to link the two figures,[9] serves rather to contrast their characters: the father does not mention (481–83) that he intends to spend his whole fortune to ransom his son (1476–80), while the wife who proclaims her love (920–27) enters dressed in the finery earned by selling her husband into captivity. The pattern of the *Samson* middle is bipartite, then. Four visitors enter two-by-two, and Summers in describing the dramatic ironies of Samson's opening encounters pairs the characters appropriately: "The Chorus and Manoa come as comforters. . . . Dalila . . . comes to seduce, and . . . Harapha to 'stare at' and 'insult' a supposedly defeated . . . and hopeless man."[10]

The typological critics explain their triadic division of the *Samson* middle by invoking a formula external to the play, the formula of the Flesh, the World, and the Devil applied by exegetes to the trials of Christ in the wilderness.[11] The explanation for the alternative binary groupings must be found within the play itself. Logic suggests that if a schematic pattern underlies the portrayal of Samson's regeneration, the key to it should lie in the contrast of act 1 (1–114) with what might be called the first scene of act 4 (1308–76) — in the contrast of the qualities of the despairing Samson of the soliloquy with those of the regenerate Samson who rebuffs the Philistine officer. In his soliloquy Samson alternates between the doubt of God and despairing self-condemnation. Samson doubts God's declared favor (23–42) — "O wherefore was my birth from Heaven foretold" — and he doubts the mission which God has given him, disparaging the gift by which he was to perform it (53–59) — "But what is strength without a double share / Of wisdom? . . . God, when he gave me strength, to show withal / How slight the gift was, hung it in my hair." The only means by which Samson can curb his doubt of God's fidelity is by transferring the accusation of treachery from God to himself (43–52) — "what if all foretold / Had been fulfilled but through mine own default? . . . O impotence of mind, in body strong!"; he can remove blame from God for preventing the successful completion of his mission only by transferring his curse to his own unsuccessful strength (60–109) — "Suffices that to me strength is my bane, / And proves the source of all my miseries." At the play's crisis, refusing the officer's command, Samson expresses confidence in God's special favor (1354–62) — "Shall I abuse this consecrated gift / Of strength again returning with my hair . . . , so requite / Favor renewed" — and he honors his mission, preparing to use his gift for the resistance of the Philistines' unjust commands (1369–76) — "who constrains me to the temple of Dagon / Not dragging?" Instead of denouncing his "impotence of mind," Samson defends his moral dignity (1334–42), his "conscience and internal peace"; and instead of cursing his strength, he refuses physical indignity (1323–32) — "Have they not sword-players, and ev'ry sort / Of gymnic artist . . . But they must pick me out . . . To make them sport with blind activity?" Logic suggests that the aspects of Samson's change should explain the significance of the four visitations which comprise the *Samson* middle, the visitations which produce the change. Summers's description of the visits of Dalila and Harapha accurately suggest the place of act 3 in the schematic design: "Dalila, that debating Circe, comes to seduce, and the giant Harapha to stare at and insult, a supposedly defeated, weakened, and hopeless man. They both retire with some fear for their physical safety from a determined, fearless, and strengthened man." Samson's two enemies ironically effect the revival of his self-respect, Dalila by testing the mind which Samson had branded impotent, Harapha by disparaging the strength which Samson had declared a bane. Summers's account of act 2 is less successful: "The Chorus and Manoa come as comforters, but they provide challenges and temptations."[12] Rather, the Chorus and Manoa, who "come as comforters," ironically receive comfort. They bring not "challenges and temptations" but doubts, the Chorus of Samson's mission, Manoa of God's fidelity. To comfort them, Samson must defend the God whom he had doubted.

An alternative to the second tenet of the typologists, that Samson is regenerated through the resistance of temptation, is suggested by Summers when he hesitates between two descriptions of Samson's encounters: "Those exchanges may be thought of both as 'debates' and as 'temptations,' but neither term alone adequately describes them." Cullen holds that Samson is tempted by figures who represent the sins of his past, but Summers suggests that Samson's visitors voice the views of the present Samson: "often" the visitors offer "what seem merely repetitions or developments of ideas or emotions" expressed by Samson.[13] Systematically developed, the alternative at which Summers glances would hold that the ideas of Samson's interlocutors relate to the aspects of the despair voiced in the soliloquy, and that by debating with these visitors, Samson learns the answers to his despairing thoughts, the answers which he voices in his defiance of the public officer.

In the first two scenes of act 2 — the Chorus's interview with Samson, and Manoa's private words with him — Samson corrects his doubts of God. The difference between the two exchanges is signaled by the difference between the kind of dismay which Manoa expresses at the sight of Samson's change and the kind of dismay voiced by the Chorus: the Chorus's theme is the fall of princes, Manoa's the vanity of human wishes. The Chorus are struck by the failure of Samson's mission. They celebrate the gift of strength which Samson disparaged, viewing it in terms of its use, the defeat of Philistia (115–50); mourning Samson's change, they "bewail" the "bondage" and "lost sight" which Samson lamented as the miseries brought him by his bane (151–63); they close with a moralizing reflection on the fickleness of worldly fortune, the precariousness of worldly glory (164–75). When they hint at the cause of Samson's fall — his "strength, while virtue was her mate, / Might have subdued the earth" (173–74) — they apparently refer in the word "virtue" to obedience to the national law, the subject of their first question to Samson (215–18) and of their final exclamation, "Just are the ways of God" (293–325). Their reflections on Samson's fall, couched in terms of crime and folly rather than in terms of sin, touch on the defect in Samson's nature by which, in his opening soliloquy, he himself had questioned God's gift: "But what is strength without a double share / Of wisdom? . . . Proudly secure, yet liable to fall / By weakest subtleties" (53–56).

Manoa laments not the failure of Samson's mission but the withdrawal of God's favor. He views Samson's reversal of fortune not as the negation of his deeds at Gaza and at Ramath-lechi but as an example of the "deceivable and vain" in human hopes (340–50), an example comparable to his own disappointment in God's promises (350–51). Developing the point — "For this did the angel twice descend? For this / Ordained thy nurture holy, as of a plant; / Select and sacred" (361–63) — Manoa cites the same angelic visitations and commands cited by Samson in his doubts of God's fidelity: "O wherefor was my birth from Heaven foretold . . ." (23ff), "Why was my breeding ordered and prescribed / As of a person separate to God . . ." (30ff). The bitter irony with which Samson expressed his sense of betrayal (40–41) is mirrored in Manoa's ironic description of his own disappointment: "I prayed for children . . . : I gained a son, / And such a son as all men hailed me happy: / Who would be now a father in my stead?" (352–55). In closing, the Chorus mentioned the cause of Samson's fall, and Manoa in his concluding protest (368–72) concedes that the failure of God's prediction may have resulted from Samson's failure — for Manoa, sin rather than folly: "if he through frailty err" (369) is a palliating euphemism. Herein Manoa echoes Samson's self-accusing explanation, "what if all . . . Had been fulfilled but through mine own default?" (44–45). The Chorus find in the fall of the champion an emblem of man's "fickle state" (164); Manoa, viewing Samson's change of fortune as the fall of God's favorite, draws from it a pessimistic religious conclusion, and voices a plaintive accusation of divine ingratitude: "Alas, methinks whom God hath chosen once / To worthiest deeds, if he through frailty err, / He should not so o'erwhelm . . . Be it but for honor's sake of former deeds" (368–72).

These initial reactions of the Chorus and Manoa continue through their scenes. Samson does not hear the Chorus's words (176–77), but he speaks as if he guessed their memories, their pity, and their moral, and wished in what Arnold Stein calls a "public lament"[14] to ease what he can imagine to be their distress. He legitimates their astonishment at his change with an emphatic metaphor, the wreck of a "vessel . . . Gloriously rigged" (198–200); he ameliorates their pity with a gallant denial of the pain of blindness (195–97); he fosters their acceptance, disarming criticism by bowing to the most extreme contempt, a contempt which he courteously avoids attributing to them (203–05): "Am I not sung and proverbed for a fool?" But then, unable to maintain the public pose, the formal self-contempt concealing a real despair about the ruin of his vocation, he tries to alleviate his pain by shifting, as in his soliloquy, from self-blame to the blame of God. He voices in public his private disparagement of God's gift: "Immeasurable strength they might behold / In me, of wisdom nothing more than mean . . . : These two proportioned ill drove me transverse" (206–09). The Chorus comfortingly quiet the blasphemy (210–14); but because Samson has broached the subject, they can voice their own version of the same doubt, courteously attributing it to the anonymous questioners of Samson's imagining (215–18). That the question of Samson's virtue in violating the Mosaic injunction against marriage to Gentiles is, like Samson's aspersions on his ill-proportioned nature, a "Tax[ing]" of "divine disposal" (210) is indicated by the Chorus's later expression of satisfaction on the point, "Just are the ways of God." When Samson satisfies the Chorus's first question, they hint at a second: "Yet Israel still serves with all his sons" (240). Their implication is that if Samson's mission were divinely ordained, it could not fail; and in the postscript to his reply Samson stresses the reality of the sanction he has claimed: "Me easily indeed mine may neglect, / But God's proposed deliverance not so" (291–92).

Samson, who does not hear the Chorus's expressions of dismay, hears his father's, and answers without formal reserve. His method of reply is the same as before — Samson lays the blame for his plight on himself — but the nature of the blame is different. He speaks not as a man who has ruined his physical self, "shipwrecked" the "vessel trusted to [him] from above, / Gloriously rigged" (198–200), but as a man who has destroyed his soul, having "prophaned / The mystery of God giv'n [him] under pledge / Of vow" (377–79). He speaks of himself not as one whose folly has been condemned by men, a man "sung and proverbed for a fool," but as one whose sin has been condemned by God: "Appoint not heavenly disposition . . . : Nothing of all these evils hath befall'n me / But justly" (373–75). To the Chorus, Samson speaks of the ruin of his mission and of his shame, to his father he speaks of the betrayal of God and of his guilt. Manoa, distracted from his theme by Samson's self-accusation, pours out old grievances, then pulls himself up, remembering that Samson is in no need of a fatherly reproof (420–33): "thou the sooner / Temptation found'st . . . To violate the sacred trust . . . , which to have kept / Tacit was in thy power; true." He then picks up his original complaint (433–47): the son for whom Manoa prayed, for whom the angel twice descended and "Ordained [his] nurture holy" has "magnified" Dagon and "Disglorified" God, bringing in place of the promised glory "shame" to himself and to his "father's house." Samson in comforting the Chorus assured the patriots that his mission was divinely guided, and they were satisfied; he comforts his father that the "pomp" he has brought to Dagon and the "Dishonor" and "obloquy" which he has brought to God are transitory shames (448–71); and, like his son, Manoa forgets as insignificant the disappointment of his private hopes in the thought of the inevitable triumph of the God whom he loves (472–78). Cullen blames the grieving Manoa for tempting his son to distrust, but Stein "conjecture[s]" that Manoa knows that the God who listens to him knows that "this is the grief of the father Manoa speaking, and not the piety of the son Manoa."[15] Stein's conjecture is validated by the fact that Manoa's complaints receive not punishment but answer: the son who had brought "reproach" and "shame" to his "father's house" (444–47), in dying brings to his "father's house" the "eternal fame" which vindicates God's gift (1718). Cullen blames the Chorus for their deficient understanding of God,[16] but God rewards them as he rewards Manoa (1745–54). Defending the Israelites, Milton places the blame for their doubts on the man who comforts them. Samson says (448–56) that his failure has opened the "mouths / Of idolists and atheists" and has brought to "feeble hearts" the "doubt" of whether God is God; it has also brought "diffidence of God," he says, and that distrust is what is displayed by the Chorus when they view his change. Samson corrects himself in act 2 by atoning for the harm which his fall has done to the pious and to the patriots of Israel.

The superiority of Hebrew to Philistine values is a crucial premise of act 3. The contrast underlies Samson's answers — answers which Milton is careful to substantiate — to Dalila's argumentative appeals: her appeal to a garrulity and to a love which she suggests are common to herself and Samson, her appeal to what she suggests is a common patriotic and religious fervor. Replying to Dalila's plea of feminine weakness, Samson disputes his wife's analogy between her revelation of his secret and his own garrulity (773–89). In his immediate response, Samson denies that Dalila is the gossip she has claimed to be; he contends that she is a venal rather than a venial sinner (829–35). His challenge is justified by the discrepancy between Dalila's initial assertion that she was ingenuously curious and ingenuously talkative (773–77) and her later acknowledgment that she consciously sought Samson's secret in order to have a hold over him (790–99), and intentionally revealed it in order to keep him her "and love's prisoner" (799–808). The charge of greed is justified by Dalila's reference to those who "tempted" her (801). Later Samson returns to Dalila's account of his garrulity, denying both that his sin was analogous to the sin which Dalila has confessed — he did not act from "levity" (880) — and to the sin which she has concealed — he acted from a generosity antithetical to Dalila's greed: he "could deny [her] nothing" (881). In rejecting her analogy, Samson accuses Dalila of moral laxness — she has extenuated her own sin, she has vulgarized his. As in his contrast of Dalila's self-condonation with his own repentance (825–29), Samson opposes Hebrew moral earnestness to pagan amorality.

In replying to Dalila's invocation of "love's law" (790–814), Samson distinguishes between love and lust, but his assertions have been questioned by defenders of Dalila. The revisionist critic Irene Samuel, for example, contends that Samson is deluded both in believing that he loved Dalila and in believing that she did not love him. Samuel follows Dalila's first defender, William Empson, in arguing that the self-sacrifice displayed in Dalila's offer to tend her ruined husband (920–27) validates her expressions of past love. The inquiry, however, undertaken by Low into what Dalila means by the term validates Samson's contrast of what a Hebrew means by "love" and what Gentiles in their fables ascribe to Cupid (836–42).[17] What Dalila calls "The jealousy of love" (791) is the desire for one's own pleasure: "Here I should still enjoy thee day and night" (807). The fact that Dalila describes herself as one who has "wrought much woe," not by a breach of love but by love itself, "well-meaning" love (813), shows that she believes that the sacrifice of another's interests to one's own pleasure accords with the nature of love. Her account of the past renders doubtful the contention of Dalila's defenders that her present offer springs from a self-forgetful tenderness.

Samuel asserts that Samson's deluded professions of love are exposed by the motive for marriage which Samson acknowledges to the Chorus but not to Dalila, that of seeking a provocation against the Philistines. Samson did have a political motive for marrying the woman of Timna, but because he was obeying a divine prompting, he can be blamed for that marriage only on the revisionist assumption that he had mistaken his own impulses for the voice of God.[18] The assumption is false. Samson declares to the Chorus that he was told by God that he should begin his mission against the Philistines by marrying the woman of Timna (219–25), and that this "intimate impulse" (223) was genuine is attested first by the fact that the marriage issued in Samson's first great triumph at Ramath-lechi (the chain of events is recounted to Harapha, 1192–216), and secondly by the fact that after that battle, God affirmed Samson's claims of divine direction by saving his life (the incident of the miraculous fountain is referred to by Manoa, 581–83). The course of the political marriage does not support Samuel's assumption that such a marriage precludes love — at least if love is thought of in Samson's sense rather than in Dalila's. Samson did not make political use of his wife. As he explains to Harapha (1195–200), it was the Philistines who turned the wedding into a political event, sending spies disguised as wedding guests. Nor did God's plan require that the marriage be unhappy. When the woman of Timna was threatened by the Philistine agents, she had the choice of betraying her husband or of appealing for his protection. If she had been faithful to her vows, God's plan would not have been thwarted: Samson would have begun his campaign by defending his wife against the thirty Philistine spies rather than by attacking their surrogates at Ascalon (1201–04). It was not Samson's political mission but his wife's decision to betray him which doomed the marriage. Dalila contends that Samson was at fault — "I saw thee mutible / Of fancy" (793–94) — but her accusation is unwarranted. Samson was angered by the betrayal at the wedding feast (382–87), but he did not "leave" his wife, as Dalila puts it (794–95), until she had committed adultery with his "paranymph" (the incident is reported by the Chorus, 1018–23). Samson mentions his divorce to his friends — "She proving false, the next I took to wife . . . Was in the vale of Sorec" (227–29) — and what he means by "false" the Chorus specify in their reference to his words, "Unchaste was subsequent; her stain, not his" (325).

When Samuel contends that Samson had a political motive for marrying Dalila, however, she misunderstands what Samson tells his friends about his second marriage (231–33). Samson explains to them that he did not have a divine directive to marry Dalila: he was under the illusion that the intimate impulse had given him a precedent for marrying a second Gentile. When he says that he was still "watching to oppress / Israel's oppressors" (232–33), his reference to his first marriage explains what he means: he was under the illusion that God would use his second marriage to further the deliverance of Israel, as he had used his first. For his second marrriage, Samson's political aim was a rationalizing justification rather than a motive. The motive was the motive which Samson tells Dalila (876–79), what Dunster calls a "violent affection."[19] It is not reasonable to suppose that Samson intended to treat his chosen wife less honorably than he had treated the wife of his arranged marriage, and there is evidence of his honorable intentions in his righteous indignation that Dalila should have violated her marriage vows for reasons of state (888–94). He, as Joan Bennett puts it, "would not have acted against

[Dalila], would not have sought 'aught against [her] life' in violation of his marriage."[20] Samson in his immediate reply to Dalila reveals what he means by "love"—the desire to give pleasure to another: "love seeks to have love" (837). In his subsequent reply Samson claims to have displayed such love, and Milton is careful to reconcile Samson's claim with the second thoughts about his violent affection which Samson reports to his father. After Dalila's betrayal, Samson saw himself as "Softened" by leisure, "pleasure and voluptuous life" (532–34), accounting thereby both for his illusions before his marriage and for his weak betrayal of God's secret after it. When Samson speaks to Dalila of his violent affection he calls it loving "Too well" (878–79), referring to the uxorious excess described to Manoa. Milton makes clear, however, that this flawed love was still love. Samson sought to have love: he "unbosomed all [his] secrets" to Dalila "Not out of levity, but overpowered / By [her] request, who could deny [her] nothing" (879–81).

Samson answers Dalila's appeals to gods and country (843–70) with a contrast of Hebrew and Philistine values. That contrast explains how Samson differs from Harapha, but as critics have sought to liken the husband and wife, so they have sought to liken the champion and giant. Explaining the difference between the values of those who uphold the Israelite rebellion and the values of those who serve Philistia, Samson distinguishes just rule from tyranny (888–94) by appealing to the criterion of obedience to the "law of nature, law of nations" (890); he distinguishes true from false deity by appealing to the criterion of moral goodness (895–900). Virginia Mollenkott contends that Samson uses a double standard in judging Dalila and himself. Dalila's choosing "above the faith of wedlock bands" (986), she argues, is justified by Samson's conduct: "If Samson can justify the breaking of law by an appeal to private inspiration, so can Dalila."[21] The critic fails to observe how carefully Milton has reconciled Samson's contention that God can give exemptions from the law (1377–79) with his contention that no true deity can command an immoral ("ungodly") deed (898). Milton confines God's power to the granting of dispensations from the statutes of the law of the covenant, from what the Chorus call the "national" law (312), the law by which God sanctified the Israelites. God does not command Samson to break the moral law, the "law of nature" which he gave to all men, to all "nations": Milton takes care not to raise the problem posed by the biblical account of the test of Abraham. Samson, then, is not granting to the god of Israel a right which he denies to Dagon, the right to break the moral law. Presumably, if the rousing motions had commanded the worship of Dagon, or the intimate impulse an intimacy with a certain wife of Gath, Samson would have doubted their divine origin. And presumably, if his wife had pleaded private inspiration, Samson would have judged her prompting by the same criterion by which he would have judged his own. But, as Low has observed, Dalila does not make that plea.[22]

Mollenkott's error stems from her belief that Milton intended to equate Samson with Dalila on the human level.[23] In fact, however, the opposite is true: Milton develops a systematic contrast between the figures. Unthinkingly accepting the arguments of the Philistine lords (849–57), Dalila resembles not the Samson of "strenuous liberty" (268–71) but the base followers of Israel's base magistrates, men obedient not to the law of nature but to the rule of force (1211–16). In her unthinking adherence to the state church (857–61), Dalila resembles not even the Chorus and Manoa, the saving remnant of Israel, men who receive no private inspiration, but who believe in the goodness as well as in the greatness of God; much less does she resemble Samson, a man whose inspiration is a sign that he is one of those whom God has "solemnly elected" (678). She resembles the Israelites of "feeble heart" (455–56), men who, oblivious to the moral difference between God and Dagon, can worship either. As Bennett explains, Milton assigns to Samson a cause which differentiated him from the base and from the feeble-hearted of Israel even when, "walk[ing] about admired of all" and "swoll'n with pride" (530–32), he made himself unworthy of that cause by his moral failure.[24] That cause — the political and religious principles which Samson explains to his wife — differentiates him from Dalila, and differentiated him even when, "swoll'n with pride," he fell "into the snare . . . Of fair fallacious looks, venereal trains" (532–33).

Cullen, who finds in Manoa the mirror of Samson's despair and in Dalila the mirror of his intemperance, finds in Harapha the mirror of Samson's vainglory when he walked "Fearless of danger like a petty god" (529). Low's reading is similar: Samson meets in Harapha his "double or inferior self: a boaster, a man of strength without wisdom, who trusts not in spiritual but in carnal weapons." Cullen argues that the giant tempts the reviving hero to believe that he is now what he once was, and Low contends that by recognizing and ridiculing the characteristics of his former self, Samson purges himself of them.[25] But the comparison between Harapha and Samson which the critics draw is not drawn by Samson himself: nowhere does the hero express the shame of a man who recognizes in his despised enemy the image of himself. The comparison between Samson and Harapha which is drawn not only by Samson but by the other characters of the scene is the comparison of the giant with the unfallen champion. Boasting his power and glory, Harapha questions the reports of Samson's former deeds (1082–90), then discounts the story of his divine gift, attributing his strength to the use of magic (1130–35). Later, boasting his moral superiority, the Philistine accuses Samson of criminality in the events leading to the battle of Ramath-lechi (1182–91). Samson, in proposing to fight armed "only with an oaken staff" (1123–29), is remembering the "trivial weapon" of his first great battle (142), and, in proposing to test the deities of God and Dagon (1145–55), he is remembering God's blessing on that battle (522–28). He answers Harapha's moral disparagement with a defence of the actions which led him to the battlefield (1192–216). Commenting on the exchange (1268–76), the Chorus contrast the "brute and boist'rous force" of men like Harapha with such "invincible might" as God put "into the hands" of a "deliverer" at Ramath-lechi. The contrast of the giant with the youthful champion links Samson's reply to Harapha with his reply to Dalila. In Samson's first challenge Milton alludes, as Steadman contends, to David's combat with Goliath, and in the second, to Elijah's contest with the priests of Baal, as Jack Goldman observes.[26] The allusions point to the heart of Samson's argument: the Hebrew is opposing to the pagan heroic code a divinely sanctioned war of deliverance. In his closing political argument, as Bennett demonstrates, Samson opposes to the tyranny of those who believe there is no right but might a view of government based on a divinely ordained freedom of conscience, a freedom operative in the political as well as in the religious realm.[27] Samson is developing the political arguments which he had touched on in answering Dalila's "feigned religion, smooth hypocrisy" (872).

Dalila enters believing in Samson's "impotence of mind." She thinks that as she won him to divulge his secret, so she can win his consent to a proposal which she dreams of unveiling at the Dagonalia. Harapha enters believing in Samson's physical ruin. In the scene with Dalila, Samson's self-correction takes the form of resistance; in the scene with Harapha, the form of defiance. He regains his self-respect by waging first a defensive, then an aggressive war against the confident upholders of Philistia. Cullen, systematically applying to *Samson Agonistes* a patristic triadic formula, finds a repeated tripartite pattern in Dalila's speeches; Balachandra Rajan, however, finds within the play itself reason for a fourfold division of the appeals: "In seeking to discover Samson's secret, Dalila prevailed only with the fourth attempt. There must be four efforts and four failures to make it evident that history will not be repeated."[28]

In the two middle efforts, the argumentative appeals, Dalila asks that Samson condone her actions, first on the basis of weaknesses common to them both (773–818), then on the basis of a common strength (843–70). But in drawing analogies between herself and Samson, Dalila unwittingly reveals the difference between her moral assumptions and Samson's, and from her arguments Samson learns the distinction between his "impotence of mind" and the total moral depravity of which he has accused himself—the "Shameful garrulity" in betraying God's secret which he confesses to his father (487–99), the "foul effeminacy" which led to that betrayal (410), the pride responsible for conditions conducive to effeminacy (526–34). Seeing Dalila's extenuation of her sin, he is made aware of the moral honesty of his repentance; he sees that his doting, if soft, was not Dalila's gravel-hearted lust; and he sees that if he made himself unworthy of his cause through pride, yet, as the "country" which he held "dear" (894) was not the government in power but a government of just principles, so the god in which he believed was not the idol of a state church but a real deity.

In her opening and closing efforts, her seductive appeals, Dalila asks for forgiveness rather than for condonation. She begins by adapting the tactics of her wheedling as these are described by Samson (392–94) to a display of contrition. She turns her reproachful "sighs" to penitent tears (732–39); for "amorous reproaches" she displays her amorous guilt (732–39); for "flattering prayer[s]" she offers humble sacrifices (743–47). She returns to seduction at the end, making more direct the emotive appeal of tears: "Let me approach at least, and touch thy hand" (951); offering to add deeds (914–19) to her words of "conjugal affection"; making specific in her offer to "fetch" Samson from prison how she means to "lighten" his sufferings (920–27). This, Dalila's fourth effort, recalls her final assault on Samson's secret as Samson describes it to his father (402–05). She offers a "blandished parley" in the erotic embellishment of her opening explanation of why she has come, and she offers a "feminine assault" in her return from argument to seduction. After her argumentative failure—"In argument with men a woman ever / Goes by the worse," she pouts (903–04)—Dalila musters all her wiles, forcing out a tight-lipped apology on the way to her final effort: "I was a fool, too rash, and quite mistaken / In what I thought would have succeeded best" (907–08); then she discharges a "Tongue-batter[y]," assaulting the weary, for, replying sarcastically to Dalila's pout, Samson, evidently thinking the interview at an end, has already fired off his parting shot: "For want of words, no doubt, or lack of breath; / Witness when I was worried with thy peals" (905–06). In resisting Dalila's two seductive appeals for forgiveness, Samson learns that there are practical as well as theoretical limits to his "impotence of mind." He has learned from experience: "Nor think me so unwary or accurst / To bring my feet again into the snare / Where once I have been caught" (930–32).

Dalila comes to see a man of impotent mind, and Harapha, stopping to view his rival on the way to the Dagonalia, comes to see a man whose strength has been broken. His three aspersions on Samson's present state recall three of Samson's own despairing assessments of himself — the description of his physical ruin in his soliloquy (60–109), and two repetitions of that description, one in Samson's ode of lamentation (641–46), the other in his reply to the Chorus's attempt to comfort him (558–76). Thinking that "Gyves and the mill" have "tamed" Samson, and disdaining to touch an unwashed captive or to "combat with a blind man" (1093 ff), Harapha hits on the miseries of which Samson most complains, his loss of sight and that "Life in captivity / Among inhuman foes" which blindness aggravates (108–09). Refusing to combat with an outcast whom God "regards not, owns not," has cut off from his people, and "delivered up / Into [his] enemies' hand" (1156–59), Harapha hits on Samson's complaint that God has abandoned him to "cruel enemies" (641–43). Finally, in refusing to fight "a man condemned, a slave enrolled" (1224–25), Harapha hits on the despair of a Samson who "blind, disheartened, shamed, dishonored, quelled" (563), asks to "drudge . . . Till vermin or the draff of servile food / Consume me" (573–75).

But before each of these aspersions on Samson's present state, Harapha makes aspersions on Samson's past. His disparagement of the blind prisoner is preceded by a doubt of the "incredible" reports of Samson's "prodigeous might and feats performed" at Ramath-lechi (1083–90); the disdain which he bestows upon the outcast follows a doubt of the divine origin of Samson's strength (1130–35); and the scorn which he heaps upon the "man condemned" succeeds an indictment of Samson's crimes at the time of his first marriage (1182–91). About the past, Samson is sure. He knows what feats he performed at Ramath-lechi, and offers Harapha a demonstration (1091); he knows the origin of his strength, and thinks of a means to convince a pagan (1145–55); he knows the political grounds of his rebellion, and, denying that he is a criminal, a private citizen who has broken the law for personal gain (1192–219), he offers his challenge as a political prisoner "maimed for high attempts" (1220–23). As Harapha moves from past to present, Samson transfers his confidence. He recognizes that "Gyves and the mill" have not made him as tame as his cowardly captors (1110–11) and that blindness has not enfeebled him (1116–29). He recognizes that the God who has cast him off "Justly" can restore him to his role as the champion of Israel (1168–77). He sees that the "baffled" Harapha (1237) has been more thoroughly "disheartened, shamed, dishonored, quelled" than he has.

Samson is helped to this transference by continual reminders of the difference between his cause and the cause of what the Chorus call "the mighty of the earth . . . Hardy and industrious to support / Tyrannic power, but raging to pursue / The righteous and all such as honor truth" (1272–76). Samson fought at Ramath-lechi for reasons other than the display of personal might, and his mission was given him by a god whose justice, mercy, and even existence are beyond the imagination of a superstitious believer in black magic, a "fool" who "think[s] not God at all" (295–98). Samson, a better judge than Israel's servile magistrates, has acted for reasons unintelligible to the unquestioning patriot of a tyrannic state. In act 3 Samson is regenerated through battle with his pagan enemies. In the first scene, the values unintentionally revealed by Dalila strengthen Samson's resistance; in the second scene, Samson's defiance is aroused by Harapha's boasts of might, of "glorious arms" (1130), of heroic honor — by his appeals to the pagan heroic code.

One episode of the *Samson* middle, the attempts of the Chorus and Manoa to comfort Samson (478–731) — it could be called act 2, scene 3 — has proved particularly problematical. The typologists, who view Manoa's offer of ransom as a temptation to despair, are faced here with an uncomfortable paradox, that Samson refuses the offer by embracing the despair. The readings of the regeneration critics, however, are scarcely less paradoxical. "The achievement of a heroic self," Summers says, "is by no means a process which makes either the hero or his audience feel consistently better and better. The conclusion of each episode finds Samson in some respects 'stronger' or 'greater' than before, yet he is more despairing after his meeting with Manoa than he was at the beginning." Low's account is similar: "There are two basic movements: a steady upward spiritual progress, and a psychological movement that first travels downward into near despair and lethargy, reaching its low point at the end of the interview with Manoa, in Samson's second great lament of the play."[29] Two puzzles are present here: Why should Samson's psychological and moral states move in contrary motion? How can Samson be more despairing after his spiritual advance than he was before it? The schematic design of the *Samson* middle can be called upon to ease these difficulties.

The answer to the psychological puzzle presented by the reading of the regeneration critics lies in the relation of act 2 to Samson's soliloquy. The distinction between psychological and moral states drawn by both Summers and Low is a false distinction, as Low's terms, "near despair" and "lethargy" reveal: these words are synonyms for what Don Cameron Allen calls sins, the sins of despair and sloth.[30] What the critics describe as Samson's psychological state corresponds to the despairing self-condemnations of his soliloquy, and the contrary motion seen by the critics is better described as a moral turn: Samson, who has answered the doubts of his friends and father, falls into a sinful self-condemnation. The explanation for this turn lies in the moral dilemma revealed in the soliloquy, that in his despair Samson can see only two equally pernicious alternatives. By answering Manoa and the Chorus, Samson answers his doubts of God's favor and of the mission which God has assigned him; but in shunning the Scylla, he is swallowed by the Charybdis of the soliloquy, viewing himself as a man alienated from God by sin (487–540) and stripped by blindness of his use to men (558–76). The turn which takes place at the end of act 2 is prepared for by the openings of the first two scenes, where the dilemma of Samson's private lament enters the public debate. The gallant admission of folly with which Samson greets the Chorus, in which he praises the "vessel trusted to me from above" (199), conceals a self-condemnation so painful that Samson can find relief only by turning on the shipwright, by resuming his "quarrel" with the "will / Of highest dispensation" (60–61): strength and wisdom "proportioned ill drove me transverse" (209). Defending "heavenly disposition" (373) from his father's objections, Samson is forced to a confession of sin so thorough that it spares him half of Manoa's fatherly reproof.

The answer to the moral puzzle presented by the regeneration critics lies in the careful placement of Samson's ode of lamentation within the moral poles represented by Samson's soliloquy in act 1 and his rebuff to the Philistine officer in act 4. The contention of Summers and Low that Samson reaches his nadir in the ode at the end of the second act rests on those expressions of despair wherein, overwhelmed by guilt and misery, Samson declares that he can find no way out but death. These expressions hark back to his soliloquy, in which Samson made an objective description of his sin (43–52). Now he makes an equivalent subjective description of his guilt (617–32). The description of guilt contrasts with the recollection of God's past favor which follows it (633–67) and issues in Samson's final request for "speedy death" (647–51). The subjective description of guilt is paired at the beginning of Samson's ode with a subjective description of his misery (606–16), which contrasts with his subsequent memory of the successful beginning of his mission (638–40). Samson's misery culminates in his despairing comparison of his death in prison to death by torture (641–46). The despair is equivalent to that expressed in the close of the soliloquy, where he objectively described the causes of his misery, "loss of sight" and the attendant indignities of "Life in captivity / Among inhuman foes" (60–109). In these respects the ungifted Chorus in their ode of commiseration prove wiser than the misjudging champion. The Chorus complain of God's treatment of his elect (667–86), yet the complaint serves to justify the preceding description of a grace which would grant to Samson the patience to bear that guilt from which he seeks relief in death (652–66). The Chorus complain of the unseemly ends of the just (687–704), but on the basis of that complaint they pray for a "peaceful end" to the sufferings of the ruined warrior, "once" God's "glorious champion" and "mighty minister" (705–09). The Chorus believe in the possibility of a change in which Samson cannot believe.

In other respects, however, Samson moves away from despair. His doubts of God's favor and of the mission which God has ordained have lightened, and in these respects what Samson says in his ode contrasts with the complaints of his soliloquy and prepares for the affirmations of his defiant speeches to the public officer. In the soliloquy Samson questioned God's prophecy and commands; now, having defended God to his father, Samson accepts that God has done his part toward him and celebrates the prophecy and commandments (633–37). In his soliloquy Samson disparaged his mission by disparaging the strength which was its means; now, having defended to the Chorus the divine supervision of his mission, Samson celebrates his strength (638–40). In these respects too Samson is set off, ironically, against the Chorus, who, moved afresh by Samson's pain, recall not only their own initial dismay, but the dismay which they have heard Manoa voice. Complaining in their ode of how God has treated those whom he has elected (678–80), the Chorus echo Manoa's complaint (368–72). Complaining about the unseemly ends of the just, the Chorus recall the emblem they first saw in Samson: "O mirror of our fickle state" (164). The cross-relation between Samson and the Chorus points up not only Samson's continuing despair but also the spiritual advances which have come through his atonement, an atonement which Milton is careful not to undercut by suggesting that it has benefited no one but Samson himself. The Chorus have not returned to their starting place: in their dismay, they, like Manoa, talked *about* God; now they speak *to* him, asking his redress. In his ode of lamentation, then, Samson is not at a nadir paradoxically at variance with his spiritual advances; rather he is at a point midway between his initial despair and his final regeneration, still despairing with regard to himself, but regenerate with regard to God.

The thematic paradox which Samson's refusal of Manoa's offer presents to the typological critics can be avoided if that incident is placed within the play's bipartite structure. The incident can be seen as part of the irony of act 2, scene 3, an irony which serves to connect act 2 with Samson's encounters in act 3. Samson refuses his father's proposal because he believes that only death can relieve his guilt. Manoa cannot assuage the guilt with his loving offer, but what he wishes Dalila accomplishes, ironically, with a parody of that offer. Samson's rejection of the Chorus's consolations, parallel to his refusal of his father's proposal, is part of a complementary ironic sequence. Hearing a repetition of Samson's opening question — "Am I not sung and proverbed for a fool?" (203) — in Samson's contemptuous description of himself shorn "Like a tame wether" (535), the Chorus try to comfort the hero with a reminder of his former Nazarite dignity (541–46). For one poignant moment the Chorus succeed, as Samson drowns in memory the awareness of his present state (547–52): "Wherever fountain or fresh current flowed / Against the eastern ray, translucent, pure . . . I drank." But when the Chorus try to extend the forgetful moment (553–57), Samson awakens, and, remembering his fall and ruined mission, longs for "oft-invocated death" (558–76). The Chorus cannot lessen Samson's grief at his lost vocation with their loving tributes to the past, but what they wish Harapha accomplishes, ironically, with slurs upon that past. These ironies culminate in the answers which are given to the Chorus's commiserating prayers for Samson. The Chorus pray that Samson may be granted "from above" the "secret refreshings" that would uphold his "fainting spirits" (664–66), and Samson's guilt is assuaged; but the assuagement comes not from Samson's reception but from his rejection, not of a holy but of the unholy return, not of a god from the heavens but of a creature from the dust, a "manifest serpent" (997). The Chorus pray that Samson's "labors" may be turned to "peaceful end" (708–09), and Samson's griefs are relieved; but the relief comes not in rest but in strife, not from a calm but from a "storm" (1061). The irony which ends act 2, that the comfort which Samson's comforters intend they cannot bring, is completed in act 3, when that comfort is brought by those who do not intend to bring it, the opposite of comforters. In the tripartite reading of the typological critics, Samson's rejection of his father's offer is parallel to his refusal of Dalila's offer and to the rejection of Harapha's supposed temptation.[31] The parallel suggests (and the suggestion has gone unchallenged even by the regeneration critics)[32] that Samson ought to refuse the offered ransom. In the alternative bipartite reading, Dalila is not the parallel but the antithesis to Manoa, and from the fact that Samson should refuse Dalila's offer it no longer follows that he should shun his father's. The alternative possibility avoids an unwelcome paradox and provides act 2, scene 3 with a welcome irony, an irony which, consistent with Summers's description of Samson's encounters, would add the scene to his sequence of ironic episodes.[33]

Milton, then, places a schematic design beneath the naturalistic surface of the *Samson* middle, a design which explains why there are four encounters there, and why they are grouped and ordered as they are. A final question remains. The typological critics account for the presence of a schematic design by supposing that Milton wished to impose upon the naturalistic events of the play an allegorical pattern. But if, as the regeneration critics maintain, the play is not allegorical, what purpose could be served by such a scheme? The answer is suggested by the fact that the revisionist critic Samuel, who denies the reality of Samson's supernatural promptings, also denies that Milton wrote "to assert divine providence" and that the play's events fall into a stylized pattern: she rejects the view that the "sequence of [Samson's] visitors enables the protagonist to assert a series of virtues" which "[annul] his earlier vices"; she is left with a material world and a transcendent god.[34]

The schematic pattern allows Milton to depict a particular kind of world, one in which events are influenced by a supernatural power that works unseen. Act 2, scene 3, makes the metaphysical implications of the design especially clear. Samson's visitors all have reasons for coming. His friends come on his only day of rest to comfort him, and his father hurries with the news of imminent release. Harapha takes advantage of the Dagonalia to meet for the first time his famous rival. As it is doubtful that Dalila comes for selfless reasons, so it is doubtful that she dresses as she does because she is too simple to understand that Samson will be unable to see her.[35] Dalila comes dressed not for Samson but for the Dagonalia, and particularly for a scene which she has imagined; before the whole great assembly, she will ask the lords, "not doubting / Their favorable ear" (920–21), for the custody of Samson. (The messenger's report, 1599–602, suggests that Samson's presence at the temple had been planned beforehand.) That scene — it would have proved the high point of the proposed reconciliation: Samson's fears for the future (938–50) are justified — requires the consent for which Dalila comes; for Samson could turn the whole splendid moment to ridicule, depriving of all her admiration a woman who is reluctant to part with even half: "My name perhaps among the circumcised . . . may stand defamed," she says (975–77), not "No doubt my name . . . will stand."

The visitors do not know that they come to aid in Samson's regeneration, and that is what the irony of act 2, scene 3, like the other dramatic ironies observed by Summers, reveals. What the Chorus and Manoa accomplish — they cause Samson's atonement — they did not intend: they came to comfort and instead were comforted. What they did intend they do not accomplish: they are unable to give Samson comfort. The audience see what they do not, that they have served God's purposes rather than their own. Character and circumstance account for the order in which the visitors arrive. Samson's friends and father hurry, drawn by love, but old Manoa hurries slowly. It takes Dalila time to hoist her sails, and Harapha time, despite his "unconscionable strides" (1245), to cover the twenty-two miles from Gath to Gaza. The visitors do not know that they come in the order required by Samson, and that is the point revealed in the irony that Dalila arrives instead of the "secret refreshings" from "above" prayed for by the Chorus.

The irony that evil comes in the place of good recalls a converse irony in an earlier arrival, the arrival of the Chorus when Samson expected his enemies "come to stare / At my affliction and perhaps to insult" (112–13). Though the audience do not at this time see the whole pattern, they know that, at the opening, good came in the place of evil, not according to Samson's expectation but according to his need. Now when the Chorus ask for what they believe Samson needs, the audience see what the Chorus do not, that God knows those needs better than men do, and arranges Samson's encounters accordingly. Samson is no more aware of God's scheduling than the visitors are: he does not recognize that the day of his regeneration is at hand. The audience learn that God has called Samson, and demands particular responses from him, by observing the schematic pattern whose outlines emerge at the center of the *Samson* middle. When Samson turns to self-condemnation from what Manoa calls "prophecy" (473), the audience learn that atonement and regeneration are not synonymous: atonement has done what it can do, and Samson still despairs. Reminded of Samson's soliloquy by his ode of lamentation, and hearing in the ode notes not touched on earlier ("I was his nursling once," 633ff, "He led me on to mightiest deeds" 638ff), they see that atonement has done something, and that what remains is the completion of a pattern now only partially realized. Remembering at Dalila's ironic entrance Samson's earlier mistaken expectation, the audience conclude that the enemies for whom Samson prematurely braced himself are now what he requires: what he began through atonement he must complete through conflict. The audience will recognize the completion of the conflict when the abstract irony of act 2, scene 3, that evil comes in the place of good, is replaced by a concrete irony in act 3, scene 2. There the enemies whom Samson was expecting when the Chorus arrived come in the person of the Chorus's opposite, Harapha: "Cam'st thou for this, vainboaster, to survey me, / To descant on my strength and give thy verdict?" (1227–28). The ironic fulfillment of the prediction of the opening will mark the completion of the pattern, and the audience will know what Samson does not, that the hero has completed his answer to God's call.

But if Milton uses the schematic design to indicate the presence of the supernatural, that presence is not his theme, as the providential critics contend. Again act 2, scene 3 is pertinent. When the Chorus pray for Samson, they are wise in believing what Samson does not, that he can change, but in praying to God to effect that change, to send "secret refreshings," to bring about a "peaceful end," they speak as if God forced the souls and actions of men. They pray as if God were the god of the providential critics, a Calvinist god of irresistible grace and predestination, who, according to G. A. Wilkes, overrules Samson's will and, "undistracted by man's errors and deserts," moves "invincibly toward the objective proposed."[36] But, in answering the Chorus's prayer, God does not bestow a change of heart but instead sends Dalila, allowing Samson to choose whether or not to yield to his former "impotence of mind." Instead of sending a turn of fortune, God sends Harapha, allowing Samson to choose between invigorating courage and helpless misery. The god who answers thus is, if not a Pelagian god, then at least an Arminian one, a god whose call can go unheeded and whose foreknowledge is not coercive. The supernatural presence in the *Samson* middle establishes the meaning and terms of Samson's change, but the subject of that middle, as the regeneration theorists maintain, is not the presence but the change.

University of Regina

NOTES

1. Joseph H. Summers, "The Movements of the Drama," in *The Lyric and Dramatic Milton*, ed. Summers (New York, 1965), p. 160.

2. F. Michael Krouse, *Milton's Samson and the Christian Tradition* (Princeton, N.J., 1949), pp. 125–26; Patrick Cullen, *The Infernal Triad: The Flesh, the World, and the Devil in Spenser and Milton* (Princeton, N.J. 1975), p. 196.

3. All quotations of Milton follow the modernized edition of Douglas Bush, *The Complete Poetical Works of John Milton* (Boston, 1965).

4. Although, as every reader of *Samson Agonistes* knows, Milton eschewed these formal divisions, I use the terms "scene" and "act" for the sake of expository convenience.

5. James Holly Hanford, *A Milton Handbook*, 4th ed. (New York, 1947), p. 285;

Krouse, *Milton's Samson*, pp. 125–26; Cullen, *Infernal Triad*, p. 199; Summers, "Movements," p. 159.

6. John M. Steadman, "Milton's 'Summa Epitasis': The End of the Middle of *Samson Agonistes*," *MLR*, LXIX (1974), 731–32; Summers, "Movements," pp. 171–73.

7. Hanford, *Milton Handbook*, p. 285; Krouse, *Milton's Samson*, p. 131; Cullen, *Infernal Triad*, pp. 234–35.

8. Steadman, "Epitasis," 740–41.

9. Krouse, *Milton's Samson*, p. 127; Cullen, *Infernal Triad*, pp. 224–25.

10. Summers, "Movements," p. 159.

11. Krouse, *Milton's Samson*, pp. 124–26; Cullen, *Infernal Triad*, p. 193.

12. Summers, "Movements," p. 159.

13. Krouse, *Milton's Samson*, pp. 131–32; Cullen, *Infernal Triad*, pp. 233–34; Summers, "Movements," pp. 159–60.

14. Arnold Stein, *Heroic Knowledge: An Interpretation of "Paradise Regained" and "Samson Agonistes"* (Minneapolis, 1957), p. 145.

15. Cullen, *Infernal Triad*, pp. 206–07; Stein, *Heroic Knowledge*, p. 150.

16. Cullen, *Infernal Triad*, p. 194.

17. Irene Samuel, "*Samson Agonistes* as Tragedy," in *Calm of Mind*, ed. Joseph A. Wittreich, Jr. (Cleveland, 1971), p. 249; William Empson, *Milton's God* (London, 1961), p. 224; Anthony Low, *The Blaze of Noon: A Reading of "Samson Agonistes"* (New York, 1974), pp. 152–55.

18. Samuel, "*Samson* as Tragedy," pp. 249–50.

19. Quoted in ibid., p. 249.

20. Joan S. Bennett, "'A Person Rais'd': Public and Private Cause in *Samson Agonistes*," *SEL*, XVIII (1978), 159.

21. Virginia R. Mollenkott, "Relativism in *Samson Agonistes*," *SP*, LXVII (1970), 99.

22. Low, *Blaze of Noon*, p. 146.

23. Mollenkott, "Relativism," 89–90.

24. Bennett, "Public and Private," 157–58.

25. Cullen, *Infernal Triad*, pp. 201, 227, 230–31; Low, *Blaze of Noon*, pp. 162, 169.

26. John M. Steadman, "Milton's Harapha and Goliath," *JEGP*, LX (1961), 795; Jack Goldman, "The Name and Function of Harapha," *ELN*, XII (1974), 85–86.

27. Bennett, "Public and Private," 163–64.

28. Cullen, *Infernal Triad*, pp. 221, 224–25; Balachandra Rajan, *The Lofty Rhyme: A Study of Milton's Major Poetry* (London, 1970), p. 138.

29. Krouse, *Milton's Samson*, pp. 126–27; Cullen, *Infernal Triad*, p. 215; Summers, "Movements," p. 160; Low, *Blaze of Noon*, pp. 169–70.

30. Don Cameron Allen, *The Harmonious Vision* (Baltimore, 1970), pp. 85–86.

31. Krouse, *Milton's Samson*, p. 130; Cullen, *Infernal Triad*, pp. 201–02.

32. Summers, "Movements," p. 160; Low, *Blaze of Noon*, pp. 168–69.

33. Summers, "Movements," p. 159.

34. Samuel, "*Samson* as Tragedy," pp. 236, 235.

35. Ibid., p. 248.

36. G. A. Wilkes, "The Interpretation of *Samson Agonistes*," *Huntington Library Quarterly*, XXVI (1962–63), 378.

APOLLONIUS OF RHODES
AND THE RESOURCELESS HERO
OF *PARADISE REGAINED**

James Tatum

T HE FIRST readers of *Paradise Regained* expected a poem on the
scale of *Paradise Lost*. They found instead one nothing like it, and
they were disappointed. Milton was impatient. He may even have preferred the second poem to the first.[1] I hope to account for some of that
impatience, if not that preference.

My context is the problem of the generic tradition or frame of reference of *Paradise Regained.* It is an abiding question about the poem.
As Barbara Lewalski observes, "the conventions of genre are of first importance in analyzing a Miltonic poem," but "the category into which
Milton appears to place *Paradise Regained* has seemed to many wildly
inappropriate."[2] Recovering the genre of a poem as a prelude to its critical description is one way to approach a classicizing writer like Milton,
though not the only one. At this point it may seem rash to suppose anything further could be said on the subject, but Anthony Low has reopened
this traditional line of critical enquiry, in his recent essay on *Paradise
Regained* as a georgic poem:

Why should Milton choose brief epic as an appropriate genre in which to outdo
the eminently successful full epic he had just written on his own terms? He would
simply be repeating himself. But if Milton wants us to view *Paradise Lost* for the
moment as pastoral, having to do with Eden and its loss, perhaps he is suggesting
that *Paradise Regained* represents the next step: georgic.[3]

Low's rereading of *Paradise Lost* as momentary pastoral is ingenious,
for the *Georgics* are an important presence in the spirit, style, and imagery of Milton's brief epic, especially in the georgic wisdom which Christ
embodies.

But there are limits to how far this identification of *Paradise Regained* and the *Georgics* should be pressed. The *Georgics* are not narrative poems. They have no continuous characters and no developed plot

---

In memoriam John Gardner (1933–1982).

or narrative line, save in isolated episodes like the Aristaeus epyllion (4.315–448). Recent criticism tends to analyze them through selected themes, images, or emblematic passages.[4] And they are explicitly didactic poems, as shown by their proems and epilogue. *Paradise Regained* is a didactic poem only by inference, no more didactic than *Paradise Lost* or *Samson Agonistes.* The didactic purpose of *Paradise Lost* is made explicit in Book I, 17–26, and that kind of declaration is conspicuously absent from the proem of *Paradise Regained* (I, 1–17). Described in barest outline, it is a narrative that moves in a straight line from its proem to the end of Book IV. It is a sequel to the narrative of *Paradise Lost* in a way that the *Georgics* cannot be a sequel to the narrative of the *Aeneid.*

The classical literary form evoked by *Paradise Regained* can be established most economically by referring to narrative poems written as sequels to full-scale epic. From what survives of Greek and Roman literature, this restricted definition eliminates epic poets commonly thought to be second-rate, or, more politely, poets who are not the equal of Vergil or Homer: Romans like Lucan, Statius, Silius Italicus, Valerius Flaccus, and the Greek Quintus of Smyrna, whose *Posthomerica (Things after Homer)* completes the story of the fall of Troy in scholarly, un-Homeric detail. Likewise the shadowy cyclical poets who wrote lost epics like the *Little Iliad* and the *Returns.*[5] Whatever shortcomings such poets had, they at least attempted to write poems of a length and an ambition comparable to the *Iliad, Odyssey,* and *Aeneid.*

A different kind of poet confronts us in Apollonius of Rhodes, and a different kind of poem. His *Argonautica (The Voyage of the Argo)* tells in four books of the voyage of Jason and the Argonauts to Colchis to recover the golden fleece. Apollonius has received scant attention in discussions of the generic tradition of *Paradise Regained,*[6] probably because he has been the exclusive concern of specialists in Hellenistic literature like Hermann Fraenkel and Giuseppe Giangrande. The first book in English of literary criticism on Apollonius was published in 1982.[7] But there are a number of suggestive parallels between the *Argonautica* and *Paradise Regained.* Both are poems about writing epic when it is no longer possible to write epic. That dilemma concentrates peculiarly, even amusingly, in the characters of Jason and Satan. Both of them strive in vain to act out the role of a classical epic hero, and neither of them succeeds. The specious lure of pagan heroism is a familiar theme to readers of Milton. *Paradise Lost* is deeply ironic in its treatment of the heroic impulse. *Paradise Regained* carries that irony further, turning the heroic quest into inconsequential comedy. Heroism could be no less comic for Apollonius.

Comparison of the two poems will show this much. Critics of Milton and Apollonius focus on similar kinds of problems, and often converge to make similar points, because both tribes of critics are concerned with the same kind of poem. Beyond that, we have more direct evidence that Milton was a reader of Apollonius. He quotes his Greek, and seems to have had an affinity for the blind seer Phineus, the emaciated victim of the Harpies whom Jason and the Argonauts rescue in Book 2.[8] We also know from the early lives of Edward Phillips and John Toland that he regarded poems like the *Argonautica* as suitable reading for students once they had acquired a thorough knowledge of the greatest authors, especially of Homer and the tragic poets.[9] Apollonius expected similar erudition in his readers.[10]

The challenge of writing epic after epic was a theoretical issue that crystallized by the time of Aristotle's *Poetics,* and it is one often restated since: how could there be a worthy sequel to Homer?[11] As Low observes, the question becomes even more poignant for Milton: how could there be a worthy sequel to *Paradise Lost,* especially if Milton himself were to write it?

Aristotle, "Longinus," and other ancient critics never supplied an answer to such a question. The Alexandrians did. Apollonius was a pupil and then a colleague of Callimachus. A fierce rivalry was long supposed to have existed between them because of Apollonius' poem. It is more accurate to say that both of them were fighting on the same side in the Hellenistic world's Battle of the Big Book.[12] Callimachean esthetics and poetic technique showed Apollonius a way toward a solution to the challenge of writing epic poetry. The essential move was to confront Homer in an oblique way: to write poetry obviously conscious of the *Iliad* and *Odyssey,* but on a smaller scale, with a carefully restricted poetic vision that complemented Homer, never challenging him. Apollonius achieved this effect by playing on his readers' expectations that the *Argonautica* is an epic poem. They would come looking for more Homer, and traditionally, they would expect to find less; instead of Homer, they then would encounter another kind of poetry altogether. This unexpected experience of reading an epic that is not really an epic at all is one of the chief delights of the new poem.[13]

Not every reader is so moved. The reactions of "Longinus" and Richard Bentley to this kind of poetry are essentially the same. Both of them could only judge the brief epic by the high standards set by true epic; naturally the shorter poem was found wanting.[14] Nevertheless, for Apollonius, and then Milton, the crucial step was to write a poem that at first looked like an epic, with an epic's external characteristics (epic meter, epic books). The change strikes the ear first of all. While both the *Argonautica* and *Paradise Regained* are in the same measure as epic poetry (dactylic hexameter, iambic pentameter), they have an unmistakably different sound from the sound of true epic verse.[15] And their structure is not at all like the structure of the *Iliad*, *Odyssey*, or *Paradise Lost*. The division into four books has been criticized as arbitrary, even meaningless. But the books are experiments in the arrangement of literary form. In *Paradise Regained* and the *Argonautica* the concept of a "book" of epic poetry is subject to as much wit and play as the idea of epic itself.[16]

Milton also follows Apollonius' example by announcing a theme sharply reduced in scope from the theme typical of epic poetry. Instead of a story of things unattempted yet in prose or rhyme, this poem will tell

> of deeds
> Above heroic, though in secret done,
> And unrecorded left through many an age,
> Worthy to have not remained so long unsung.   (I, 14–17)

This is not an implicit challenge to any predecessor, like *arma virumque cano*. Even less so is it an open declaration of war, like that adventurous song "That with no middle flight intends to soar / Above the Aonian mount" (*PL* I, 14–15). The only connection with epic is the "I" of line 1: the singer of the present poem once sang of the happy garden lost. His new theme, to tell of deeds above heroic, only characterizes those deeds; it does not follow that the poem that recounts them is an epic. Apollonius is even more discreet. His reader must watch carefully to catch what declaration there is. The poet is off and running with his story after only four lines:

Beginning with you, Phoebus, I shall recall the famous deeds of men who lived long ago, those who through the mouth of the Pontus and Cyanean rocks at King Pelias' command sped the well-benched Argo, for the golden fleece. For such was the prophecy that Pelias heard . . . (*Argonautica* 1.1–5)

Deeds "Above heroic . . . unrecorded left through many an age" is a recognizable variation of Apollonius' *palaigeneōn klea phōtōn*, "the famous deeds of men who lived long ago." It is also a pointed departure from the classical deal of *kleos*, the fame or glory for which Achilles, Odysseus, and Pindar's heroes all strive. The ideal of "deeds / *Above heroic*" cancels the ideal of *kleos* ("fame," "glory") and *klea* ("famous deeds").

Such parallels and variations may be traced also in the more substantive matter of the story or myth of each poem and in the way each poem tells it. *Paradise Lost* follows Homer and Vergil by hastening into

Horace's middle of things. Neither the *Argonautica* nor *Paradise Regained* observe Horace's precept. Both poems follow a strictly chronological order. The *Argonautica* opens with Pelias' challenge to Jason to recover the golden fleece and closes with Jason's return to Greece. *Paradise Regained* opens with Satan planning to test Christ and ends with his defeat. As plots, these seem simpler and more straightforward than the complex narratives of the *Iliad, Odyssey, Aeneid,* and *Paradise Lost.*

But this simplicity is only an apparent one. Both poems are set in a complicated frame of reference to what has been narrated in epic poetry. Apollonius shifts his story to an earlier period of mythical history, to a time before the rape of Helen and the Trojan War, in the generation of the fathers of the heroes who went to Troy. On the voyage to Colchis, Jason is accompanied by Peleus, the father of Achilles, and Telamon, the father of Ajax. These and other companions are the generation Nestor refers to — I am tempted to say, will refer to — in the *Iliad.* This technique of turning prior texts into successor texts anticipates Milton's use of the myth of Adam and Eve in *Paradise Lost.* As David Quint and Patricia Parker have shown, that choice of theme reverses Milton's relationship to all his predecessors: he creates the original, sacred epic, making Homer, Vergil, Dante, and all his rivals secondary imitators of his primal story.[17]

Apollonius' aim is more modest: to remove his poem as much as he can from rivalry with the *Iliad* and *Odyssey.* A charming indication of the remoteness of the world of the *Argo* from the Trojan war comes early in the poem. As the ship is sailing out from Greece, the wife of the centaur Chiron holds up the little boy Achilles for a last glimpse of the Argonauts (1.553–58). The hero of the *Iliad* has yet to grow up. Only one mature heroic figure appears. From his stature everywhere in Greek literature, Heracles might be expected to dominate the poem. But this greatest of all Greek heroes is treated in a peculiar way. By the end of the first book he disappears, never to return (1.1272). He becomes an unavailable, idealized character whose absence is often regretted by Jason and others (1.1286–89, 2.145–48, 2.774–810, 4.1432–84). The heroic world of Achilles and Heracles is beyond reach. It is at once passé (Heracles) and under age (Achilles).[18]

At first Milton's strategies seem to tend in the opposite direction from this design. *Paradise Regained* is a sequel in biblical time to the events of *Paradise Lost.* But it is not a sequel in heroic action, not even as redefined in the proem to Book IX, 13–19. Milton pushes heroism completely out of the poem. If Christ's patience seems incomprehensible to Satan, or to the reader, that is because Satan or the reader can only grasp heroism in the satanic sense.[19] As God declares, Christ's deeds above heroic lie far in the future. They have no place in the present contest.

> But first I mean
> To exercise him in the Wilderness;
> There he shall first lay down the rudiments
> Of his great warfare; 'ere I send him forth
> To conquer Sin and Death the two grand foes;
> By humiliation and strong sufferance.
> His weakness shall o'ercome Satanic strength
> And all the world, and mass of sinful flesh.　　　　(I, 155–61)

Earlier in his life Christ had entertained thoughts of heroic deeds — "Victorious deeds / Flamed in my heart, heroic acts" (I, 215–16) — but now he has put them aside, in obedience to his father's will.

> And now by some strong motion I am led
> Into this Wilderness, to what intent
> I learn not yet, perhaps need not know;
> For what concerning my knowledge God reveals.　　　(I, 290–93)

Only Satan strives for heroism. *Paradise Regained* has the same relationship to epic poetry that we can observe in the *Argonautica*. Heroic deeds on the scale of epic poetry are either lost in the past and unattainable (for Satan), or far in the future and of no present concern (for Christ). At the same time, both poems are filled with constant reminders of epic poetry and epic heroes. For Jason, those reminders are embodied in Heracles, whether he is present or absent; for Satan, they lie in his own memories of the events of *Paradise Lost*.

　　The main event in both poems is a struggle to be a hero in a world where it is no longer possible to be one, or even desirable. Since heroism in the classical sense of the word is achieved preeminently by deeds, the real interest in both poems finally centers not on whatever deeds Jason and Satan manage to accomplish, but rather on their efforts to act heroically, and on their constant frustrations when they cannot be what they want to be. Because they live in worlds bounded by disappointment and failure, their psychological state becomes as interesting for the reader as anything they say aloud, or anything they do.[20]

　　Jason's adventures begin with the test imposed on him by Pelias, who hopes for Jason's defeat and death. If Pelias does not succeed in this scheme, the reader must always wonder whether Jason succeeds, either. The most common circumstance he finds himself in throughout the poem is helplessness. His *amēchaniē* (from *amēchanos*, literally, "resourceless," "without tricks or wiles") recurs as a formulaic parody of the traditional epithet of Homer's "resourceful Odysseus" *(polymētis Odysseus)*. Jason's dilemma of trying to be a hero in a world where heroism is no longer achievable parallels the dilemma of Satan, who is an enfeebled version of his old self in *Paradise Lost*.

Not being Odysseus, Jason has greatness thrust upon him. Before the voyage begins, he proposes to the assembled Argonauts that they elect a leader. It is a reasonable idea, but the outcome is surprising:

"But friends, we share a homecoming to Greece after this, common too our journey to the land of Aeetes; choose then without further ado the best man to be our leader, one who will take care for everything, one who will make war and peace when we are in the company of strangers." So he spoke. The young men turned their eyes toward bold Heracles sitting among them, and with a single cry they named *him* their leader. (1.336–42)

Heracles handles this awkward turn of events very well. He insists that Jason be chosen leader, and he is. Jason is reduced to silent weeping at the prospect (1.460–61). Throughout the voyage, even after the landing in Colchis in Book 3, he is constantly uncertain and prone to make the wrong move. When the Argonauts visit Lemnos, he gullibly accepts an offer from the queen Hypsipyle to stay with her as her consort. But the women of Lemnos had murdered their husbands, and Hypsipyle had given Jason a carefully sanitized version of events. Only Heracles is able to pull Jason back on course: to stay on Lemnos would mean an end to the search for the golden fleece (1.864–74) — and, incidentally, an end to the poem.[21] Once Heracles has gone off in pursuit of his lover Hylas, Jason finds others to help him in his misfortunes: Telamon, for example, who rebukes him for collapsing on the ground and grieving at Heracles' departure (1.1284–89).

At his best, before Colchis, Jason is a communal hero who requires the constant support of his crew to survive every challenge (2.621–47). Unlike Achilles or Odysseus, he is incapable of sustaining even a moment of isolation from others. And there is always the reminder of Heracles: how Heracles would have stopped a quarrel if only he had been present (2.145), how Heracles would have managed the voyage to Asia (2.774). Comparisons with Heracles are everywhere, and they are never favorable to Jason. Perhaps the worst moment comes when the *Argo* sails past the imprisoned Prometheus in the Caucasus (2.1215–47). The Argonauts hear his cries in the distance, but sail on nevertheless. The same spectacle will elicit a different response from Heracles, for we know that *he* is destined to free Prometheus from the eagle of Zeus. Now Prometheus is merely noted in passing, as if he were one of the local tourist attractions.[22]

By the second half of the poem and the *Argo*'s arrival in Colchis, the outcome of this unheroic odyssey is as uncertain as ever. In a real sense, in this poem as in *Paradise Regained*, there is no progress or development in plot.[23] Even the gods are afflicted with momentary helplessness at the thought of what they could do to aid Jason (3.6–35). For his part, Jason reaches the nadir in his career as a hero when the time comes for him to confront Medea's father Aeetes, the guardian king of the golden fleece. Like an Athenian sophist, Jason attempts to use clever words rather than heroic deeds to win the fleece (3.171–93). The result of this strategy is disastrous. Aeetes' fierce speech is so rhetorically effective that Jason is once again reduced to helpless silence: "Thus Aeetes spoke. But Jason fixed his eyes on the ground and sat there, speechless, resourceless in his unhappiness" (3.422–23).[24]

Happily for Jason and his mission, Aphrodite intervenes. He falls in love with Medea because Eros is bribed by his mother to make Medea fall in love with Jason. The failed odyssey thereupon turns into a success as a love story. Because of Medea, but only because of her, Jason will at last win the golden fleece. And Medea brings more than success to Jason. Her love transforms him into a different man, one who is not at all resourceless before Aeetes. His center of values shifts from the dubious realm of heroic adventure to the intimate world of a man and woman in love. He becomes, at last, a competent hero and achieves the famous deeds *(klea)* Apollonius speaks of in the proem of the poem. Medea makes even his notorious resourcelessness charming: only now it is the shyness one lover feels in the presence of another (3.1022–24). She introduces him to a paradise within, where interior values acquire more meaning than public shows of virtue. In this domestic context Jason becomes the master of every situation: he has forethought (3.1189), undergoes any trial easily (3.1220). With Medea's help, he accomplishes things he (and we) previously thought only Heracles could accomplish (3.1233–34). The contrast between the old and new Jasons is very pointed.[25]

Salvation through Eros does not last. Nor does Jason's domestic heroism. Even as he succeeds in stealing the golden fleece (4.187), the happy fabric begins to unravel. The Argonauts mutter about returning this barbarian princess to her father, and a certain death (4.355–91). Medea herself devises a solution by betraying her brother Apsyrtus; his murder is described in grisly detail that clashes rudely with the rhetoric of love and romance (4.392–482). Jason and Medea finally return to Greece, in what might be termed a technical triumph of heroic values, but their spiritual impoverishment is oppressive. Eros was Jason's salvation as a hero, and now it is his undoing. By the end of the poem, the reader knows with increasing certainty that the tragic events of Euripides' *Medea* are fast approaching:

> *Nurse:* Would that the ship Argo had never flown through the dark Symplegades to the land of Colchis, nor that the fir had ever fallen in the glades of Pelion to furnish oars for the hands of heroes who sought the golden fleece for Pelias. For then my mistress Medea would not have sailed to the towers of Iolcus' land, struck with love for Jason. (*Medea* 1–8)

The resourceless hero of *Paradise Regained* is most evocative of this Apollonian world of dubious heroism. From the moment Satan first appears in the poem, there is a sharp contrast between this diminished fiend and that resourceful leader who appears at the opening of *Paradise Lost.* He can measure this new struggle only in terms of past conflicts:

> I, when no other durst, sole undertook
> The dismal expedition to find out
> And ruin Adam, and the exploit performed
> Successfully; a calmer voyage now
> Will waft me; *and the way found prosperous once*
> *Induces best to hope of like success.*   (I, 100–05; my emphasis)

Satan cannot grasp the altered world in which he now moves. He imagines that the task at hand can be met in the old heroic way, and this failing will bring him as much frustration as Jason. Like Jason, he is doomed to a succession of bafflements. He suffers from an increasing sense of his own impotence in the face of an adversary he thought he could master. As Stanley Fish observes, "activity only serves to accentuate the anticlimactic nature of what happens when the scenes are played out and the confrontations actually occur."[26] Often compared to a stage manager, he is just as nicely described as a setter of mouse traps, trivial snares that seem to be ingenious but are not.[27]

Satan's vividness and activity do not add up to success. This perception comes to us again and again, with that same repetitive quality characteristic of Jason's continual exposures to failure and frustration. Satan's disguise and his first temptation are ludicrously inept. Christ brushes them aside with a brusqueness reminiscent of Heracles in Apollonius' poem.

> Why durst thou then suggest to me distrust,
> Knowing who I am, as I know who thou art?   (*PR* I, 335–56)

Such was the way he [Heracles] upbraided the gathering. No one there dared to
look him in the eye, or answer him with a speech; they broke the meeting up and
hurried off to prepare for departure. (*Argonautica* 1.875–78)

Satan's response to this new adversary is pure Jason. He is overwhelmed
by the contest before him and is sustained only by his infernal crew.

> "Therefore I am returned, lest confidence
> Of my success with Eve in Paradise
> Deceive ye to persuasion over-sure
> Of like succeeding here: I summon all
> Rather to be in readiness with hand
> Or counsel to assist, *lest I who erst*
> *Thought none my equal, now be overmatched.*"
> So spake the old Serpent doubting, and from all
> With clamor was assured their utmost aid
> At his command.   (II, 140–49; my emphasis)

Since Satan cannot free himself from judging the present conflict
in terms of past wars, he contrives what he supposes are more intricate
variations of the temptation of Eve. The banquet seems a more gorgeous
version of the temptation of *Paradise Lost* IX, 494–779.

> Alas how simple, to these cates compared,
> Was that crude apple that diverted Eve!   (II, 348–49)

But the poet is being ironic; Satan's Lucullan feast is a test of a far cruder
kind than the temptation of the knowledge of good and evil. His pomp-
ous delicacies could appeal only to baser appetites, yet he cannot see the
comedy in the contrast: "these are not fruits forbidden;" that is, "This
is not *Paradise Lost*."

> no interdict
> Defends the touching of these viands pure,
> Their taste no knowledge works, at least of evil.   (II, 369–71)

When Christ rejects this silly trap, there is a lovely touch to the characterization of Satan's banquet.

> With that
> Both table and provision vanished quite
> With sound of Harpies' wings and talons heard.   (II, 402–03)

The feast offered Christ is in reality no more appealing than the ban-
quets of Phineus with the Harpies: no nourishment whatever, rotten
food — if any food at all — left behind in exchange (*Argonautica* 2.223–35).
Why wonder that Christ can remain everywhere imperturbable in the

face of such tests? His passivity is underscored by the formulaic nature
of his responses: "To whom then Jesus patiently replied" (II, 432), "To
whom our Saviour calmly thus replied" (III, 43). For his part, Satan experiences the infernal dilemma of the *amēchanos*, the resourceless hero
without effective means to deal with his foe. And he suffers, like Jason,
formulaically:

> and Satan stood
> A while as mute confounded what to say,
> What to reply, confuted and convinced
> Of his weak arguing and fallacious drift.   (III, 1–4)

> and here again
> Satan had not to answer, but stood struck
> With guilt of his own sin, for he himself
> Insatiable of glory had lost all.   (III, 145–48)

> Perplexed and troubled at his bad success,
> The Tempter stood, nor had what to reply,
> Discovered in his fraud, thrown from his hope,
> So oft, and the persuasive rhetoric
> That sleeked his tongue, and won so much on Eve
> So little here, nay lost.   (IV, 1–6)

The reason for his mounting sense of frustration may be traced to Satan's
attempt to relive the triumph over Eve.

> But Eve was Eve;
> This far his overmatch, who self-deceived
> And rash, beforehand had no better weighed
> The strength he was to cope with, or his own.   (IV, 6–9)

If Satan could have his way, *Paradise Regained* might amount to
nothing more than a repeat performance of Jason's troubled heroics in
the *Argonautica*. Christ his presumed adversary makes the crucial difference. The two similes at the climax of the poem sum up all that remains to be said about Satan the resourceless hero:

> To whom thus Jesus. "Also it is written,
> 'Tempt not the Lord thy God.'" He said, and stood.
> But Satan smitten with amazement fell
> As when Earth's son Antaeus (to compare
> Small things with greatest) in Irassa strove
> With Jove's Alcides, and oft foiled still rose,
> Receiving from his mother Earth new strength,
> Fresh from his fall, and fiercer grapple joined,

> Throttled at length in the air, expired and fell;
> So after many a foil the Tempter proud,
> Renewing fresh assaults, amidst his pride
> Fell whence he stood to see his victor fall.
> And as that Theban monster that proposed
> Her riddle, and him who solved it, not devoured,
> That once found out and solved, for grief and spite
> Cast herself headlong from the Ismenian steep,
> So strook with dread and anguish fell the Fiend,
> And to his crew, that sat consulting, brought
> Joyless triumphals of his hoped success,
> Ruin, and desperation, and dismay,
> Who durst so proudly tempt the Son of God.   (IV, 560–80)

The myths of Antaeus and the Sphinx are a pointed commentary on Satan's heroism. All his machinations culminate in a rise and fall as stunning as the rise and fall of Antaeus, who lost his powers once he lost contact with his mother Earth. Alcides (Heracles) raised Antaeus from the earth, then killed him easily; Satan contrived to raise himself into Air, the realm he thought his old dominion:

> O ancient powers of Air and this wide world,
> For much more willingly I mention air,
> This our old conquest, than remember Hell
> Our hated habitation.   (I, 44–47)

But Air, the old conquest of *Paradise Lost* (I, 630–43), becomes merely the scene of his newest defeat.

The allusion to the Sphinx of Thebes contains the same reflexive ironies. She attempted to destroy every man who passed her way by posing her famous riddle, to which the answer was "man." When Oedipus answered the riddle correctly, she cast herself down to her death.

> His first-begot we know, and sore have felt
> When his fierce thunder drove us to the Deep;
> Who this is we must learn, for Man he seems
> In all his lineaments, though in his face
> The glimpses of his Father's glory shine.   (I, 89–93)

The man whose identity so puzzled Satan at the beginning of *Paradise Regained* now is revealed, and this revelation causes him to cast himself down like the Sphinx. For the answer to the riddle he has posed is not "man" (Adam and all his descendants), but the man first named by God in *Paradise Lost*.

So man, as is most just,
shall satisfy for Man, be judged and die,
And dying, rise, and rising with him raise
His brethren, ransomed with his own dear life.   (III, 295–97)

The mythical paradigms of Antaeus and the Sphinx put Satan's second rise and fall into a double perspective: against a superior Heracles he is not very strong; against a superior Oedipus he is not very bright. Here is the total defeat of the heroic impulse, in both the physical and intellectual spheres.

The poem itself wins a kind of victory in the way it advances beyond the considerable achievement of Apollonius of Rhodes. By writing *Paradise Lost* and *Paradise Regained*, Milton wrote epic and its Apollonian sequel, and in effect accomplished as much as Homer and Apollonius combined. Before he published this poem, epic had by definition been the all-embracing story, with no possible successor text. Vergil died writing the *Aeneid*, literally; Dante completed the *Commedia* shortly before his death. Milton wrote epic, then lived to tell another tale. Joan Webber has an excellent comment on the peculiarly consuming task of being an epic poet: "It cannot be wholly coincidental that the writer's last work on epic is often done just before his death. Young men do not write epics before going on to other things, nor is an epic often put aside because it is finished to the author's satisfaction: it is in process as long as he is."[28] In *Paradise Regained*, Milton breaks free of the mortal and artistic constraints described here. He has the power to finish an epic to his satisfaction, then proceed in a briefer poem to evoke Apollonius's revision of the traditional ideas and images of classical heroism.

Paradise Regained marks an important development in Milton's rhetoric of literary forms after *Paradise Lost*.[29] This development is not without its theological significance. By transforming Apollonius's brilliant solution to the Alexandrian (or Bloomian) anxieties of Homer's influence into a Christian poem, Milton does more than identify Satan with Jason. In Pauline terms, he creates an opposition between Christ's faith and grace and the works and boasts of Satan. Because of the priority of Satan in all manifestations of the satanic, Satan in *Paradise Regained* actually anticipates the inadequate hero invented by Apollonius of Rhodes. Jason is demoted to an even lower status than Apollonius could conceive: nothing but one specimen of a general type, the diminished Satanic hero, for which Satan in *Paradise Regained* sets the standard. To compare great things with small, *Paradise Regained* repeats the process whereby Achilles in the *Iliad* is revealed as a later manifestation of the prototypical, and incomparably more resourceful, hero of *Paradise Lost*. Milton achieved all these artistic and theological revaluations in a poem so brief that no one could wish it a line shorter than it is.

Dartmouth College

NOTES

I am grateful to James Kelsey, Kenneth Bleeth, David Kastan, Robert Hollander, and the anonymous referee of *Milton Studies* for their help with earlier drafts of this essay. All citations and quotations of Milton's poetry are from *John Milton: Complete Poems and Major Prose*, ed. Merritt Y. Hughes (New York, 1973). For the Greek text of Apollonius, I have used *Apollonius de Rhodes: Argonautiques*, Tomes I–III, ed. Francis Vian et Émile Delage (Paris: Société d'Edition "Les Belles Lettres," 1976–1981). All translations are my own.

1. See the biographies of Edward Phillips (1694), John Toland (1698), and Jonathan Richardson (1734), in *The Early Lives of Milton*, ed. Helen Darbishire (London, 1932) pp. 75–76, 185, 247.

2. Barbara K. Lewalski, *Milton's Brief Epic: The Genre, Meaning and Art of "Paradise Regained"* (Providence, 1966), pp. vii, 5; see also Elizabeth Marie Pope, *"Paradise Regained": The Tradition and the Poem* (Baltimore, 1947), p. xiv; J. B. Broadbent, "The Private Mythology of *Paradise Regained*," in *Calm of Mind: Tercentenary Essays on "Paradise Regained" and "Samson Agonistes,"* ed. Joseph Anthony Wittreich, Jr. (Cleveland, 1971), pp. 71–92.

3. Anthony Low, "Milton, *Paradise Regained*, and Georgic," *PMLA*, XCVIII (1983), 158. See also Arnold Stein, *Heroic Knowledge: An Interpretation of "Paradise Regained" and "Samson Agonistes"* (Minneapolis, 1957), pp. 6–7; Burton Jasper Weber, *Wedges and Wings: The Patterning of "Paradise Regained"* (Carbondale, Ill., 1975), p. 1; Louis L. Martz, *The Paradise Within: Studies in Vaughan, Traherne, and Milton* (New Haven, 1964), pp. 171–202.

4. See C. G. Perkell, "A Reading of Vergil's Fourth *Georgic*," *Phoenix*, XXXII (1978), 211–21, and Jasper Griffin, "The Fourth *Georgic*, Virgil and Rome," *Greece and Rome*, XXVI (1979), 61–80. For the *Georgics* as the middle poem in Vergil's career see Brooks Otis, *Virgil: A Study in Civilized Poetry* (Oxford, 1964), pp. 144–214.

5. See Jasper Griffin, "The Epic Cycle and the Uniqueness of Homer," *Journal of Hellenic Studies*, XCVII (1977), 39–53.

6. To my knowledge, only Anthony Low refers to him, in connection with the four-book structure of the *Georgics* and *Paradise Regained* (Low, "Milton, *Paradise Regained*," 169, n. 1).

7. Charles Rowan Beye, *Epic and Romance in the Argonautica of Apollonius* (Carbondale, Ill., 1982); see pp. 169–78 for a bibliographical survey. Helpful also are E. V. Rieu's introductory essay to his Penguin translation, *Apollonius of Rhodes: The Voyage of Argo* (1959), pp. 9–32, and the commentary and introductory essays in the Budé edition of Francis Vian and Emile Delage, *Apollonios de Rhodes: Argonautiques*, vol. I, *Chants I–II* (Paris, 1976); vol. II, *Chant III* (Paris, 1980); and vol. III, *Chant IV* (Paris, 1981).

8. *A Second Defense of the English People* (1654) quotes *Argonautica* 2.181–84; *Letter 24 to Philaras* (September 28, 1654), 2.205.

9. Darbishire, *Early Lives*, pp. 60, 98.

10. Cf. Beye, *Epic Romance*, p. 11: "We are expected to notice how he has recast the Homeric poems and their world view."

11. See *Ancient Literary Criticism: The Principal Texts in New Translations*, ed. D. A. Russell and M. Winterbottom (Oxford, 1972), p. 127 and n. 4 (on Aristotle, *Poetics* 1459 b), p. 388 (on Quintilian, *Institutio Oratoria* 10.54), and p. 492 (on "Longinus" 33.1).

12. See Mary R. Lefkowitz, *The Lives of the Greek Poets* (Baltimore, 1981), pp. 117–35; cf. W. Clausen, "Callimachus and Latin Poetry," *Greek, Roman, and Byzantine Studies*, V (1964), 181–96.

13. Cf. Beye, *Epic and Romance*, p. 17: "One of the sources of creative tension in the poem is the precarious balance between the narrator, the characters, and the epic tradition: no one element is consistently authoritative," and p. 79: "The critical problem does reside in our expectations. Apollonius has contrived to write what is *formally* an epic, yet in a sense *not* an epic."

14. With "Longinus'" remark at 33.1, "Apollonius makes no mistakes in the *Argonautica* . . . but would you rather be Homer or Apollonius?" compare Bentley's strictures on *Paradise Regained:* "a dry, barren, and narrow ground to build an epic poem upon" (*Paradise Lost* [1732], on X, 182).

15. See Enrico Livrea, *Argonautica: Apollonii Rhodii Argonautikon Liber IV* (Florence, 1973); Lewalski, *Milton's Brief Epic*, pp. 325–56.

16. E. M. W. Tillyard, *Milton* (London, 1930), pp. 316–18; Broadbent, "Private Mythology," p. 77; Lewalski, *Milton's Brief Epic*, p. 331; Beye, *Epic Romance*, pp. 34–38, 142–43.

17. David Quint, *Origin and Originality in Renaissance Literature: Versions of the Source* (New Haven, 1983) pp. 213–14; Patricia A. Parker, *Inescapable Romance: Studies in the Poetics of a Mode* (Princeton, 1979), pp. 114–58, esp. 143: "The reader is set before events which have already happened as if they were about to happen, still a matter of choice."

18. See G. K. Galinsky, *The Herakles Theme* (Totowa, N.J., 1979), pp. 108–16, esp. 109: "Apollonius took pains to demonstrate that Herakles' heroism was clearly of the kind that was beyond Jason's reader."

19. Cf. Stanley Fish, "Inaction and Silence: The Reader in *Paradise Regained*," in *Calm of Mind*, pp. 25–47; cf. Fish, *Surprised by Sin: The Reader in "Paradise Lost"* (Berkeley and Los Angeles, 1967), p. 162.

20. Beye, *Epic and Romance*, p. 24; Joan Malory Webber, *Milton and His Epic Tradition* (Seattle, 1979), p. 215.

21. This is a rapid sketch of a complex part of the poem; for a detailed reading, see E. V. George, "Poet and Character in Apollonius' Lemnian Episode," *Hermes*, C (1972), 44–63.

22. Cf. Galinsky, *The Herakles Theme*, p. 108: "In no other epic are the protagonist and most of his companions afraid so often, and nowhere else is an epic hero so continually overwhelmed by resignation and despair in the face of a never-ceasing series of dilemmas."

23. Cf. Beye, *Epic and Romance*, pp. 102–19, and Stanley Fish, "Things and Actions Indifferent: The Temptation of Plot in *Paradise Regained*," *Milton Studies*, XVII, ed. Richard S. Ide and Joseph Wittreich (Pittsburgh, 1983), pp. 163–85.

24. On Jason's problematic heroics, see Gilbert Lawall, "Apollonius' *Argonautica:* Jason as Antihero," *Yale Classical Studies*, XIX (1966), 119–69.

25. On the interiorization of values in Milton, see Annabel W. Patterson, "*Paradise Regained:* A Last Chance at True Romance," *Milton Studies*, XVII, pp. 187–209. For similar reasons, *Argonautica* 3 and 4 are an important anticipation of the ancient Greek romance; see Arthur Heiserman, *The Novel Before the Novel* (Chicago, 1977), pp. 46–77. Cf. Beye, *Epic and Romance*, p. 142.

26. Fish, "Inaction and Silence," p. 29; cf. Lewalski, *Milton's Brief Epic*, p. 136, on Milton's "destruction of genuine dramatic action."

27. On the triviality of Satan's temptations, cf. Fish, "Things and Action Indifferent," p. 177, and Lewalski, *Milton's Brief Epic*, p. 162.

28. Webber, *Milton and His Epic Tradition*, p. 91.

29. Barbara K. Lewalski, *Paradise Lost and the Rhetoric of Literary Forms* (Princeton, 1985), 3–24, 254–80.